Disorderly Women
and Female Power

in the Street Literature

of Early Modern

England and Germany

Feminist Issues: Practice, Politics, Theory
Kathleen M. Balutansky and Alison Booth, editors

Carol Siegel, *Lawrence among the Women: Wavering Boundaries in Women's Literary Traditions*

Harriet Blodgett, *Capacious Hold-All: An Anthology of English Women's Diary Writings*

Joy Wiltenburg, *Disorderly Women and Female Power in the Street Literature of Early Modern England and Germany*

Diane P. Freedman, *An Alchemy of Genres: Cross-Genre Writing by American Feminist Poet-Critics*

Disorderly Women
and Female Power
in the Street Literature
of Early Modern
England and Germany

Joy Wiltenburg

University Press of Virginia
Charlottesville and London

The illustration on chapter opening pages is from Hans Sachs, *Von den neun Häuten der bösen Weiber* [16c], broadside (courtesy of the Germanisches Nationalmuseum, Nuremberg).

The illustration facing the Contents page is from *Halfe a dozen of good Wives: All for a Penny* [1634], broadside (reprinted from *The Roxburghe Ballads*, 1, ed. William Chappell [Hertford, Eng.: Ballad Society, 1872]: 451 by permission of the British Library).

THE UNIVERSITY PRESS OF VIRGINIA
Copyright © 1992 by the Rector and Visitors
of the University of Virginia
First published 1992

Library of Congress Cataloging-in-Publication Data

Wiltenburg, Joy.
    Disorderly women and female power in the street literature of
early modern England and Germany / Joy Wiltenburg.
        p.   cm. — (Feminist issues)
    Includes translations from German.
    Includes bibliographical references and index.
    ISBN 0-8139-1350-0. — ISBN 0-8139-1351-9 (pbk.)
        1. English literature—Early modern, 1500–1700—History and
criticism.   2. German literature—Early modern, 1500–1700—History
and criticism.   3. Women and literature—England—History—16th
century.   4. Women and literature—England—History—17th century.
5. Literature, Comparative—English and German.   6. Literature,
Comparative—German and English.   7. Street literature—History and
criticism.   8. Disorderly conduct in literature.   9. Women and
literature—Germany.   10. Feminism and literature.   I. Title.
II. Series: Feminist issues (Charlottesville, Va.)
PR418.W65W55   1992
820.9'352042'09031—dc20   91-22327
                                                                        CIP

Printed in the United States of America

For my brothers

Contents

Acknowledgments / ix

Introduction
1. Prologue / 3
2. Gender and Disorder in Early Modern Europe / 7
3. The Literature of the Streets / 27

Disorderly Women
4. Woman as Protagonist: Virtue and Disorder / 47
5. The Locus of Power: Marital Order / 71
6. Marital Disorder / 97
7. Sex and Power / 141
8. Women and Violence: Tragedy and Comedy / 183
9. Women and Crime: A Return to the Family / 209

Conclusion
10. Perspectives / 253

Abbreviations and Short Citations / 269
Notes / 271
Bibliography / 303
Index / 347

Acknowledgments

I would first of all like to acknowledge my debt to Erik Midelfort, without whose inspiration and support this work would never have been undertaken, let alone brought to two conclusions, first as a dissertation and now as a book. I am very glad of this opportunity to offer him my thanks, both for my share in the intellectual adventures of his teaching and for his continued encouragement and enthusiasm.

The book has benefited greatly from the comments and criticisms of scholars who have read it at various stages, although I am sure I have failed to take full advantage of their wisdom. I am especially grateful to Ann Jones for her exhaustive commentary, as well as to Phyllis Rackin, Keith Moxey, and J. A. Sharpe for their extensive suggestions. I would also like to thank Richard Dunn, Nicholas Edsall, Elizabeth Fox-Genovese, Ruth Karras, Thomas F. X. Noble, David Noble, and Karl Otto, who have read part or all of the work and offered me advice and/or support. Marianne S. Wokeck deserves special thanks for reviewing my translations from the German in addition to commenting on the whole. I have also had valuable suggestions from two anonymous scholars who reviewed it for publication. I would like to thank Eric Carlson, Sigrid Brauner, and Frances Dolan for generously sharing unpublished work with me.

I have incurred a large number of more diffuse intellectual debts; and of these I must mention especially those to teachers who have shaped my view of the historian's calling (in chronological order): Robert Kreiser, Laura Oren, Eugene Genovese, Elizabeth Fox-Genovese, and Lenard Berlanstein.

My research in Germany was supported by a grant from the German Academic Exchange Service (DAAD), and my work on the manuscript by the American Council of Learned Societies and the National Endowment for the Humanities. My work was also greatly assisted by the kindness of the staffs of the Deutsche Staatsbibliothek (Berlin), the Deutsche Staatsbibliothek Preussischer Kulturbesitz (Berlin), the Herzog August Bibliothek (Wolfenbüttel), the Germanisches Nationalmuseum (Nuremberg), the British Library, the Bodleian Library, the National Library of Scotland, and the Society of Antiquaries. I would particularly like to thank David Paisey of the British Library for his invaluable aid. I also thank my colleagues of the Papers of William Penn and the Biographical Dictionary of Early Pennsylvania Legislators for tolerating my absence while I worked on this book.

I am very grateful to my husband, Rick Womer, for his unflagging support, and to my children, Ellen and Jim, for their nonhistorical perspective.

A Note on Quotations

In quoting sources I generally have retained the original spelling, capitalization, and punctuation, with some exceptions: superscript letters in older German texts are treated as umlauts or omitted; tildes are expanded; and italics are omitted, as is capitalization of any letter in a word other than the first. In cases where I have used modern editions, I reproduce the editors' version unless there is a significant difference between the original and the published version. The English translations of German texts are my own unless otherwise indicated. For both English and German sources I give the location of the copies consulted. Occasionally I cite additional locations to show that a text exists in multiple copies (suggesting some popularity), but with no attempt at comprehensiveness. Many of the English pieces are also available in the microfilm edition of works listed in Pollard and Redgrave, *Short-Title Catalogue*, and Wing, *Short-Title Catalogue*. For original early modern English sources, the place of publication is London unless otherwise noted.

Introduction

I.

Prologue

 This book arises out of an interest in two separate but interrelated issues. The first and broader one, and perhaps the less susceptible to any fully satisfying analysis, is the problem of male dominance. Modern feminism has exposed its injustice and shed light on the ways in which it is socially constructed, but has been somewhat less successful in explaining why it exists or, in more concrete terms, why and how women have allowed it to exist and accommodated themselves to it. It is certainly appropriate, and has now become easy, to condemn the misogyny of the dominant male culture; but unless we are willing to accept a view of women throughout history as oppressed ciphers with negligible influence, we must seek to understand them as cultural actors, as people whose actions and attitudes affected the shape of their culture, albeit in ways that might not fit our modern views of their enlightened self-interest. At the same time, as other feminist scholars have noted, we need to integrate our understanding of male dominance into our conceptions of how culture works as a whole; just as culture cannot be understood without reference to gender, so gender rules acquire meaning only as part of their culture. My focus on depictions of disorderly women addresses the issue of control under male dominance by examining expressions of the cultural conviction that women were out of control. The fascinating recurrence of this theme, the preoccupation with women's unwillingness to conform, brings to the forefront key questions about the politics of gender: Were women really resistant to domination? If so, how

was their resistance contained? Were the images of disorder used to exorcise male fears? To warn women against their own potential disorder? To offer women imaginary power while depriving them of the real thing?

The second issue is that of recovering the thoughts and feelings of ordinary people in a world three or four centuries removed from our own. While it was once believed that most people could be ignored for historical purposes, historians have now recognized the need to understand what went on below the level of the elite. We are no longer satisfied with the upper crust alone; we want the whole pie. This is not idle curiosity, either: widely held social attitudes underlay patterns of familial, economic, and political life that shaped whole social structures. So it matters what people thought, and how they thought; but it is not easy to discover. Like the problem of understanding women, the study of popular culture is hampered by the scarcity and bias of our sources.

This book attempts to contribute to the understanding of both these historical problems, or at least to suggest fruitful ways of thinking about them in the context of early modern European culture. Since neither problem can be approached directly, I have adopted an oblique approach through street literature—the cheap pamphlets and ballads purveyed to a wide audience in streets and markets. To some this approach may seem excessively oblique, dealing as it does not only with materials that were produced by biased authors and put to uncertain uses, but also with creations of the imagination that in large part do not even pretend to be descriptions of real life. In my view, however, it is precisely because their meanings are so tricky and elusive that we must devote our careful attention to these works. Human beings do not build their social identities on a logical compilation of rules; they draw, instead, on a wide range of models, associations, identifications, and prescriptions, linking them together in ways that are both idiosyncratic and culturally bounded. While the ways in which people combine these elements depend largely on their complex of social relationships, the elements themselves are drawn partly from the public discourses of their culture. This is where street literature comes in, and it becomes clear from a reading of these works that one of their key aims is to help people solidify their social identity. These widely distributed texts provided cultural images for people to think with. What kinds of meanings did they hold? What can they tell us about how their cultures conceived of social identity and the place of gender within it?

The book's comparative approach is intended to underline my contention that conceptions of gender can be interpreted only within their social and cultural contexts. While similar misogynistic elements appear in the texts of both England and Germany, this is only the starting point for analysis. The two sets of depictions of female disorder, which at first might seem attributable to a monolithic male dominance, in fact reflect rather different conceptions of the sexual order, and of social order as well. These findings point to central questions about the relationships between gender and social order in early modern European culture and about the changes wrought in both by the developments of the sixteenth and seventeenth centuries.

To establish the need for cultural context in analyzing attitudes toward women's place and power, it would perhaps serve equally well to compare any two countries. For early modern Europe, however, the Reformation offers exceptional opportunities to examine ideas about sexual order. While the degree and direction of change in sexual politics brought about by the Reformation remain matters for debate, the reformers showed a newly intense concern with issues of sexuality, familial hierarchy, and gender identity. Thus I have based this study on two countries, England and Germany: both were deeply affected by the Reformation, and both produced large numbers of popular texts to address issues of sexual politics. The chronological bounds of the study, roughly 1550 to 1680, are designed to capture the post-Reformation ferment in gender ideology and to include major flowerings of popular literature in each country.

It should hardly need to be said that the problems addressed in this book, like all historical problems, are of interest not because they existed in the past but because they hold meaning for the present. Nothing in the past is historical until we make it so by looking back and attempting to understand it. My interest in these issues stems from the conviction that we cannot fully understand a culture without paying attention to the elements it seeks to suppress and control, and that the "powerless" often exert power of which neither they nor their superiors are fully aware.

2.

Gender and Disorder
in Early Modern Europe

The societies of early modern Europe placed strict limits on the exercise of power by women. Although their roles in the family and household economy carried some legitimate authority, and although exceptional women had their impact on public affairs, the cultural conception of social order required that women be subordinated and controlled by men. Indeed, in some ways the confines of patriarchy were tightening during the sixteenth and seventeenth centuries, with increasing restrictions on women's economic, political, and social pursuits.[1] Yet in the images of popular literature, this picture of the sexual order dissolves, as women were constantly depicted escaping from male control. Whatever women's real-life disabilities, the female characters of popular literature are often powerful—powerful and subversive. Perhaps subliminally aware of problems in keeping the upper hand, male authors often depict women as disorderly creatures, whose licentious urge for dominance threatens to disrupt the carefully constructed social hierarchy. The cultural perception of women's power as disorder, and of their disorderliness as power, reflects male anxieties about the success of patriarchal rule. At the same time, the partial mirror of popular literature may provide a glimpse, though a distorted one, of some women's strategies for coping with that rule.

The disorderly women of early modern popular literature share in a tradition that was inherited from medieval fabliaux and passed on to the world of modern soap operas. The imaginative tradition of female unruliness has a long history, and its various embodiments reflect a persistent undercurrent of misogyny as well as the distinctive qualities of each time and culture. In order to assess the shifting cultural uses to which misogyny can be put, it is useful to examine some of its roots, and here anthropology offers some suggestive ideas. Sherry Ortner has noted a tendency across many cultures to view women as closer to the forces of nature, less civilized and less disciplined than men. Both biological and social factors have fostered such perceptions: just as female bodily functions underline nature's power, women's social roles in such tasks as food preparation and the socialization of children can be seen as mediating between nature and culture, assimilating the natural into the forms of civilization.[2] Such conceptions of gender differences and of the interaction between human society and the natural world have had particularly strong resonance in the cultures of Western Europe. Thus women, sharing in the mysterious forces and processes attributed to nature, have been seen as powerful and threatening despite their subordination in objective social terms.

Further light on such imagined female threats emerges from Mary Douglas's analysis of ideas about pollution and danger: the crossing of boundaries is always perilous, especially any venture into the natural chaos outside the culture's rule, and order is preserved by hedging the borders with taboos.[3] Women's sexual and maternal roles represent a dual blurring of boundaries: between individual and individual, as bodies join and separate in intercourse and birth; and between mind and body, reason and appetite, as in sexuality the cultured understanding is ruled by the imperatives of nature. To be sure, men play an equal part in the disorderly aspect of intercourse, but this reality has been overshadowed by the perception of women as the source of natural urges.[4] Thus women, in their mediatory role with nature, can be seen as prime sources of danger; and cultural fears of female power are closely linked to the need to banish and contain natural disorder. This need and the fears associated with it are common to both sexes; and although primal male fears of female sexuality have contributed their share, it should be noted that misogynistic ideas and perceptions are by no means the exclusive province of men.[5] On the other hand, given the suppression of female power inherent in the preservation of male dominance, the tradition of female disorder represents conscious or unconscious cultural recognition that women harbor an element of potential resistance to the structures of patriarchal society.

While some aspects of these ideas appear to be universal, differences across time and culture in the expression of such fears can shed light not only on their societies' attitudes toward women, but also on the links between sexual symbolism and ways of thinking about the world in general. Natalie Davis has pointed out such relationships between the idea of female disorderliness and the symbolism of ritual inversion in early modern Europe: on the one hand, the sexual reversal of the "woman on top" bolstered the accepted sexual order by shaming or ridiculing those who departed from it; on the other, it presented an image of female license that could provide both sexes with a potential relief from authority.[6] In male-dominated societies, the comic reversal of sexual roles toys with the accepted social hierarchy in ways that can amuse both sexes, providing both a humorous debunking of authority and a subtle reinforcement of it. The exploration of such connections between sexual imagery and social mentality can illuminate a wide range of cultural issues, from social stratification and authority to ideas about familial relationships, violence, individuality, and the supernatural.

Gender relations in early modern Europe, as in other societies, were far from the inevitable expression of natural and divine necessity, despite persistent attempts to define them as such. The cultures of this period expended considerable energy on defining and shaping these relations, in efforts that affected all areas of the social order, from law and custom to the literature of popular entertainment.[7] The period has long been noted for its misogyny, from the widespread literary attacks on women to the antifemale impact of witchcraft persecutions. The early modern preoccupation with the proper ordering of sexual roles, and the tensions over their definition, suggest widespread uncertainty and unease about these issues. Gender relations were changing, or threatening to change; but scholars are still far from a full understanding of what was happening, and of how gender relates to the general changes in early modern society and culture. However historians are ultimately to explain early modern developments, it is important not only to bring general issues to bear on women's history, but also to recognize that the ordering of gender relations forms an integral part of general cultural structures. The analysis of early modern thinking about women and the sexual balance of power deals not with a sidelight but with a central issue in cultural thinking about hierarchy, society, and the self.[8]

Early modern economic developments offer one clear source of tension in sexual politics. Early in this century, scholars documented women's declining control over their economic activities in the sixteenth and seventeenth centuries, as capitalist organization increasingly displaced guild and household production.[9] With the more recent growth of feminist social history, scholars have been extending and refining this picture. During the sixteenth and seventeenth centuries, women suffered a substantial decline in economic power across wide areas of Europe, as population pressure and economic distress led to increasing restrictions on women's work, and as advancing market organization tended to remove control of production from the household.[10] In trades controlled by guilds, early modern regulations frequently reserved skilled work for male workers. In areas outside guild control, where production was moving away from household organization to rely increasingly on wage labor, women tended to lose the managerial responsibilities that had fallen to them in household workshops. With the growth of cottage industry, under the "putting-out" system, women often predominated among the workers hired by merchant capitalists to work up raw materials in their homes, but under conditions that left them no control over the marketing of their goods or the price of their labor.

In the early modern household, the wife held legitimate authority over children and servants as her husband's lieutenant—one of the few areas in which female authority was orderly, as long as it remained within its bounds. Supervision of a household involved substantial administrative responsibilities, and this work gave some women significant power, particularly when the household was also the center of economic production. Wives of the gentry frequently managed estates in their husbands' absence, while at lower social levels women often assisted their husbands in trade or carried on separate businesses, particularly in retail sales, brewing, innkeeping, and sewing. Women were sometimes admitted to guilds, carrying on either their own trades or those of their deceased husbands, though their opportunities to do this were being curtailed. In the absence of a male family head, women took over completely, a situation that was common in German cities but was fraught with risks, for the many female-headed households were often among the poorest.[11] Though women's economic contribution to the household was substantial, their labor was considered marginal to that of men, who were expected to provide the family's main income. Women everywhere were paid much less than men for equivalent labor, and they were especially subject to poverty when they had to earn their own support.[12] The view of women's labor as marginal placed them in an extremely vulnerable position in the hard years of the sixteenth century, when increased population both intensified competition for jobs and pushed real wages down. In Languedoc, for example, as real wages reached their nadir in the last decades of the century, women's pay as a proportion of men's also reached its low point, falling substantially below the usual one-half of men's wages.[13] In England, too, the gender gap in wages widened.[14] Thus both demographic pressures and the structural changes of developing capitalism worked against women's economic interests.

Of course, earning power was far from being the sole determinant of women's economic fortunes. Marriage was an economic partnership, and a key factor in a woman's ability to secure adequate provision for herself was the size of the dowry she was able to bring to the union. There is evidence that dowries generally were rising during this period—at least at the upper levels of society—apparently because families of newer wealth were paying for the privilege of marrying their daughters into families of higher status. The impact of higher dowries on women's economic power, and even on their economic well-being, is ambiguous, however. On the one hand, women whose wealth formed a substantial prop to the family's fortunes could use this as a source of informal authority over husbands; and in most areas women retained some rights over the sale of dower or marital property, even if they might have little say in its management or the use of the income during the marriage. Thus in street literature unruly wives sometimes point to the wealth they brought to the household. On the other hand, higher dowries meant that daughters would be viewed as greater economic burdens by their families, and also that a girl of a given fortune would have to settle for a poorer husband. From this point of view, the woman was getting less for her money. Furthermore, the stiffer competition among prospective brides meant that women of lesser wealth might be the real losers, having to settle for poor marital bargains or none at all.[15] At the same time, the dowry often served as a substitute for inheritance and could be paired with curtailment or elimination of further rights in her family's property.[16] In general, there may be a correlation between increased reliance on female dowries in establishing households and low levels of economic opportunity for married women: when a wife must be supported, it may become essential for her to offer a premium, conditions that would not apply where her labor is an economic asset. Thus rising dowries could be linked with declining economic productivity for women.[17]

The problem of women's economic status was reinforced by other

features of early modern society. Some studies have indicated a surplus of
women in the towns of the late Middle Ages, as women's longevity
overtook that of men. These findings have recently been disputed, but
whatever their numbers, the decline in women's means of support was
making women—especially unmarried women—a relatively greater social problem.[18] At the very time that women's economic activities were
being restricted, the Reformation placed a new emphasis on marriage as
women's sole calling: both nunneries and brothels were to be eliminated,
and all loose individuals placed under the authority of a male head of
household. Theoretically, of course, if all women did marry, their economic needs would be taken care of by males, with the exception of a few
unavoidable widows and orphans; and the disorderly prospect of women
outside male control would be eliminated.

The problem with this ideal in the context of early modern society
was how poorly it fit with reality. While Luther was advocating teenage
marriage and marriage for everyone, the actual pattern of marriages
across northwestern Europe was distinctive precisely for its violation of
both these precepts, and the Reformation had no success in reversing the
tendency of social practice. Average marriage ages for both men and
women were relatively late—in the mid-to-late twenties—and a relatively
large proportion remained unmarried.[19] This pattern has wide implications for the history of early modern family and society. From the point of
view of women's economic dilemma, of course, it meant that many women
went unprovided for. At least for the long period of adolescence leading
up to marriage, and often for their whole lives, women of the middle-to-
lower classes had to earn a living—which was becoming more difficult.
Before a couple could marry, they were expected to accumulate, from
their families or from their own labor, the economic resources to set up
an independent household, with a livelihood sufficient for the support of
the couple and their future children. Both sexes began their work lives
early, often leaving their parents' home for service or apprenticeship in
another household and saving up earnings for marriage. The need for
self-sufficiency posed economic barriers to marriage that delayed it for
many and placed it outside the reach of others. The reformers could urge
everyone to marry and praise marriage as women's route to an honorable
life, but they could not make it possible for everyone, and the closing off
of alternatives left many women without a secure social place.

The history of marriage and family life is, of course, closely intertwined with the history of women, since the family was the central institution for the articulation of gender rules. In recent decades historians have come to recognize that familial organization plays a decisive role in economic and political structures as well, though they have yet to arrive at an integrated understanding of the interplay of gender, class, family, authority, and culture. The early modern family has received a great deal of scholarly attention and remains a subject of debate. The clearest evidence has come from historical demographers, whose painstaking research has laid out the key structural features for northwestern Europe: the European marriage pattern outlined above; the prevalence of nuclear households without wider kin but often with servants or other nonrelatives in residence; the low life expectancy, which made broken households common; and high infant mortality, which kept the numbers of surviving children lower and the households relatively smaller than one might expect. The evidence also shows significant differences in household structure across class lines, with the elite tending toward larger households with more children, servants, and kin. The upper classes also married earlier, and upper-class women spent a greater proportion of their lives in active childbearing: their earlier marriages made for more years of marital fertility, and their children could be more closely spaced when wet nurses were employed, since this eliminated the contraceptive tendency of lactation.[20]

Historical demography thus has taught us a great deal about how people lived and about the differences and similarities between early modern families and our own. While the structural features of family life appear to have been relatively stable between 1500 and 1700, historians also have sought to trace changes in early modern family relations. Since it has become evident that the family does change over time, it would be more surprising to find complete continuity than to discover changes during these two eventful centuries. But because the main changes are in the realm of attitudes and ideology, they are more difficult to pin down than demographic patterns. Most scholars agree that there was a long-term development favoring a focus on companionate marital relations, allowing selection of spouses by the partners rather than their families, and intensifying concern for familial privacy; but the chronology and degree of the changes are less well established, partly because of wide variations in familial practices and ideas according to region and class.[21] Early attempts to draw a general picture, such as Lawrence Stone's sweeping treatment of the early modern English family, tended to overstate the changes.[22] Especially vulnerable have been early assumptions about the lack of emotional intimacy in premodern families. In recent years historians have presented ample evidence of close relationships between husbands and wives, courting couples, and parents and children; and the street literature examined here offers more.[23] Studies of English society have particularly stressed continuity during this period, and Alan Macfarlane has even treated the whole period from 1300 to 1800 as one in which the essential features of English family life remained the same.[24] Though this picture of continuity is overdrawn, it cautions against the overhasty charting of contrasts.

The thesis of major change in early modern familial relations has fared better for the Continent, though here, too, some evidence of early companionate family relations has raised questions. For Germany, scholarly debate turns on the impact of the Reformation, which has long been lauded as rescuing families, and women along with them, from the devaluation of sexuality and reproduction in medieval Catholicism. Against the earlier exaltation of virginity, Luther insisted that marriage was equally blessed and that a healthy marriage was far more pleasing to God than the false chastity of lustful celibates. Divinely instituted as an outlet for God-given sexual drives, marriage was now seen as the natural destiny of both sexes and the basis of social, religious, and moral order—a highly honorable estate. Steven Ozment has painted a positive picture of Reformation family life, which he sees as affectionate and rational within its hierarchical framework.[25] For Lyndal Roper, on the other hand, the Reformation advanced an intensely patriarchal system of gender order, in which women were more firmly subjected to male discipline both within the household and without.[26] In England, too, scholars have noted the Reformation's renewed focus on the authority of fathers. Though the reformers, and particularly the Puritans, once were credited with originating the ideal of companionate marriage and being responsible for its spread, it appears that they were merely repeating ideas put forward by others.[27] Thus the Reformation's reputation as a chief promoter of modern family harmony has been called into question.

Its reputation as a positive development for women has suffered as well. On the plus side, of course, the Reformation offered some women an encouragement to independent spiritual commitment, since believers of both sexes were to relate directly to God, with no priestly intermediary.

The Reformation endorsement of lay Bible reading helped spread literacy more widely among both sexes. In domestic relations, reformers emphasized and publicized the ideal of marital companionship, even if they did not originate it. A male rule based on reason and affection was still conceived of as rule, but it was undoubtedly more favorable to women than a rule based on unmediated force. On the other hand, the new conception of the father as his family's spiritual guide may have intensified men's control over wives who no longer could turn to a priest as an alternative authority.[28] Some of the more radical sects offered women greater latitude, even allowing them to preach, and these few women clearly felt empowered by the conviction that God could inspire women as well as men.[29] Such opportunities were rare, however, as it was only during the early days of the Reformation in Germany, and during the Civil War and Interregnum in England, that religious radicalism flourished. Women's losses from the Reformation also were substantial. By doing away with the veneration of female saints and the Virgin Mary, the Reformation stripped women of these powerful (though ambiguous) role models. Perhaps even more significant was the closing of nunneries, which had provided opportunities for women to gain highly responsible administrative positions and relative freedom from male rule.[30]

The Reformation's challenge to received authority and hierarchical rule unintentionally helped undermine some of the props to the established sociopolitical order. Conservative forces in the movement fought hard to get the genie back in the bottle when confronted with rebellious peasants and Anabaptists in sixteenth-century Germany, Levellers and sectarians in seventeenth-century England. Women never threatened to mount a parallel movement of their own during this period; but reformers were keenly aware of the danger of female insubordination and intent on preserving gender order, both for its own sake and as an emblem of general social hierarchy and authority. The Reformation theoretically recognized women's individuality—since their salvation, like that of men, depended on their own inner conviction—but its attitude was highly ambiguous. The dissolving of older ideas of social and religious hierarchy could make women's status problematic and require renewed justification of their subordination. Christina Larner has pointed to the tensions inherent in the view of women as both fully responsible individuals and their husbands' permanent subordinates. Larner and others have noted a significant change in legal conceptions of women's accountability for their actions during this period. While the law had formerly tended to excuse women on the grounds that they were under male authority and not fully answerable for their actions, the early modern period brought a new tendency to prosecute women, most notably for the sex-linked crimes of witchcraft and infanticide. Larner has speculated that the contradictions of the Reformation's view of women—defining them as spiritually independent and therefore powerful but insisting that they remain socially powerless—contributed to the fears that fueled early modern witch-hunting.[31]

The early modern tendency to invest women with greater accountability was not exclusively Protestant, however, just as the increased focus on individual religious responsibility was common to both Protestant and Catholic Reformations.[32] In France, Jean-Louis Flandrin has found that between the sixteenth and eighteenth centuries confessional manuals and catechisms shifted from a view of husbands as responsible for their wives' morals and behavior to a conception of the woman as fully accountable. Confessors were even coming to expect that wives might exert substantial influence on the religious conduct of their husbands.[33] The fact that this new recognition of women's responsibility appeared in Catholic France, as well as in Protestant England and Scotland, shows that the phenomenon transcended religious differences. The pressures in sexual politics that informed the Protestant Reformation extended to the Catholic Reformation as well.

The sixteenth century marked a notable shift in European attitudes toward sexuality, a development which similarly crossed confessional boundaries. Across wide areas of Europe, authorities and moralists sought to suppress illicit sexuality and exercise more effective control over public morals. Concubinage and prostitution, which had been widely tolerated during the Middle Ages, came under attack, particularly in Protestant areas. The Reformation brought widespread closing of public brothels, and informal unions were increasingly condemned in Catholic countries as well.[34] The Reformation's attitude toward sexuality, like its attitude toward women, was ambiguous. On the one hand, sexuality was natural, created by God, and therefore good. On the other hand, the fallen flesh was so suffused with sin that sexual relations always tended toward evil desires. Only marriage could legitimize the dangerous sexual impulse; and with the establishment of marriage as the universal norm, all extramarital sexual activity was intolerable. It had always been considered sinful, of course, but post-Reformation Europe took this sin much more seriously. It could even be seen as the archetype of all sin; it was in the sixteenth century that artists began portraying the fall of Adam and Eve as a fall into sexuality.[35]

Like the early Christian recoil from sexuality, the sexual fears of the sixteenth century rebounded on women. From the male perspective of theology and public discourse, women were the source of temptation; their bodies posed a danger to the souls of men, and to their own souls as well. The double standard of sexual morality, in which women's sexual failings were seen as more damaging than men's, was also well established. The Protestant reformers attempted to enforce a common code of chastity for both men and women, but the double standard was too strongly entrenched. In practical terms, of course, the closing of brothels, like the closing of nunneries, deprived women of an alternative to marriage, though at a much different social level. In a broader cultural sense, the campaign against illicit sex both drew on and fostered misogynistic attitudes. The early modern drive for public morality was linked both to a wider movement to suppress social disorder and to a wider attempt to restrict the power of women.[36]

Social historians have noted an increased rigor on the part of early modern governments against crime and disorder of all kinds. The standards of public order became stricter, and the definitions of what constituted disorder broadened. The use of violence in social interactions both public and private was increasingly curtailed—a change that brought increasing social disapproval of violent marital discipline as well as of tavern brawls.[37] At the same time, authorities sought to suppress older popular customs that were now coming to be viewed as unseemly, licentious, superstitious, or cruel. Peter Burke has dubbed this development the "triumph of Lent," as the values and behavior of religious seriousness succeeded by the eighteenth century in taming much of the irresponsible, carnival-style behavior of earlier popular culture. The reformation of morals and the reform of popular culture fit into a general pattern of increasing, or at least redirected and more focused, social control.[38]

This pattern is very much of a piece with early modern attitudes toward women, who paralleled carnival in their potential disorderliness. Legal systems in many areas of Europe tightened restrictions on women's economic rights during the sixteenth century.[39] Misogynistic literature reached new heights (or depths). Martha Howell has suggested that the misogyny of late medieval popular literature may have reflected fears aroused by a temporary upsurge in women's economic power in the later Middle Ages. If so, the reaction intensified in the following centuries, encompassing economic, legal, and ideological changes. As early modern state building and economic development drew stricter lines between public and private, women were increasingly confined to a shrinking domestic sphere. In this situation, as Joan Kelly has argued, women's opportunities for political and economic power were much reduced.[40] In addition to the intentional limitations placed on women's options, changes in standards of conduct worked against their traditional spheres of power. Kin relationships and personal influence, through which women often exerted considerable power, were increasingly viewed as inappropriate determinants of public action. Ideal models of behavior were shifting from a reliance on personal and corporate loyalties to a demand for objective principles and individual responsibility.

In the realm of social interaction, the civilizing process described by Norbert Elias was demanding a fuller suppression of drives perceived as "natural" and a sharpening of the boundaries between individuals. New rules of bodily comportment increasingly regulated behavior from table manners to the handling of body wastes, first in courtly society and gradually spreading to wider social levels that aspired to civility. While the Middle Ages had found it acceptable to spit or blow one's nose on the floor, to eat and drink from common vessels, the early modern period ushered in changes symbolized by the fork and the handkerchief. Body functions were increasingly to be kept private, hedged about with rules and restraints. This had little to do with ideas of contagion, which did not develop until much later; rather, the changes were motivated by conceptions of propriety and decorum. Both the reformation of sexual morals and the growing restraint on violence fit into this pattern of stricter civilization, which Elias has connected with an increased control and separation of individuals in social life. Europeans believed themselves to be steadily conquering and subordinating the natural functions of uncivilized life. These growing requirements for order could make female disorderliness seem especially threatening, despite the fact that upper-class women played an important role in promoting changes in manners. In fact the meticulously ordered lady can be seen as the obverse of the natural disorder that women could otherwise represent; and the disorderly image could be even more disquieting to her than to her male counterparts.[41]

The growth of individualism in early modern Europe was problematic for gender relations. Though the triumph of rational individualism eventually brought a new recognition of women's potentialities, the early steps in this direction undermined the old sexual order without providing a clear alternative. Developments in religion, law, politics, and economics all furthered the gradual spread of a conception of society as a collection of self-sufficient individuals. This idea was nowhere near gaining full currency, but it began to make inroads in older social conceptions of hierarchy, kinship, and corporatism—most notably perhaps in religion, with the Reformation's exaltation of the individual conscience. It was by no means clear, however, how women were to be fit into an individualistic framework. For one thing, their reproductive role presented a constant reminder of human interdependence. Partly because of this, few could imagine a world in which independent individuality for women was possible. Even more telling, perhaps, was the evil prospect that loomed when people did begin to imagine this—for women represented disorder, the aspects of nature that man could not control. If this disorder was not held in check by tight patriarchal authority, human order might collapse entirely. It was perhaps only when men began to gain confidence in the power of reason to tame and conquer the natural world that the threat posed by female disorder could seem less intense.[42]

I should emphasize, to avoid misconstruction, that the issue here is the place of women and gender in cultural thinking about authority, order, and individuality, not the views of individual men about their female relatives and acquaintances. There is plenty of evidence of mutual respect and satisfying relationships between women and men on an individual level, and also plenty of evidence that the cultural conception of woman need not bear any obvious relationship to actual women. Similarly, the tensions in early modern sexual politics do not imply a decline from a medieval golden age. The Middle Ages had their own problems, and indeed many of the tools for the expression of early modern concerns about women and gender were inherited from earlier centuries. At the same time, it is important to recognize the substantial power that, despite cultural prescription, could be exercised by early modern women, often with male connivance; and the analysis of tensions should not obscure the benefits that could accrue to both sexes from the accumulation of wealth and rising standards of living attendant on the growth of capitalism. My intent is not to argue that the sixteenth and seventeenth centuries were worse for women overall than other centuries, but to examine some of the components of this period's conceptualization of women and gender relations.

This general picture of the social and cultural changes that affected thinking about women and gender in early modern Europe forms the background for a closer look at the two countries to be examined in this study. While they shared much common ground, there were also significant differences; and while some of these differences are easy to describe, others are still not well understood. In addition to the specific differences between Germany and England, historians have noted ways in which England appears exceptional in the general European context: in its early adoption of companionate marriage and individualism, for example, and, of course, later in its early development of constitutional government and industrial capitalism. It remains difficult to account fully for these contrasts, making the need for more comparative studies especially pressing.

Both England and Germany shared in the general changes of early modern Europe, political and economic as well as cultural: both experienced the sixteenth-century population growth and inflation, religious tension and conflict, the seventeenth-century economic slump, and politico-religious war in the mid-seventeenth century. The divergences of the two countries are equally striking. Germany was the core of the Holy Roman Empire, but with authority scattered among hundreds of principalities and towns; England, a country more peripheral to the politics of Europe but far more cohesive in itself, had in London an ever-growing political, economic, and cultural nucleus. By the seventeenth century the economy of the previously flourishing German towns was entering upon a long decline, while England was beginning to establish itself as a major commercial center. Germany's intermittent and, in the seventeenth century, shattering experience of war contrasted with the relative calm of England, broken by a mid-seventeenth-century crisis that brought civil war without large-scale devastation. While German society erected sharply defined barriers between different estates and classes, England seems to have had a more fluid and mobile social structure. By the seventeenth century Germany's middle classes were in eclipse, and its literary culture was dominated by a mannered style that catered to the aristocratic elite; England, with a more flexible economy and a growing individualistic ethos, was developing a more diversified culture.

The geographical dispersion of German political and cultural life contrasted sharply with the cultural hothouse of London. The self-contained German cities had perhaps more in common with provincial English towns than with the London metropolis. Unlike English towns, however, German towns, and especially the imperial cities, often were independent in both government and culture, subordinate neither to a strong central authority nor to an exclusive cultural center. Both the smaller German towns and the English metropolis attracted immigration, especially of young women and men who could find work there more readily than in the countryside. Yet the difference in scale between the German city of at most 40,000 and the London of 200,000 in 1600, and 400,000 by the mid-seventeenth century, probably involved a difference in the quality of life as well.[43] London's large population may have led to an increased confusion of classes and loosening of the controls that would operate in a more self-contained community. E. A. Wrigley has suggested that the big city's large number of casual contacts encouraged a shift to "rational," contractual relations in place of reliance on tradition and custom.[44] Some of the differences in outlook between German and English popular literatures undoubtedly are linked to this contrast in their urban scenes. The German towns of the sixteenth century had passed their peak of cultural influence and were to fall still further in the seventeenth, when the Thirty Years' War completed the destruction that economic depression had begun. English provincial towns were also declining in independence and prosperity; but London, the hub of English culture, politics, and economy, was gaining the ground they lost. In broad outline, the fortunes of popular literature in the two countries followed the fortunes of their urban environments: from prosperity to stagnation in Germany, from gradual growth to soaring activity in England.

In both England and Germany, the Reformation modified traditional social orthodoxy even as it redrew the lines of religious orthodoxy. The change in Germany was perhaps more dramatic, because here an indigenous movement took hold of communities that could often induce the authorities to follow their lead; and also because, with its division into conflicting sects, post-Reformation Germany was to become a religious as well as political battleground. In England, where the break with Rome was more or less peacefully imposed from above, it was only in the later sixteenth and seventeenth centuries that a widespread religious movement—that of Puritanism, supplemented by the seventeenth-century multiplication of sects—gained significant cultural, social, and political influence.

Contemporaries recognized England as a less restrictive environment for women than Germany and the rest of Europe.[45] The English women's freedoms, however, lay mainly in the informal realm of attitudes toward behavior, for their legal rights differed little from those of their German contemporaries. According to the legal and social norms of both countries, women remained throughout their lives subject to the direction of men, first of fathers, then of husbands. Widows might gain somewhat more independence, but in parts of Germany they still needed a guardian to transact certain legal and financial business, and in both countries women (like men) usually remarried promptly when they could.[46] In England and much of Germany control of a wife's property fell wholly into her husband's hands, unless her family took elaborate measures to prevent this. In England married women were legally nonpersons, unable to take any legal action; German wives could do so only with their husbands' consent. In some German areas wives formally retained some rights over their property, but in practice these rights were difficult to enforce against a husband's will.[47] In both countries women could engage independently in trade and for this purpose were seen as legally and economically distinct from their husbands, but in both countries women's economic opportunities were declining during the sixteenth and seventeenth centuries. Men were legally entitled to physical as well as economic power over their wives; they could, of course, claim sexual service and fidelity, and in other matters legal authorities upheld their right to enforce wifely obedience by beating, as long as the women suffered no serious injury. In parts of late medieval Germany, in fact, even a wife's death from beating entailed no punishment for the husband if he swore his blows had not killed her.[48] Moralists in England counseled against the use of violence, while those of Germany accepted it more readily.[49] In practice women could hope for little legal protection, though fortunate ones might be able to rely on families or neighbors for help.

The injunctions of moralists and preachers reinforced this legal framework, repeatedly telling both women and men that women should be chaste, modest, submissive, and silent.[50] German opinion strongly held that a woman should stay at home unless she had a compelling reason for venturing out, such as going to church; certainly she must never leave the house against her husband's will. Visits to female friends, which could lead to nothing but pernicious gossiping, seem to have been frowned upon in sixteenth-century Germany almost as much as trips to taverns. English women were granted more freedom of movement, though they too were to look to their husbands for permission to venture from home. The chief aim of restrictions on women's movements and behavior was to preserve their chastity, a slippery thing which might forsake them at any moment. Men's sexual misbehavior might be a sin and folly, but it was nowhere greeted with the same opprobrium as that of women. Women's modest, humble, and sober conduct was to discourage even the suspicion that they might go astray; the appearance of lightness was almost as bad as the sin itself. An early sixteenth-century German pamphlet exhorts women to careful regulation of their bearing lest they seem proud and wanton; an honest woman should walk "wie eine müde Kuh [like a tired cow]."[51] Given the frequency of complaints about contrary sorts of female behavior in both countries, it is doubtful how widely women adhered to such rigorous precepts. Still, for those who wished to be considered good, convention dictated downcast eyes, silent and retiring ways, and a dutiful submission to the commands of their menfolk.

Perhaps the most striking divergence between English and German treatment of women, and the most egregious link between early modern cultural misogyny and social reality, appears in the prosecution of witchcraft. While no one would argue that misogynistic fears were the sole cause of witch-hunting, they cannot be left out of account, especially given the strong focus on sexuality and its perversion in the literature on witchcraft.[52] From the late fifteenth century through the seventeenth, European communities prosecuted and executed tens of thousands of people, mostly women, for mischievous sorcery and heretical pacts with the devil. Germany was the center of large and recurrent panics; torture was used to extract further accusations from those arrested, resulting in massive trials and burnings of "witches" from all social levels and both sexes, though women always predominated. England had its share of witch scares also, but on a much smaller scale. Here again the majority of those accused were women, but the numbers of arrests and convictions were much lower.[53] Part of the explanation for this difference lies in contrasting criminal procedures: since England never adopted the inquisitorial Roman law prevalent on the Continent, English witch-hunters were unable to make systematic use of torture. Thus, they could not elicit confessions of massive witches' sabbaths, with the huge multiplication of victims such confessions allowed. It has been suggested, also, that in England the learned construct of demonic heresy failed to impose itself on the more popular fear and resentment of damage caused by unseen forces.[54] While Keith Thomas and Alan Macfarlane have seen the victimization of women in witchcraft trials as the result of their economic vulnerability, Erik Midelfort has linked it with demographic and economic conditions that fostered a fear of "loose" women, and Christina Larner has connected it with the Reformation and the intensification of cultural misogyny.[55] All of these factors are closely interrelated.

In both England and Germany the family fulfilled central economic and social as well as religious functions. Training of apprentices, as of courtiers, took place within the household, with master artisan or noble patron filling the father's role as guardian, instructor, and disciplinarian. Popular literature took this familial setting for granted in its depictions of contemporary life. Parents often exerted decisive influence over their children's careers and marriages, as social theory prescribed and practice had confirmed. At the same time, however, the sixteenth and seventeenth centuries saw increasing criticism of parental control over marriages, and English popular literature strongly endorsed the demand for freedom of choice for the young. In England, according to Stone, children were gradually gaining first the right of veto and then, by the eighteenth century, the right to choose their own mates.[56] For the mid- to lower social levels, control of courtship was solidly in the hands of the young even in the sixteenth century.[57] In Germany, Luther and other moralists condemned parental tyranny, even though it was the Protestant reformers who insisted most strongly on the need for parental consent to children's marriages.[58] In contrast to the English situation, the tightening of legal control over marriage in Germany during the sixteenth and seventeenth centuries bolstered the power of parents, whose consent was increasingly required for valid marriage.[59]

The familial structures of the two countries appear basically similar, making it more difficult to account for attitudinal differences. Alan Macfarlane has advanced a wide-ranging characterization of England's unique and early development of individualism and capitalism, interweaving this with a broad conceptualization of the familial system; but it remains a puzzle to explain why, if England was indeed so different, this should have been so.[60] Macfarlane's analysis of the "Malthusian" marriage system—characteristic of modern Western Europe and, in Macfarlane's view, of England as early as 1300—raises interesting issues for the comparison of England and Germany. In this system marriage is seen not as inevitable and universal but rather as the result of a carefully calculated personal choice. Because marriage is deliberately chosen, postponed, or avoided, Macfarlane has argued, fertility in such societies can respond to the economic situation and avoid the Malthusian disasters of overpopulation, famine, and pestilence. Macfarlane has linked this distinctive marriage pattern to a wide range of attitudes and practices of early modern marriages: most notably a relatively egalitarian conception of the relations between husband and wife, a central focus on this relationship rather than on wider kin ties, and a perception of children as costly rather than as a source of wealth. The analysis of street literature suggests that various elements of the system, which in Macfarlane's analysis appear logically interconnected, are separable, for while Germany and England shared some distinctive features of this pattern, they diverged markedly on others.

3.

The Literature
of the Streets

In many ways the study of women's history and the study of popular culture pose parallel problems. Current understanding is limited not only by the youth of these fields of scholarship but also by the difficulty of reconstructing the lives, thoughts, and roles of people whose activities were largely restricted to the fringes of the well-documented, male, upper-class culture. Even if authors of popular literature had a humble readership in view, works produced by, and for the profit of, a more educated class can hardly present a direct expression of the attitudes and concerns of their consumers.[1] Similarly, in an age when authorship remained almost exclusively male, literature is bound to reveal more about men's views of women than about how the women addressed may have viewed themselves. Despite these limitations, however, the evidence of popular literature provides insights into a decisive link between the mainstream, literate, male culture and the groups dominated by it—the illiterate, the semiliterate, women, the poor. Many works in both England and Germany made explicit attempts to appeal to women, evidently seeking to include them among their readers, hearers, and singers. Especially in works that focused on female exemplars, authors clearly anticipated a substantial female audience. Many of the ballad singers and sellers of later seventeenth-century England seem to have been women, and in Germany, too, they participated in the trade.[2] Even if women saw popular literature as the product of a foreign milieu, it informed their sense of the attitudes and expectations of society and of their fellows.

Any attempt at historical interpretation of literary sources has numerous pitfalls to avoid, some obvious and some less so. To begin with the obvious: literature is not life, and though everyone knows this, it is easy to be lulled by the repetitive reading of literary patterns into assuming that they reflect reality. Analysis of such sources requires alertness not only to distortions of real actions and social relationships, but to distortions of actual attitudes as well. Cultural ideas about women and gender are only one of a combination of influences shaping an author's presentation of women, including such factors as literary conventions, commercial or political aims, the author's temperament and artistic skill, and even, to an uncertain extent, the author's experience of "real life." On the other hand, none of these factors is a static category, as all interact and react upon each other. Literary convention, for example, both responds to and helps shape cultural thinking about women, which likewise bears a reciprocal if convoluted relationship to real social interaction between the sexes. Thus, there is no such thing as "mere" literary convention. But the unraveling of these tortuous cultural connections is not so obvious and requires both caution and sensitivity.

Of course, the significance of the texts of street literature is not fixed by their authors: these texts would be much less interesting if they had been written merely for the authors' private amusement. It was in their audience's reception of them that the texts became culturally powerful. Just as authors drew on common language and assumptions about gender in producing these texts, the audience drew on these assumptions in reading or hearing them; but just as the texts promoted their own versions of the ideas they borrowed and embodied, the audience in its reception and uses of the texts participated actively in the shaping of common assumptions. The performance of street literature, particularly of songs, made it especially susceptible to independent use and interpretation by audiences who might themselves become performers. Singers in the ballad audience, for instance, undoubtedly chose to remember portions of songs that pleased them while forgetting portions that did not, or devised their own replacements for segments they disliked or forgot. The oral history of folkloric ballads attests to this practice, so that the printed texts preserve only the audience's starting point. Such uses and interpretations need not have meshed with the authors' intentions. Differences in the assumptions brought to a text could change its meaning, and it is likely that differences of sex, class, and geographical location gave many texts different cultural meanings for different audiences. Thus while from one point of view commercialized street literature can be seen as a hegemonic tool, purveying mostly moralized justifications of the dominant cultural order, it could not be exclusively that. If the texts exerted power on their audience, the reverse was true as well, partly through authors' commercially motivated attempts to respond to popular tastes, but more importantly through audience uses of the texts themselves. Unfortunately, any analysis of such uses must remain speculative in the absence of direct evidence about audience reception.[3]

With the growth of printing, both England and Germany developed a flourishing market for broadsides and pamphlets containing songs, jokes, news, and stories. Sold at markets or fairs, hawked in the streets of towns, or carried to the country by peddlers, these productions reached a far wider audience than more sedate volumes of sustained discourse. The songs, as well as some of the other rhymes and tales, were designed more for oral presentation than for silent reading. Many who were unable or unwilling to buy or read the texts heard them sung or spoken in taverns, fairs, and streets. Authors and publishers catered to buyers rather than to an informal, nonpaying public; but it was an advantage for sellers to draw a crowd, even if only a small minority would buy. Even the poorer and less literate, whether or not they thought these productions expressed their own outlook, would have experienced their performance, in what may have been one of their closest contacts with the world of print. Such works of popular entertainment, the least common denominator of public discourse, formed a bridge between oral and written cultures.

In England the dominant form of this entertainment was the broadside ballad, a single printed sheet, usually decorated with rough woodcuts. A huge variety of subjects—including knightly adventure, ill-fated love, grisly news of murder or war, religious and moral precepts, jests, prodigies, and portents—appeared in songs, to be sold by street singers and country peddlers. Tunes were indicated by name, with no musical notation; audiences either knew the tune beforehand or learned it from the ballad seller. These sheets grew popular during the second half of the sixteenth century, and by the seventeenth they had become a flood.

Ballads were sung in streets, fairs, and markets, where presumably anyone with a little time to spare could hear them; but the precise numbers and class identity of their public remain uncertain. Authors frequently include direct exhortations to listen or buy, and these are addressed to both sexes and all social levels: good Christians, young men, maidens, wives, fathers. Occasionally these addresses are more socially specific, as in appeals to gallants or masters, but the obvious intent is to cast the net as widely as possible.[4] Ballads were regularly sold for a penny in the sixteenth and seventeenth centuries.[5] This was the same price as admission to the pit of the Globe theater; and according to a jestbook from around 1600, a penny would buy "a pot of ale,"[6] though the price of the latter undoubtedly varied with the pretensions of the establishment that sold it. Chapbooks, short pamphlets printed on cheap paper, ran to three or four pence, with prices rising into shillings and pounds for longer pamphlets and bound volumes. Since paper accounted for a significant portion of the cost of printed matter in both England and Germany, shorter generally meant cheaper. According to J. E. T. Rogers, carpenters' wages in England stood at about twelve pence per day from the late sixteenth century through about 1630, when they began to rise, reaching twenty pence by 1680; but London wages were well above average, hovering close to three shillings (thirty-six pence) per day in the 1670s. A laborer working for such an artisan was paid about two-thirds of this rate.[7] Of course, these levels of pay applied to workers fortunate enough to have steady work and a marketable skill. Even with secure wages, the high cost of necessities left little to spare, particularly for those with a family to support.[8] This may have been one reason for the ballads' tendency to pitch their appeals to unattached youth. Wages lagged considerably behind the price inflation of the sixteenth century but began to recover in purchasing power from about 1630. Ballads and cheaper pamphlets would certainly have been a luxury, though not a completely inaccessible one, for better-off workers who thought such entertainment worth the price of a few drinks. They became more affordable during the course of the seventeenth century, as their price remained steady while wages rose.

Of course, relative cheapness is no proof of a humble readership; upper-class readers were not above spending pennies for popular works, as the preservation of these pieces by elite collectors attests. Though literati often denigrated ballads as mere amusements of the rabble, it would be a mistake to take this assessment at face value. Printed ballads had a substantial clientele among the well-to-do, both the wealthier merchant and craft families of London and the gentry, nobility, and their retainers who frequented the court and capital. Early ballads from the sixteenth century appear in the songbooks of minstrels who performed in the houses of the nobility, suggesting an established audience at this social level.[9] Printing lowered the prestige of ballads even as it expanded their audience, but it by no means excluded the upper classes.

The ballads' audience spread beyond the circle of their purchasers, however. They were not only sold and sung in the streets but also decorated the walls of drinking houses. References to them in contemporary literature associate them with a motley crowd of hearers and performers, though here again satirists probably exaggerate the base status of the ballad audience for comic effect. A character in a 1640 play comments that condemned criminals

> are sure
> Ere they be scarce cold, to be chronicled
> In excellent new ballads, which being sung
> In the streets 'mong boys and girls, colliers and carmen,
> Are bought as great memorials of their fames,
> Which to perpetuate, they are commonly stuck up
> With as great triumph in the tippling-houses,
> As they were 'scutcheons.[10]

In 1656 a mock elegy dedicated to the balladist Martin Parker celebrated his numerous songs,

> Which (as was us'd of old) did kindly greet
> The peoples ears as they did pass the street;
> Sung to the pleasant Treble and the Base,
> The Small or Great, the Sharp or Flat, to grace
> Thy sublime Sonnets; was not every Song
> Of thine applauded by the thirsty throng.[11]

Governments repeatedly sought to regulate or suppress the circulation of ballads, with their potential for disruptive and seditious effect. The 1557 incorporation of the London Stationers' Company provided for some measure of government control, as it granted the company a monopoly of printing and required it to oversee the registry and licensing of all printed matter.[12] An edict of 1649 imposed heavy penalties for the singing and sale of ballads, apparently with some success, but after the Restoration they regained their vigor.[13]

Most of the authors wrote anonymously, though a few—notably Thomas Deloney in the sixteenth century and Martin Parker and Laurence Price in the seventeenth—became known for their ballad writing.

Parker, an especially witty and prolific versifier of the first half of the seventeenth century, sometimes stirred up public demand by answering his own ballads with others that took the opposite view. All the known ballad authors were male, but details about their lives are scarce. Those engaged in more respectable literary production—playwrights, for example, or even snobbish pamphleteers—viewed balladists with scorn.[14] As Thomas Nashe complained in 1589: "What politique Counsailour or valiant Souldier will ioy or glorie of this, in that some stitcher, Weauer, spendthrift, or Fidler, hath shuffled or slubbered vp a few ragged Rimes, in the memoriall of the ones prudence, or the others prowesse? It makes the learned sort to be silent, when as they see vnlearned sots so insolent."[15] Although imputations of low social status were a stock libel, the balladists' reputation as plebeian and ale-sodden may have had some basis in reality: William Elderton was a famous toper, and Deloney was a silk weaver, while Parker is said to have been a tavern keeper.[16] Contempt for their inelegant, commercialized literary efforts played an equal part in their low repute, though some respectable men of letters were known to have written an occasional ballad.[17] Evidence on the pay of professional ballad writers is inconclusive, but for most it could hardly have been enough to provide their sole support.[18]

Many of the ballads show their authors to have been educated enough not only to grind out doggerel rhymes, but to have gained a passing familiarity with some characters and conventions drawn from classical and courtly literary traditions. The names of Venus, Cupid, and Vulcan might casually be dropped, or the balladist might sing of Dido's frustrated love for Aeneas. Sometimes such classical themes and names were drawn from the contemporary theater—building on the popularity of a successful play, or perhaps helping advertise a play to the wider ballad audience.[19] In other cases ballads were modeled according to the conventions of artificial pastoral love scenes, with "Phillis," "Amintas," "Corinda," and their ilk tumbling into each other's arms or lamenting their unhappy love. While such pieces as these may have appealed especially to an audience that knew the world of courtly fashion or aspired to know it, it seems likely that they spread beyond the social circles they described. Most ballads did not owe such obvious debts to the fashions of elite culture.

Chapbooks were somewhat more expensive than ballads, and they usually lacked the musical appeal that could fix the latter in people's minds. Like the songs, however, they could blend the elements of oral and written culture, presenting jests, riddles, and tales to while away the time with company. A late seventeenth-century chapbook called *Canterbury Tales*, by "Chaucer Junior," recommended itself as "Composed For the Entertainment of All Ingenuous young Men and Maids at their merry Meeting, upon Christmas, Easter, Whitsontide, or any other time; especially in long Winter Evenings." It included humorous tales, together with songs for the various holidays.[20] Throughout the period under review here, chapbooks were less numerous than ballads, and their typical cheap format became fixed only in the second half of the seventeenth century. Before that time, the appeal of pamphlets seems generally directed to a more sophisticated audience than that of ballads.

It remains difficult to estimate the proportion of people who were capable of reading even a literature as simple as that provided by broadsides and chapbooks. Levels of literacy differed dramatically between country and town, and wide differences between different districts make generalization difficult. David Cressy has estimated, on the basis of signatures on loyalty oaths, an overall figure of 30 percent literacy for rural England in the 1640s. London, the center of production and distribution for popular literature, showed a much higher degree of literacy; even among women, who in other areas were nearly all illiterate, over 20 percent could sign London court depositions. Cressy found that proximity to trading centers played a significant role in the literacy of a given area, while within each community literacy was closely correlated with social status. According to Cressy's findings, literacy levels fluctuated throughout the sixteenth and seventeenth centuries, with a generally upward trend, to reach in the early eighteenth century a level exceptionally high for early modern Europe: 45 percent for men, 25 percent for women.[21]

The evidence of court depositions, as Cressy has pointed out, relates to a group of people who were selected for respectability and reliability; thus, they probably tended to be more literate than the population at large. Loyalty oaths also probably omitted some of the more marginal members of the community. This overestimate may be offset, however, by the fact that reading was taught before writing during this period; thus, many may have acquired the limited reading skills needed for perusal of simple popular literature without learning to sign their names.[22] This could be especially likely among women, for whom reading was considered spiritually valuable even if writing seemed superfluous. For a metropolis like London, therefore, and to a lesser extent for other towns, a majority of the population potentially could have been exposed to ballads and chapbooks. Those who could not read had a good chance of knowing someone who could or of hearing the songs retailed in the streets and taverns. In rural areas the opportunities certainly were not as great; but if the overall rural literacy rate was near 30 percent, as Cressy has suggested, there could have been a considerable literate audience, especially in areas within striking distance of market towns.

The chronological pattern of popular literature in Germany differed from that of England, but they shared much in character and tone. The early development of printing gave Germany a head start, and the controversies of the Reformation brought a boom in popular literature. While broadsides had been used for songs and pictures from the fifteenth century in sixteenth-century Germany the short pamphlet became the most widespread format for cheap popular literature. Ranging from flimsy song pamphlets of two or four leaves to substantial religious tracts of fifty pages or more, *Flugschriften* provided a medium for polemic, news, religion, and entertainment. Like the English ballads and chapbooks, short German pamphlets and broadsides were hawked in the streets and markets, though their distribution is even more difficult to trace because of Germany's regional diversity. Towns repeatedly issued ordinances to curtail or prohibit the singing and selling of unseemly songs, satires, caricatures, and pictures. A Saxon ordinance of 1546, directed against libelous satires, noted "daß etzliche Mannere, Weibere und Knaben, gedruckte Büchere, Liedere, Reime und Gemelde vmbtragen [that many men, women, and boys go about selling printed books, songs, rhymes, and pictures]."[23] As in England, the authorities' concern was mainly political: in 1547, during the Schmalkaldic War, the Nuremberg council forbade "alle lateinischen und deutschen Schmachschriften, Büchlin, Lieder und dergleichen Druck und Gemäl, sonderlich diese Kreigsläuft belangend [all Latin and German lampoons, pamphlets, songs, and the like printed works and pictures, especially those concerning the present war]."[24] Officials might also wish to preserve their community's moral tone, but the spread of broadsides and pamphlets apparently was difficult to control. A song pamphlet of 1569, *Ein Schön New Geistlich Lied / so wider das vnfletige Schandt Huren liedlein / das Jagts jm zu gemacht ist worden / so man jetzundt gar gemein pfleget zu singen* [A lovely new spiritual song, against the monstrous, shameful, whorish song, *His hunt is done*, which people now are singing everywhere], complains of the lewd songs and jokes retailed in streets and taverns among all ages and sexes:

Da hört man seltzam schwenk /	One can hear jests most rare Over bench and table there
vber tisch vnd vber benck /	When they have all been
wann sie haben getruncken /	drinking.
. . . da singt schon / Jederman	. . . there sings everyone, it's true,
vnuerschämpte grobe zotten /	Shameless, dirty jokes and ditties,
wie sies gelernet han.	As they have learned to do.
Es ist auch jetzt der sitt /	And now the custom is
man schont niemant hiemit /	That no one's spared from this;
Weibshild [*sic*] oder Jungfrawen /	Now women and maidens young
zu hören vnd drauff schawen /	Learn to listen when it's sung,
lernens nun / jagts jm zu.	Unto *His hunt is done.*[25]

Such songs and rhymed pamphlets held their prominent place in German popular literature throughout the sixteenth century, but after 1620 they became much rarer. During the Thirty Years' War, broadsides became the commonest form of street literature, but many of these, with their elaborate engravings, consequent high prices, and rather sophisticated subjects, were limited to an educated and prosperous audience. The war, together with the decline in the towns' prosperity and independence, seems to have stifled the lower levels of popular literature in Germany just as these productions were reaching their heyday in England. A trickle of songs and rhymed pamphlets persisted, and news sheets on current events abounded; but street literature aimed at entertainment or edification generally languished at a level far below that of the sixteenth century.

Information on the prices of German popular literature is much more scattered and contradictory than for England, where organization under the Stationers' Company fostered early standardization of prices. For news pamphlets and small tracts, prices seem to have ranged from 3 to 6 pfennigs in the sixteenth and early seventeenth centuries.[26] Song pamphlets were often smaller than news tracts and thus might have been cheaper; but they also seem to have used woodcuts more regularly, which may have evened things out. While English ballads were frequently decorated with reused woodcuts, the German pictures usually appear to have been original. Some German song pamphlets have gilt-edged pages, an expensive touch, but one that at least in some cases was added by later collectors. Broadsides seem to have been more expensive than pamphlets and often were sold at least as much for their pictures as for their text. Rolf Wilhelm Brednich, in his study of song sheets, notes that a broadside sold for 20 pfennigs at the close of the fifteenth century, which would have consumed the lion's share of the daily wage of 24 to 28 pfennigs for reapers and masons.[27] Prices decreased in the early sixteenth century with a fall in paper prices.[28] William Coupe, in his work on the seventeenth-century broadsheet, dismisses earlier estimates of 10 to 50 pfennigs for the price of engraved broadsides, asserting that the price must actually have been 100–200 pfennigs; but both ranges are undocumented. Coupe sees the broadside as appealing to all levels of society, collected by both burghers and their serving maids; though if his estimate of the price is correct, one might wonder about his picture of the maid gluing into her trunk a piece of paper worth two months' wages.[29] According to Walter Krieg, the daily wage of a master mason or carpenter in the early sixteenth century was about 24 pfennigs, while a day laborer would earn 60 pfennigs a week.[30] By 1600 a mason in Klosterneuburg earned 48 pfennigs or more per day, but prices had risen even more dramatically. Wheat, for example, cost more than three times as much in 1600 as at mid-century, and the price of paper seems roughly to have paralleled that of food.[31] The chaotic wartime inflation after 1620 makes estimates especially difficult. There is some evidence that wages were keeping better pace with prices after about the 1630s, but both yearly and regional variations make generalizations risky.[32] On the whole, the popular literature of early modern Germany was more expensive than that of England; nothing seems to have matched the standardized cheapness of the English broadside ballads, though pamphlets may have been roughly the same price as their English counterparts. The simpler and cruder broadsides decorated with woodcuts may have reached down to the price level of short pamphlets, but more elaborate ones must have appealed to a higher social level, especially as the more costly copper engraving tended to replace woodcuts during the seventeenth century.[33]

Most of these pieces were printed anonymously, but there were many authors who did sign their names. They ranged from clerics to artisans and included poets who identified themselves as soldiers, nobles, and merrymakers (Schlemmer). The best-known and most successful, Hans Sachs, was a shoemaker of Nuremberg in the sixteenth century. Even one woman, Barbara Münchheym, signed her name to her pamphlet on the adventures of Saint Ita.[34] Most were not professional writers; even more than in England, there was hardly enough money in literature, let alone street literature, to eke out a living. According to Krieg, authors' pay in the second half of the seventeenth century averaged 12–16 groschen (144–192 pfennigs) per sheet, plus some free copies; thus short, cheap pieces would have paid especially badly.[35]

Literacy in Germany has not yet received as systematic a study as that of Cressy on early modern England, and most of the available evidence is literary or anecdotal. Rolf Engelsing, in his survey of this evidence, has noted that an early sixteenth-century Basel schoolmaster expressly advertised his services to artisans, women, and girls. Lübeck schools at the close of the century similarly extended their teaching beyond the elite. As in England, women were certainly less literate than men.[36] Both the growth of schools and the vigor of popular literature in sixteenth-century Germany suggest a considerable spread of literacy, and Gerald Strauss has concluded that "by the middle of the sixteenth century literacy was taken for granted in the elevated ranks of society, regarded as normal among artisans, and noted without astonishment in the peasantry."[37] The same probably could not be said about England until the following century, but Germany's sixteenth-century advantage in literacy was lost in the seventeenth. The long disruptions of war hampered education in Germany even as English elementary education, despite setbacks, was gaining ground. Regional diversity was also great, and the discrepancy between town and country may effectively have limited popular literature to towns and their environs in Germany even more than in England.

While the production of popular literature in England was concentrated in a single center, London, the German sources for this study were printed in over fifty different towns (including Swiss ones). This variety is somewhat deceptive, however: many towns printed only an odd news pamphlet or two when something startling happened nearby, and production of the bulk of this literature was limited to a few major centers. Of the sources whose place of origin is identified, Nuremberg accounts for over a third, followed by Augsburg with about half as many. These two cities were the chief producers of popular literature designed as entertainment rather than journalism, and they were active particularly in the sixteenth and the first half of the seventeenth centuries. Other significant sources of street literature include Erfurt, Basel, and Cologne.[38] In the sixteenth century especially, the printing of popular street literature was concentrated in Protestant areas. The Reformation had made highly effective use of pamphlet and song in spreading its message, and the audience built up in part by religious ferment also was tapped by printers with more secular aims. Of the German sources for which printing location can be determined, at least 180 were printed in Protestant areas, against only about 30 for Catholic ones. This disparity has made it difficult to analyze religious differences in the literature on disorderly women, as the Catholic sample is simply not large enough. Even for crime literature, in which the balance is somewhat better (15 to 9), consistent patterns are elusive.

The German street literature shares much with the English in tone and theme. Both drew on a common European tradition of jests and anecdotes; often different versions of the same tales appear in the popular literature of both countries. In the simple and direct language of their songs, also, the two parallel each other. In the German literature as in the English, there is a distinct shift in tone, and probably also in audience, between popular song and nonmusical pamphlets in rhyme or prose. Discursive pamphlets in both countries were more heavily larded with Latin phrases, classical allusions, and satirical references to the doings of the fashionable world. As pamphlets grew longer, they tended to add dedications, prefaces, mottoes, and similar paraphernalia of cultivation. Even when they claimed to be addressing a general readership, their aim was set higher than that of the songs.

The pamphlets and songs offer internal hints about the social class of their readers, though speculations based on these can have no pretension to certainty. Ballads and pamphlets in both countries frequently relate the doings of tradesmen and craftsmen of various levels of prosperity and with varying degrees of humor and seriousness. They commonly assume that only the industriousness of both sexes can ward off poverty. In England they often champion the virtue of the humble against the arrogance of the rich, while in Germany many show a keen sense of the economic precariousness of life. On the other hand, fashionable English love ballads, with their modish scenes of pastoral lovemaking, make arcane references to Diana or the Greek fate Atrapos, while German pamphlets are sprinkled with Latin tags which only the educated could fully comprehend. Similarly, the many admonitions against wasting one's fortune at the alehouse assume that one has a fortune to lose.

It is probably a mistake, then, to look for a homogeneous audience for popular literature in either country; different songs and pamphlets might appeal to different social groups, but the evidence suggests an overall audience distributed widely across the social scale. Given the variation of literacy with social status, the commercial aim of publishers, and the role of oral performance, one can distinguish two distinct, though overlapping, levels of consumption. The paying public possessed both literacy and disposable income, however modest; it was probably made up mostly of urban merchants and craftsmen, together with some of their wives, apprentices, and children, in addition to some members of the upper classes and their retainers, and a more limited rural audience which probably did not extend much below the class of yeomen or prosperous peasants.[39] This was the group whose tastes authors and printers cared most to consult. The nonpaying crowd of listeners and singers, who might enjoy the performance without expecting to hear their distinctive views represented, could include humbler workers, and possibly greater numbers of women. In casting their net this widely, ballads and songs assumed a broad social consensus of shared values, and they promoted this consensus by embodying it in public discourse. In this the German conception of the common man was matched by English notions about public opinion, although the higher German prices made for a more restricted primary audience.

These printed songs and stories formed a bridge between written and oral cultures, both in their own oral performance and in the exchange of texts. While the printed sources sometimes were adaptations of songs or stories that had first gained oral currency, the reverse process—from ballad or pamphlet into oral tradition—is better documented and possibly more common. The great majority of printed works in both countries appear to have been written by individual early modern authors, even in cases where the themes were borrowed from earlier written or oral sources. The oral folklore materials that have been collected since the nineteenth century provide valuable hints about the lasting popularity and later transformations of certain themes or works—such as those of Adelger and Tannhäuser in Germany or Robin Hood in England—but they offer little help in assessing the realities of early modern authorship, performance, and audience.[40]

Hints about the songs' oral history may be gleaned from the printed word, but much remains obscure. Natascha Würzbach has analyzed the ways in which the demands of performance shaped the texts of English balladists. Beyond this, however, the passage into oral culture removed the uses of texts from control or definition by authors, even more than the ordinary act of reading would. The performance and reception of ballads, a field for which our knowledge is unhappily scant, were central to their impact, and particularly to their impact on early modern women. While women's role in the creation, transmission, and transformation of the materials of oral culture was undoubtedly considerable, the printed works under study here must be seen as largely the product of male culture—at least of male selection, and usually of male authorship. As members of the audience, however, and in the oral adoption of the printed texts, women had a much more significant role to play. Authors who hoped for commercial success in a mixed audience, as many seem to have done, had to appeal to women's tastes as well as men's. The authors' conceptions of women's preferences may or may not have matched women's real attitudes, but the attempt to reach them had important effects on popular literature. This was true even when the technique employed was to rouse women's irritation in order to provoke mirth, and thus increase sales, among the male audience. Though their influence was indirect and difficult to assess, real women and their reactions found a dark reflection in the mirror of street literature.

In both countries street literature had special appeal to the tastes of youth. Complaints about the undesirable moral effects of ballads and songs pointed particularly to the corruption of the young, and many songs advertised themselves as pleasant for young men and maids to sing. Deriders of ballads described their singers not only as people of vulgar class but as "boys and girls," while in Germany young girls were chided for learning songs of lovemaking which would undermine their virtue.[41] Many of the songs' prevailing themes—especially love, sex, and courtship—are matters of particular concern to youth, while others—ballads showing the trials of marriage or celebrating the carefree bachelor's life of the tavern—similarly could have captured youthful imaginations. A married woman's complaint, *A Woman's Work is never done*, is presented as "a Song for Maids to sing,"[42] while another ballad, *The Maidens sad complaint for want of a Husband*, combines the young girl's desirous lament with two lines of letters illustrating the alphabet, presumably as a help in learning to read.[43] Moralizing songs similarly tend to address their messages to the young, in such works as *The Virgins A.B.C.*, *The Young-Mans A.B.C.*, and *Du junger man merck vnd versteh / Vnd wilt du greyffen zu der Ehe* [Young man, unto this song give heed / If thou to marriage wouldst proceed].[44]

Most songs take the part of youth against age, especially in England; they condemn parents who marry off their children against their will, and they humorously sympathize with the young man married to a hideous old woman (in Germany) or the fresh young maid tied to a decrepit miser (in England). The large numbers of young people living and working in London and in German towns offered a tempting market. Moralists hoped to feed them sugarcoated pills while they were still impressionable, and booksellers might find it easier to coax pennies for frivolous expenditure from the young than from their elders. This concentration on youth probably contributed to both the playful tone of much street literature and the contempt of literati for the genre. At the same time, however, its youthful audience must have given street literature an especially powerful influence on the popular imagination. As both pastime and primer of the young, these pieces helped shape the conceptions and aspirations of people who were not yet securely locked into their place in society, who were seeking ways to satisfy dreams and yearnings even as they moved toward marriage and a settled position in life.

The great diversity of street literature complicates the analysis of its themes and images. With informal abandon, its authors adopted, adapted, or parodied existing literary genres, even as the common aims of popular appeal and oral performance imposed common structures on street literature itself. While some pieces were drawn directly from medieval sources or built on medieval models, others were based on contemporary life. Authors and audiences may have viewed material drawn from certain traditions—of chivalric adventure or fabliaux-style adultery, for example—as conventional amusements with no relevance to everyday existence. Even if the audience recognized such themes as dated, however, their persistent appeal testifies to the imaginative life they enjoyed in early modern popular culture. After all, old jokes are retold only as long as someone laughs. Interestingly, the German sources show a greater tendency to relate stories from the past or from foreign milieus than do the English, which rely more heavily on contemporary themes (the English material is less than 10 percent past or foreign, the German over 20 percent).

While the sources resist any systematic typology, it is useful to note sharp contrasts in form: to distinguish topical news reports from chivalric adventures, jests from religious meditations or moralizing fables, satire from serious love songs. Different types, which may well have been appealing to different audiences, gained popularity at different times in each country—a phenomenon which is only partly literary accident, for it also reflects changes in cultural tastes. Of course, the various forms often overlap and blend into each other. For street literature, the most significant generic distinction is that between spoken rhymes or songs and the prose pamphlets meant for reading. The division between literature designed for the ear and that designed for the eye is central, as oral presentation has its own imperatives about the kinds of statements that can be made, the manner of making them, and their uses for hearers.[45] Also, since the oral forms were uniquely accessible to nonreaders, the distinctive features of oral style went along with a difference in audience.

For all its richness as a source for the study of popular culture, street literature presents some problems that require caution. Information on authorship and distribution is often elusive. Questions of the popularity and typicality of individual pieces also pose difficulties, though one can pay particular attention, as I have here, to works that were printed repeatedly. Further indications of popularity include the reuse of tunes named for earlier songs and the mention in other contemporary sources of a song, its theme, or its characters. In many cases the dates of these fugitive items remain doubtful, especially since popular works in both countries often were reprinted from earlier editions. Thus the date of a particular copy tells nothing of the work's origin and later history, and changes across time can be difficult to trace. Though I have sought to analyze chronological developments where possible, the conclusions must remain tentative.

Interpretation of early modern popular literature is further complicated by the vagaries of survival. Most of these productions have perished, and we owe the preservation of those that still exist to a handful of collectors and libraries. While these modern collections are wide-ranging, there is no guarantee that they are fully representative of what once existed. For England, the registers of the Stationers' Company provide some clues about the survival of ballads printed between 1557 and 1709. Of those registered, less than a third seem to be extant today; conversely, a relatively small proportion of those now extant appears in the registers.[46] Even allowing for gaps in the record, this suggests both a very partial survival and a great deal of unlicensed printing. For Germany the situation is more complicated. Since there was no contemporary record comparable to the Stationers' registers, we do not know what proportion survives. Germany and its libraries have suffered much from the destruction of wars, in this century as in the seventeenth; thus a greater proportion has been lost than in England, which increases the chance of imbalance in the sources now available. Collectors naturally preserved only the pieces they found interesting; the Wick collection in Zurich, for example, concentrates on accounts of miraculous or horrific occurrences. Other collections are more comprehensive, like the large Meusebach collection of pamphlets, now in the Deutsche Staatsbibliothek, Berlin; but the possibility of skew is worth remembering.

The period considered here, roughly 1550–1680, is designed to include times of flourishing popular literature in both countries. After the Reformation-era flood of confessional pamphlets, popular literature prospered in Germany up to about 1620; thereafter news and political pamphlets continued to thrive, but those dealing with social topics became relatively scarce. In England the boom in street literature dates from the later sixteenth century on, with a lull during the 1640s and 1650s, when political pamphlets replaced ballads as the staple of the popular press. The London Stationers' registers list numerous titles for the second half of the sixteenth century, but disappointingly few sixteenth-century ballads survive.[47] The chronological gap between English and German popular literatures complicates the comparison between them, as apparent contrasts could reflect a difference in time rather than in culture. Overall, the median date for German sources falls just after 1600, as against the 1640s for the English; and the spread of sources is far from even for either country.

Of course, differences across time are as much worth knowing as differences across cultures: the point is to distinguish between them. One would like to know, for example, whether the greater vigor of English heroines reflects English attitudes as opposed to German or seventeenth-century attitudes as opposed to sixteenth. If the sources were evenly spaced through time, such issues would be easier to determine; but the relative scarcity of sixteenth-century English and seventeenth-century German materials makes it more difficult. Fortunately there are ways of compensating for the imperfections of the surviving sources. One can pay special attention to the cases where direct parallels exist, either across time in one country or at the same period in both countries. In addition, since some offerings survive even from the lean years in each country, one can attempt to assess the direction of change. In the case of the contrasting heroines, the English development is toward increasing adventuresomeness, while in Germany the earliest heroines are among the most vivid. A factor that makes dates more difficult to trace, but also makes the chronological disparity somewhat less troubling, is the slow pace of change in popular literature. Many pieces in both countries were reprinted across spans of fifty or one hundred years (or more) without undergoing major change, and the continuity of some popular themes extended well into the eighteenth century. With all this said, the chronological uncertainties remain a caution against hasty generalizations about Anglo-German contrasts.

This study is based on a review of about 4,000 works of popular literature, with closer study of about 900 that deal directly with disorderly women—those who stepped outside the normal bounds of social prescription. Of the English items, about 2,500 are broadside ballads, which probably accounts for over half of those extant; the total number surviving has been estimated at seven to eight thousand, with possibly half of these duplicates.[48] The 350 English pamphlets scanned are necessarily a smaller proportion of the many thousands of these that survive. For Germany, I have reviewed about 1,000 pamphlets and 250 broadsides, making close readings of 350 of these pieces. There is no doubt that fewer of these ephemeral works survive for Germany than for England, and at least in the case of ballads it seems likely that fewer were originally printed in Germany than in England. A nineteenth-century count recorded about 3,500 extant song broadsides and pamphlets.[49] More have been discovered since, though others have been lost, and the number surviving now is uncertain. I have generally excluded pamphlets longer than about ten pages as likely to be too elaborate or expensive to cater to the street literature market.

Disorderly Women

4.

Woman as Protagonist:
Virtue and Disorder

 The ideal social and cultural order of early modern Europe called for women to play a secondary role, as helpmates to men rather than principal actors. But literature often departed from this idea, bringing women to center stage. As villainesses such women make their disorderliness clear, but even as heroines they can pose an implicit threat to order—a threat to be contained by rigid adherence to social rules or deflected by ascription of all women's achievements to their love for men. In both England and Germany the female characters of popular literature, though they often played to a sexually mixed audience, were created almost exclusively by men. The adoption of women as protagonists implied for male authors a shift of perspective beyond that required for the simple depiction of women as characters among other characters. Whether for praise, blame, or ridicule, the author imagined a female point of view and a female actor, even though her accomplishments might be negative and passive. The authors' styles of perception and presentation of their heroines and other female protagonists reveal much about the assumptions that they and their audiences brought to the consideration of women in general. The models adopted for these, and particularly for heroines, deserve special attention.

These depictions of women served various aims for male authors and for their male and female audiences. In upholding models for female emulation, authors worked within the socially accepted schemes of female virtue, praising chastity and passivity, but also occasionally admiring active courage. Though some, as moralists, attempted to dictate female behavior, the central aim of this imaginative literature was to entertain, and to entertain not only men but also women, who in both countries were often seen as major consumers of literature that focused on the actions of their own sex. Thus the judgment of what was admirable relied not only on men's conceptions but also on an expectation of women's endorsement. Authors considered what women would accept as well as what they should accept, and their messages both impressed social values on women and solicited women's participation in the reinforcement of those values.

In addition to imagining female endeavor, authors ventured to imitate the female voice. In both countries they devised direct speech for female characters, and in England they often adopted a female character as the main speaker. The female voice was commonly used for caricature; nevertheless, it required from male authors a more vivid conception of femaleness than other forms of characterization. They attempted, if only in play or parody, to imagine what it was like to be a woman, so as to cast in her own words their, and her, message to the public. If the song was intended to be sung by women, as some professed to be, the author faced a still greater challenge: to imagine female experience in a way that women could accept as an entertaining or moving, if not true, representation of their outlook. Use of the female voice was much less common in Germany, partly because of the greater general tendency of English popular pamphlets and broadsides to dialogue and direct speech. Even allowing for this difference, however, women's appearance as central speakers was disproportionately rare in Germany.[1]

The satirical aim is especially strong in the first-person songs of lustful young women, which appeared in both countries. Satire is also evident in the complaints of seduced and abandoned maidens who appear to warn others against the faithlessness of young men, an especially common theme in seventeenth-century England. Such parodic use of the female voice was a timeworn device, whose antecedents in medieval Latin—a language inaccessible to most women—illustrate its distance from real female speech.[2] In both countries many, and perhaps even most, of these female-voiced songs retain male perspective despite their adoption of the female voice. Even in England, the female voice is often "overheard" by a male persona who frames and introduces the female monologue. The female protagonist reveals in her own words what men have always suspected about women, evoking laughter that resounds at women's expense. Women's follies, and particularly women's lasciviousness, are the dominant themes, and the characters range from matrons lamenting their husbands' sexual inadequacies to whores explaining how they gull men into serving their purposes. The device of attributing first-person speech to an absurd character is applied to men also, of course, and such figures as henpecked husbands bring ridicule on themselves as well as on the women of whom they complain.

Not all adoptions of the female voice invite mockery, however. Ballads on English crimes, which frequently impersonate the criminal to give a vivid first-person portrayal of his or her fall and repentance, often take female criminals for their subjects.[3] Their scrutiny of the women's motivation and their imaginative sympathy with the sinner's suffering penitence closely parallel similar treatments of male criminals in their "last good-nights." The processes that lead women to criminal violence are considered to be as interesting as those that tempt men, and the sexes share equally in the cathartic public confession that, if their "own" accounts can be trusted, enables them calmly to face their shameful executions, secure in the hope of forgiveness and salvation.

In both satirical impersonations and gallows confessions, the first-person voice served three paradoxical functions. First, it represented a more fully imagined characterization than third-person narrative, offering, if only in parody, a version of the speaker's subjective experience. On the other hand, it could undercut audience identification with the speakers by presenting them as deviant; the public airing of private matters was hardly respectable, whatever the objective merits of the case. Third, it gave to deviance, instead of a silence imposed by shame, a powerful public voice. This is especially evident in the last good-nights, which often cast evildoers as instructors of the public on proper moral behavior. Thus the first-person voice sent ambiguous messages to its audience, and its ambiguity was intensified by the fact that audiences were also performers. Encouraging both emotive identification and social distancing, the first-person mode invited imaginative play that promoted a view of the self as determined by conscious choice out of a wide range of possibilities.

Other English songs feature more sympathetic women and come closer to adopting a female point of view. Ballads giving counsel to maids on the selection of husbands, or against the selection of any husband, often appear in the first person, with an independent young woman telling others how little she needs male interference in her life. Women complain of their husbands' mistreatment or their lovers' cruelty in terms that make their claims seem reasonable. Even the workaday life of a married woman, in *A Woman's Work is never done*, draws sympathetic scrutiny and detailed expression, though with some satiric touches.[4] Such pieces attribute to women a high degree of self-consciousness, a weighing of their life's pattern against other possible patterns instead of a stolid acceptance of their lot. The female voice of many English ballads represents a recognition of women's subjective experience which goes far beyond the views offered in the German literature.

The clearest difference between the German and English heroines of popular literature is the prominence of religious achievements among the German. Saints and other godly women far outnumber secular heroines in the German literature of both centuries, while in England only a handful of women are celebrated for their piety. More often the English women win renown for their steadfast love, wit, obedience, or courage. The two countries shared an admiration for passive female endurance, and both could be charmed by tales of the long-suffering Griselda, who would have borne even the murder of her children without a disobedient whimper. But English heroines generally take a more active and independent path than those of Germany, and while the English become increasingly intrepid in the seventeenth century, the German heroines show no such development. The earlier celebration of chivalric ladies admired active bravery, but seventeenth-century German authors tended to abandon this theme in favor of suffering sainthood. The English showed a greater preference for contemporary settings and a constant stream of newly invented heroines. Most of the English heroines appear not as worthy models from bygone days but as modern women inhabiting the same world as their audience. They also spread more widely across the social scale, and shift their social status more readily, than the more elite and socially static German heroines. At once less remote and more lively than their German counterparts, the English heroines more often take an active role in determining their own fates.

Authors of both countries joined in praise of such passive virtues as chastity and devotion to husbands. Thus in Germany songs appeared in praise of Lucretia, Susannah, and a series of faithful wives of biblical and classical traditions, while English writers and audiences also paid tribute to such standard heroines as Penelope, Griselda, and Susannah.[5] Even here, however, English pieces tend to allow more scope for female independence and personality. A sixteenth-century German song on the chaste Susannah urges good women to imitate her, emphasizing conjugal piety as the essence of her virtue:

Wie sie hat thun betrachten /	The way that she regarded
gehalten jren Mann.	And treated her husband,
Für jren Herrn vnnd Hawpt	And knew him as her lord and
erkendt /	head;
als ein yede Frawe /	As every woman still
soll jr nachuolgen bhend.[6]	Should follow in her tread.

A sixteenth-century English song, reprinted well into the seventeenth, gives the story a somewhat different thrust. It shows some hesitancy about adopting a female hero, as suggested by the first line, "There dwelt a man in Babylon"; the husband receives first mention despite his negligible role in events. Still, the song presents Susannah as a model not only for submissive wives but for all: "Why should wee not of her learne thus / to live godly?"[7] Not faithfulness to her husband but faithfulness to God is her key virtue, making her a worthy model for both sexes, albeit one whose prominence requires justification.

Differences in the treatment of women in the two literatures are related to the greater English recognition of an individualized pursuit of happiness—an idea to which the German literature opposes a more static moral and social outlook. Thus the same story could be used to illustrate somewhat different morals in the two countries. A heroine of both literatures is a woman of ancient Rome who saves her imprisoned father from starvation by secretly feeding him milk from her breasts. The emperor has forbidden anyone to take him food, but she successfully begs to be allowed to see him. The authorities cannot understand how he survives; when she finally explains what she has done, they free her father out of admiration for her faithfulness.[8] The German version emphasizes her cleverness and presents her as a shining example for all children, many of whom neglect their needy parents.[9] The English ballad turns the episode into a tale of tensions between parents and young lovers, as well as filial loyalty. Here the daughter has been estranged from her father.

Yet now, behold, one daughter dear,
  he had, as I doe find,

> Which liv'd in his displeasure great,
>   for matching 'gainst his mind:
> Although she liv'd in mean estate,
>   she was a vertuous wife,
> And for to help her father dear,
>   she ventured thus her life.

Emphasizing the advancement won by her virtue and the vindication of her earlier rebellion, the song upholds youthful independence against parental control:

> And much admiring at the same,
>   and her great vertue shown,
> He [the emperor] pardon'd him, and honour'd her
>   with great preferments known.
> Her father ever after that
>   did love her as his life,
> And blest the time that she was made
>   a loving wedded wife.[10]

The moral example here is presented as the daughter's personal success story, though within the limits of the role of a virtuous wife. While the German author uses the story to reinforce parental claims, the English version encourages freedom of choice. On the other hand, the German version points to the young woman's personal quality of intelligence, while the English stresses the way in which her ability to help her father was conferred by marriage. The English promotion of women's individual development is persistently imagined as culminating in a sexual relationship with a man.

The German focus on religious heroines usually honors such passive virtues as the preservation of chastity, as in the case of Susannah, or uncommon devotion, whether to God or to their husbands. In the mid-sixteenth century Hans Sachs's song of *Die zwölff durchleuchtige Weyber des alten Testaments* [The twelve illustrious women of the Old Testament] repeatedly stresses the themes of obedience and self-sacrifice in praising such worthy dames as Sarah, Rebecca, Leah, and Ruth; so much so that he has some difficulty reconciling Jael and Judith with his principles of female virtue.[11] Though he draws his heroines from religious tradition, their key accomplishments are earthly, like those of the heathen women also singled out for admiration: loyalty to husbands is their most important duty.[12] Not their relations with God but their relations with men determine their praiseworthiness. Only a few religious heroines, like Judith, gain fame by their own dramatic actions. Most of these sixteenth-century works on religious heroines are Protestant, and they share an overriding concern with the secular submissiveness that religion should induce in the faithful woman; or rather, they view submissiveness as itself a religious trait.

While most of Germany's religious heroines belong to the past, some contemporary women gain a brief fame through visions, trances, and prophecies that inspire and enlighten their communities. Printed mostly in Protestant areas, the reports on such phenomena accord the women a special spiritual quality. Occasionally men boast such experiences also; but in both Germany and England women, especially young women, dominate the field of religious ecstasies as well as that of demon possessions. In a number of German pamphlets clustered in the second half of the sixteenth century, girls ranging in age from seven to eighteen appear to warn of God's wrath and tell of their visions of angels. Several of these girls have returned from the very verge of death, some even reviving at their funerals to tell of the sufferings in store for sinful mankind. They warn of pestilences, fire, war, earthquakes, and depredations by the Turks, all to punish Germany and Europe for the prevalence of sin and vice. Some are reluctant to leave their visions, for though they have learned of miseries to come on earth, they have also been entertained by angels and shown the beauties of heaven. The authors view these visions as divinely inspired and expect the girls' prophecies to arouse awe in pious hearers.

A Nuremberg pamphlet of 1560 tells of an eighteen-year-old peasant girl who has fallen into a dramatic trance. Giving a detailed description of her speeches and gestures, the work urges all to heed her call to repentance. She predicts harsh punishment for the world's vice and pride, and in condemning sinners she is moved to violent gestures: "jn dem schloß sie die hend in einander / vnnd thet sie wider auß einander / mit einem finger sie Drowet / damit sie die gantz handt auff thet / als het sie eine Rutten vnd wolte steupen / Behielt die Hend empor / vnd sprach Ach betet / der Herr kombt / vnd weheklaget darauf hefftig vnd / Erbermlich schlug sie an die Brust vnd hub die hende auff / vnd saget / Wenn jr diesen spiegel verachtet / so habt jr Gott im Himel verachtet [then she clasped her hands together and brought them apart again. With a finger she threatened, and then she raised her whole hand, as if she had a rod and would inflict punishment. She held her hands up and said, 'O pray! The Lord is coming!' and lamented then vehemently, and pitifully she struck her breast and raised her hands and said, 'If you scorn this example, you have scorned God in heaven'].”[13] A learned doctor has endorsed her sayings, pointing out their accordance with Scripture. In 1577 a widow's beloved eight-year-old daughter has lain as if dead for fourteen hours and is about to be buried when she awakes at her mother's kiss. She describes a sweet sleep in which an old man has told her of pestilence and war to come.[14] A virtuous maiden of eighteen falls into similar trances in 1594, and on awakening she reports the same contrasting visions of joy in heaven and calamities on earth.[15] The ordinarily passive simplicity and naïveté of young girls makes the supernatural quality of their prophecies all the more striking. These virginal children, though earthly, are not yet fully engaged in human society and its processes, nor yet completely tainted with its sin. Their loving but earthbound parents and relations recoil in fear and grief from the prospect of the children's death or affliction, while the young prophets enjoy a direct link with divine spirituality and can speak with a certain detachment of the disasters in store for the sinful world.

Young women in England show similar ecstatic leanings and are held up for similar admiration, though their messages are generally less bleak and their appearances come later, in the seventeenth century. *A Wonderful Prophecy*, a ballad of 1656 by Laurence Price, tells the story of twenty-year-old Christian James, a godly maid who has refused many suitors in order to preserve her virgin life, wears homely clothes despite her parents' wealth, goes to church often, and aids the poor. She falls into a deadly swoon for twenty hours, and when her frantic mother is finally able to restore her, she awakes and says she has been on her way to heaven. Having learned that the day of doom is nigh, she exhorts men to leave their sinful ways. Then she dies, to the playing of sweet, heavenly music, and the parish magistrates order her prophecy printed.[16] Elizabeth Stretton, the "Godly Maid of Leicester," appears in a ballad printed in the 1670s and 1680s. On her deathbed she falls into a trance in which she fights with Satan and vanquishes him. She wakes briefly to tell of the struggle:

> I have been in a combat great,
> Even with the Black Prince of the Ayr,
> By craft, and by his strong deceit,
> Did seek to bring me to despair.

Satan tries to convince her that her sins must lead to damnation, but she retains her faith in Christ's redemption:

> When he perceiv'd my faith so strong,
>   Satan began to hide his head;
> I did by him receive no wrong,
>   So presently he vanished.[17]

Christ sends her back to tell her friends of God's mercy and the salvation of his elect; after urging them to a godly life, she commends her soul to God and dies.

A similar song of the late seventeenth century shifts its focus from supernatural vision to familial affection but continues to emphasize young women's spiritual mission. *The Sorrowful Mother; Or, The Pious Daughter's Last Farewel* features a dialogue in which the dying daughter tells her distraught mother not to grieve but to look forward to their meeting in heaven. The mother proves difficult to console, and her speech casts maternal love in the strongest terms:

> My daughter dear, and is it so,
>   That I indeed must part with thee?
> This fills my heart with grief and woe,
>   From sorrow I shall ne'r be free;
> But languish here in deep despair,
> My grief is more than I can bear.

The girl repeatedly tells her relatives not to weep, as she is going to eternal joy, but still the survivors suffer greatly from her loss:

> No tongue is able to express
> Their sorrow, grief, and heaviness.

> A tender mother did express
>   Those words unto her friends, and said:
> "My grief and sorrow is the less,
>   To see the happy end she made:
> A worthy pattern may she be
> To Damsels now of each degree."[18]

The virtues held up for female emulation are at once spiritual, emotional, and social. Women of youth and innocence gain glory and admiration for their special links to the world of the unseen, but women are also the preservers of domestic affection, overflowing with earthly tenderness. Their religious affinities embrace the same passive qualities that give ease to domestic life. Resignation, obedience, and even, for the most heroic, a masochistic joy in suffering as a badge of honor buy for women the highest esteem. The virgin's denial of the earthly embodies a higher truth than her mother's confinement to the earthly, but both nurturing mother and suffering saint represent an ideal of feminine pliancy.

While Protestant printing dominated the field of female religious heroism in sixteenth-century Germany, the seventeenth century saw a marked rise in the production of songs about Catholic female saints. Like the Protestants, the Catholic authors admired passivity, with the women gaining praise for their martyrdom but also for their spiritual achievements. While the stories themselves derived from a long tradition of medieval hagiography, they found a new resurgence in the popular literature of seventeenth-century Germany. A song on the martyred Saint Dorothea appeared in at least three editions from 1600 to 1668—interestingly, in Lutheran Nuremberg as well as in Catholic areas. A pious young maid, she is dutiful, obedient, and humble:

Schamhafftig vnd fein stille /	She always acted, as is right,
hielt sie sich alle zeit /	With quiet modesty,
vnd lebt nach Gottes wille /	And lived uprightly in God's
acht keiner üppigkeit.[19]	sight;
	Cared for no vanity.

Enraged by this spectacle of godliness, the Devil inspires his heathen servants to persecute her. Dorothea stands fast against every pressure, refusing to forsake Christianity. Even when condemned to death, she merely prays for the conversion of her enemies, and after death she miraculously converts her judge by sending him flowers from heaven. In a Catholic song of 1613, Saint Barbara, daughter of a noble but godless house, converts to Christianity in spite of her father's violent opposition. She undergoes the most terrible tortures, but Christ miraculously heals her wounds, and after her martyr's death she continues to perform miracles for those who appeal to her.[20]

Saint Catherine, heroine of at least three seventeenth-century songs, takes a more active path to martyrdom. Having dedicated her life to Christ, this princess resists a heathen king's insistence that she marry his son. Despite her female weakness, she emerges victorious from a disputation against fifty philosophers gathered to confute her. The saint prays in all humility for God's help:

| Gib ware wort in meinem | Put true words in my mouth, I |
| Mund / | pray |

| Daß ich die warheit reden kund / | So that I now the truth can say; |
| Ich bin fur mich selb zschlecht vnd zblöd.[21] | Myself I am too weak and mean. |

An angel appears promising both the needed inspiration and a blessed martyr's death. This divine intervention infuriates the pagan tyrant,

| Daß solt ein Weib vil stärcker seyn / | That a woman should be stronger quite |
| Als er vnd all sein Gwalt in gmein.[22] | Than he and all his gathered might. |

Following a period of imprisonment, hunger, and torture, she is executed, but only after a terrible engine designed to kill her has been struck by a miraculous thunderbolt. Catholic songs tell of the wonders performed by her bones and promise that God will grant what is asked in her name.

One of the few song pamphlets written and signed by a woman deals with the sufferings of Saint Ita, a countess unjustly abused by her husband because of the Devil's intrigues. Showing his usual spite against the virtuous, Satan steals her wedding ring. One of her husband's hunters finds the ring and unwittingly wears it, stinging the count to fury. He will listen to no explanations, but has the hunter killed and casts his wife down from a high window. Ita escapes the worst effects of her husband's mistrust and violence, as God brings her through the fall unharmed. She then pledges her life to him: "Ach Herr nimb mich zum Gmahel an / ich will für hin kein andern Mann [O Lord, take me to be thy bride; / I'll have no other man beside]." She lives for seventeen years in a humble hut, till finally her innocence is revealed to her husband, who begs her to come back—but in vain, for she is now espoused to God. She ends her days in a cloister, and her tomb becomes the site of many miracles. The author, Barbara Münchheym, prays that Saint Ita will intercede with God for her. In her closing lines Münchheym identifies herself with suffering: "Barbara Münchheym ist mein Nam / Vom Glück bin ich offt gar verlahn [Barbara Münchheym is my name; / Fate oft leaves me in lonely pain]."[23] The status of innocent sufferer for the sake of virtue is the most widely praised of women's roles in the German literature. Even as it offers women a route to social approval, it presents an ideal within women's reach and a consolation for their frequent powerlessness.

It is telling that this rare female author, Barbara Münchheym, chose a saint for her theme and explicitly identifies herself with the suffering

virtue the saint represents. Münchheym recounts the legend straightfor-
wardly as it appears in earlier sources, but she adopts the saint directly as
her own protector and as a model who invests women's powerlessness and
humiliation with religious value. At the same time, Ita's story offers hope
of a spiritual escape from earthly subjection. Unlike the religious heroines
often praised by male Protestant authors, St. Ita is notably resistant to the
structures of familial patriarchy. Though she does not actively rebel
against her husband, her devotion to God frees her from his power: he
cannot get her back. For the Catholic Münchheym, the saint clearly
offered a means of validating her own experience, in a mode of self-
justification and implicit revolt that was less open to Protestant women
but that also discouraged any active pursuit of power. Her theme of female
religiosity and her endorsement of self-abnegation made her authorship
acceptable. In both England and Germany, devotional literature was
considered more appropriate for women than secular subjects, as long as
the women avoided theological arguments.[24]

The commonest heroine of the Catholic saint songs, of course, is the
Virgin Mary, who appears sometimes as the sinless, godly, simple maid of
old and sometimes as the wise and powerful queen of heaven.[25] Though
Mary has led a blessed life and is now in glory, she too knows the meaning
of human suffering. A song of 1686, praying Mary to intercede with
Christ for sinners, asks her to

Erzehl Jhm die Schmertzen /	Tell Jesus of the pain
die du in deim Hertzen /	Thy heart did then sustain,
wie brennende Kertzen /	Like candles all aflame
gelitten hast /	With burning grief,
jn selber drey Stunden /	In those three hours that he
da Jesus voller Wunden /	Lay wounded on the tree
ja gar hingesuncken /	And dying was truly
am Creutz ohne Rast.[26]	Without relief.

Even in her position of heavenly power, she retains the feminine virtues of
pity, love, humility, and obedience. Women are urged to imitate her
goodness by preserving chastity themselves and extending pity and charity to others.

The seventeenth century also found special appeal in the figure of
Mary Magdalene, pictured as the repentant prostitute whom Christ had
converted to a life of ascetic chastity. Two pieces from mid-century

Augsburg feature the scantily draped saint in pictures that probably catered to lust as well as devotion. It is hard to tell how serious the publishers
were in the pious purpose these productions avow, though they had good
medieval precedents for viewing the Magdalene's piety as an insatiable
desire that parallels her former lust.[27] One of them casts the saint as a
fashionable, contemporary strumpet, who tells young "cavaliers" of her
penitence and warns them that she will no longer be available. Giving her
tale in the first person, the song emphasizes passion as the driving force of
both her life and her conversion. She formerly loved many but now
focuses her desires on one alone:

Hab all geliebt mit schlechtem nutz /	I once loved all to no good end; I made of love a habit.
der Lieb war ich gewohnet:	Now all my love on one I bend.
Jetzt lieb ich ein allen zu Trutz /	. . . . .
. . . . .	My heart afire burns with desire
Mein Gemüt entzünd / jetzt anderst brinnt /	Much different from before.
mit gantz liebreichen Flammen.	

Now it is Jesus who will be her bridegroom:

Auß Liebes-Brunst vnd nit vmb sonst /	With love aflame, and not in vain,
sitz ich zu seinen Füssen:	There at his feet I sit.
Mein Hertz voll Sünd /	My sinful heart
sicht was da findt /	Then sees its part
will seine Füß begiessen.	And wants to wash his feet.

Living happily in repentance and love, she is devastated by the news that
her beloved Jesus has been condemned to death, and she expresses her
dismay in typical lover's fashion:

O Todt Tyrann / was hast gethan /	O tyrant death, thou steal'st my breath,
mein Hertz möcht mir ertrincken.	My heart will drown within me!
O Jesu mein / wer bild jhm ein /	O Jesus dear, who can bear to hear
deines zarten Leibs so schwere Pein?[28]	Of thy sweet body's pain severe?

She resolves to forsake the world and vanity, spending her life doing
penance in the wilderness. After years of constant weeping and suffering,

she hopes to gain eternal life through God's love. The song's amalgam of temptress and suffering saint produces an odd but in some ways characteristic figure. Like the female martyrs, she proves her worth by voluntary suffering. Her bond of love with Christ repeats the standard bridal image of nuns and other religious women, but her lustful past and her penitential dishabille in the wilderness add a salacious element to her message.

Though women could be seen as spiritually blessed creatures, they also predominated among the spiritually afflicted. Moralists and theologians assumed that women's bodily weakness was paralleled by weakness of mind and spirit, making them especially vulnerable to demonic assault. Frankly misogynist texts like the witch-hunting manual *Malleus maleficarum* made much of this susceptibility, but it was widely assumed in popular thinking as well, buttressed by evidence stretching back to Eve's original seduction by the demon-serpent. In the popular texts demons apparently prefer females as targets for both possession and persecution; though men are also subject to these evils, they appear in the reports far less often than women. While exceptional, saintly women could emerge with credit from demonic encounters, the woman possessed is usually seen as a helpless victim who, though passive in relation to the devil, becomes a living embodiment of demonic disorder.

A few religious adepts, such as Elizabeth Stretton and Saint Ita, wrestle with the Devil and win. During the latter's long life of holy seclusion,

Der Teuffel thet jhr vil zu leyd /	The Devil did her much
vexieret sie zu aller zeit /	torment:
wich doch zu letzt mit schanden	Against her still his will he bent,
ab /	But did at last in shame depart,
deß sie sich hertzlich frewt	Which greatly did rejoice her
darab.[29]	heart.

But women who lack the saint's prodigious faith often face the assaults of demons with less happy results.

Innocence alone is seen as insufficient protection. A German song of the mid-sixteenth century, printed in at least four editions, recounts the news of a "frumm Gotsforchtigs kindt [good, God-fearing child]" named Anna who has been possessed by the Devil. She unwittingly swallows him in a drink at a carnival time, and after four weeks of illness she finds herself unable to pray at Easter. Her torments begin as soon as she names Christ:

der Feindt wider begunt /	The Devil in revenge set out,
der jhr die augen außdrennen /	Her eyes within their sockets
den kopff auff die achßlen	churned,
wenden /	Her head round on her shoulders
die zung gewunden auß dem	turned,
mund.	Her tongue he twisted from her
	mouth.

She is carried to church, where all pray for her deliverance, and the Devil finally flies out the window. The author urges readers to replace disorderly popular customs like carnival with pious temperance:

O mensch thu dich bekeren /	O sinner, turn from gluttony,
vor fressen sauffen vnd	From drinking and swearing
schweren /	viciously,
Got wirt vns sonst straffen	Else God will sharply chasten us.
hart.[30]	

Another victim, in a work with a different but equally obvious polemical purpose, has been led astray by Lutheran heresy and is attacked by Satan only when she is about to return to the Catholic fold. As the possessing spirit explains, the Lutherans are already in the Devil's hands, so the demons ignore her until reconversion threatens to snatch her soul away from them. This unfortunate, Veronica Steinerin, is possessed by thirty-odd spirits, who speak through her in strange voices and blasphemous words, make her body swell, and cause her much suffering. The Jesuits finally cure her with a ten-hour exorcism, but this is a "trawriges / jämerliches Spectackel [pathetic, wretched spectacle]," as "Die Teuffel rumorten vnd polderten in der Junckfrawen vnsäglich / vnd . . . fiengen an / die Magd auff das erschröckligist zu peinigen vnd quelen / alle glieder zu recken vnd strecken [the devils fought and quarrelled in the maiden unspeakably, and began to torment and plague the maid in the most terrible way, pulling and stretching all her limbs]." As each devil is driven out, he "ließ der Junckfrawen ein solche letze / daß sie allweg muste / wie ein todte inn onmacht hinfallen [gave the maiden such a final blow that each time she fell down in a swoon as if dead]."[31]

The English literature shows similar examples of hapless innocents who fall into the Devil's clutches, though here again the English incidents belong to a later period, and they appear mainly in prose pamphlets. In a text from 1677, a beautiful and virtuous young maid of Buckinghamshire has been possessed for over twelve years. The demon, sent by certain evil women who hold a grudge against her father, often tosses the girl up and down, causes strange contortions of her face, and makes her fall on the ground; but the blasphemies and temptations he injects into her mind are far worse than what he does to her body. Strong men are unable to restrain the Devil's violence in her, and despite long years of prayer and fasting the family has yet no sign of her deliverance.[32] Later in the century the ballad of *The Distressed Gentlewoman* tells of a godly damsel, "a pattern of true Piety." Seeing her religious inclination, Satan plots to blast her happiness, and gradually he gains control of her through melancholy and madness.[33]

In another young woman, Joyce Dovey, the Devil's manifestations are more violent. Not only does she swear in a strange voice, but "She is oft thrown against the walls, and into the fire [by the Devil], but all without any hurt. . . . She hath snatched a paire of Cizzers from a womans girdle, and applyed them to her throat; and another time a knife from another, in an admirable quick way, and strook her breast, yet both without so much as a scarre in either place."[34] She, too, has so far found no relief. The grotesque tortures and contortions undergone by victims of demon possession, together with the sufferers' own unseemly violence, both authenticate their supernatural disorder and emphasize its uncanny evil by violating all rules of human, and especially feminine, decorum. The participation of women in violence as both victims and aggressors calls up conflicting associations whose incompatibility underlines the frighteningly unnatural quality of these incidents. The women are wild and disorderly, spouting blasphemy, looking ugly, and doing ill; but their torments recall the women of religious martyrdom, for their seeming rampage is also a passive endurance of the Devil's manipulations.

The positive side of women's affinity with the unseen, their religious fervor and martyrdom, dominates the German visions of female heroism. The German heroines who win fame for secular achievements typically show similarly passive virtues, chiefly chastity and devotion to their husbands. Occasionally, however, the German literature celebrates an active and adventurous wife, as in some early songs of chivalric theme that were reprinted frequently during the sixteenth century and into the early seventeenth. The consort of Alexander of Metz rescues him from captivity among the infidels by means of courageous travels and disguises, together with divine aid that enables her to charm his captors with song. Yet despite all her accomplishments, chastity is her crowning virtue, a virtue constantly subject to suspicion and in need of proof.[35] In another courtly adventure, the gallant and faithful Floredebel saves her husband from death in still more trying circumstances. This beautiful princess falls in love with the virtuous knight Trinumitas, proposes to him, and obtains her father's consent to their marriage. When Trinumitas hears that the French queen is lovelier than his wife, however, he is seized with a desire to see her, unable to believe that there could be a finer woman than Floredebel. At the French court the queen seduces him, their adultery is discovered, and he is thrown into prison; but when Floredebel hears the news, she rushes to help him. Bribing her way into his prison, she switches clothes with him so that he can escape. At the trial she reveals herself as a woman and clears the queen's honor. The intrepid wife and her loving Trinumitas are reunited in joy.[36] While such highborn medieval ladies were widely admired, their exploits found no contemporary or bourgeois imitators. Dominated by the genre of chivalric romance, secular female heroism all but disappeared in the seventeenth-century decline of fictional popular literature in Germany.

In England also love is often seen as the motive behind women's heroism, but such adventures are far more common, and increasingly so. Since the English heroines are usually young virgins, their stories lack the element of submission to the social laws of marriage and chastity implicit in such German songs as that of Alexander of Metz. On the other hand, of course, they promote the treatment of marriage as an unexamined "happy ending," a myth which still dominates much popular fiction. For young female audiences, the emphasis on youthful independence and freely chosen marriage could well obscure the legal subordination that marriage would bring. The English texts often focus on contemporary women, while the settings for German heroines usually are remote in time or place; Alexander's wife, for example, performs her heroics at the time of the Crusades, while other virtuous wives were drawn from biblical or classical lore. The English heroines also spread more widely across the social scale, ranging from the nobility to women of humble degree. The contemporaneity and social spread of the English texts encouraged audience identification with female adventures.

Many English songs deal with women who follow their lovers across the sea or into battle, and some of these heroines save the men from imprisonment or death. *The Merchant's daughter of Bristow*, printed from the late sixteenth century to the later seventeenth, tells how Maudlin follows her lover to Italy after her relatives prevent their marriage. Disguised as a lad, she arrives at Padua to find her love condemned to die for his religion. He will not deny his faith even for love, so she professes the same faith in order to die with him. "But when the judges understood, / The faithful friendship in them all that did remaine," the pair is sent home to England. As her father has died in the meantime, they are happily married.[37] Another heroine of a seventeenth-century ballad similarly faces parental objections to her love for a poorer man. When her father has her lover pressed to sea, she follows in man's clothing and works as a surgeon's mate on the same ship:

> Fierce fights at Sea this Couple did valiantly endure,
> As fast as one did aime to kill, the t'other striv'd to cure;
> The Souldier and the Surgeon's Mate did both imploy their parts,
> That they, each way, did win all the Seamens' hearts.[38]

On their return they, too, find the impediments to their union removed. Such ballads as *The true Mayde of the South* and *An Admirable New Northern Story* recount similar adventures.[39]

The English texts feature many variations of female heroism, ranging from the self-abnegation of patient Griselda to the valor of sturdy viragoes. Though many of them include romance in their adventures, the women are often endowed with an independence that disregards male authority and belies male superiority. This maiden liberty and strength exalt the female even as they make her lover's ultimate possession of her seem all the more triumphant. However playful and fleeting the freedom they celebrate, the English texts endow heroines with far more independence than the German ones do. Some women are even allowed to use violence with impunity: Long Meg of Westminster gains praise for cudgeling unjust men, though she proves submissive to her husband; and Mary Ambree wins fame by leading men into battle against England's enemies.[40] Most heroines are less aggressive than this in their self-assertion, but many are equally brave and unconventional. A ballad of Robin Hood from the second half of the seventeenth century describes his encounter with Clorinda, "Queen of the Shepherds," a woman of both beauty and vigor:

> Her gait it was graceful, her body was straight,
>   and her countenance free from pride:
> A bow in her hand, and quiver and arrows,
>   hung dangling by her sweet side.

She plans to kill a fat buck for Titbury feast, and Robin offers her two or three, but when they pass a herd she quickly shoots the fattest of them all, winning Robin's admiration:

> "By the faith of my body," said bold Robin Hood,
>   "I never saw Woman like thee;
> And com'st thou from East, ay, or com'st thou from West,
>   thou needst not beg venison of me."[41]

He asks her to marry him, she blushingly agrees, and they live happily in Sherwood Forest.

The English celebration of maidenhood and its prerogatives reaches its height in a number of ballads that recommend the single life for women. Like their counterparts in praise of bachelorhood, these pieces contrast the bonds and cares of marriage with the liberty of the unmarried and often urge the carefree young to avoid the trammels of wedlock. Though both sexes usually concede that marriage will be their eventual fate, both also emphasize the importance of free choice, and some assume that they can remain bachelors or maids indefinitely. *A Fairing for Maids*, from the first half of the seventeenth century, takes a dim view of the restrictions that marriage imposes:

> Whilst you are single, there's none to curb you:
> Go to bed quietly and take your ease.
> Early or late there's none to disturb you,
> Walk abroad where you [will], and when you please.
> A single life is free from all danger;
> Then, maids, embrace it, as long as you may.
> For when you are bound then you needs must obey.[42]

Besides the authority of a husband, marriage brings the cares of children, and a maid should marry only if she finds a true, loving man who can turn marriage into a blessing. In a ballad of the 1680s by Tobias Bowne, an independent West Country lass asserts a firmer intention to remain single, celebrating her economic self-sufficiency as well as her freedom. Courted by a young man of higher station, she gives him a firm rebuff:

> Good Sir, I do fancy you jeer at me,
> Your Riches and mine will never agree,
> For I am a poor Man's daughter, it's known,
> I work for my Living abroad and at home.
> Sometimes Ime at home, to spinning of Yarn,

> And sometimes abroad to reaping of Corn,
> Sometimes in the Field to milk the Cow:
> I get what I have by the sweat of my brow.

Her poverty and labor give her control over her life, a prize she resolves not to relinquish by marrying:

> I live as well contented as any Maid can,
> What need I entangle my self with a Man?
> I walk where I please at my own command,
> I need not say "Shall I, pray shall I, husband?"
> Now I have my self to guide and to rule,
> In marrying some people have played the Fool.[43]

Though marriage officially places the woman and not the man in subjection, bachelors' ballads advance similar warnings that husbands are bound and must obey. The bachelor life is free from care:

> No cradle have wee to rocke,
>   nor children that doe cry,
> No land-lords rent to pay,
>   no nurses to supply:
> No wife to scould and brawle.

Few are inclined to dispense with marriage entirely, however; and most reach the same conclusion as their female counterparts, that only a virtuous and loving partner is worth having:

> Except a vertuous wife
>   a young man chance to find,
> That will industrious be
>   and beare a modest mind,
> Hee better were to live
>   still single, as wee see.
> For 'tis a gallant thing
>   to live at liberty.[44]

This evenhanded treatment of young people's options sanctions women's independent evaluation of their lot in life, even though the objections raised against marriage are humorously treated. While the German literature generally directs advice on marriage and its choices to men, the English treats women's alternatives as similar to those of men. Marriage is the expected and accepted destiny of both sexes, and the songs of each on *cf. MacFarlane*

youthful freedoms and pleasures generally view them as fleeting; yet both women and men are depicted as faced with a free decision that will determine the course of their lives.

In real life, of course, this literary vision of equality was belied by the severe restrictions on women's economic opportunities. Though marriage was the standard route to full adulthood and social status for both sexes, it was undoubtedly much easier in practical terms for men to forgo it than for women. The West Country heroine of Bowne's ballad is poor, and it is largely her willingness to accept poverty and hard work that enables her to resist seduction by an upper-class male. The author is using a romanticized pastoral vision to highlight the flaws of civilized life, a well-worn literary theme among elite authors. There is no reason to suppose that his depiction reflects either the real options of a lower-class country woman or any real desire on the part of young women in general to embrace poverty over marriage. Nevertheless, these texts uphold an imagined liberty and a view of marriage as freely chosen, applying these conceptions to both sexes.

The German texts give women no claim to this sort of independence. Maidens are sometimes shown in the act of accepting or rejecting suitors, but without direct expression of their views and with a moral far different from the English: girls who are proud and choosy about marriage are sure to come to grief. A song from the mid-seventeenth century tells of a pretty maiden who has refused a dozen suitors in hopes of getting the particular young man she wants, but she allows undue liberties and is repaid with shame:

Der Dreyzehend ließ sie im blossen stahn /	She was jilted by the thirteenth lad,
was sie den andern hat gethan /	As before she all the others had;
er ließ sie sitzen zu Spott und Hohn /	He left her to sit in mockery,
sie kam hernach in die Wochen schon /	And soon after that with child proved she:
das war jhr rechter verdienter Lohn.[45]	A just reward for her vanity.

In another song a merchant's daughter, brought up to think herself fine and clever, thinks no one good enough to court her, until a penniless rogue dupes her by pretending to be fabulously rich. Against the advice of her family, she marries him, but she soon learns of her mistake. She has to work for the family's support, while her husband drinks, gambles, and beats her. Though she complains to her parents, they ridicule her because she defied their wishes, and finally she accepts their judgment and laughs at her own folly. The song points to her fate as a warning to maids against disobeying their parents and wanting to marry above their station.[46] Another seventeenth-century song complains about uppity housemaids who are not only lazy but also finicky about suitors, not wanting to marry men who get dirty at work.[47] All authors seem to agree that no good can come of such pretensions.

The German literature thus discouraged women from seeking to direct the course of their lives, and particularly from seeking to choose or change their social station. Advice to men also disapproved of social mobility, but it was in women's fashions, manners, and pride that authors found the most infuriating signs of social restlessness and confusion of status. Denunciations of women's prideful fashions appeared in England as well, but there they were balanced by stories of poor girls raised to high station by virtue alone, or by songs on marriage that urge suitors to put aside considerations of wealth. The English texts draw heroines from varied walks of life, imagining poor servants outwitting cruel and lustful merchants, and depicting the duchess of Suffolk reduced to poverty and hardship so that she can show her true mettle. In the less fluid German context, nearly all heroines are wealthy, if not aristocratic. Mary Magdalene appears as a prosperous strumpet, renouncing all her jewels and directing her maid to distribute her wealth among the poor, before she retires into the wilderness.[48] With a more limited audience, and in a society intent on preserving stability against the forces of disorder and change, the German literature did not encourage either sex to take an expansive view of its options. The aspirations of women, especially subversive because of women's subordinate position, were most firmly suppressed.

Both German and English women are depicted as readily able to achieve sexual satisfaction through either heroic or disorderly conduct, but the ambiguous character of women's sexual freedom qualifies their claims to independence in both German and English popular literature. English heroines are shown choosing paths that often lead to adventure, but the adventure is usually ruled by their romantic involvement with a man and ended by their marriage. German heroines are seldom granted such exciting courtships, but their achievements as wives or saints allow them a scope that is bounded more by social and religious rules than by devotion to a single male personality. Religious pursuits especially can free them from ordinary human law by subjecting them to a higher one, and the inner drive of pious heroines makes them uniquely immune to earthly pressures. The freedom defined by love or sex, a freedom which both German and English characters can readily achieve, brings women back into a direct relationship with men—a relationship which, especially in German texts, usually means domination by the male.

The characterizations of female protagonists in the popular texts of Germany and England reflect disparities in outlook that inform all their treatments of women, and particularly of those who step outside the normal bounds set for female behavior. Both countries hold up for admiration the virtues of passivity and loving or pious self-sacrifice; and both sometimes present women as specially attuned to the supernatural world, whether for good or ill. For the German literature, however, these qualities bulk much larger in the total picture of women's nature and activities. Heroic women tend to be saintly women, or if their achievements lie in the secular realm, they show their virtue by subordinating themselves wholly to their men. The English literature allows more latitude for female adventure, bestowing praise on vigorous women who occasionally pursue their goals irrespective of men, or who rebel against parental authority to gain a life with men of their own choice. At the same time, the personalities of women are given fuller expression in first-person songs, of which some mock their subjects, but others seem to identify with them. The greater English emphasis on individuals and their choices produces narratives in which women as well as men seem to possess a measure of control over their lives that the German characters usually lack. Less preoccupied than their German counterparts with the need for a rigid social and moral structure, English authors often contemplate with calmness disorderly or heroic behaviors that German authors would be swift to condemn. Women's accepted scope remains limited, but is imagined within more flexible bounds that allow at least the illusion of free choice.

5.

The Locus of Power: Marital Order

The household was the ultimate center of the sexual balance of power. Marital relations, for authors of popular literature as for other moralists and social commentators, presented a model for the proper ordering of both sexual and social hierarchies. All agreed, of course, that the natural order of things called for subordination of the female, though they might differ on details of its enforcement and extent. In a didactic vein, popular authors depicted the salutary working of this natural order and its beneficial effects for all concerned. More often, however, they opted for the more dramatic portrayal of threats, either humorous or serious, to the established structure. English and German views of marriage, as expressed in the writings of leading moralists, share the conviction that wives should be submissive and obedient, while husbands should rule but not tyrannize their wives and households. Within this general framework, much scope remained for differences in emphasis and outlook. German writers tended to see marital love as a duty owed by the wife, to be returned by the husband only as a reward for good behavior; the English laid more stress on mutual love and comfort. In keeping with this concern, the English allowed more scope for wifely influence over a husband's conduct. If wives proved undutiful, German moralists more readily permitted husbands to use physical correction; like the English, they thought peaceful means were preferable, but the Germans were less troubled by the prospect of violence.[1]

The ideal marital relationship as depicted in popular literature generally corresponds closely to that called for by more established moralists. Wives are to love, honor, and obey their husbands, while men in turn will love a virtuous wife, respect her affectionate counsel, and make allowances for her feminine weaknesses. The emotional content of the union rests on a proper economic basis: the wife is frugal and industrious in her care of the household, and the husband works hard to provide responsibly for his family's needs. This emphasis on frugality as the wife's most important economic trait underlines the urban sensibility of street literature: in peasant households the emphasis was on strenuous labor, and it was among craft families in towns that saving was erected into an ideal.[2] Both German and English texts show concern for the dual nature of a successful marriage, noting the need for both practical and psychological cooperation. The English ballads, however, give far more graphic expression to domestic companionship and love. While both literatures reserve a more prominent place and more vivid treatment for discord than for peaceful coexistence, the English more often dramatize marital companionship instead of merely tacking pious wishes onto depictions of strife.

This distinction between straight didactic admonition and the multivalent messages of fiction overshadows other differences of genre and marks a gap between the two literatures, for the English seem far more comfortable with unglossed fiction than the Germans. In both countries most pieces dealing with marriage present a mixture of jest, fable, and satire, often drawing on medieval sources and often appending a "serious" moral to a seemingly frivolous tale. To some extent, such morals undoubtedly were employed to avoid censorship. Nuremberg authorities, for instance, considered whether a questionable text was edifying (promoted *Erbauung*), and in both countries authors often had to secure prior approval of texts.[3] Censorship may well have been more effective in well-regulated German towns than in England, where large numbers of ballads were published without the required registration. Whether a genuine reflection of the authors' concerns or a ploy to deflect criticism, the moral pronouncements sometimes bear little relation to the imaginative texts. In the belief that a pious moral would counteract the ill effects of a bad example, even respectable authors could purvey unsavory material. Their attempt to serve a serious moral purpose affected both their treatment of the tales and the uses to which they were put, but the stories' independent meanings might well speak to the audience long after the explicit moral was forgotten. Each type of expression poses its own interpretive demands, and the analysis of this literature requires attention to the differing and contradictory meanings of assertion and imagination.

During the seventeenth century English popular literature shows a decline in the depiction of domestic violence against women. This change parallels the decreasing acceptance of such violence in seventeenth-century English society, but—as a caution against hasty conclusions about the literary reflection of social reality—the depiction of violent wives continues and intensifies. The female characters are increasingly dominant, using slapstick-style violence against their helpless mates. For Germany the scarcity of seventeenth-century sources makes definitive conclusions difficult, but while there is certainly a decline in the number of productions that deal with marriage, no decrease in violence is evident. The depiction of male victories over shrewish wives fell from its sixteenth-century peak, but without the English exaltation of shrews. In fact, the German wives' most successful uses of violence appear in texts of the earlier sixteenth century. At the same time, while seventeenth-century English street literature develops an increasing concern for marital affection, the German pieces suggest a continuing focus on the proper filling of roles as the key to domestic happiness.

A number of sixteenth-century German songs devote themselves to didactic praise of marriage, furthering the Reformation's goal of upholding the institution against alleged Catholic contempt. They are usually careful to point out its drawbacks also, as in this Swiss celebration of harmonious unions:

Nach allen Creaturen	In all of God's creation
gfalt mir vff erd nit me	There's naught I'd rather see
by Edlen vnd by Buren	In high or lowly station
dann ein früntliche Ee.	Than wedded harmony.
die wol vergutt thunt haben	They bear all well together
in freüd vnnd ouch in leid,	In joy and woe alike,
nüt von eyn ander klagen.	Not grumbling of each other.

But the author laments the prevalence of the contrary:

noch find man vil der groben,	Yet there are many wretches
die achtend es gantz ring,	Who set all this at naught,
die by ein ander sitzen	Who like unthinking cattle
wie vnvernünfftig vych	With one another live,

mit schlachen vnnd mit	With constant blows and battle,
schmützen,	At which I daily grieve.
als ich täglich gsich.	

He condemns wives who stray from home, whether for gossip or adultery, as well as men who mistreat their wives or waste the family's sustenance on wine. Each should behave virtuously; and when quarrels occur, the wife should submit and the husband forbear:

Ob es sich thäte fügen,	If it should come to pass,
als etwann dick beschicht,	As oft perchance it may,
vnd das sy wurden kryegen,	That man and wife should clash,
so sol es bald synn gricht.	Then settle it this way:
die frow soll nitt lang strytten,	The good wife never will
dem mann nit wider stan,	Long strive against her man,
ouch soll der man zü zytten	And he should sometimes still
jhr schwachheyt sehen an.[4]	Her frailty understand.

Perhaps the greatest of woman's frailties, in this view, is her inability to reconcile herself to her subordinate position.

Wedding songs often paint a relatively optimistic picture, though without neglecting to instruct the parties in their respective duties. *Zwey Schöne Lieder / wie man ein Braut Geystlich ansingen soll* [Two pretty songs to sing to a bride in godly fashion] exalt marriage as the analogue of Christ's relation to his church. While the husband is the wife's head, a good wife is her husband's crown. The man must work hard to support his family, and the woman must suffer in childbearing, but in marriage they can help each other bear these burdens:

Ein ander helffen leiden /	Help one another to endure
tragen gemeine beschwer /	The common trials you face,
allen zanck ohn vrsach meiden /	And ever causeless strife abjure
mit hübscher weyß vnd ber.	With kindness and with grace.

In lieb vil vber sehen /	In love you much should
	overpass,
vnd lassen vber gan /	Each other's faults ignore;
In Gottes wort veriehen /	Thus human love will longer last
so mag die lieb bestan.	If you God's word adore.

Das Weyb soll gehorsam	The woman should obedient be
leisten /	Unto her head, the man;
dem haupte jrem man /	

Doch sol der man am meysten / jr schwachheit sehen an.[5]	But still the man her frailty Must fully understand.

The second song in this pamphlet explains that the woman's duty of obedience to her husband is a punishment for Eve's original sin. If both partners hold to their duty in love and godliness, husband and wife will be one in body, mind, and heart.

Another sixteenth-century wedding song gives more grudging praise to the institution. Assaulting the false chastity of the old religion, the author recommends marriage mainly as an alternative to whoredom, and asserts that though unlawful love may offer greater enjoyment, God-fearing people should marry to avoid sin:

Ehestand du wirst so gar
    veracht /
das kumpt allain auß der vrsach /
nyemandt wil kummer leyden /
   . . . . .
	Marriage, thou now art set at
	    naught;
	This by one cause alone is
	    brought:
	No one will trouble bear.
	   . . . . .

Ob gleich dar inn sind bösse
    tag /
so sey man darumb vnuerzagt /
Gots wordts nymmer mer
    vergessen /
in dem schwaiß deins
    angesichts /
solt du dein brot ia essen.
	Although it brings some evil
	    days,
	Let none therefore be now
	    dismayed.
	God's words never more forget:
	In the sweat of thy brow,
	So shalt thou eat thy bread.

Besser ist böß tag on sünd han / denn in den güten in sünden stann / das creütz wil sein getragen / die zeyt ist kurtz / die frewd wirdt lang / die Christus vns zu saget.[6]	Better are bad times without sin Than good ones to be sinful in; The cross must be endured. Time here is short, But long the joy That Christ has us assured.

The author reports that he has sung these pessimistic sentiments to his bride, presumably to urge her to conscientious bearing of their common cross. Even for its proponents, marriage in sixteenth-century Germany did not always present an inviting face.

Such song pamphlets in praise of marriage became much less common in the seventeenth century. The German Reformation's concern with marital issues seems to have fallen from popular view by the later sixteenth century, though some of its ideas had insinuated themselves into common assumptions. Marital ideals do find occasional expression in broadsides, such as the mid-century *Spiegel einer Christlichen vnd friedsamen Haußhaltung* [Mirror of a Christian and peaceful household], which clearly directs its message to an audience of thriving, industrious householders. This piece features an engraving of a prosperous-looking family, along with verses in which husband and wife urge each other to virtue. Each is to love the other first after God, respect the other's moods and humor, and save criticisms until the couple is alone. The wife is to discipline the children, take diligent care of the household, stay at home, keep her husband's secrets, be patient with his faults, and preserve her honor. The husband should instruct the children and servants to obey her, work hard to support the household, stay home at night, and give no cause for jealousy. Both partners emphasize the need for privacy and decorum in their relations. The wife promises that if he instructs or reproaches her only in private, she will gladly obey; "Doch so es käm zu einem Keib / so schmäht doch nicht ewr Ehlich-Weib [But if it still should come to strife, / Do not abuse your wedded wife]."[7] Both note the importance of friendly attention to the moods of the other, and the wife particularly emphasizes the need for enjoyment of evenings together after a long day's work. While the wife can only modestly remind her master that their duties are reciprocal, the husband has a threat to make: if she wishes to retain his favor and love, she must follow his precepts. There is, of course, no question of her withdrawing affection from him in case of his noncompliance. The sexual hierarchy is to be clearly established, and quotations at the top of the sheet warn against the folly of letting a woman have her will. Still, male ascendancy is to be assured by psychological means, not by brute force. The wise husband appeals not just to his wife's sense of duty and religion but also to her desire for his affection and benignity. This broadside's combination of concerns reflects a strong sense of the need for privacy, propriety, and companionship in marital relations. The well-ordered family is to be ruled by reason rather than violence, will foster intimacy between husband and wife, and will shield marital relations from the eyes of the outside world. This concern for reasonable rule, mutual respect, and respectability echoes the sentiments of such sixteenth-century writers as Hans Sachs. Significantly, however, such ideals are most often expressed in works depicting their opposite.

While such relatively harmonious scenes between husband and wife

appeared in didactic form, they seldom made their way into more informal works designed mainly for entertainment. Pamphlets and songs
sometimes celebrate the exploits of virtuous, faithful wives, but they focus
their attention on the women's self-sacrificing loyalty rather than on
married life or its intimacy. Hans Sachs, in *Die neun getrewen Hayden* [The
nine faithful pagans],[8] praises nine steadfast wives of antiquity to match
the nine faithful men featured in the title. The women owe their celebrity
to their extraordinary love and loyalty, as attested by such deeds as killing
themselves after their husbands' deaths, following their husbands into
exile, dying of fear that their husbands might be dead, and killing themselves either before or after rape. The song of *Alexander von Metz*, dating
back to the late fifteenth century and printed in many editions and
variants, similarly exalts a loyal wife, but with little concern for the
relationship between her and her spouse. Its medieval themes of chastity
and loyalty retained their appeal into the seventeenth century. The song's
female paragon, whose name we never learn, both preserves her chastity
against assault and rescues her husband from captivity. The knight Alexander leaves his wife for the Holy Land despite her entreaties, with threats
of punishment if she should besmirch her honor. With the help of an
angel she makes him a shirt which will remain white as long as she is
faithful. When Alexander falls into slavery among the heathen, his wife
again receives celestial aid in proving her virtue. Disguised as a monk, she
frees Alexander by gaining the heathen king's favor with her heavenly
music and song. On his return home, her mother-in-law accuses the noble
wife of unchastity on account of her long, unexplained absence. This
charge elicits more threats from Alexander, despite the continued white-
ness of the magical shirt. Finally the wife reveals her exploit and gains his
praise and gratitude:

zart liebste Frauwe mein /	My sweet and dearest wife,
ich gib dir deß mein trewen /	I pledge thee on my honor
ich will dein stähter Diener sein /	That I will serve thee all my life
vnd will dich deiner grossen	And will reward thee for thy
Trew ergetzen.[9]	great devotion.

For all his apparent regret of his earlier mistrust, the knightly marriage
here appears as a distant relationship cemented only by the wife's chastity.

A seventeenth-century song in praise of Susanna brings her marriage
into closer accord with contemporary ideals; but its virtues are those of
duty, religion, and practicality. She loves both God and her husband, and

In Gottes furcht sie lebte
  vnverborgen /
darinn auffzog jhre Kind /
  Gesind mit sorgen /
Sie war auch gantz hefftig in
  jhrem Hause /
Kein lediggang sie wolte han /
sie blieb allzeit auff rechter
  Bahn /
das steht noch wol den Frawen
  an /
sie sind daheime / oder auch dort
  ausse.[10]

In fear of God she lived most
  notably,
Therein with care brought up
  her family,
With diligence her household
  path she trod.
To looseness she would never
  stray,
Kept ever in the narrow way,
As still becomes good wives
  today
Whether they are at home or
  else abroad.

Her admirable behavior, a model for German wives to imitate, arouses the Devil's ire and prompts him to arrange assaults on her honor and life. Vainly enticed and falsely accused by two lecherous judges, Susanna clings to God and is saved by the inspiration of the God-fearing Daniel. Beyond supplying the required background for wifely virtue, the marital relationship receives little attention.

Where marital relations come under more direct scrutiny, cynicism about women and marriage is far more common than praise. *Ein lied von einem eelichen volck* [A song of a married couple], a sixteenth-century song, exposes the false grief of widows, a standard theme of medieval satire which appears in England as well. Here a celebration of marital love is presented only to be undercut by an attack on female faithlessness. The song opens with an admiring description of a couple so lovingly united that they never fought:

Ein eelich volck eins mals ich
  kant /
kain grossere trew ich nie
  entpfandt /
dann von den zwayen leüten.
  . . . . .
jr kains dem andern übel redt /
man dorfft nit weyter fragen /
es wer mit trinckenn schlaffenn
  oder essen /
jr kains da kundt vergessenn
des andern spat oder frü.

A married couple once I knew,
I never saw a pair more true
Than these two people were.
  . . . . .
Neither would speak the other ill
Of this there was no question;
Whether at drink, at sleep or else
  at meat,
Neither would e'er forget
The other at any time.

The man sickens and dies, and the wife is frenzied in her grief. On the way to his burial, she urges the bearers not to stop and rest under a particular tree; the bearers of her first husband's coffin stopped there, only to have the corpse revive, and the widow explains that she wishes to leave this husband's soul in peace. She offers them wine to take him to the cemetery without delay, and within a week she remarries. The author presents this behavior as typical of women and warns against trusting them:

Das beyspill merckt jr lieben geseln /	Mark this example, young men all,
wol von der weyber liste /	Of women's sly deceit,
sie waynen vnd klagen wenn sie wöln /	For they at will can cry and bawl,
wenn jnn schon nit vil priste /	Though their hurt be nothing great.
sie haben kurtzen mut vnd lange klayder /	Their temper's short, although their dress is long;
das klagt vil mancher layder /	Many have felt this wrong,
das noch teglich geschicht.[11]	As daily happens still.

Very few German authors depict love as central to marital relations. One song, printed in the latter half of the sixteenth century and reprinted early in the next century, advances unusual claims for the importance of true love in determining the fitness of marriage partners. Citing Aristotle, the author sees such love as arising from the blood and drawing two individuals irresistibly together. Instead of parting such natural lovers to marry their children according to wealth or station, parents should allow their sons to marry according to their inclinations (note that it is assumed that the young man, not the woman, will make the decisive choice). Then couples will greatly enjoy each other and be blessed by God with many children.[12] Far more common, however, is the hardheadedly respectable view of Hans Sachs in *Der Buler Artzney* [Medicine for lovers]. The author meets a distraught lover whose secret liaison with his mistress (apparently a woman of higher social station) has just been discovered and ended by her family. Desolated by the separation, the lover also worries about the fate of the woman

Die jch inn schanden hab gesetzt	Whom I have brought to shame, and now
Auch schwanger worden ist / zu letzt	She's gotten pregnant; O, think how
Wirdt auch veracht die junge frucht	The child too will be put to scorn.

Auch reyt mich starck die eyffer sucht Sie werdt sich an ein andern hencken.	By jealousy I'm also torn For fear that she'll take up with someone new.

The poet advises him without more ado to forget her completely. Illicit love can bring nothing but loss of health, wealth, and honor. To quench his amorous flames, he must seek out and marry a respectable woman of his own social standing. The married couple will be able to love each other legitimately and openly; and the virtuous wife will give industrious care to household and children, helping him to bear his troubles. The prudent husband can train her in her youth to be obedient and virtuous:

Das sie sich redlich an dir heldt Vnd dir auch leyst was dir gefelt Wie man den spricht / ein biderman Ein frummes weyb jm ziehen kan.	So she acts rightly toward you And does what you would have her do. As people say, a good man can Train up a wife to fit his hand.

This kind of love, pleasing to both God and man, will bring peace, happiness, wealth, honor, friendship, health, good conscience, and God's favor. Enlightened by this counsel, the erstwhile lover thanks the poet and resolves to follow it forthwith:

Nun will jch schawen auff das mein Vnd Huren lassen Huren sein.[13]	From now on I'll beware of ill, Let harlots live as harlots will.

The rhyme closes with reflections on the evils of illicit love, citing Saint Paul on the usefulness of marriage for avoiding whoredom. In this piously pragmatic view, mutual affection of individuals matters far less than proper enactment of the social roles of husband and wife. For those who accommodate their behavior to the moralist's prescriptions, marriage offers both an outlet for physical desires and a source of all the social, economic, and religious goods available to the respectable man. The woman who has violated sexual norms is dismissed as a whore, and Sachs implies that her partner owes nothing to her or her bastard child. Women appear here as interchangeable objects to be put to good or bad use; and with fair-minded consistency, Sachs in other pieces assumes women's point of view and treats men as similarly interchangeable role fillers.

English popular literature generally takes a far more sentimental view of conjugal relations, though here also marital love is often seen as a matter of virtue rather than inclination, particularly in the earlier works. Even didactic and moralizing pieces tend to emphasize the happiness in store for faithful couples, putting their pictures of wedded bliss in more personal and vivid terms than their German counterparts. *The Bride's Good-morrow*, a sixteenth-century ballad, addresses the bride with words of pious advice, urging her to remain faithful to both God and her husband. At the same time, it extols the joys of marriage and cheers her with promises of comfort and companionship:

> This day is honour now brought into thy bosome,
>   and comfort to thy heart:
> For God hath sent you a friend for to defend you
>   from sorrow, care, and smart;
> In health and sicknes, for thy comfort day & night
>   he is appointed and brought,
> Whose love and liking is most constant, sure, and right:
>   then love ye him as ye ought.

Love is seen here as a duty to be enjoined on both bride and bridegroom, but also as a constant source of solace in married life.

> There is no treasure the which may be compared
>   unto a faithfull friend;
> Gold soone decayeth and worldly [wealth] consumeth,
>   and wasteth in the winde:
> But love, once planted in a perfect & pure minde,
>   indureth weale and woe:
> The frownes of fortune, come they never so unkinde,
>   cannot the same overthrowe.
> A bit of bread is better cheare,
> Where loue and friendship doth appeare,
>   then dainty dishes stuffed full of strife.[14]

While in Germany paeans to marriage might acknowledge its miseries, in England even songs criticizing marriage can point to the expectation of emotional intimacy. The sixteenth-century *Song in Praise of a Single Life*, after detailing the ills of an unhappy marriage, warns of the pitfalls of a happy one:

> How greatly are they grievèd,
> And will not by joy be relievèd;
> If that death doth call,
> Either wife or children small,
> Whom their virtues do commend;
> Their losses whom they thus lovèd,
> From their hearts cannot be movèd.[15]

Domestic bliss is pictured as very real, its loss a bitter danger of married life.

The *Poor Man's Counsellor*, from the 1670s, similarly pictures the happiness of an affectionate marriage:

> If thou hast a Wife that is loving and kind,
> Great comfort in her at all times thou wilt find;
> Whatever betide thee, she will bear a share,
> And help to advize thee, in woe or welfare;
> Then strive not her patience at all to provoke,
> But freely submit to draw both in a yoak.

In keeping with its general recommendations of prudence, industry, and contentment with one's earthly lot, this ballad gives special emphasis to the good wife's economic virtues. While a bad wife squanders her husband's goods, a true and loving companion preserves his fortune:

> A wife that is froward I do not comend;
> What thou dost take pains for she'l lavishly spend;
> And do what thou canst for to humour her still,
> She'll hold thee in scorn if she want of her will;
> Make much of thy Wife that is loving and chaste,
> For she will be saving and fearful to waste.

The husband, in return, should spend his leisure time at home, avoiding the bad company at alehouses that will waste his money, and instead enjoying his wife's companionship: "A cup of good liquor at home with thy wife, / Will chear up your hearts and prevent further strife."[16]

Women receive parallel advice in *The Wonderful Praise of a Good Husband*, a ballad from the 1680s (to the same tune as the *Poor Man's Counsellor*) which presents a mother's counsel to her marriageable daughter. Unlike the bad, improvident husband, the hero of the title never wastes money carousing but works hard to care for his wife and family. "Good Husbands are Jewels far better than Gold," and their fortunate spouses must show similar virtues of both economy and affection:

> If such a kind Husband you happen to have,
> Your duty, dear Daughter, will then be to save;
> And likewise be loving, not given to scold.

The ideal couple's industrious harmony goes hand in hand with affectionate relations:

> When Wives by their Husbands are dearly ador'd,
> No greater a Blessing the world can afford;
> In troubles or crosses, or what may befall,
> Good Husbands will still bear a share in them all;
> And in their kind arms their sweet Wives will infold.[17]

In addition to the relatively straightforward didacticism of such pieces as these, however, some ballads depict domestic companionship in more dramatic form. Thomas Deloney's ballad of *The most rare and excellent History Of the Dutchesse of Suffolke's Calamity*, written in the sixteenth century and reprinted throughout the seventeenth, recounts the trials of the Protestant duchess and her family during the reign of Queen Mary. The lady flees to the Continent with her husband, child, and nurse, where they are robbed and beaten by thieves and deserted by their servant. Friendless and penniless, they are caught in a storm but help each other to bear their troubles:

> Sometimes the Dutches bore the child,
>   all wet as ever she could be,
> And when the Lady, kind and mild,
>   was weary, then the child bore he:
> And thus they one another eas'd,
> And with their fortunes were well pleas'd.

With no money to pay for lodging, they take refuge in a church porch, where the husband makes a fire to warm his wife and child:

> She sate downe by the fire side,
>   to dresse her daughter, that had need;
> And while she drest it in her lap,
> Her husband made the infant pap.[18]

The ballad's appreciation of their parental and conjugal care is heightened by its sense of the incongruity of nobles' needing to concern themselves with such earthy matters. The couple's humble resignation, combined with their gentle status, makes them fit models of a pious virtue which includes mutual comfort as well as submission to God's will. The refugees ultimately come before the governor, after the husband has assaulted a sexton who attempts to drive them from the church. When their story is revealed, they are treated with honor, and on Elizabeth's accession the loving family gratefully returns from exile.

The joys depicted in an ideal marriage sometimes include romantic love as well as mutual kindness and assistance. *The valiant Commander with his resolute Lady*, dating from the mid-seventeenth century, sings of the defense of Chester against Roundhead besiegers. The gallant Cavalier commander leads his men bravely but laments that his beautiful and beloved wife is there with him instead of safe at Shrewsbury:

> O my own heart's delight, my joy and turtle Dove,
> More dear than my own life, Heavens know I do thee love.
> Those beautious looks of thine my sences set on fire,
> Yea, though I love thee well, thy absence I desire.[19]

When the town's plight appears hopeless, the courageous lady sends for male attire and fights beside her true love.

Even songs that deal mainly with the pleasures of fornication often expect marriage to be a continuation of the lovers' joy. German songs on this theme, following the medieval *Tagelied* tradition, usually part the lovers at dawn, with the man riding off and his return uncertain. *The Maid's Comfort*, from the mid-seventeenth century, depicts a liaison of passionate English lovers. The man courts the maid, urging her to be his marigold as he will be her sun, till she yields to his desire and they enjoy love's pleasures. She then entreats him to be constant, and he lovingly agrees:

> Comfort she found, and straight was made a Wife;
> It was the onely thing she did desire:
> And she enioyes a Man loues her as life,
> And will do euer, till his date expire.
> And this for truth, report hath to me told,
> He is her Sunne and she his Marigold.[20]

Defenders of the comforts of marriage also found exemplars from humbler walks of life than that of Cavaliers and duchesses. *A constant Wife, a kinde Wife, A louing Wife, and a fine Wife*, dating from the first half of the seventeenth century and reprinted several times, presents a man singing in praise of his constant mate. Her family is wealthier than his and tries to block the match, but he fights for her and she proves steadfast.

> Then ioyn'd we hands in Hymens bands
>   to loue and liue together,
> She lov'd me not for house nor lands,
>   for I had none of either.
> Her loue was pure, and doth endure,
>   and so shall mine for euer:
> Till death doth vs so much iniure,
>   as part vs from each other.[21]

He goes on in a tone of pleasantry to describe her various charms of both mind and body. *The Benefit of Marriage*, a ballad from mid-century, is a paean to marriage sung by

> A man that had a pretty young Wife,
>   who closely unto him did cling, Sir,
> And lov'd him as dearly as her life,
>   which to him much comfort did bring, Sir:
> They liv'd in love and true content,
> And oftentimes in merriment.

Wedlock not only has brought him happiness but also has helped save him from shameful and wasteful lewdness in the company of whores:

> That man is worse then a mad man I think,
>   who doth a Whore maintain, Sir:
> For though she helps him away with his chink,
>   she will not at all take pains, Sir;
> But live an idle lazie life,
> When as an honest careful Wife,
>   doth many a shilling gain, Sir.[22]

The combined emotional and economic benefits of a good marriage also can ease the pains of poverty. *The Housholder's New-Yeere's Gift* features a dialogue between a husband and wife threatened by hardship and debt. The husband, bowed down by the sorrows of hard labor and encroaching poverty, is on the verge of despair, but his wife consoles him with her loyalty and piety. Urging him to trust in the Lord's providence, she promises to work hard along with him, carding, spinning, and saving his income carefully. She reminds him that honest poverty is better than riches tainted by discontent. Her heartened spouse responds gratefully, "Deare Wife, thy gentle speeches / revive me at the heart." She concludes with assurances of her constant affection:

> What thou want'st in riches
> I will supply in love;
> Thou shalt be my honey,
> and I thy turtle dove:
> Thou art my beloved,
> no sorrow shall remove:
> And God send a merry new yeere![23]

This ballad appears to exist in only one copy, but the theme recurs in a ballad from the later seventeenth century, *The Chearful Husband: or, The Despairing Wife*, which depicts the same scene with the sexes reversed. With his wife despondent at the threat of poverty, the husband comforts her—"Chear up, my kind and loving wife, / The joy and comfort of my life"—appealing to Providence and hard work. The wife profits from his consolations and adopts the same pious contentment:

> Well, loving husband, since I find
> That thou art so exceeding kind,
> God's Providence I'll not distrust,
> For He is merciful and Just.[24]

The interchangeability of roles underlines the mutuality celebrated in these works; either spouse can be imagined offering advice and consolation to the other.

Such pieces aim more directly at edification than at entertainment but take care to embody their ideals in a livelier form than that of dry precepts. Many ballads similarly cast lessons for the husband on thrift and responsibility in individualized and dramatic form. In the model of marriage they advance, women remain subordinate but have the right, and even the duty, to give their husbands good counsel and turn them away from sin. *Robin and Kate; or, A bad husband converted by a good wife* explicitly lays down the limits of wifely admonition. Robin sits at the alehouse day and night; Kate urges him to stay at home with her, warning of poverty to come if he wastes all their money. Insisting on his freedom to do as he likes, Robin spurns her advice: "Out, out, hold thy twattle, and doe not thus preach, / Ile not be ruld by thee, whatever thou say." She fears that she has lost his love and laments that he is weary of her company; he assures her of his affection but is moved to new assertion of his male prerogatives:

> I love thee as well as I did the first day;
> And yet when I list, I will goe or Ile stay;
> To be at command of my wife I doe hate,
> For I must, and I will have my humor, sweet Kate.

Kate protests that she has no mischievous desire for dominance:

> I doe not command thee, that's not my intention,
> For my humble duty unto thee is such,
>   that one word of anger to thee Ile not mention;
> Examine thy heart, and thou shalt understand
> I give thee good counsell, I doe not command.

Robin, assured that his resistance has been based on a misunderstanding of her motives, can bow to her wisdom rather than to her will:

> Ah! now my sweet Kate, I perceive very well,
>   Thy words doe proceed from a hearty affection;
> Now all my delight in thy bosome shall dwell,
>   Ile ever be ordered by thy direction.[25]

Thenceforth he vows to devote himself to good husbandry.

Similar messages are advanced in such pieces as *A new Ballad, Containing a communication between the carefull Wife and the comfortable Hus[band]*, *A Dainty new Dialogue between Henry and Elizabeth*, and *The Carefull Wife's Good Counsel*.[26] A ballad from the 1670s, *A Good Wife is a Portion every day*, lauds the good wife for her effective but submissive influence:

> A wife that is vertuous and civil beside
>   will honour her Husband, his words she'l obey,
> She'l not strive to cross him what ever betide,
>   but make all things well when there should be a [fray?]:
>   With fair words she'l him draw
>   To submit to her Law,
> Though his Beard it be frozen, in time she'l it thaw,
>   Although he be given to wander and stray,
>   A good wife will lead him into the right way.[27]

Young men should choose such a woman even if she is poor, as her virtue will include thrifty care for his estate while her "fair words" soothe his humor. In this context, the wiles and flattery that are condemned among loose women can be commended and even demanded as skills of the good housewife; her rule can be tolerated if it uses these methods.

Theoretically, German women also could wield legitimate influence in marriage, as long as it remained humble in aspect and morally conventional in effect; in dramatic terms, however, success eludes them. Like the English, German pieces argue that "ein frumes weib kan Iren man wol ziehen [a virtuous wife can train her husband well],"[28] just as a wise and virtuous husband can lead his wife into good behavior. This faith in the curative powers of virtue in either spouse is often expressed in both countries, despite the many counterexamples popular literature has to offer. Yet while the English literature presents many dramatizations of the bad husband's reform, the German only seldom portrays a wife subduing the vices of her mate. A sixteenth-century counterpart of English bad husband songs, *Ein schön new Lied / wie ein fraw jren Mann strafft / vnd weret jm er sol nit zum wein geen* [A pretty new song of how a wife scolds her husband and tells him not to go out drinking wine], leaves the effect of the wife's prudent counsels in doubt. Like the heroine of *Robin and Kate*, she pleads with her husband to stay home with her instead of wasting his money on drink. The man complains that "Wenn ich gee inn der wochen auß / so muß ich haben vor ein strauß [On weekdays when I'd quench my thirst / I have to fight a battle first]," but the wife appeals to honor and respectability. Not only will drinking and good company lead him to neglect the economic needs of his household, but he is setting a bad example for his children. Her unshakably moral counsels elicit no contrite response from her husband, however, and the song closes with a jocular rhyme of praise for wine over water.[29]

In another song from the mid-sixteenth century, a good wife does succeed in teaching her husband a lesson, though a rather limited one. The woman is submissive and industrious, but her quarrelsome husband is never satisfied:

In ainer stat da wz ain man /	There was a man once in a town
der het ain weib die jm gar schon	Whose wife him as her head did
zu aller zeit wz vnterthon /	own,
Ein Ehrenweyb thet sich	Had always true submission
vntugent schemen.	shown,
	An honest wife who shrewish
Sy fliß sich stets wie sie nur	ways did shun.
mecht /	

zufriden sein vnnd hausen recht /
auff das es kainen hader brecht /
aber Ir man wolts vergut nicht
    annemmen.

She always tried her very best
To live content, in peace and
    rest,
Avoid all strife and bitterness,
But still her peevish man would
    not be won.

He finds fault with her constantly, so she finally asks him to write down in a letter what she ought to do. He gladly complies, and she faithfully follows his directions. One day, on their way home from a church festival where the man has drunk too much, he falls into a stream and calls to his wife for help; but "sie sprach Ich gee vor haim vnd schaw ob es auch stant geschriben Inn meim brieffe [she said, 'I'll go home first and see if that is written in my letter']." After pulling himself out of the water, he goes home and tears up the letter, telling his wife to "thu selb was du mainst das recht sey [do what thou thyself thinkest right]."[30] This modest achievement—of relative autonomy in household work and freedom from her husband's ceaseless abuse—is apparently the best a model German wife can hope for. Passive endurance, obedience, and, in this case, wit, are her only legitimate weapons.

English street literature offers similar jesting support for the woman's claim to freedom from domestic interference. In *The Woman to the Plow, And the Man to the Hen-Roost,* a seventeenth-century ballad extant in several copies, the husband finds fault with his mate's housewifery, and she criticizes his work. He angrily suggests that they exchange jobs, and he proceeds to bungle all the household tasks, even as his wife spoils the plowing. Realizing the loss that has resulted from his meddling, the husband thenceforth leaves his wife alone:

> He would be twatling still before,
> But after that ne'r twattled more.
> I wish all Wives that troubled be,
> With Hose-and-doublet Huswivery,
> To serve them as this woman did.
> Then may they work and ne'r be chid.[31]

In both this and the previous example, the husbands not only treat their wives unfairly but also demean themselves by their concern with women's affairs, thus opening themselves to ridicule for their folly.

In such cases, where the wife aims merely at recognition of her legitimate household sphere or her right to responsible financial support from her husband, authors of both countries support her. The man appears as erring or even absurd; and so long as the wife's self-assertion does not reach the point of rebellion against her subordinate position, she is treated with sympathy. Often, as in the German song of the woman and her husband's letter, and in *Robin and Kate*, authors are careful to emphasize the woman's humble adherence to the norm of submissive behavior. Concerned to uphold fair play within the established sexual hierarchy and to lampoon departures from the proper performance of marital roles, these pieces exalt the "good" woman who knows her place and is intent on filling it.

Though authors of both countries usually reserve their fullest sympathy for submissive wives, popular texts sometimes treat a husband's transgressions as a fair occasion for his wife's seizure of domestic authority. Especially when his sexual misbehavior has been exposed, a wife's relative innocence can provide her with an effective weapon. In *The Knight and the Beggar-Wench*, the hero's dealings with a prostitute come to light when his horse runs off with her beggar's pack. On chasing the horse home, he faces the ridicule of his wife and neighbors and finds that his adultery has lasting consequences:

> My Madam doth make it slight,
> But I have got nothing by't,
>   for when she wants of her wish
>   it is thrown in my dish,
> I'd better been hang'd out-right.[32]

Other wives are less subtle in asserting their rights. In a ballad from the 1680s, a rich broker attempts to seduce a joiner's wife, offering her twenty guineas. She and her husband contrive to give the lecher his just deserts: they send for the broker's wife and have her take the other's place in the dark. The unsuspecting broker speaks loving words to her, explaining that he doesn't love his wife, and

> At length she began for to rant and revile;
> She teas'd him and tore him about in his shirt,
> Nay kickt him and thumpt him and beat him like dirt.[33]

He is forced to beg forgiveness and promise never again to offend. In anther ballad from about the same time, a tailor's wife gains a more thorough recognition of her authority. Tailors were frequent butts of

ridicule in English street literature and were assumed to be both effeminate and dishonest. Authors could invest women with power over these
absurd figures without questioning the rule of real men. In this first-
person song, the tailor tells how he constantly resorts to whores, though
his own wife is young and fair. One night he is left naked and penniless by
a harlot who steals his watch, money, and clothes while he sleeps. In the
morning he has no alternative but to send for his wife:

> When she came in, she rang me a peal,
>   Ay, and her fist she forc'd me to feel.
>   . . . . .
> There with her fist my face she did maul,
>   till at length I was forc'd to fall
> Down on my knees, her love to obtain,
>   vowing I'd ne'er offend her again.
>
> "Rascal! (said she), I'll pardon thee now!
>   If that this day you solemnly vow
> To be obedient still to your wife."
>   "Yes, if you please to spare but my life."
>
> Ever since then she bears such a sway,
>   that I am forc'd her Laws to obey,
> She is the Cock and I am the Hen:
>   this is my case, Oh! pity me then.[34]

Though this subjection to female rule gives him some claim to the
audience's pity, he has to admit "That I am fairly serv'd in my kind." His
rightful male superiority, already undermined by his status as a tailor, is
destroyed by his profligacy and foolishness. He is in a state of subjection
no man should suffer—hence the pity—but he has brought it on himself.

The German literature offers a similar scene in *Der Rolandt*, a
sixteenth-century song whose tune served for several other songs in the
early seventeenth century, an indication of its popularity. When Agnes
brags about how much her husband Jan loves her, her friend Clara charges
him with unfaithfulness and advises Agnes to test him by pretending to be
dead. On learning of his wife's demise, Jan laments mightily and threatens
to kill himself. Soon, however, when he thinks he and Clara are alone, he
declares his love for her and gives her the ring from his "dead" wife's
finger. The enraged Agnes springs up and violently demands its return:

Cla. Gibs wider zu deiner Frawen Gaist /	Give it to your wife's ghost again.
Jan. Nein es ist der Teüffel das ich wol weyß /	No, it's the devil, that is plain, A ghost could never hit so hard.
Ein Gaist nit so hart schlagen kan.	

Admitting himself at fault, he begs forgiveness, which the implacable Agnes grants only on condition that he swear obedience to her:

Ag. Heb auff zwen Fingr / vnd schwere hier	Two fingers raise, and swear to me
Daß du gehorssam leistest mir /	That you'll henceforth obedient
Vnd haltest mich für deinen Herrn /	be And recognize me as your lord
Vnd diene mir in grossen Ehrn.	To serve in faithful deed and word.
Jan. Das will ich thun.35	I will.

In these humorous pieces, the men's moral failings allow their women to seize both physical and moral authority. Though an unnatural and humiliating reversal, female dominion here is seen as a fitting punishment for derelict males; the domineering woman, ordinarily an object of distaste and derision, here serves as an ironical instrument of moral and social vengeance.

In general, however, patient submission is the wronged woman's proper response, especially in Germany. Virtuous victims of unworthy husbands gain the German authors' pity but are usually given little recourse against their husbands' ill-treatment. The males may be seen as unjust, but good women generally remain limited to passive suffering. Their predicament is depicted similarly across a wide range of genres, from moralistic fiction to news reports. In Hans Sachs's *Der Lose Mann* [The good-for-nothing man], a slothful husband leaves his family in want, forcing his wife to sell her honor for their support. She would gladly live a chaste and industrious life, but her husband's preference for dissolute luxury leaves her no option; her honor lies in his hands, not her own.36 Another woman, in a news sheet from 1594, suffers constant abuse from her violent and drunken husband. When the pregnant wife gently urges him to change his ways, he raves and curses the child in her womb, invoking the Devil. She soon goes into labor and after five days of great suffering bears a monstrous child, which kills its godless father. Her own fate is left unclear.[37] In a seventeenth-century song, the chaste Saint Ita is nearly killed by her unjustly suspicious husband; only divine intervention preserves her so that she can devote her cloistered life to God.[38] Similarly, the pregnant women sold to murderers in several news sheets of the late sixteenth century survive only through the providential assistance of hunters. Only one of these victims thinks to express doubts about her husband's intentions to a neighbor, and none resist their spouses' commands; indeed, if they did, such behavior would undermine their status as innocent martyrs.[39]

The English literature also approvingly depicts patient suffering of the wrongs inflicted by one's husband. The tale of Patient Griselda, popular in English as well as German and other European languages, provided matter for both ballad and pamphlet.[40] Authors of both countries noted that this story annoyed real-life women, who had no intention of following Griselda's example; but it was recommended to them nevertheless. Chosen by a nobleman as his wife because of her beauty and virtue, the lowborn Griselda willingly swears never to question his commands. Even when her husband tests this resolve by taking away her children and leading her to believe they will be killed, she makes no complaint and shows no displeasure. Not satisfied with this, the nobleman casts her out, then summons her to assist at his wedding to a new bride; this too she bears patiently, and he finally recognizes her worth and reunites her with her children. Griselda, like Saint Ita, attains ultimate honor and vindication through passivity, taking no action whatever in her own defense, but submitting wholly to the power of her husband as the saint submits to both her husband and God. In *Constance of Cleveland* the wife similarly suffers neglect and ill-treatment from her whoremongering husband, but she loyally offers her own life for his when he is unjustly condemned to death.[41]

In most English depictions, however, women do not brook such abuse without complaint. Some women are able to reform their backward husbands, and even those who fail to change the men's delinquent behavior often give free voice to their grievances. Several pieces from the 1630s, written by the popular balladist Martin Parker, vividly present the women's side of marital discord, usually in response to his own ballads representing the trials of unhappily married men. *A Hee-Diuell*, sung to the tune of an earlier ballad on *The Shee-diuell*, is the lament of a woman who married in haste to be free of her maidenhead but now repents her bargain:

For he is such a dogged wretch,
   and doth so basely vse me,
Many a sorrowful sigh I fetch,
   when he doth beat and bruise me.
I marryed him for loue
   that was not worth a farthing,
And yet he doth ingratefull proue,
   iudge, is not this a hard thing?

He wastes the fortune she brought to the marriage by carousing in lewd company:

And if I speake to him,
   in kindnesse, to reclaime him,
Heele with his girdle lace my skin,
   though all the neighbours blame him.

She tries her best to please him, but to no avail. He forbids her to keep a maid, so she has to do all the household work; and his extreme jealousy prevents her from going out with friends. These complaints hint at the author's mildly satirical view of her, as they point to her husband's grievances: from his perspective, she may well be proud, shrewish, and lazy. Both complaining wives and complaining husbands are figures of fun, and their shares of the good lines are roughly equal. She closes her song urging maids to beware,

And you good wiues,
   that heare my wofull Ditty,
If you ere bought Ballad in your liues,
   buy this, for very pitty.[42]

The Married-womans Case, to the tune of *The Married-mans Case*, similarly warns young maids to choose carefully, as a bad husband will bring all sorts of suffering upon his wife:

For when to the Alehouse he bringeth a Fox home,
   hee'l finde some occasion to baste her:
She seldome shall goe without her face blacke,
She shall not want blowes, though vitle she lacke,
Although from a man hee'l perhaps turne his backe.[43]

This text suggests that it is a cowardly man who beats a woman, an idea that has been used to shame violent husbands in later centuries as well. It further warns that the wife of a whoremonger risks disease in performing her conjugal duty, while the wife of a drunkard or gamester will be left in want together with her children. A ballad from later in the century, *The Married wives complaint*, offers the same message. This wife sighs that if only her husband would leave off his brawling and whoring they would be happy, as there is no greater joy than that of a loving married couple; here even a song of marital discord pays tribute to the ideal of love. Yet he persists in beating her, spending his all on whores while she languishes in rags. She counsels maids not to trust young men, as they will swear undying love to get a woman's fortune, "But when they have won you your sides they will bang."[44]

Women in the German texts seldom voice such public complaints. When they do, in Hans Sachs's *7 clagenden weiber* [7 complaining wives], they draw the poet's condemnation for airing family linen in public and being intolerant of their husbands' faults—just as he evenhandedly blames husbands who complain about their wives instead of teaching and reasoning with them.[45] Authors of both countries concede that both sexes have some ground for marital dissatisfaction, but respectable people keep their gripes to themselves; characters who complain are fair game for satire. Still, though their actions are not fully endorsed, the English women are given a more public presence. While English wives regularly appear as speakers in their own songs on conjugal ills, the German songs and pamphlets generally reserve this central role for men. The overall picture presented to German audiences was one in which good wives kept silent. English authors subscribed to this precept in principle, but they treated it loosely in practice, perhaps encouraging women to view their grievances as matters to be spoken of rather than merely endured.

Though German and English conceptions of marital order were similar in theory, the German depictions presented their audience with a less positive picture. While love and companionship dominate English accounts, at least those about the entry into marriage, in Germany they are seldom stressed and are very seldom shown as being put into practice. For German authors, a happy marriage comes less from mutual sympathy than from a proper understanding of marital duties and hierarchy. The English are concerned with duties and control as well but depict them as leavened by strong emotional ties. In the street literature of both countries, however, the ideal of marital order pales before the prevalence of disorder. Despite all pious injunctions, marriage in the popular texts is presented primarily as a struggle for power between the sexes.

6.

Marital Disorder

Though the popular texts sometimes vindicate women in disputes with erring husbands, marital discord is usually cast in terms of female resistance to male authority. Since marriage was conceived as a hierarchical relationship, conflict, whatever its initial cause, nearly always involved an element of this rebellion. In these texts insurgent women, who choose to pass the bounds of respectful exhortation, have many weapons at their disposal. Some stop short of direct confrontation but make their husbands' lives difficult by various means. They may gain their ends by wiles and flattery, cajoling husbands into doing their bidding. Others simply fail to comply with a husband's wishes, leaving him to look for ways to enforce his authority. In a more active but still indirect approach, some wives turn to adultery to deprive husbands of full mastery. Others use gossip to enlist public opinion on their side, or in extreme cases even take their grievances before the law. More dramatic than these indirect methods, though not necessarily more effective, is either an active self-defense or a frontal assault, depending on which partner is the aggressor. Here the tongue, women's proverbial source of power, stands at the head of their arsenal, often proving triumphant in battle and usually opening the fray even when the outcome is determined by more substantial weapons. Only after an initial bout of scolding are women likely to use violence, unless their husbands have taken the offensive and used it first. Once violence does occur, however, it is likely to be the decisive factor in a quarrel's resolution. To emerge victorious, women

must either subdue men by physical force—a conscious and usually humorous reversal of the ordinary state of things—or prevent men from
resorting to their tradition weapon of superior strength.

In both countries critics of the female character often remarked on
women's persistent strivings for liberty and dominance. The requirement
of obedience in marriage was not based on women's natural docility, as a
few theorists optimistically professed to believe; rather, it was usually seen
as a rule directly contrary to women's inclinations, an order which could
be sustained only by vigilant suppression of their unruly drives. One of the
reasons why conforming wives were so highly praised was that they had
successfully resisted the natural but sinful temptation to assert their own
will. Male supremacy could be justified both by man's natural superiority
in strength, intelligence, and virtue, and by God's explicit imposition of
female subjection as a punishment for Eve's sin; but few deluded themselves with the notion that its triumph was a mere matter of course. In this
world of sin and folly, female insubordination, like other forms of human
sin, would plague the righteous and unrighteous alike. Only the fortunate
few would be blessed with good wives, rare jewels whose exemplary piety,
constant virtue, and meek submission raised them almost to the level of
angels. Like the mass of men—and, as the "weaker vessels," even more
than men—most women could be expected to indulge their sinful desire
for power.

Many women in the popular texts find ways of evading the strict
application of male control without abandoning a formal adherence to the
norm of marital order. By wiles, flattery, wheedling, and tears, women
exercise power without seeming to fight for it. It seems to have been such
methods as these—or even women's mere possession of characters strong
enough to belie accepted wisdom about their weakness—that inspired
popular literature's frequent jokes about the rarity of true male supremacy.
In Hans Sachs's *Narrenfresser* [Fool-eater], the fearsome monster of the
title grows fat on fools; his opposite, who habitually feasts on men who
rule their households, nears starvation. This theme was a European commonplace and had its English equivalent in jests and tales about "Fill-
Gut" and "Pinch-belly." In Sachs's text, male dominance has suffered a sad
decline:

Mein herr, ich bin der man,   I am the man, good Sir.
Die männer ich gefressen han,   I've always eaten men who were

Die selber waren Herr im hauß
Und gingen darynn ein vnd aus
Und die weyber nicht fürchten
   thetten
In schlössern, dörffern, märck
   vnd stedten.
Darvon hab ich mich lang
   genert.
Aber yetz hat es sich verkert.
Wo ich hungriger yetz hin geh,
Findt ich der männer wenig meh,
Die herschen in eym hauß alleyn.

Sole masters of their houses, so
That as they pleased they'd come
   and go
And never feared their wives at
   all,
In village, city, town and hall.
In this way long my food I
   found,
But now all things are turned
   around.
Where e'er I look, though
   hungry sore,
I now find few men any more
Who even rule a single house.

The poet flees in terror of the *Narrenfresser,* but the other poses no danger:

Des thüren mans ich gar vergaß,
Der doch die Männer fryst allein,
Die Herr in jrem hause sein.[1]

The thin man, though, I clean
   forgot,
Who after all will eat no fool,
Just men who in their houses
   rule.

A seventeenth-century German broadside suggests the stringent requirements of true male mastery. "Herr Uber-Sie" offers valuable horses to anyone "Wer Meister ist in seinem Haus / Wer sein Weib nicht förchtet durchauß [Who master is of house and hall / And never fears his wife at all]."[2] Those subject to female rule will instead receive an egg. "Jann Alleman" claims a horse but wants to consult his wife about the color, so he gets only an egg. Similarly, "Gally von Kempten" takes a horse but is unwilling to dirty his clean shirt; he, too, has to settle for the egg. Any indication that a husband cares about his wife's opinion or does not want to displease her stamps him as a victim of "Weiber Herrschaft [female rule]." Such pieces show recognition that the realities of human interaction contradict the dogma of male supremacy. The male authors and characters poke fun both at themselves and at the mass of humanity; still, their ridicule is directed less at the impossible standard of iron masculinity than at their own weakness in failing to live up to it. Human folly tarnished many an ideal, and though in a perfect world there might be neither sin nor female influence, the real world's shortcomings offered a fertile field for satire. At the same time, such examples indicate that pervasive complaints of female rule need not reflect a very high level of power among women; the slightest departure from male absolutism could be denounced as feminine tyranny.

English ballads, pamphlets, and jestbooks offer similar assurances that few husbands are free from female usurpation. *Pasquils Jests*, reprinted often during the seventeenth century, tells of a knight who invites his tenants for Christmas dinner but will not allow the men to drink until a man who is master of his wife has sung a carol. After much hesitation one dares to sing in feeble fashion, and all drink with relief. At the women's table, one who is master of her husband is required to sing, "wherevpon they fell all to such a singing, that there was neuer heard such a catterwalling piece of musike."[3] The same tale appears commonly in German jestbooks.[4] Similarly, in *A Banquet for Soueraigne Husbands* by Martin Parker, men flock to a feast of roast ram established for true lords of the household, but most dare not eat "For feare their wiues ere they had dinde / Would fetch them home with words vnkind." One scolding wife appears and prevents her husband from eating, while other men slyly find fault with the meat. The author comments that

> If none but ruling women might
> Haue come, it had been swallowd quite
> In the forenoone, for sure I am
> they best deseru'd to eate the Ram.[5]

He goes on to jest about the horns they give their husbands. The behavior of these women leaves no doubt of their active pursuit of domestic power. The English women take a more aggressive stance than the German wives, who are characterized as dominant but remain shadowy, background figures. Each literature adopts stock, traditional complaints about female dominance, and both seem equally convinced of and amused by its prevalence; but they differ in the content they give to the charge and in the degree of female power they recognize as threatening.

These pervasive complaints about female power undoubtedly had complex implications for their audiences, and particularly for women. On the one hand, of course, they laid almost any female self-assertion open to the charge of "female rule," implying that women had no right to the liberties they were taking. Yet in both countries the view of these liberties was indulgent, and the ridicule directed against these mildly "henpecked" husbands was of a different order than that directed against men who really allowed their wives to overturn the domestic hierarchy. It was conventionally acceptable even for the author of a German pamphlet attacking unruly women to confess that his wife ruled him—but only by the sweet words she used to control and deflect his anger.[6] These texts thus urge women to use the indirect means of attaining influence that work within the system. At the same time, they encourage women to interpret this domestic influence as empowerment. This again is a two-edged sword, offering women the satisfaction of feeling in control—and of exercising some control at the level of individual interaction—and discouraging them from seeking to disturb the hierarchy itself. They are also encouraged to view their de facto power as a sort of inside joke: men's pretensions are debunked, but in the process female power is defined as comic. This formula probably also helped men to cope with women's mild usurpations of everyday authority. At the close of *A Banquet for Soueraigne Husbands*, Parker addresses the women in the audience:

> If here be any scolding wiues,
> I wish them if they loue their liues,
> In any case not buy this song,
> Which doth to gentle wiues belong.[7]

Women are invited to enjoy the idea of female power but to distance themselves from any open rebellion.

In addition to generalized complaints of female mastery, the popular texts complain of various behaviors that vitiate the marital chain of command. Some forms of disobedience are pursued without the husband's knowledge or in indirect ways that make them particularly hard to control. The German literature is especially concerned about the problem of bad housewives who neglect domestic work, gossip with friends, and secrete dainty snacks or strong drink for their private enjoyment. Bad English wives also scorn household drudgery; they often force their husbands to do it for them and generally take a more belligerent stance than their German counterparts. Similarly, English wives who amuse themselves with friends usually go beyond gossip and find male playmates to share their pastimes. Women in both countries also come under fire for extravagant dress, drinking, and general orneriness.

Wives who seek the loosening of marital discipline often are shown appealing to public opinion in an attempt to gain encouragement or immunity from punishment. This can work both ways, and husbands sometimes expose their erring wives to the neighbors' condemnation or ridicule. Women, however, with their network of gossip and their (apparently) lesser sensitivity to shame, are given a distinct edge here. Adulterous wives hold an even more formidable weapon, especially when, as often happens in the English works, they show little concern for their own reputations and taunt their husbands with the public shame of cuckoldom. In a singular twist on the double standard, this seventeenth-century English fear of cuckoldry shifts the burden of a wife's adultery to her husband. The authors treat female sexual transgressions as more serious than male ones, but the undermining of the husband's masculinity is even more shameful than the wife's immorality. While this damage to the husbands' prestige wins the women many literary victories, it cuts both ways, for the female characters who triumph by exposing their husbands' weaknesses or their own unruliness are trampling on widely accepted notions of honor and propriety. Both literatures show a keen awareness of the shame that insurgent women should be feeling, even when their misbehavior is not sexual. While allowing his wife to dominate him, one English husband warns:

> But let not my neighbours of this understand;
> For that if thou dost, I know it will be
> A shame to thy selfe, [and] disgrace unto me.[8]

Similarly, a sixteenth-century German song notes that when a woman retaliates against her husband's blows by striking him in turn, "damit beschleüst fraw Ehr [that was the end of honor]."[9] The depiction of women as void of this honorable shame suggests that men rather than women are the possessors and guardians of honor; at the same time, it calls on women to feel shame or embarrassment at the outrages being committed by members of their sex. This apparent attempt to buttress the supports of patriarchy parallels such customs as the mocking processions directed against beaten husbands and their wives, in which a neighbor or the victim himself rode backwards on an ass to the hoots and laughter of the multitude. Such shaming rituals were practiced in both Germany and England, and their currency suggests that women's internalized values provided insufficient controls on their behavior.[10] Interestingly, according to Susan Amussen, English defamation cases indicate that early modern women valued their reputations for chastity but not for submissiveness.[11] Popular literature's persistent blurring of the distinction between adultery and insubordination thus clashes with women's own evaluation and underlines the literature's strong male bias.

Neighbors and their opinions are frequently an important factor in treatments of marital discord, and the street literature suggests that they offered a support system more for women than for men. Gossiping friends sometimes egg wives on into defiance of their husbands, as in the *Neun Häuten der bösen Weiber* [Nine skins of bad women] of Hans Sachs or the sixteenth-century English *Scole house of women*.[12] Authors of both countries also denounce women who complain to neighbors about their husbands. The speaker of *Ein new Lied von eynem bösen weib* [A new song of a bad wife] tells how his vain and useless wife gossips about him for hours at church:

Hör zu mein gfatter Margret zwar /	Good neighbor Margret, now I swear,
mein schelm mich gestern nam beym har /	My knave did take me by the hair,
vnd gab mir vil der maul biren /	And gave me many a nasty blow,
Das jch vmb den tisch vnd wend /	So that I o'er the table fell,
da mit thet vmbher zwiren.[13]	And round the room did go.

Such gossip could be useful in deflecting male violence, as Martin Parker notes in *Have among you! good women*. Two men are discussing the local scolds; they are appalled by the behavior of "Jone that cries pins," who

". . . has broken her husband's shins,
    and sweares shee'll be drunke before hee."

"Why, wherefore all this doth he suffer?"
    "why, if he should give her a check,
She tels her friends how he doth cuff her
    and threatens to break her neck:
So he, for feare shee'll cry out,
    dares neither to strike nor chide her,
For shee'll give the word all about
    that his Queans will not let him abide her.["][14]

In both German and English pieces, spirited wives yell murder when beaten by their men, in hopes of attracting neighbors to intercede. The surrounding community is seen as playing an important role in maintaining or modifying the balance of marital power.

The most intractable and infuriating of female departures from true obedience in these texts is adultery, which offers women the double pleasure of sexual enjoyment and defiance of their husbands' rights. For the wives in English texts, the exercise of their sexual prowess can mean accession to substantial new domestic powers; in the German literature, the seditious aspect of adultery has less dramatic results. Women of both literatures sometimes acknowledge rebellion in addition to lasciviousness as a motive for their escapades, though the English gain more from flouting their mates. The "witty Westerne Lasse," finding herself pregnant and abandoned, resolves to have the child secretly and then, passing for a virgin again, to marry a tradesman in London. If he proves a kind husband, she will treat him with honor and obedience;

> But if he crabbed be and crosse,
>   And basely beat me, back and belly,
> As Vulcan's Knight Ile fit him right,
>   And scorne to cry, alack, and welly!
>
> A secret friend Ile keepe in store
>   For my content and delectation,
> And now and then in the taverne rore
>   With joviall gallants, men of fashion.[15]

A similar response to male violence, but at a much higher social level, appears in a German song from the early seventeenth century. When a nobleman strikes his wife for interrupting him, she swears that he'll regret it and quickly runs off with another man.[16] Other forms of mistreatment, such as excessive jealousy or miserliness, can produce the same result, but without the English wives' seizure of domestic authority.[17] In an English pamphlet of 1651, *The Joviall Crew, Or, The Devill turn'd Ranter,* the author depicts women as consciously using sexuality to gain marital power, and as attracted to a deviant sect mainly by this possibility. The Ranters, conversely, are imagined as subversive particularly in the encouragement they give to female disorderliness. Two citizens' wives, Mrs. Idles-by and Mrs. Doe-little, hear that the Ranters indulge constantly in pleasure, drinking, and the feats of love. Intrigued, they set off to join in the orgies: "*Idlesby.* The breeches are my own, henceforth I'le rant. / *Doelittle.* No way but this to be predominant."[18] Other wives are shown similarly pouring scorn on vows of obedience, deriding their cuckolded husbands and claiming a right to mastery of the household.

While the German texts anticipate no dramatic reversals of authority as a result of female adultery, women's sexual irregularity still is seen both as a consequence of inadequate marital discipline and as women's most serious transgression against conjugal order. A vain and lusty woman makes a fool of the man she marries:

Die sach würd sich erst schicken ein /	Affairs would them be set up fine;
jr man müst decken mantel sein /	Her cloak would be her husband kind.
dann würd siß erst wol schaffen /	
wenn er sich nur fein narren ließ /	Well managed would her fun be: If he'll just be a proper dupe
sie macht auß jm ein affen.[19]	She'll make of him a monkey.

In Hans Sachs's piece on *Die Zwölff Eygenschafft eines boßhafftigen weybs* [The twelve qualities of a vicious woman], unchastity appears as the crowning vice of a woman whose many bad qualities drive her husband to the brink of suicide. The unhappy victim complains that his wife is negligent of the housework, lazy, drunken, deceitful, vain, extravagant, insolent, quarrelsome, shrewish, violent, and hateful, among other faults. The poet suggests various means of taming her: patient instruction, scolding, appeal to the influence of neighbors, and violence; but the husband has tried all these in vain. He could bear it all if she preserved her honor, but she now dallies with a worthless fellow and her spouse is powerless to prevent her infidelity. The author recommends beating to correct this fault; but when beaten she complains to her family and even to the authorities, making them believe that her husband abuses her. Sadly the man regrets that he indulged her too much at the start, so that she has become used to getting her way:

Des hat sie nun bißher gewonet,	And she's accustomed now to this,
Das sie thut selber, was sie wil,	That she will do things her own way,
Geyt vmb mich weder weng noch vil.[20]	Gives not a pin for what I say.

The poem warns that a man who fails in his duty to control his wife must look forward to misery and dishonor.

From the dissatisfied wife's point of view, adultery is depicted as providing not only sexual freedom but economic independence as well.

Cuntz Haß, in a sixteenth-century pamphlet on marriage, chides men and women alike for irresponsible behavior in marriage. While young men often waste their money on drink and abuse their wives, vain young married women neglect their households and pine for fancy clothes. Grumbling at their husbands' insufficient wealth, they "suchen raht / Bey einer alten Kupplerin [get help from an old bawd]" and find men to support them on the side.[21] Similarly, in *All is ours and our Husbands*, country alewives justify the wanton tricks they employ to supplement their taverns' income: "Perhaps our husbands would repine, / If they of this should know." But

> You know their gains come by the pains
>   Of only me and you,
> They must not frown to wear the horn.[22]

The threat of such behavior likewise provides leverage against a husband's resistance to his wife's will, as in *A Crew of kind Gossips*, a pamphlet by Samuel Rowlands. One brave gossip tells her hard-drinking companions that when her husband objects to her extravagant dress, she menaces him with cuckoldry, saying:

> But well, within my head I haue a tricke,
> Some haue their Foreheads swell that be not sicke:
> Ile haue my will to be maintain'd in all,
> And if one will not, then another shall.[23]

Her access to an independent source of livelihood—along with her small concern for religious and moral strictures—seriously limits her husband's authority. These images of wives using sex to gain money serve to impugn the chastity of women who strive for economic power. This, it is suggested, can lead to only one thing—a charge which undoubtedly was connected to the constriction of women's economic options.

If a female character engages in direct assertion of independence or control, her primary weapon is her tongue. In England this instrument at times practically acquires a life of its own, with overtones of both sex and violence. In German street literature, while women's scolding is considered a plague, the female tongue does not attain the same status as an invincible weapon and a symbol of female power. Though women are shown engaging in physical violence as well as tongue-lashing, hostile speech appears in both countries as the female analogue of male violence.

Not only does shrewish behavior escalate into violence, but scolding words—and in some German examples, even the withholding of desired words—regularly provide the provocation and justification for men's violent reaction. The wife's angry or spiteful words, an attack as stinging as the husband's retaliation with fist or stick, form a standard prelude to battle.

While German and English popular texts share this common pattern of domestic discord, their treatment and development of it differ substantially. Though in both cases the wife usually is presented as the guilty party in marital troubles, in England the women nevertheless emerge on top far more often than the men; for Germany, it is more often the men who keep the upper hand. Over the whole period female victories outnumber male by more than three to one in English pieces, while in Germany men win almost twice as often as women.[24] Most of this discrepancy arises from sixteenth-century male victories in Germany and seventeenth-century female victories in England; in both countries the proportion of women on top increases over time. But the fullest triumphs of German wives also date to the early period: their victories increase in quantity but not in quality. Both literatures depict marriage as a relationship determined as much by force as by love, law, or tradition. Men of both countries are shown readily using violence to subdue their wives, though the German husbands are more unrestrained and more successful in this venture. Shrews, similarly, use violence in an attempt to gain mastery; but while the English seize on it with independence and bravado, often against a peaceable victim, the German women use violence more defensively and gain fewer substantial benefits from it. Even the tongue, though powerful enough to make husbands miserable, usually earns the German women no permanent power and brings down beatings on their heads from infuriated males. English scolds, by contrast, often intimidate men into compliance, with or without violence; some husbands will do almost anything to avoid "The onely hell vpon this earth, / to haue an angry wife."[25]

An essential feature of marital violence in both German and English texts is its comedy. The chief aim of all these depictions was to amuse the audience, and it is important to keep this in mind while examining texts that, to current tastes, often seem more repellent than ridiculous. A modern audience has less trouble understanding the humor of the violent shrew than of the violent husband; the comic figure of the angry wife

wielding a rolling pin is still familiar in twentieth-century popular culture. The incongruity of her violence helps explain its comic appeal and distance it from real life—though one needs to guard against any assumption that enjoyment of the shrewish character is normal or culturally neutral, for the amusement depends at least partly on the shrew's reversal of normal order, and thus on a cultural assumption that it is really the man who should be in charge.

The violent husband is another matter: even in the early modern context, his was a different kind of comedy than that of the shrew. This is clear from the authors' tacit assumptions about their audience: while both sexes were expected to laugh at the triumphant shrew, authors recognized that shrew beating was funny only to men. Women were expected to take offense, a reaction that is easy to understand given the real danger to them of domestic violence. But why did the men laugh? It appears that the humor of shrew beating derives in part from the turning away from marital violence among sober-minded moralists. It would hardly be so funny if it were universally accepted as the proper way to do things. Rather, the humor of wife beating belongs to a transitional stage in which violent marital discipline is no longer an unquestioned procedure, but has not yet come to arouse revulsion among its potential practitioners, who can still relish the vicarious enjoyment offered by street literature. This revulsion appears to have come sooner in England than in Germany, though it is far from complete anywhere.

Both shrews and shrew beaters draw humor from their transgression of the developing ideal of harmonious marital relations. From one point of view, of course, such laughter at the overturned ideal can leave the ideal itself intact, or even reinforce the ideal by ridiculing deviance. Probably this is what pious authors were aiming for in their depictions of discord, but this could not have been their only effect. The comic satisfaction of this marital violence depends on its being directed at a victim who is culturally defined as a culprit, deserving of punishment. This stigma was attached to both weak or wastrel husbands and insubordinate wives, but with an important and obvious difference: husbands were socially empowered to administer punishment to their wives, even by violent means, and the humorous portrayals of wife beating undoubtedly reinforced that empowerment even as they testified to the questioning of it.

In both countries popular texts address admonitions to women against scolding and to men against wife beating. Martin Parker, in a pair of ballads printed in 1634, explicitly treats scolding as the female counter-part of male violence. In the first, *Keep a good tongue in your head*, the speaker tells how he married a woman with countless good qualities but one besetting fault:

> She is a girle
> Fit for an earle,
> Not for a churle;
> She were worth pearle,
> If she could but rule her tong.

He married her for love and values her virtues, but he bemoans this failing, for "No venemous snake / Stings like a woman's tongue."[26] The second ballad, *Hold your hands, honest Men*, sung to the tune of *Keep a good tongue*, represents the woman's point of view. The speaker praises her husband's looks, wisdom, strength, learning, and other fine qualities, but she laments that he "cannot rule his hands."

> As he is wel qualifide,
> Which no way can be denide,
> So I, with my heart,
> Doe honor his desart,
> He hath my affection ty'd:
> Though sometimes I speake,
> My sex being weake,
> A man that understands
> So much as he
> Should patient be,
> And beare with me:
> How well were we
> If he could but rule his hands.[27]

Scolding and wife beating, then, are equally disruptive of domestic order, and the two complaints form an even exchange.

Many pieces in both countries casually assume that violence is a male prerogative, the natural and expected response to female scolding. In *The Cruell Shrow: Or, The Patient Man's Woe*, the husband describes the un-happy life he leads with his "unquiet wife":

> When I, for quietnesse-sake, desire
> my wife for to be still,

> She will not grant what I require,
> but sweares she'le haue her will.
> Then if I chance to heaue my hand,
> straight-way she'le "murder!" cry.[28]

Though beating is usually unsuccessful in taming the shrews of English street literature, it is often recommended. *The Dumb Maid: or the Young Gallant Trappan'd* tells of a young man who has married a beautiful and industrious maid but is troubled because she cannot speak. Finally he gets a doctor to cure her, only to find that once her tongue is loosened, she instantly becomes a scold and gives him no peace. Returning to the doctor, he is told there is no way to reverse the process; but the sage suggests:

> So, as you to me came, return you back again,
>   And take you the Oyl of Hazel strong;
> With it anoint her body round,
>   when she makes the House to sound:
>   So perhaps you may charm her tongue, tongue, tongue.[29]

German songs offer more elaborate prescriptions to cure women's prating, and violent remedies are applied even for such nonaggressive offenses as gossiping. Hans Sachs, in *Ein recept vur der weiber klappersuecht* [A prescription for women's chattering], asks a doctor for a way to cure gossipy females who

> haben vnpeschaiden
> Die klappersüecht im mawle,
> Vnd sint doch sünst stüedfaüle

> with their shameless mouths
> For gossip are half crazy,
> And otherwise bone lazy.

The consultant recommends:

> Scheit krawt, gerten salate
> Vnd pengel sueppen glate,
>   . . . . .
> Tromel praten nit schaden,
> Dar zw starcke plew fladen.
>   Nem auch vest schlegel
>   küechen,
> Füesmilch thw darzw süechen,
> Fewst opfel 4 pfünt schwere,
> Nem auch elpogen schmere

> Rod cabbage, cudgel slaw,
> Hot switch soup will her thaw;
>   . . . . .
> Good paddle roast won't hurt
>   her,
> Strong cuff cake will her nurture,
> Firm birch cake also take you,
> And foot-milk for her make you,
> Fist apples 4 pounds' weight,
> And elbow grease a spate,

Vnd auch perwein mit namen.	With bastinado wine.
Diese stueck allesamen	These items all combine,
Mit füenffinger krawt zwire	Mixed with five-finger-plant;
Jr alle tag auf schmiere	Smear this each day by hand
Am leib durch alle ende,	The woman's body o'er,
Kopf, arm, schenckel vnd lende,	Head arm, loin, thigh, and more,
Pis der plab schwais her dringe.[30]	Till the blue blood comes through.

Such treatment, followed up if necessary by "hünger krawt [hunger plant]," "mangel kraut [shortage plant]," and "Prunen saft [well juice]," is guaranteed not to fail.

In a perennial German favorite, *The Nine Skins of Bad Women*, even a silent rebuke rouses the male's violent ire. In Hans Sachs's original version, the bad wife's offense is a negative one: giving her husband the silent treatment. Later seventeenth-century renditions of the tale make her a more aggressive shrew. All versions profess disapproval of the violence they show, but it remains central to their action and appeal. In Sachs's verses, a scratched and battered husband meets the poet and tells of a violent battle with his wife. Returning home from drinking wine, he finds that his wife will not speak to him. He has heard the old wives' tale that bad women have nine skins; growing angry, he tests the theory on his mate. He beats through the cold fish's hide to reach, in turn, the growling bear, the squawking goose, the barking dog, the fleeing hare, the kicking horse, the scratching cat, and the grunting sow. When at last he reaches the human skin, she begs his forgiveness, explaining that a neighbor has led her astray and that she will never treat him so again. Despite his victory, the husband is unhappy: his wife's defensive scratches not only hurt, but present visible evidence of her insubordination that damages the honor of both parties in the eyes of their community. Sachs, the moralist, draws a lesson from this for all young husbands:

Sey nicht zu schnell / zu toll / vnd hitzig	Be not too hasty, hot, and mad, As if no sense at all thou had.
Als ob du werest gar nicht witzig.	If thy wife's looks are not all kind
Wann dichs Weib nit stäts süß ansicht /	Or all her words not to thy mind; For thou thyself at some times art
Oder dir nach deim Sinn zuspricht.	Not friendly, kind, and light of heart.

Da du doch selbs bist nicht
    allzeit
Häußlich / freundlich / vnd
    voller freud.
Wilt dann mit schlagen alls
    außrichten /
Das zimmt ein Biderman mit
    nichten.

Then solving everything with
    hitting
Is for a good man most unfitting.

Wise and virtuous men rule their wives with reason, patiently pointing out their shortcomings in a fair-minded way:

Mit Freundlichkeit sie stäts
    vermahn /
Mein Weib / das steht dir vbel
    an:
Schaw / diß ist schand / vnd
    jenes schad /
Wilt haben meine Gunst vnd
    Gnad.
Geh solches müssig / folge mir /
    So will ich auch gehorchen dir.
Wann mir etwas steht vbel an /
    Will handeln als ein feiner
    Mann.

Admonish her with kindness still:
My wife, that thing becomes thee
    ill;
Look, this is bad, and that brings
    shame.
Now if thou wilt my favor gain,
Then shun such things and
    follow me,
As I will also hark to thee
When anything becomes me ill;
Act like a proper man I will.

Such pacific and rational behavior should bring a wife to know her duty. Only if she obstinately persists in wrongdoing should violence be used, and then only "mit Bescheidenheit / Daß euch nit rew hernach allbeyd [with measure due / That it not cause you both to rue]." Sachs is constantly mindful of the couple's common interest in preserving their communal honor, which requires an appearance of domestic order, with all correction and dissidence hidden from public view. Through discretion and the timely application of both "sour and sweet," an ideal marriage is achieved:

Dadurch euch hie auff dieser Erd
Fried / Frewd / vnd
    Freundlichkeit auffwachs
Jm Ehestand: das wünscht
    Hanß Sachs.

Thus ev'n in earthly marriage
    will
Grow peace, good will, and
    gladness too;
And this does Hans Sachs wish
    for you.

Though the husband depicted here has made himself absurd by his excess and indiscretion—attested to by the very fact of his appearing in public as a man whose wife fights with him—Sachs sees nothing wrong with the private enjoyment of violence against an unruly wife. If she stubbornly neglects her duty, "So kanstu wol zu streichen greiffen / Vnd jhr zum dantz ein Liedlein pfeiffen [You surely can to blows advance / And pipe a song to make her dance]." Although Sachs presents the husband of this piece as an example of what to avoid, the action of the piece advances a different message: clearly it is the successful violence, along with the humorous descriptions of the woman's various skins, that gives the verses their wide appeal. Besides, to draw a different moral from that appended by Sachs, one has only to read the rhyme atop the mid-sixteenth-century broadside:

Welcher Mann ein solch neunhäutig Thier Strafft / vnd macht ein fromb Weib auß jhr / Verdient durch jeden Tritt / vnd Streich Ein Staffel in das Himmelreich.[31]	The man who such a nine-skinned cur Tames and makes a good wife of her Will earn for every blow struck here A higher place in heaven's sphere.

Both this and other editions offer a series of nine pictures, reiterating the images of violent male dominance and of female behavior as animal. The scenes depict progressive stages of the battle, with the woman flanked by the appropriate beast in each. Instead of a single couple throughout, however, the pictures present different couples in different dress at the various stages, thus underlining the universality of the battle: the battering husband is conceived not as one man but as everyman, and his story is seen as one that all men can enjoy. Similarly, the scenes imply, all women are the same. The gestures and positions of the figures convey the escalation of the conflict: the husband appears angry and threatening from the outset, but the wife at first adopts a confident stance. Only gradually does she lose her composure, as her hair becomes disheveled and she attempts to fight back by kicking and scratching. In the last pictures the husband, evidently finding his bare hands unequal to the task, has seized a stick and gives the wife her final comeuppance. The last scene finds her on her knees, in a stark and, from the text's point of view, satisfying contrast with her initial haughtiness. (See illustration used on chapter opening pages.)

By the later seventeenth century an updated version of the piece appeared. The end of the opening rhyme is altered—perhaps to correspond with a more secularized atmosphere—to "Verdient alsdenn für iedem Schlag / Ein'n recht vergnügten Ehstands-Tag [Will earn for each stroke at his wife / A happy day of married life]." The text has changed as well, though the outline of the tale remains the same. The young husband, now called "Philander," appears with his face scratched from a fight with "Dorilis," his wife. He complains to his friend that she is crazy and tells how it all began:

Als ich am Abend kam nach Hause von dem Wein,	Last night from drinking wine with friends I did come home
Und mit ihr reden wolt im Bette gantz allein	And wished to talk with her in bed we two alone;
Da fieng sie hefftig an auf mich sehr hart zu fluchen:	Then she did violently begin to curse and shout,
Muß man dich Huren-Schelm in Huren-Häusern suchen?	Thou whorehound, must one then in brothels seek thee out?

The wife has become the verbal aggressor, and the battle is now linked to their sexual relations. While Philander wishes to continue normal marital intimacies, Dorilis accuses him of sexual irregularities. Like his predecessor, he becomes angry and resolves to try beating his way through the nine skins. By starting the fight with her scolding, this version spoils the earlier fish-skin analogy; but here the emphasis lies less on the witty comparison of different sorts of female behavior with that of animals than on the rage an unruly woman can arouse and the satisfaction of beating her. Having disposed of several skins, Philander perseveres to the end:

Und hätt ihr die Natur noch eine Haut verliehen	Had nature given to her yet another skin,
So etwa von der Sau; ich achte solches nicht,	As of a sow, perhaps; to that I paid no heed,
Mein Prügel gleicherweis sein kräftig Werck verricht.	But still my cudgel strong performed its mighty deed.
Ich wolt die (8) Sau-Haut ihr so tapfer schlagen, blauen,	I wanted that same (8) sow-hide to so bravely thump and beat
Daß jedes seine Lust vergnüget könte schauen;	That every man could see his satisfaction there complete.

Ich wolte schlagen fort, bis	I wanted to keep thrashing until
man recht sehen könt	one could truly see
Die schöne (9) Menschen-	That soft and lovely (9) human
Haut bis an ihr letztes End.	skin had come through
	thoroughly.

Finally, he is rewarded with her submission:

Ach göldner, lieber Mann! Ach!	O precious husband dear! O
Schatz, laß mich doch leben!	darling, spare my life!
. . . . .	. . . . .
. . . Ich wil hinfort nicht mehr	I'll ne'er do so again, I swear that
So schändlich garstig thun;	from this day,
All Liebe, Treu und Ehr	I'll not shamefully treat thee,
Soll dir von mir, als Weib,	but love and honor pay,
treulich gegeben werden.	And will devoted be, as a good
	wife befits.
. . . . .	
Ich wil dir flehentlich auch	. . . . .
fallen um den Hals,	I also will imploringly thee hug
Damit du mir nur magst	and kiss,
vergeben dieses alls.	To plead that thou wilt only now
	forgive all this.

She too was misled by a neighbor and promises not to repeat her error. Though he is gratified by the outcome, Philander realizes that this is a bad way to conduct a marriage: "Das ist ein schlechte Lust, dacht ich, auch schlecht Beginnen [That is a bad desire, I thought, and bad beginning]."[32] Like Sachs, he advises men to rule their wives with reason rather than tyranny.

Though it endorses the standard edifying message, this piece goes even further than the original in offering men a dramatic identification with its violence and anger. The earlier contrast between the wife's passivity and the husband's aggression apparently is no longer satisfying—either because it offers less scope for humorous exchanges between the discordant couple or because the provocation seems inadequate to the punishment. By allotting the wife a more active role, this version makes the conflict more equal and Dorilis a more vivid personality; on the other hand, however, it weakens the piece's moral case against the impulsively violent husband. Sachs's protagonist can be condemned as "Zw müetwillig, dol, tüm vnd frech [Too willful, wild, witless, and insolent]," typical of intemperate young men who explode into violence "Wen eüch ein weib nür krüm ansicht [If a woman only looks at you sideways],"[33] but Philander's is a less one-sided quarrel. Also, in contrast to the earlier husband, who is scolded by Sachs for his crude behavior, Philander arrives independently at a "reasonable" view of the situation and voices the moral himself—adding to his recommendation of rational rule in marriage an admonition to wives:

Hingegen soll das Weib sich auch vernünftig stellen,	The woman, too, however, should not this reason lack,
Dem Mann nicht allezeit nach Hundsart wiederbellen	Nor always like a dog at her man be barking back,
Sie soll sich jederzeit fein freundlich stellen an:	But ever should behave in friendly wise and kind,
Das er sein Hertzens-Lust an ihr auch möge han.	So that in her he still his heart's delight may find.

The woman's fractious tongue parallels the man's resort to violence.

The street texts of both countries cater to men's delight in seeing a shrew trounced, and her violent subjugation is comic by its very nature. In the parallel sixteenth-century adventures of the German *Korbmacher* [Basketmaker] and the English *Pinnyng of the Basket*, female perversity humorously succumbs to masculine force. The German basketmaker, hero of both song and verse, finishes a basket one Sunday and wants his wife to praise God for it; but she rudely rebuffs him:

Sie wolts nicht thun war eygensinnig sprach vngschlacht /	She wouldn't do it, Was obstinate and rudely said,
ist er gmacht so sey er gmacht gilt mir gleiche.	Well if it's done, it's done, what do I care?
Er sprach mein liebs weib mich gewer /	He said, dear wife, do this for me,
sprich Gott sey lob das der korb gmacht ist woren /	Say God be praised, the basket now is done.
ist er gmacht so sey gmachet er / sprach sie /	If so, it's all the same to me, She said, and now his anger was begun,
da ergrimmet der Man im zoren /	That she refused those words to speak.
das sie nicht sprechen wolt die wort /	With right good will he did her poke and thump,

vnnd sie ein gute müh rauffet
vnd schluge /
die Fraw die schrey zetter vnd
mord.

The wife did bloody murder
shriek.

The mayor happens by, and the amusing scene sets him laughing all the way home. When he tells his wife about it, however, she sympathizes fully with the basketmaker's wife and proudly insists that she would never say it either: "Sie sprach . . . ich sprech es nit vnd kost es mir das leben / Da schlug er sie in das Angesicht [She said, I'll never say it, though it cost my life; / Then he hit her in the face]."[34] She remains obstinate and threatens to tell her family of his abuse. The husband's servant then tells the kitchen maid how the mistress, like the basketmaker's wife, has "veracht [scorned]" her master. The maid asserts that no one could force her to say it either, whereupon the servant gives her a beating. While this song sanctions the men's violence, another pamphlet version condemns it:

Sie hattend eingleit kleine ehr /
Man find noch vil der selben
lappen /
Hand kein verstand seind groß
diltappen /
Vnd wölln doch gar fast witzig
sein /
Wenn sie heim kommen von
dem Wein /
So sticht sie der Narr vnd die
Grillen /
Wöln dweiber zwingen vmb
nichts willen.

. . . . .

Welcher sein Fraw also veracht /
Vnd meint dest höher zsein vnd
ferrer /
Derselb geht wol zum Narren
bschwerer /
Vnd lest sein Fraw dieweil
vngirt /
Biß das er wider nüchtern wirdt.

In truth their honor was but
small.
Such idiots one often finds,
Great oafs with nothing in their
minds,
And yet they think they're wise
and fine
When they come home from
drinking wine.
Fond notions then these fools
possess,
So they for naught their wives
oppress.

. . . . .

The man who thus will scorn his
wife
And thinks this makes him high
and tall
Must seek a cure from folly's
thrall,
And meanwhile leaves his wife
free rein
Until he sobers up again.

The author goes on, somewhat inconsistently, to insist that "Der Spruch trifft an allein die bösen [This rhyme concerns only the bad]," implying that for bad women such violence is appropriate. He apparently feels that this "schimpflicher Spruch [comical verse]," though amusing, needs clarification to counteract its dubious moral tendency.[35] Such efforts to salvage the story's moral illustrate its currency even among those who professed respect and honor for women.

The "pretie jeste" of the *Pinnyng of the Basket* tells a similar tale. A chandler's wife, angry because he is out drinking and gaming instead of minding the shop, seeks him out, and "When she hym founde, the bedlam beaste / Beganne to scolde." He patiently goes home with her, serves the joiner's page who has come to buy his goods, and then tells his wife to pin the basket—that is, to fasten the package of goods—and give it to the customer. She bluntly refuses and verbally abuses him:

> Knowe thou, quoth she, sir knaue, that I
> The basket will not pinne!
>
> Her housebande, sore insenste, did sweare
> By stockes and stones,
> She should, or els he would prepare
> To baste her bones.
> . . . . .
> Then with a bastion that stoode by,
> Whiche he did smell,
> At her he freely did let flie,
> And bumbde her well.
> . . . . .
> Vnguentum Bakaline
> Did make this houswife quickly pinne
> The basket passyng fine.

As in the German versions, men find this event exceedingly funny, while women greet it with indignation. "This pastyme pleased well the page," who goes home and tells his master:

> The joigner ioyes at this,
> But sure his wife, to heare this tale,
> Was quite bereft of blisse.
> . . . . .
> Quoth she,—For all his bloose,

> The knaue the basket should haue pinde
> Hymself, spight of his nose!

She declares that she would not have pinned it, and the couple go to bed to discuss the matter. Meanwhile the maid pounces on the troublemaking page:

> Caulyng hym knaue and sot,
> And vsed hym, that, in the ende,
> A broken head he got.

> Henceforthe take heede of makyng strife,
> Thou knaue, quoth she,
> Betwixt thy maister and his wife,
> Where loue should be.

Here, in contrast to the German version, the female is the aggressor; but the page does not take this abuse passively:

> Yet vp he stept full stoutly then,
> And bomde me Jone;
> That she lent he so paide againe,
> He made her grone.

Then he makes her sit and eat supper with him. This encourages the master next day to assert his authority; when his wife persistently refuses to pin the basket, "Then with a bedstaffe he to baste / Her doeth beginne." Still unwilling to submit, she runs and complains to a justice's wife, who lays the case before her husband; but men's solidarity proves even stronger than women's:

> Her housebande, hearyng by this tale
> How all thynges stood,
> In mynde he at this ieste so stale
> Did laugh a-good;
>
> . . . . .
>
> A little more adoe,
> This Justice would have taught his wife
> To pinne the basket too.

> Now all good wiues, beware by this
> Your names to blot;
> The basket pinne with quietnesse,
> Denie it not.[36]

Though the English women show more initial aggression than the German, the latter match their sisters in stubborn defiance. The author of the English ballad, who recognizes his theme as timeworn, makes no excuses for the treatment meted out to unruly wives, but apparently expects that women will be included in his audience. Pinning the basket became a proverbial phrase for wifely submission, just as the nine skins of bad German wives recurred as a proverbial excuse for marital violence in German texts.

It is noteworthy that the English version of this theme halts the violence at a lower social level than does the German, possibly suggesting a view of wife beating as more appropriate for the lower orders. The English ballad also preserves the movement of violent example from lower to higher, even when this interrupts the flow of the action: thus the joiner does not immediately beat his wife but instead goes to bed with her, in an example of the persistent English analogy between sex and violence. Only when encouraged by his servant's example does he take up the cudgel—a bedstaff, in another underlining of the sexual element. The German mayor instantly hits his wife when she seconds the basketmaker's wife, while the English justice, though approving of the other men's actions, stops short of violence himself.

While these beatings apparently do their victims no permanent damage, in other texts comic violence against wives causes jarringly real injuries. In some German works it goes to the extreme lengths of maiming and even death without disturbing the joyous mood. The *Tagweyß / wie man die bösen weyber schlahen sol* [Song of how one should beat bad women], described by Franz Brietzmann as "das allerwiderlichste Opus dieser Art, das in seiner selbstverständlichen Roheit nicht gut zu übertreffen ist [the very most revolting work of this sort, which in its unabashed brutality can hardly be surpassed],"[37] gives men elaborate instructions for beating their wives. Printed together with another song on marital discord, it appeared in at least two editions in the mid-sixteenth century. It opens with a jocular recommendation of irresponsibility and violence:

Frölich so will jch singen /	Now will I sing so gaily,
schlag dein weib vmb den kopff	Hit thy wife on the head,
mit knütteln soltn sie schmiren /	With cudgels smear her daily,
vertrinck jr mantel vnnd rock.	And drink away her dress.

Then come more specific directions:

Vnd schmir sie vmb die lende /
mit einem heslin stab /
stoß jr den kopff vmb dwende /
vnd trit sie in den sack /
der streych soltu dich fleyssen /
erschlag sie doch nit gar /

Her body be sure well pound
With a strong hazel rod;
Strike her head till it turns
 round,
And kick her in the gut.
With blows be ever zealous,
Yet see thou don't her kill.

One should try not to kill her but need have no fear of other damage, which might be the only means of keeping her within the bounds of marital obedience and honor:

Also solt du sie straffen /
wiltu sie haben zam
fleis dich bey deynen ehren /
soltu sie schlagen lam /
an henden vnd an füssen /
das sie nit lauff daruon /
also solt du sie straffen /
so laufft sie zu keim pfaffen /
erst wirts dir vnterthon.

Thus shouldst thou thy wife
 punish
If thou wilt have her tame;
Car'st thou about thy honor
Then must thou beat her lame
Of hand and foot also
So she can't run away.
Thus must thou beat and damp
 her
So to no priest she'll scamper;
Then first she'll thee obey.

One might expect the author of such a scurrilous piece to show little concern for either the justice of his prescriptions or their reception by a female audience. Nevertheless, he explains in closing that such treatment applies only to bad women: "Ich sing von bösen weyben / die guten geets nit an [I sing of women bad, / To the good this won't apply]." And apparently anticipating that some women will still be listening, he clarifies the moral for them:

Hüt euch jr Frawen alle /
vor diser Tageweis /
ob sie euch nit gefalle /
so solt jr haben fleyß /
gegen ewern mannen alle /
vnd seyt jn vnterthan /
das jr des werdt vertragen /
als vbel nit geschlagen /
das ist alzeyt mein rat.[38]

Take care, you women all,
Of this song's argument;
And if it should you gall,
Then be you diligent
To please your husbands all.
Obey in meek subjection
So they with you will bear,
And bad wives' beatings spare,
That's ever my direction.

Whether the song was actually sung to women or mainly to men who enjoyed the prospect of their wives' taking such a message to heart, the author does not hesitate to address women. Like the author of the *Pinnyng of the Basket*, he jokingly threatens violence for female misbehavior, but with a casual acknowledgment that violent punishment can cause women injury or death.

While the brutality of this song may have been unsurpassed in the sixteenth century, some seventeenth-century broadsides carried the effects of violence still further. These productions, with their large and elaborate engravings, were certainly more expensive than simple song pamphlets and thus probably were aimed at a rather more prosperous audience—an audience with a well-developed taste for extreme violence in the depiction of marital relations. *Offt Probiertes und Bewährtes Recept oder Artzney für die bösse Kranckheit der unartigen Weiber* [Often tested and proven prescription or medicine for the evil sickness of misbehaving women], an engraved broadside from the Nuremberg workshop of Paul Fürst, offers the final solution to the plague of women's shrewishness. The hero of the tale innocently marries, not realizing the misery in store:

Der gute Kerl dacht nit / wie daß das Weibernehemen / ein nöhtigs Ubel sey / die Eh ein Weh und Grämen.	The good man little thought how taking of a wife Was just a needful ill that brought woe to man's life.

Soon he is tormented with constant nagging and abuse; he cannot even drink in peace:

Das bitterböse Weib das war sein Fegefeuer auff Erden seine Höll /	That furious raging woman his purgatory was, His hell here on this earth.
. . . . .	. . . . .
Trug etwan ihn der Wein zuhaus auß einer Zeche / da riefe sie: daß dir der Blitz den Hals zerbreche / du Schlauch / du Säufer du. Da war sie Hundetoll /	If he from drinking wine with friends did come home to his wife, At him she then would fume and shout, "May lightning blast your life,

gesegnet ihm den Trunck mit
    Teuffeln Tonnenvoll.

You sot, you drunkard you!"
    Thus would this rabid she
Bless him his drink with barrels
    of curses fiendishly.

She accuses him of neglecting household responsibilities for drink, robs him of his rightful authority, and with her motherly doting foils his attempts to discipline their children. The man, finally driven to ask a friend for advice, is told that he has erred in not subduing her from the first, a mistake which authors of both countries warn against repeatedly. Still, it is not too late to act, and he is given a slip of paper which reveals the sure cure for his difficulties. Following these instructions, the man cuts himself a cartful of cudgels and takes them home. When his wife greets him with curses, he is ready:

        meine Pillen
die sollen dir die Gall / du böser
    Teuffel / stillen.
Ich bring jetzund das Kraut / das
    fromme Weiber macht;
du solst mir frömmer gehn zu
    Bette diese Nacht.
Thun / Dencken / war hier eins.
    Er nahm ein derben
    Prügel /
lief / fasste bey dem Haar den
    Jgel / den Höllrigel.
Puff / gieng es / platz / klip /
    klap! auff jedes Ort
    zweymal.
Es fielen da von ihr acht Häute
    an der Zahl.

        these pills I bring,
You devil of a wife, will still your
    vicious sting,
For now I have the herb that
    makes bad women tame;
You'll go to bed tonight a far
    more docile dame.
Here thought and act were one.
    A cudgel strong he found,
Ran and grabbed by the hair that
    hedgehog, that hellhound.
Bang! it went, pow! smick!
    smack! all o'er her body
    twice.
Then from her duly fell her eight
    skins in a trice.

She, like the "böse weib" of Sachs's piece, has nine skins; but in this case either they do not lend her the same immunity to harm, or the enraged husband does not stop when he reaches the human skin. "Sie lief halb tod hinweg / verschloß sich in die Kammer [She ran half dead away, shut herself in the chamber]," where she laments her sufferings but confesses that they are deserved and urges other women to obey their husbands. At length she dies of her injuries, to her husband's great delight:

der Holtzbirn hatte sie so viel zu sich genommen /	So many sturdy blows did she that day receive
daß sie nit kondte mehr zu Kräfften wieder kommen /	That never after that could she her strength retrieve,
daran ersticken must. Da ward erst froh der Mann.	And so from this she died. Then the man's joy began.

Free at last, he invites his drinking and gaming companions to make merry in honor of her funeral.

In the series of six engravings at the top of the broadside, the couple depicted is very prosperous, with a well-appointed home, framed pictures on the walls, and a nurse for the baby as well as a serving maid. The altercations between husband and wife are shown taking place in the relatively public space of this private family circle, with children and servants looking on. In one scene, when the wife prevents her husband from beating a misbehaving child, another child, a little girl, beats her brother with a stick. The pictorial message endorses the text's interpretation: in thwarting her husband the mother is overturning the sexual hierarchy and destroying familial discipline, and the children reflect and imitate her disorder. Still more striking is the depiction of the final beating: the wife is flanked by four children and a maid, all seeking to dissuade the father from further blows, but to no avail; in the background appears a funeral procession. Unlike the intemperate husband of Sachs's *Nine Skins of Bad Women*, this husband is shown as suffering no shame or loss of honor because of his marital battles. By providing witnesses, the pictures intensify the man's arrogant assumption that he can do as he likes.

Far from considering himself a misogynistic *Frauenschänder*, the poet of this text takes care to assert his fair-mindedness and respect for good women. The treatment described, it went almost without saying, should be reserved for bad women who bring it on themselves by their evil conduct. This limitation leads him, in the course of his denunciations of the overly indulgent mother, to imply (accidentally, no doubt) that good women need not obey their husbands:

Ein Weib darff selber Zucht / das ungezämte Thier /	Woman herself, that untamed beast, needs constant rule.
das leer ist an Vernunfft / ein Sklave der Begier:	Of reason she is void, and of desire the tool.
(Sie sind nit alle so; ich meine nur die Bösen /	(They are not all like this; the bad alone are meant,

von denen wollest du /
    O Herr Gott / uns erlosen.)
Drumb halte sie der Mann
    in Furchten allezeit.
gehorchen müssen nur /
    nit herschen / solche Leut.[39]

From whom may God's
    deliverance be swiftly to us
    sent.)
Let her therefore e'er fear her
    husband's rightful sway;
Such people must not rule, but
    only must obey.

With such disclaimers and encouragements to female virtue, the depiction of wife murder can present itself as a production laden with social, moral, and religious value.

A similar broadside from earlier in the seventeenth century celebrates a similar denouement. Having married a disobedient wife with a poison tongue, a young man solves his problem in nine days, his activities represented in a series of pictures. On Monday he drives to the woods, Tuesday cuts a cudgel, Wednesday beats his wife soundly. By Thursday she is ill from the beating but takes it patiently as her husband's just punishment of her. Friday she takes to her bed, says farewell to her neighbors, urges the wives to take example by her and be obedient, and arranges to leave all her goods to her husband. Saturday she dies, Sunday he buries her, and Monday he celebrates in a bout of drinking with his friends. Like other such pieces, this closes with a "Protestation" telling good women not to be offended, as the rhyme refers only to bad ones:

Derhalb bitt ich ohn alles
    wanckn /
Es wols ein jed zum besten
    verstehn /
Vnd denckn / es thet sie nit
    angehn.[40]

Therefore I ask without a qualm
That each will take this in good
    part
And think it does not her regard.

There could hardly be a more explicit statement of the way in which such texts put pressure on women to dissociate themselves from rebellion and model their behavior on the ideal of submissiveness—to the point, the author hopes, where the violent punishment of a bad woman can be seen as having nothing to do with them. However, the fact that such protestations were considered necessary shows that women were not so easily fooled. The repetition of these disclaimers suggests, in fact, that such texts made women angry—perhaps a reassuring thought for modern feminists. But the women's annoyance was part of the texts' purpose, and authors did their best to reduce it to helpless sputtering: a woman who complained could be ridiculed for identifying herself as a shrew. No doubt many women were prepared to risk this, but women's lack of an independent public voice made it difficult for them to combat such texts effectively.

A contemporary English satire of uncertain provenance offers a similar message but is somewhat less explicit about the woman's fate. Headed "A New Yeeres guift for shrews," it pictures the various stages of the man's triumph, with an explanatory rhyme below:

> Who marieth a Wife vpon a Moneday,
> If she will not be good vppon a Twesday,
> Lett him go to ye wood vppon a Wensday,
> And cutt him a cudgell vpon the Thursday,
> And pay her soundly vppon a Fryday,
> And she mend not, ye Diuil take her a Saterday.
> Then he may eat his meat in peace on the Sunday.[41]

The picture shows the undesirable wife being chased off by the Devil after the husband's beating—implying death, but hardly as bald as the German version.

Comic violence of the sort that could inflict palpable injury does occasionally appear in English popular literature, though usually not in the fatal forms it takes in Germany. Its depiction is generally limited to longer and more elaborate pamphlets and jestbooks—productions which, like the German broadsides, probably appealed to an audience more elevated (economically, at least) than that of simpler ballads and songs. The sixteenth-century *Wife lapped in Morels skin*, a small book in rhyme decorated with several woodcuts, tells a "mery jest" of a young man's sadistic victory over his shrewish wife. Before their marriage she warns him of her hasty temper and insists that he agree to bear it patiently— which he promises to do, but with a mental reservation. After their marriage, when he rebukes her for mistreating the hired hands, she falls to railing and finally seizes a staff to beat him. At this he goes off in a rage, resolving to tame her by force if necessary. In preparation, he has his old horse, "Morell," skinned, and the hide salted. When his wife hits him with her fist, calling him "whoreson," he drags her to the cellar, strips her, and beats her bloodily:

> In euery hand a rod he gate,
> And layd vpon her a right good pace;
> . . . . .

> Euer he layde on, and euer she did crye,
> Alas! alas! that euer I was borne;
> Out vpon thee, murderer, I thee defye,
> Thou hast my white skin, and my body all to torne:
> Leaue of betyme, I counsayle thee.

But he persists:

> He gaue her than so many a great cloute,
> That on the grounde the bloud was seene.
> Within a whyle, he cryed newe roddes, newe!
> With that she cryed full loude alas!
>
> . . . . .
>
> And sodainely with that in a sowne she was.

This is only the first stage of her punishment; next he wraps her in the salted skin, making her wounds smart. He threatens to keep her there forever, and in her great distress she begs forgiveness, promising to serve him faithfully ever after. She is put to bed and healed, then astounds everyone with her diligence at her parents' next visit:

> The husband sate there like a man,
> The wyfe did serue them all that day;
> The good man commaunded what he would haue,
> The wyfe was quick at hand.

When the young man explains his method, his wife's mother is angry, but her father heartily approves, and

> All they that were there held with the yong man,
> And sayd, he dyd well in euery maner degree.

The author agrees:

> Forgeue the yongman if he did sin,
> But I thinke he did nothing amisse,
> He did all thing euen for the best.[42]

Though less deadly in its effect, this violent treatment matches the German in its enjoyment of the deserved suffering inflicted on an ill-natured, disobedient woman. This tale also especially savors the wife's astonishment and helpless indignation; she clearly expects immunity from abuse, relying on her class status and the support of her family for protection, and she is shocked to find herself subjected to such treatment.

Like other English shrews, she gives greater provocation than the anti-heroines of similar German pieces, none of whom goes so far as to lift a hand against a husband. In contrast to the scrupulous explanations of many German works of this kind, the author here contents himself with a halfhearted apology in case anyone is offended. His stance is ambiguous, suggesting either a supreme contempt for women's indignation or a recognition that there is no hope of reconciling them to such a tale as this. German authors, adding conciliatory limitations and excuses even to their least edifying pieces, take more pains than the English to justify their work: it must be instructive as well as entertaining, a concern which illustrates the lesser differentiation in German literature between fiction and admonition.

This type of graphically injurious violence against disruptive wives found little place in the popular literature of seventeenth-century England. Its scattered appearances seem limited to productions with a clearly restricted audience, such as the mid-century periodical *Mercurius Fumigosus*. This satirical series of pamphlets featured caricatures of low life, spiced with misogyny, for the delectation of "gentlemen." An issue of 1655 recasts an old antishrew tale as the triumph of a "merry conceited Smug" (blacksmith) over his wife, who comes railing after him to the alehouse, calling names "without any respect of Persons," even when he is drinking "with some Persons of great quallity." When they get home he strikes at her with an iron bar, breaking her arm. He pays the bonesetter a double fee, saying the extra money is for setting the other arm, which he will break the next time she follows him. She swears never to do it again:

> So Smugg did cure the fashions in his Wife,
> And now lives happy without care, or strife.
> If any man be troubled with a Shrew,
> Smugg's Cure is most approv'd and certain true.[43]

As in the *Pinnyng of the Basket* (but unlike *Morels Skin*), the violence is a plebeian activity; people of "quality" observe it with amusement and approval but are not shown engaging in it themselves. This redefinition of violence against women as a lower-class activity offered respectable audiences a means of distancing themselves from the violence while still enjoying it, and suggests that violent shrew taming was increasingly seen as a forbidden fruit. In works aimed at a broader audience in seventeenth-century England such extreme cures are seldom applied, at least in so blatant a manner. A similar joke appears in several seventeenth-century German jestbooks, but without the English element of elite amusement at the uninhibited doings of artisans.[44] The rarity of such graphic violence in seventeenth-century England's street literature, with an apparent waning of faith in the efficacy of force against shrewish behavior, contrasts with the persistence of violent solutions in Germany. In England the laughter that had been roused by shrew beating in the sixteenth century now resounded mainly in response to the women's reversal of the standard order.

Though violence, as an instrument appropriate for use by superiors against inferiors, was claimed by men as their exclusive right, women in the popular texts of both countries often fail to honor this claim. English scolds are shown gaining substantial power by use of the tongue alone, but most do not stop at railing. When their will is thwarted or when they simply need to relieve their ill temper, they violently abuse their mates. Their violence increases in seventeenth-century texts but is depicted in the sixteenth as well. A song of the 1550s presents the complaint of an unfortunate husband whose wife laughs him to scorn, refuses to do any work, and beats him "Both bak and bon." She brought substantial property to their marriage and now will not be ruled.[45]

Another husband tries to beat his wife when she shirks her duties, but with ill success:

> The god man for to beate his wyffe
>   In hande a pase he went;
> He caught two blowes vpon his head
>   For every one he lent.
>
>   . . . . .
>
> He was so stowte and sterne and stoure
>   And fearsse with her in fyght,
> That even vpon the stony flowre [floor]
>   She knockt his head full ryght.
> The good wyffe was wonderous wake [weak] in hande,
>   Fearefull, and nothing bold.
> But he had never a fott [foot] to stande
>   When she of hym caught hold.[46]

The Batchelor's Delight, from the first half of the seventeenth century, warns against marriage with a shrew, who torments her husband day and night, forcing him to do her work as well as his own:

> And if he doth the same refuse,
> The durty quean will him abuse,
>   and beat him with the ladle.
>
> He cannot quietly rest in bed,
>   but, every little season,
> The childe doth cry and must be fed,
>   and then, she saith, 'tis reason
> That he should do't, and let her sleep;
> The poor man he must silence keep,
>   for talking would be treason.[47]

Later in the century, "Poor Anthony" has submitted to his wife's yoke, obeying her commands and doing all the housework, even washing diapers, but still:

> A dismal Peal to me is rung,
>   while I Rock Bearn in Cradle,
> Oh! bless me from her scolding tongue,
>   and from her basting Ladle.
>   . . . . .
> My Wife doth lug me by the ears
>   if I but ask for Bacon,
> And flouts and taunts and scolds and jears,
>   but she must have her Capon:
> She kicks me up and down the house,
>   and roars as loud as Thunder,
> While I am silent as a Mouse,
>   hold up my hands and wonder.[48]

In another comic tale of woe, the speaker confesses that

> To tell you the truth both plain and flat
> Though I am the Head my Dame is the Hat.

He is forced to make the fire, warm her clothes, even hold the chamberpot for her when she comes home drunk:

> Or else with a bed staffe my noddle she'l greet
> In such a rude manner you'd laugh for to see't.

He resolves to assert himself and make her change her tune, starting tomorrow: "Ile knock her bold face against the wall / and make her for to know sorrow."[49] But if he fails in this bold attack, he fears all the neighbors will mock him.

Other henpecked husbands, like the "West Country Weaver," make similar resolutions to fight their wives' fire with fire; but once an "invincible shrew" has achieved such sway, few can tame her. The helpless and, by the later seventeenth century, usually unresisting victims face a life of subjection to arbitrary female violence. Many "turbulent" wives compound their shrewishness with adultery, which increases both their husbands' humiliation and their own authority. Pouring scorn on the men's sexual inadequacy, they indulge even more freely in violence, invective, and general abuse.[50]

For all its efficacy as a tool in subduing fainthearted males, these women's slapstick violence retains the unreal quality of farce. The angry wives' ladles, frying pans, and bedstaffs may crack their husbands' pates but seem to inflict no lasting damage. The humorous reversal of authority leaves the husband thoroughly beaten, but only so that he can more entertainingly bemoan his fate. This style of coarse but relatively innocuous female violence is shared by both German and English pieces on such themes as the shrew's triumph over the Devil[51] and the wife's punishment of her adulterous spouse. In some German pieces, however, women exercise a violence which parallels some of the feats of German husbands in its graphic realism, though not in the degree of injury suffered. While the English women's aggressive, independent, but stylized violence often wins them mastery, the German women's more defensive though occasionally damaging violence seldom brings more than temporary gains.

Like the English, the German shrew attacks first with the tongue, often in anger at her husband's habit of staying out drinking with his friends. She can make a strong verbal attack, including threats of violence, but nearly always leaves initiation of violence to the man. The most successful of German shrews is also one of the earliest: the villainess of *Der bös rauch* [The terrible smoke], an early sixteenth-century song, makes her sway complete and became a proverbial example of female dominion. Here it is the shrew who strikes the first blow, though not in an entirely unprovoked and independent attack. This "frembde abentheür / von ainem weib so vngeheür [strange tale of a wife so monstrous]" tells of "ain gütter ainfeltiger man [a good, simple man]" who "auff erd kain gutes wort / von ir bekumen kunde [On earth no good word ever / Could from his wife obtain]." Resolving to settle matters with her once and for all, he tells her that if she wants to be the man of the house, she must win the breeches from him. He procures a pair of blue breeches and two cudgels:

der frawen er den ainen bot /
sy gund sich kurtz beraten /
er wolts vor mit ir tragen auß /
warbey es solt beleyben /
die fraw schlug dar mit starckem
    sauß /
gund jn im hauß vmbtreiben /
zwo stiegen auff er ir entgieng /
die ain fiel er bald wider ab /
vor schlegen groß die er
    empfieng.

He offered one unto his wife,
Who quickly got her ready.
He wished her first to
    understand
How the fight should be
    bounded,
But she struck home with heavy
    hand,
About the house him hounded.
Of two steps up that he might go
He quickly fell down one again,
For he took many a grievous
    blow.

She beats him senseless and throws water on him; he eventually manages to get out the door, and then: "von hertzen wainen er began / des lasterß vnd der schande [He from the heart began to cry / For his disgrace and shaming]." In answer to a friend's sympathetic questions, he replies that his house is on fire and the smoke has driven him out. The neighbor enters the house to help, but is also beaten out, and agrees with the husband that he has never seen such dreadful smoke. This formidable woman rules the household ever after:

also die fraw die bruch gewan /
vnd trug sie darnach selber an /
vnd zoch für baß jrn mane /
nach jrem willen maysterlich /

And so the wife the breeches
    won,
Herself thereafter put them on,
And thenceforth ruled her
    husband
Firmly according to her will.

The author closes with a virulent attack on such domineering females:

ja wolte got vonn hymelrich /
das sy weren begraben /
die noch solichs gewalts begern /
so stünd es in der welte baß /
vnd blib vil manig man bey eern.

I would to God in heaven above
That they were dead and buried,
All wives who still such power
    crave;
The world would be a better
    place,
And many men their honor save.

He berates the fool who gives her the opportunity and thus brings shame on his whole sex, and he urges other men to comport themselves better:

es ist allen mannen ain schant /
ich rat dir man ob dich anzant /
dein weibe vmb dich mauset /
leg ir fünff finger auff den kopff /
das sy zur erden tauchet /
thustu das nit du bleibst ain
    tropff.[52]

'Tis shame to all men
    everywhere.
I tell thee, man, if thy wife dare
Against thee vent her itches,
Then lay five fingers on her head
So that to earth she pitches,
Or else you'll stay a sap instead.

But the husband must not delay to beat her down, as he who hesitates is lost. The author complains that his own wife makes a fool of him, cooling his anger with sugared words, so that he rules the house only when she is out. Like many other complaints of female rule, his comment clearly refers to women's subtle undermining of male absolutism rather than to any outright claims to power.

The "böse rauch" poses a real threat to her husband's well-being. He lies unconscious for several minutes before he is revived by the water she throws on him. Her violent beating "fart jm seines leben [endangered his life]," and he is lucky to escape out the door. Another husband, in the seventeenth century, similarly faces real injury when he attempts to punish his wife for drinking:

sie fiel jhm in den Bart /
und rupfft jhn also hart /
das jhm das Blut thet fliessen /
über den Bart hinab.[53]

His beard then grabbed she
And pulled so mightily
That soon his blood was flowing
Over his beard and down.

He quickly resigns the breeches to her. For all the fame of the terrible smoke, however, such complete ascendancy is rare for the German women, and its incidence does not increase over time.

Another shrew, in the mid-sixteenth-century *Ein kurtzweylig Lied / von eynem liederlichen man vnd seynem weyb* [An amusing song of a wastrel and his wife], takes the verbal offensive; and though her husband strikes the first blow, she gains the final victory. While she shares the qualities of other "böse Weiber," her husband's dissolute character gives her some excuse and makes her a humorous instrument of moral vengeance. The speaker, a bad husband who constantly stays out late drinking and gambling his family into poverty, complains of his wife's reaction:

Meyn fraw hebt an / vnd ist mir
    gram
es thut jr etwan notte /

Then starts my wife this ugly
    strife;
Perhaps it troubles her head

die kind die haben kein brodte /	That the children have no bread.
Du öder laur / es wirt mir saur /	"Thou worthless sot, I'm getting
wenn du auß geest /	hot,
vnd mir nichts lest /	If thou go'st out
wie sol jch mich erneren /	And leav'st me naught,
Ich sag dir nun / laß bald	How shall I be supplied?
daruon /	Heed what I say, stop this today,
jch thun dir die haut erberen.	Or else I'll tan thy hide."

Despite her indignation he persists, losing his coat, hose, and finally their bed; after this he is afraid to return home:

Mein fraw vnrein /	My wife so bold
jch dorfft nicht heym /	Might well me scold;
jch förcht sie wurd mich	I hardly dared go home.
schelten.	

And, indeed, she does not spare her curses:

Du voller narr /	Thou drunken fool,
du gleichst eim farr /	Thou'rt like a bull,
. . . dz dich got schend	. . . may God shame you,
kan dich der teufel nit füllen.	The Devil cannot fill you.

Unable to quiet her with mild words, he decides to assert his authority:

Jch sprach schweig stil /	I said, be still,
das ist mein wil /	That is my will,
oder jch ler dich geigen.	Or else to squeal I'll teach thee.
Ich schlugs zum kopff /	I hit her head
bey jrem schopff	And by her braid
thet ich sie lang vm ziehen.	Long pulled I her around me.

When she makes as if to flee, he hurries after her but trips over a stool. Instantly she turns on him, and in his drunken state he cannot escape:

sie fiel mir zwar /	Raging she there
grimlich ins har /	Did grab my hair,
mit jren beyden henden.	With both her hands me tearing,
. . . . .	. . . . .
Unter die banck sy mich	And forced me then beneath the
bezwang /	bench,
thet mich mit füssen tretten.[54]	Where she kicked me with her
	feet.

Usurping the male prerogative of violence, she pummels him without mercy and throws him out into the street, where he lies in helpless humiliation. Though the man is seen as culpable, her berating and name-calling make her a blameworthy shrew even before she turns to actual violence. Like those of the Devil, her inflictions are deserved by the victim without being justified for the perpetrator.

Though the drunken man is an absurd figure, weakened by inebriation to his unruly wife's advantage, the wife's shrewish behavior remains an offense against propriety and an intolerable interference with manly freedom. In the often-reprinted song of *Ein Streitt / zwischen einem bösen Weib / vnd einem versoffnen Mann* [A battle between a shrewish wife and a drunken husband], the man's sodden condition is established at the outset; but this does not detract from the guilt of his female tormenter. The song is cast in dialogue form, though some versions apparently present only the man's side of the quarrel. The combatants vie with each other in name-calling, charges, and countercharges. The husband opens hostilities: "O Weib / O Weib / das sey Gott klagt / wie sehr bin ich von dir geplagt [O wife, O wife, to God I cry, / How sorely plagued by thee am I]"; her constant wrangling leaves him no peace. Not to be cowed, she retorts that he is a drunken sot and has wasted her inheritance. His exasperation mounting, the man vainly seeks to outdo her in abusive language, wishing he could be rid of her:

O Weib / O Weib du böser
    Wurm /
dein Maul macht offt manch
    wilden Sturm /
daß ich dir muß / offt mit
    verdruß /
geben ein Kopffstoß /
wolt Gott daß ich dein were loß.

O wife, O wife, thou dragon foul,
Thy maw makes many a stormy
    howl,
So that I must in my disgust
Oft punch thy head;
Would God I could of thee be
    rid.

Worse yet, she has scratched his face—apparently in retaliation for his blows—and used craft to get his money and spend it on dainty tidbits for herself. For all his escalating revilements, however, the husband is no match for his voluble wife. He has brought no wealth to their marriage:

drumb laß mich vnverachtet auch /
du fauler Schlauch /
viel leyden ist nicht mein
    Gebrauch.

So I advise thee scorn me not,
Thou lazy sot,
For I'm not one to take a lot.

Furthermore, he would run after young women if she were dead. He acknowledges that he wishes fervently to God for her death, and he menaces her with violence:

ich will dich nemmen bey dem Haar /	I'm going to take thee by the hair,
vnd mit dir sauber kehren auß /	With thee the house I then will sweep
die Stuben vnd Hauß /	And clean it keep,
vnd dir wol machen ein grauß.	And really teach thee how to weep.

Undeterred by either hatred or threats, this harridan offers to meet him blow for blow:

O Mann / . . . glaub mir ohn schertz /	This is no jest, when I speak out,
ich hab auch ein frisches Hertz /	For my heart too is bold and stout;
ich hett jetzt gleich ein Lüstlein /	I too now have an itch, you see,
ob ich gleich bin klein /	Though small I may be,
wolt ich doch schlagen mit Fäusten drein.	I'd like to pound my fists on thee.

At length he is forced to admit defeat, though:

was soll ich doch mit dir fangen an /	Alas, what shall I do with thee, Poor husband me!
ich armer Mann /	The last word ever thine must
das letzte Wort muß ich dir lahn.	be.

The song's conclusion pities the poor man saddled with such a burdensome creature:

Wer bekompt ein solch vngehewr /	The man who marries such a shrew
der hat allhie das Fegfewr /	Lives e'er in purgatory true;
wann sein Nachbarn vnd Freund allzeit /	And since his friends and neighbors all
auff jhn tragen Neyd /	Him fortunate do call,
darff er niemand klagen sein Leyd.[55]	To none dares he lament his thrall.

This proud wife doubtless gains much of her self-assurance from the fortune she brought to the marriage, a possibility which led authors to advise against marrying women for their wealth.

This pamphlet's cover illustration shows a woman beating a man in the foreground, while in the background a man beats a woman. The picture visually assimilates the violent woman to the woman being beaten: their postures are the same, the two figures are at the same level, and the disheveled hair of the beaten woman echoes the straying headdress of the foregrounded wife. The facelessness of the background couple suggests universality, while the greater realization of detail in the foreground highlights the foibles of the deviant pair: the man's fashionable clothes may suggest his improvidence and vanity, the woman's plain clothes and haglike features her shrewishness. Though this wife is dominant, the picture undermines her victory, pointing to the norm of male discipline of unruly women and suggesting that this is what she deserves. The man also wields a more solid weapon and maintains a more erect posture. It is only because her husband is so low that this wife remains above him. (See illustration on following page.)

Though some German shrews triumph over their husbands, their achievements are far outweighed by those of wife-beating males; and those depicted in the seventeenth century do no better than their fore-bears. Their victories, often temporary and seldom depicted beyond the first moment of male capitulation, do not establish the comprehensive and continuing rule of the English shrews, in which husbands are forced into actual slavery rather than mere defeat. Female dominance in Germany remains a "frembde abentheür," a strange tale, while in the English texts it is an everyday occurrence, especially by the mid-seventeenth century.

In both literatures, for all the pious commendations of domestic harmony, marriage emerges as a relationship governed ultimately by force. One partner has to dominate, and though authors of both countries pay tribute to women's considerable influence within an orderly marriage, in dramatic terms violence is the fundamental arbiter. The English can envision a companionate bond of shared affection which grants the wife a subsidiary but significant and legitimate power; by casting this ideal in concrete, imaginative form, some English works offer an alternative to the standard of superior force. Some German authors favor a union of re-ciprocal affection and rationality, but they seem able only to recommend it, not to embody it in their works. While German authors seldom depict domestic peace, they imagine domestic violence in a starkly realistic and literal way. Here the battered bodies can bleed, sicken, or die, despite the texts' comic tone, while most English spouses bounce back from their wounds with little harm done, especially in the seventeenth century.

Drey schön neue

Weltliche Lieder. 59

Das erste: Ist ein Streitt/ zwischen einem bösen Weib/ vnd einem versoffnen Mann.

Das ander: So fang ich aber an/ vnd sing ein newes rc.

Das dritte: Mein Hertz ist mir bekümmert so sehr/rc.

Gedruckt zu Augspurg/ bey Johann Schultes.

The violence of English domestic quarrels, especially that exercised by women, is a comic formula out of touch with the possible effects of violence on flesh and bone. In this comic setting, it appears as a natural extension of the strong-minded shrew's power, and domineering wives use it with abandon. German works, with more concern for verisimilitude, limit most wives to defensive scratching or kicking; those who go further are pitted against a foe handicapped by drink or by a surprise attack. The English husbands' weaknesses are more tangible: often sexual inadequacy or simple spinelessness. Both literatures relish the taming of a shrew, but the English can more readily imagine alternative methods to violence. They also can concede a shrew's "invincibility" with undisturbed amusement. German authors, while they find a shrew's reversal of authority entertaining, are careful to add indignant denunciations of her; just as, in the same apparent fear of misconstruction, they insist that the beatings applied to bad women are not meant to affect the good. The English literature is more comfortable with imaginative license, though it too retains a strong moralizing strain. With their companionate ideal on the one hand and their freewheeling shrews on the other, English songs and tales are far less strict than the German in the limits they place on female power.

From *Drey schön neue Weltliche Lieder. Das erste: Ist ein Streitt / zwischen einem bösen Weib / vnd einem versoffnen Mann* (Augsburg, [c. 1640?]), 4 fols., DSB Ye 1746 (courtesy of the Deutsche Staatsbibliothek Berlin in der Stiftung Preußischer Kulturbesitz, Abteilung für seltene und kostbare Drucke.

7.

Sex and Power

If the open power struggles of marriage in street literature are determined mainly by force, the more subtle balance of power between the sexes is conceived as strongly dependent on sexuality. The depiction of female sexuality is closely linked to issues of power: women's power over men, men's power over women, women's potential escapes from male power, and women's power or powerlessness in relation to their own bodies. Conversely, the texts' conception of female power persistently tinges it with sexuality; love and lust appear as the keys to much of women's influence, especially in England. Even the powers of mind and speech often are charged with sexual significance. Thus, female wit is presented as seductive wiles, and female speech is embodied in the tongue, an unruly member which threatens to usurp male potency. Such sexual emphasis often places women in a separate category of being, even when their activities have clear parallels with those of men.

Women's sexual power takes various forms in both English and German popular literature. Most commonly, it is shown as the result of men's physical desire, which women can intentionally excite or manipulate for their own ends. Female sexual power is also extended to qualities of mind: men can use craft and deceit but never *Frauenlist* or women's wiles, a cunning which retains its sexual element even when used for nonsexual ends. Furthermore, women's bodies in themselves are shown to possess powers foreign to men: pregnancy and lactation, which entail both prerogatives and vulnerability, and a sexual capacity that can outstrip male ability to compete. German and English authors share a recognition of women's potentially formidable strengths but diverge in the focus of their concerns.

The English strongly emphasize women's sexuality as an instrument of control over men: not only can women's beauty charm men into doing their bidding, but their sexual prowess can cow inadequate mates into domestic subjection. Like German wives, English characters use wiles to secure sexual freedom despite their husbands' watchfulness; the English, however, extend their claims beyond mere liberty to actual command. This possibility, hinted at in some sixteenth-century works, emerges full-blown in seventeenth-century English ballads; German authors, by contrast, hardly consider female sexual freedom as a source of marital power in either century. In England, the domestic self-assertion of adulterous wives parallels the activities of simpler shrews, who use speech or violence to attain a similar ascendancy. Neither in sexual relations nor in marriage are the German women given so complete a dominance. They assert considerable control over male lovers, but concern with this influence is less pervasive than in England. German authors write tributes to the irresistible force of women's charms but are in fact less apt than the English to depict sexual attractiveness as a purely feminine trait. With their wiles women gain secret triumphs and freedom of action but no marital authority.

In both countries the power of sexuality can be turned against women as well. Men who succeed in satisfying women's sexual requirements are seen as dominant both within marriage and without. Illicit sex is especially risky for women in these texts, as it certainly was in real life, and here power often hinges on differences of class. Class difference, of course, serves to mark a sexual encounter as illegitimate; in both countries, real-life fornication between partners of equal status was usually a prelude to marriage rather than a casual escapade. Both German and English texts present pictures of lower-class women engaged in illicit relations with men of higher status, and the relations of power between them are depicted in highly ambiguous terms. The English texts span the widest extremes here, with seduced and abandoned maidens represented as utterly helpless, while "whores" in the same situation jauntily make plans to support themselves by deceiving yet another well-heeled male. The German texts treat unwed mothers much more matter-of-factly, while making the women's vulnerability clear. Maternity wins the German characters more influence over their children than the mothers of the English literature can boast, but pregnancy in both literatures appears less as a power of women than as an aspect of their subjection. Women's bodies harbor forces that lie outside their control, and especially for the German women these are often linked with mysterious dangers that can bring them harm as well as gain.

In the English street literature, particularly that of the seventeenth century, sexual attractiveness is women's commonest and most effective source of power. German authors also note the significance of such power, but in dramatic terms it has a relatively smaller place in their women's arsenal. At the same time, manipulation of men through sex, beauty, or love draws almost universal condemnation in the German literature, while in England some forms of this attraction are seen as benign and even praiseworthy. In general, passive beauty arouses English sympathy, while active exploitation of her charms brands a woman as mischievous. The difference between love and lust lies not in the original feeling—all lovers are assumed to be after the same thing—but in the woman's reaction, either to male pursuit or to her own desires.

In street literature the virtuous and beautiful English maiden can effect a transformation of lust into conjugal love by preserving her chastity against male assaults. This opportunity is thrown into strong relief by the more common fate of maids who spoil their chances by yielding before marriage, only to face abandonment by lovers who now see them as strumpets. The potential rewards for chaste behavior include wealth and high social status as well as marriage, and authors in both centuries endorse the crossing of class lines by fair maidens. The beauteous Peggy, a serge-weaver's daughter, attracts the love of a young knight who offers vast riches and "All the Pride of London City" if she yields her virtue. She remains firm but humble, and this impresses him so much that he marries her and makes her a lady:

> You may think her friends consented,
> And that she was well contented:
>   and I'm sure so was the Knight;
> All the day they kiss and play,
>   and God knows what they did at night.
> Now you see how she regarded,
> For her vertue how rewarded.
>   made a Lady for her parts;

> Rais'd to power, without Dower,
> only by her own deserts.[1]

Another "witty maid" gains a similar reward for resisting seduction by a lawyer: "now she is a Lawyer's Wife, her Husband do's dearly love her, / So that she leads a happy life; there's few in the town above her."[2] This power of beauty, of course, can only be legitimized by virtue, a virtue which precludes any active pursuit of the eventual prize. Beauty may receive homage but must never court it. Still, the promise is clear; and these late seventeenth-century examples show the same spirit as the subtitle to a 1619 pamphlet on the beautiful and patient Griselda, *Shewing, How Maides, by her example, in their good behauiour may marrie rich Hvsbands.*[3] It becomes difficult to distinguish between passive possession of virtuous beauty and active desire for the benefits it might bring. The happy endings of these texts belie the probable realities of cross-class sexual exploitation. The tale of Peggy's being "Rais'd to power" obscures the fact that her fate is wholly dependent on the power of her upper-class would-be seducer. Instead, the texts seek to assure women that chastity will be rewarded and that class lines are more fluid—and more reflective of personal worth—than was in fact the case.

The unconventional "Beautiful Shepherdess of Arcadia," heroine of a ballad that was highly popular in both the sixteenth and seventeenth centuries, flouts the established patterns of virtue and gains her husband through vigorous self-assertion. "Sweet William," a knight stricken by her beauty, wishes to lie with her, and she readily agrees. When he rides away from what he thinks has been a casual encounter with a lower-class woman, she follows him to the royal court and accuses him of stealing her maidenhead. Ordered by the king to marry her, William tries to put her off with a bribe and spare himself the disgrace of wedding below his degree. But the intrepid damsel retorts:

> A Shepherd's daughter as I was,
> you might have let me be;
> I'd ne'r a come to the King's fair court
> to have crav'd any love of thee.

Branding him as the aggressor, she can preserve the vestiges of maiden modesty. In the end she proves to be a duke's daughter, while he is only a squire's son. The revelation of her noble status restores all to its proper order. Here the text has merely been playing with the idea of cross-class sexual relations and with the incongruousness of imagining marriage as their result. In the end,

> Their hearts being so linked fast,
>   and joyned hand in hand,
> He had both purse and person too,
>   and all at his command.[4]

The linkage of hearts is smoothly grafted onto a purely physical relationship by the magic of marriage. Here, as elsewhere, there is no distinction between the emotions aroused by "good" women in "good" men and those evoked by the other kind. The good woman's sexual nature is justified by marriage, but the feelings she arouses and the power her beauty exerts over men share the same physical basis as the attractions of loose women. The urges felt by Peggy's knight and Sweet William match those of any rake. With the addition of a legal tie and the esteem it brings, they are transformed into husbandly affection, but the element of sexual desire retains an important place in their conjugal feelings.

German popular texts generally eschew such intertwining of sexual desire and marital esteem. This is especially true of pieces with a contemporary setting; those modeled on the tradition of chivalric romance are less severe, though they do not wed knights to lower-class girls. Appreciation of physical enjoyment is practically limited to adultery and fornication, while marriage typically appears as a soberly practical arrangement, scarcely connected with frivolous courtships and "true love."[5] Unlike English fornication, which often turns on a promise of marriage, the German version rarely involves more than a vow of silence. Marital relations, of course, were supposed to involve affection and friendship: young men were warned against the *Flitterwochen* or honeymoon, when their loving and naive indulgence could accustom young wives to having their own way; and moralists repeatedly urged couples to love and esteem one another instead of fighting. Marriage was also viewed as a means of satisfying the physical drives of both men and women. In works devoted to love, however, marriage usually appears, if at all, as an obstacle rather than an aim. Accordingly, for moralists, women's capacity to arouse desire was not the basis for a happy ending but an invitation to vice. On the other hand, with women at least as susceptible to sexual allurements as men, sex was seen less as a special source of power for women than as an impersonal force drawing both men and women to pleasure and sin.

Despite tributes to the power of *Frauenlieb*, the women of German street literature rely far less than the English on sex as a means of attaining power. Both literatures depict women as lusty, expecting them to enjoy sexual activity as much as men. In spite of this, however, the English pieces tend to view sexual pleasure as a benefit controlled by women, one that they can withhold at will. At the same time, the women's desire for pleasure is a challenge to their partners' virility. In the German texts the balance of sexual desire and power falls far closer to the center. Though women subdue men with their beauty, they are also smitten by the beauty of men. While the English siren is a coldhearted schemer, her German counterpart often lays out her snares and charms only when driven to it by irresistible desire. The German men, on the other hand, are shown as feeling little anxiety about their ability to satisfy a woman's sexual needs if they so choose. Failure in this regard, the source of so much humiliation to sexually inadequate males in English texts, causes relatively little concern for the lovers and husbands of German street literature.[6] The German women sometimes take the initiative in lovemaking but usually are depicted as content with any sexual attention they get. This contrast suggests not that German men were sexually secure but that German authors did not invest female sexuality with the same significance as their English counterparts.

In an often-reprinted pamphlet, *Der Weltlich Joseph. Wie er von dem Egyptischen weib / in vnordenliche liebe gereitzt / vnd jhn vnschuldigklich in gefäncknuß bracht* [The secular Joseph: How the Egyptian woman enticed him to illicit love and unjustly had him imprisoned], lust drives Potiphar's wife to attempt the seduction of "Joseph den schönen jüngling [Joseph the handsome youth]." She dresses in her most alluring clothes, offers him money, and tries every temptation she can muster, but to no avail:

Joseph, biß nit so fromb,	Joseph, don't be moral so!
Ich wolt gern bey dir schlaffen,	I want to go to bed with you;
Yetz hasts in eyner summ.	That's it in short, you know.
. . . . .	. . . . .
Thus dapffer mit mir wagen,	Now do it with me daringly,
Wir hand jetz fug vnd glimpff.	For we have every right.
Glaubs frölich, was ich sagen,	Believe me now unsparingly,
Dann es ist mir nit schimpff.	I'm serious tonight.
So zierlich han ich mich angethan,	I've dressed as daintily as I can,
Du kanst mirs nit versagen,	So thou canst not refuse me
Bist du ein frauwen man.	If thou'rt a woman's man.

When Joseph stands firm against her seductive challenge, rage leads her to accuse him of attempted rape. He protests his innocence, pointing to the dubious quality of female testimony:

Herr, thünd mit mir nit gähen,	Think, master, don't judge
Secht an mein state treüw,	hastily;
Das dweyber etwann schmähen,	I always have been true.
Fürwar, das ist nit neüw.	That women may speak nastily
	Is really nothing new.

He is nevertheless cast into prison. The author comments that women who are annoyed by this song merely reveal their own lasciviousness:

Thät das ein weyb verdriessen,	If any woman this annoy
Sy wurd dardurch erkennt,	It only goes to show
Das sy auch gern hät vnnütz	That she would like an idle boy
knecht,	To do her will also.
Die jrem willen dienten.[7]	

In another song, reprinted from the early sixteenth through the early seventeenth centuries, an evil French queen practically rapes men who please her, threatening them with death if they refuse to comply and killing them in the morning. She beckons a hapless young man from her window and throws herself on him:

Die Königin was auff jn	The queen on him her lust had
verbeint /	bent.
Er wust nicht wie sie es da	He had no thought of what she
meint /	meant,
sie het sie noch mit jhm vereint /	But with his body hers she blent;
er mocht sich gegen jr nit	Against her he could no
auffenthalten.	resistance make.
Sie blickt jm in das Hertz	Into his heart she cast her eye:
hinein /	"Take my body and with me lie;
meins Leibs must du gewaltig	This I command or thou shalt
sein /	die."
das beüt ich dir bey hoher pein /	His honor had he then no power
der Ehren sein / het er da kein	to save.
gewalte.	

Here, as in the case of Potiphar's wife, the woman's status gives her power over the men she desires; but she herself is the slave of lust. The male is for her a purely sexual object; she tells another unwilling lover:

mein edler leib soll dir sein vnderthenig.	To thee my noble body I submit.
Das beüt ich dir bey meiner Kron /	My royal crown will here attest That thou must honor my behest.
das du alsbald nun wöllest thun / ich laß dir weder fryd noch rhu / all mein begir / will ich an dir volleyste.[8]	I'll give thee neither peace nor rest; Through thee will I fulfill all my desire.

The language of sexual relations here underlines the reversal involved in this female assumption of the active and aggressive role: the young man must "gewaltig sein [have power]" over her body, though over his own honor and fate he has "kein gewalte [no power]"; the queen's body is "vnderthenig [subject]" to the male whom she is using to fulfill her desires. Both participants are dominated by the power of sex itself.

Here, though the women are in a sense "on top," the men appear as the dispensers of sexual pleasure as well as wisdom. Similarly, in a tongue-in-cheek broadside of the mid-seventeenth century, "Herr Weiberherr [Mr. Wifemaster]" links sexual potency with male dominance and claims that women like it that way:

Alle Männer müssen siegen / Alle Weiber vnten ligen. Und kömpt ja eine Klage So ist es nur am Tage. Man hat noch nie gehöret Daß sich ein Weib beschweret / Daß jhr der Mann zu Nachte Auß Ehstand Wehstand machte.	All men must gain the victory, All women on the bottom be; And if they raise a fray, It's only in the day. No one has ever yet Heard any woman fret That her husband in the night Made marriage a bitter plight.
Ihr Weiber folget hier so seyd jhr gute Knechte / Bekommet gute Zeit vnd lauter güldne Nächte.[9]	You women be good servants, and do as here you're told, And you'll have happy daytimes and nights of purest gold.

The sexual satisfaction their husbands provide will make women docile and submissive. In the seventeenth-century English ballads, conversely, one hears constant complaints from women about their husbands' nocturnal performance; men apparently are failing to supply the price of female

subjection. At the same time, accounts of sexual encounters between unmarried lovers sometimes jestingly point out the man's inability to match
his partner's perseverance. Sex, particularly in the seventeenth century, is
depicted as a decisive test for the male; a demonstration of potency affirms
his dominance, while failure to satisfy the female brings him shame and
subordination. Impotence, even the merely relative impotence of cuckoldry, implies a complete upheaval in the sexual order and gives the
woman power to flout, ridicule, and sometimes command her mate.

Even in the sixteenth century, when English street literature was
somewhat less preoccupied with sex than in the seventeenth, songs mock
men's uncertain powers as well as women's lustfulness. In *A Ditty delightfull of mother Watkins ale*, a lad offers a girl some "Watkins ale" to save her
from dying a maid. She enjoys the first taste and after some conversation
asks for more, but her partner wants to talk longer:

> With that the mayd began to smile,
> And saide, good sir, full well I know,
> Your ale, I see, runs very low.

Abashed, he gives her more and she goes her way, only to become ill in
nine months "With taking much of Watkins ale."[10] *Loves Power*, a ballad
from the 1680s, enlarges further on this theme. Two lovers meet and
eagerly fall to "the sport." With the first bout the young man "had both
his wish and desire," but the woman has only begun:

> The Damsel was mightily pleased,
>   and kist him a thousand times o're,
> Quoth she, now my sorrows are eased,
>   but I must have a little touch more;
> O lye down a while for to rest thee,
>   that I may enjoy my desire,
> I hope that the fates they will bless thee,
>   I quench, but thou kindlest my fire.

After a while they continue; but eventually

> The young-man began for to tyre,
>   and his Cudgels began to lay down,
> Which made the young Damsel admire,
>   and straight she began for to frown:
> Quoth he, I have done what is fit,
>   no reason can more require,

> But her brows then upon him she knit,
> and she still did want her desire.

The ballad advises young men to be "lusty,"

> For Maidens look sowre and crusty,
>   when their wants cannot be well supply'd:
> But 'twas an Old Proverb I heard,
>   though Men burnt with amorous ire,
> That Damsels when once they come near,
>   could quench their most vigorous Fire.[11]

In *Enfield Common*, another woman urges her "Lusty Gallant" to more energetic efforts: "Quoth she you vapour, and draw your Rapour, / but yet methinks too soon you seem to tire." In this case, however, the song combines female insatiability with its obverse of macho prowess, for the male triumphantly satisfies her:

> With joys I crown'd her, for then I found her,
>   to have a heart far lighter than a feather.
>   · · · · ·
> The loving creature, of pure good nature,
>   she gave me twenty kisses when we parted,
> Because she never had found such favour,
>   in loves soft pleasures to be so diverted.[12]

In the context of marriage, women are shown making equally exacting demands. Most obvious and traditional is the complaint of the young bride wedded to a "Doting Old Dad."[13] Such ridicule of the aged husband appears also in the German literature, though without the English focus on the woman's point of view.[14] Similarly, the German authors usually notice only simple impotence, while the Englishmen's problems often stem from lovemaking that is technically adequate but leaves their female partners unsatisfied.[15] In England women saddled with a "fumbler" freely assert their right to roam. *The Forc'd Marriage; Or, Unfortunate Celia* expresses the defiance of a young woman whose unfeeling parents compel her to leave her young lover for an old man:

> I have now got a man
> I must love if I can,
>   But I fear my first dear,
>   I must love now and than.

If I chance to transgress,
As I shall you may guess,
   You may shame me, not blame me,
   for not loving him less.

My Husband's a Sot,
Deform'd, and what not,
   All Day He's at play,
   with his Nose o're a Pot.

. . . . .

When my fumbler's in bed,
& has laid down his head,
   He lies with closed eyes,
   just [as] though he was dead.[16]

She plans to indulge in pleasures at will and may even leave her husband if his presence interferes with her enjoyments.

A man does not have to be old, however, to prove sexually incompetent. In *The Lamentation of Chloris for the Unkindness of her Shepherd*, a young wife complains of her "Strephon's" neglect. He leaves her alone all day to pine, and then

At night he doth think
   for to make me amends,
And with his fair looks,
   for to make us good friends:
But alas, he's so weary,
   he cannot be kind.[17]

If he does not mend his ways, she will cuckold him in order to become a mother. Satirical pamphlets from the 1640s depict women voicing similar grievances. *The Parliament of Women. With the merrie Lawes by them newly Enacted. To live in more Ease, Pompe, Pride, and wantonnesse: but especially that they might have superiority and domineere over their husbands* shows a motley congress of women arguing over proposed legislation on marriage. In describing the ridiculous results, the royalist author lampoons both unruly women and the parliamentarians who similarly upset the established order. The disputants agree, among other things, to allow women more than one husband. After all, they point out, many men cannot please their wives; women ought to be allowed at least two. A tailor's wife says hers "hath no more mettle in him then a Mouse. . . . He will sow and sow, and yet when he hath done all hee can, it proves but so and so." Another recounts how her husband once threatened to thump her, whereupon she told him to "thump me but where thou shouldst thump me, or Ile make it the dearest thumping that ever thou didst thumpe in thy life: and I thinke I hit him home, which was more than ever he did to me."[18]

The authors of street literature generally depict wives as scorning to bear such deprivation patiently: they commit adultery at the first opportunity. Authors agree, in Germany as well as England, that it is impossible to prevent a wife from straying if she so desires. Many are the jesting consolations directed to the unhappy English cuckold. In *Household Talke*, a ballad by Martin Parker, the jealous Simon is tormented by the specter of cuckoldry and asks a friend for advice. His companion urges him to forget his fears, since even if they were true he would be helpless:

> If thou seeke
> Her use to breake,
> Rather strive to stop a Billow
> of the Sea; tush! never speake.

At length Simon recognizes the wisdom of this counsel, resolving thenceforth to banish jealousy:

> Nor will I mistrust my Scull;
> Ile be merry with good fellowes;
> Home Ile hie,
> By and by,
> Kisse my Wife (with due submission);
> thankes, sweete Roger, heartily,
> For thy holsome admonition.[19]

Others take the "due submission" of the complaisant cuckold to more extreme lengths. The woman's sexual victory over her husband, begun by his inability to satisfy her and consummated by her selection of a superior lover, often extends to complete usurpation of his domestic authority. The emasculated male becomes feeble in both body and mind: he is subject to violence from his wife and/or her lovers, forced to perform menial tasks ordinarily assigned to women, and afraid to complain by word or sign. While shrews are also shown achieving such dominance purely by means of their tongues or fists, the sexual element of conjugal battle and conquest receives special emphasis. Particularly in the later seventeenth century, the wholly subjugated cuckold appears as a stock figure of fun in English ballads.

An early ballad, from the mid-sixteenth century, hints that allowing a woman to make sexual demands is tantamount to relinquishing male rule. A husband admonishes his restless young wife that she must never scold or mock,

> Nor Venvs game vpon me craue,
> Nor yet your honestye for to spill,
> And make me neyther boy nor slaue,
> But do good, and therin take your owne wyl.[20]

Again, in the early seventeenth century, a ballad warns against cuckoldry and condemns the husband who

> neuer dares reprooue her,
> But letts her haue her will;
> Nor cares how many loue her,
> So shee the purse do fille.[21]

In a 1638 ballad, *Cuckold's Haven, Or, The marry'd man's miserie*, the complaining husband has not yet fully abdicated, although his wife openly and impudently engages in adultery:

> My wife hath learn'd to kisse,
>   and thinkes 'tis not amisse:
> Shee oftentimes doth me deride,
>   and tels me I am hornify'd.
>
> What euer I doe say,
>   shee will haue her owne way;
> Shee scorneth to obey;
>   Shee'll take time while she may;
> And if I beate her backe and side,
>   In spight I shall be hornify'd.

Though the man tries his best to maintain his authority, all his efforts are useless, and the wife's assertion of sexual freedom makes him feel that she is dominant:

> be we great or small,
>   we must be at their call;
> How e're the cards doe fall,
>   we men must suffer all.[22]

The protagonist of *My Wife will be my Master*, a popular ballad from about the same time, has practically given up the struggle. He does the housework, gives his wife the best of everything, and pleases her as best he can, while she lazes all day at the alehouse; still she abuses him and strives for mastery:

> And when I am with her in bed,
>   she doth not use me well, Sir;
> She'l wring my nose, and pull my ears,
>   a pitifull tale to tell, Sir.
> And when I am with her in bed,
>   not meaning to molest her,
> She'l kick me out at her bed's-feet,
>   and so become my Master.
>
>   . . . . .
>
> But if I were a lusty man,
>   and able for to baste her,
> Then would I surely use a means,
>   that she should not be my Master.[23]

The ambiguity of "baste" equates the powers of sex and violence, implying that the man lacking in one will also lose the other. *Mirth for Citizens; Or, A Comedy for the Country* relates more explicitly the origins of the wife's ascendancy. A young farmer tells how he married a woman of beauty and fortune, only to fail the test of his wedding night:

> She shewed me Venus School
>   and with me she did daddle,
> But I a young puny fool,
>   did quickly fall out of the saddle.
> . . . then on the morrow morn,
>   O she laughed me to scorn:
> She drank sack and canary in Silver,
>   and made me drink out of a horn.

With this female superiority established, all further efforts to restore the normal order of things are vain:

> She told me she would be Master,
>   and all the whole houshold guide,
> I told her it gave disaster,
>   she said it should quickly be try'd:
> Then against her I took stick,
>   thinking she durst not come nigh,

> With a cudgel my bones she did lick,
>   that for pardon I quickly did cry.[24]

Like other "henpeckt cuckolds," he is condemned to domestic servitude and to constant ridicule and violence from his haughty wife.

His complaints found echoes in many other ballads of the 1670s and 1680s, in which helpless husbands humorously lament their fate and warn others against the dangers of marriage to wanton and willful women. Forced into such demeaning tasks as washing diapers and fetching piss pots, they become completely demoralized, deprived even of the woman's traditional weapon, the tongue. One bleats:

> Before I'd been Wed a Week
>   her Cruelty she did show,
> And would not suffer me to speak,
>
> . . . . .
>
> Sometimes I would her embrace,
>   then straitway she'll fling and throw,
> And call me Cuckold to my Face.

Before he was married he lived in freedom; "But since I am married to this cross wife, / the world is turn'd upside down."[25] The tongue serves as a symbol of potency for the shrew, and the husband's loss of even this outlet reveals his utter castration: she has usurped all his power and reversed the sexual order.

The seventeenth-century English preoccupation with cuckoldry, common in drama as well as in street literature, casts female usurpation in terms of sexual dominance, joining verbal, physical, and sexual insubordination in a single symbolic complex. The female tongue, like the weapons used against husbands, acquires strong phallic associations.[26] It is a cudgel for battering her spouse, the scepter of her potency, a member at which men may well tremble, knowing that their own puny tongues are helpless against it: the man attacked by a woman's tongue hardly dares to raise his own. This symbolism of the tongue reflects contemporary views of female nature. Women's bodies were seen as both disorderly and disordered: not only were they apt to stray from their proper functions; they were flawed from the start, lacking a key prerequisite for authority. The cuckold complex endows the shrew with substitute penises—the tongue, the instruments of violence, even the member of her adulterous partner—that offset the lack of adequate equipment in the cuckold himself. The tongue as phallus was an especially apt image for the disorderly female body, in which the lower was always apt to overthrow the higher, and in which it was seen as no strange thing for the sexual organs to dominate the head.[27] This suggestion that sexuality was paramount in marital insubordination served to reinforce the shame that unruly women were supposed to feel. As Susan Amussen has found, early modern English court records suggest that women felt shamed by aspersions on their sexual conduct but not by charges that they had failed to preserve the proper respect and obedience toward their husbands.[28] Thus the sexual tinge in the ridicule directed against shrews could add powerfully to women's embarrassment at fitting the image.

As Martin Ingram has pointed out, the laughter directed against dominated husbands in popular shaming rituals not only discouraged deviant behavior but also reflected men's uneasiness about their ability to keep the upper hand.[29] Similarly, the mockery of cuckolds and of sexually powerful women both reflected male anxieties and helped to ease them. The intensification of such mockery during the seventeenth century, from the ballads about female sexual demands to the purported self-revelations of "ranting whores," suggests a heightened sense of male inadequacy. By placing the problems of male dominance in the sexual arena, such ballads depict them as private ones that can be solved in bed. Denying their political aspect even while serving the political function of discouraging female deviance, they reaffirm the notion of woman as a purely sexual being. Yet the sexual aspect of the fears is also genuine. Coppélia Kahn, in her analysis of the Shakespearean patriarchal ideal, has pointed to the "emotional vulnerability" of men whose identity and prestige depend on their women's fidelity. The clash between men's public power over women and women's private power over men fed male anxieties about their control of female sexuality.[30] An increasing focus on affective relationships, with its demand for recognition of both male and female individuality, combined with the persistence and even partial intensification of patriarchal ideals to create strong tensions in the sexual politics of the later sixteenth and seventeenth centuries.[31] The exclusion of women from public activity, with the attempt to define their powers as purely private, may well have heightened the sense of discomfort at women's continued influence and at the impossibility of wholly containing it within domestic bounds. The evidence of street literature suggests that these sexual tensions retained their hold on the popular imagination into the eighteenth century, perhaps giving way only when the desexualization of women's image provided an improved cultural strategy for dealing with their threat.

In German popular texts the balance of marital power is much less affected by women's uses of their sexuality. Though the *verkehrte Welt* [world upside down] is a common conceit in early modern German popular literature, the reversal there does not extend to complete upheaval in sexual relations. The German adulteress, proverbially resourceful at evading her husband's control, takes her pleasure at will; but her achievement of sexual liberty implies no new domestic authority. Though she has flouted her husband's rights, she remains formally subject to his command, and her triumph usually remains covert. The freewheeling English wife often is shown using sex to amass further power, but for the German wife sex appears more as an aim than as a tool. Once she has gained sexual freedom, getting the better of her husband by keeping him in the dark, she has reached her goal and generally shows no loftier ambitions. Though the wiles of her sex endow her with substantial power, she typically uses them to gain liberty rather than authority.

The German texts often cite wiles as women's most formidable weapon, and songs and pamphlets repeatedly warn against the power of *Frauenlist*. No man, they claim, can outwit a crafty woman, nor even prevent her from making a fool of him. In both countries women's wiles are closely related to their sexual power, as conscious manipulation of physical charms is considered an exercise of feminine craft. Yet the female cunning admired by German authors is less related to women's sexual allure than its English counterpart, even though it flows from their female nature; it is an activity of mind rather than body. At the same time, it expresses a general quality of the sex rather than an individual personality. "Wiles" can be extended to include almost any use of intelligence on the part of a woman. Authors seldom make precise distinctions between different sorts of female power; it seems to make little difference to them whether a woman outwits a man or charms him. Still, it is *List*, far more than sex, on which German antiheroines, and even at times heroines, depend for their power. While this skill can be applied to a variety of purposes, good as well as bad, the accomplishment of secret adultery is by far the most common.

Drawing on such sources as the tales of Boccaccio and the *Cent Nouvelles Nouvelles*, German *Schwankliteratur* of the sixteenth century made adultery a favorite theme; and many of the jokes and anecdotes found their way into short, popular pieces. Again and again women are depicted pursuing illicit liaisons and pulling the wool over their husbands' eyes. In a typical episode, taken from Boccaccio, a dyer's wife is in bed with her husband when her lover comes knocking. She convinces her simple mate that it is only a ghost, and with a carefully worded "exorcism" sends the lover off to find a feast she has prepared for him.[32] In a less commonplace escapade, a Roman empress secretly cuckolds her husband in defiance of a magical "Eeren bildt [image of honor]" designed to expose adultery and perjury. If the woman transgressed, a horn would grow on her husband's forehead. The wife would then stand trial, with two of her fingers placed in the statue's mouth; in case of perjury the fingers would be bitten off, the horn would fall from the man's head, and the adulteress would be executed. Nevertheless, desire drives the empress to continue her lovemaking while her husband is out of the country:

Sol ich schöns lieb nicht mer der liebe pflegen /	Dear love, if I no more love's game can play,
so ist meins hertzen Trost vnd frewdt so gar verlegen /	It takes my heart's content and joy away.
. . . . .	. . . . .
Wer weiß ob kunst auch helff in fremden landen /	Who knows if magic works in foreign lands?
mein grosses trawren will ich lassen vnterwegen /	My sorrow great will I now put to flight
mit meinem leibe so wil ich stäter frewden pflegen /	And with my body ever take delight.
. . . vor dem Bild wil ich mich wol fristen /	. . . from the statue I can well escape
mit so listigen banden.	By my cunning wiles.

She cheats the test by having her lover disguise himself as a mad fool and hug her before the assembled company. She can then swear, without lying, that no man has come closer to her than her husband and the fool. The author comments that women often make fools of wise men, citing several examples:

Durch frawen lieb hat sich Adam versundet hart /	Through woman's love fell Adam into sin below;
durch Frawen lieb Troy die statt auch zerstöret wart /	Through woman's love the town of Troy destroyed was also;

Fürst Olifernis von einem Weyb getödtet wardt /	Prince Holofernes fell before a woman's blow;
Durch Frawen lieb der Starck Sambson /	Through woman's love Samson the strong
wart lesterlich geblendet.[33]	Was treacherously blinded.

Though the empress triumphs by means of her cunning rather than love, the author apparently sees no need for such distinctions: he treats the powers of women, love, and wiles as basically the same.

English women have similar wiles at their disposal and are shown gulling either husbands or other males virtually at will. Like the German women, they use cunning to mask adultery and to gain covert triumphs over their husbands, though in England these exploits are more common in jestbooks than in ballads. Jestbooks of varying lengths repeat in both centuries such tales as that of the wily wife who subjects her husband to both cuckoldry and violence, without arousing the slightest suspicion. Wishing to make love with a young servant, she tells her husband that the lad has propositioned her. She urges her spouse to dress in her clothes and take her place at their appointed meeting so that he can beat the would-be adulterer. At the same time she sends her lover out with a staff to beat his master. Pretending to take the disguised husband for the wife, the servant reviles him as a whore, says he had only been testing his mistress's chastity, and cudgels him soundly. The husband goes away delighted at the virtue of both wife and servant, who are now above suspicion and can do as they please.[34]

The English wives' behavior seems to grow increasingly bold from the sixteenth to the seventeenth centuries, and by the late seventeenth they hardly bother to hide their sins. Even when the adventures begin secretly, they can be revealed without causing the women much chagrin.[35] In *Touch and Go; or, the French Taylor finely Trappann'd*, a tailor and his wife each go in search of illicit pleasures and by accident meet at the same house of ill repute. Furious at finding her there, the husband rails at his wife, but she gives as good as she got:

> Then up his wife did start,
>   and said, "My dear Sweetheart,
> You are as deep i' th' mire,
>   as I am in the fire.
> Therefore I you desire
>   to mitigate your ire.["][36]

A roving husband can even recognize the justice of this view:

> Why should we repine
>   that our wives are so kind,
> Since we that are husbands,
>   are of the same mind?
> Shall we give them Feathers,
>   and think to go free?
> Believe it, believe it,
>   that hardly will be.[37]

Whether married to fumblers or rakes, these female characters view their sexual freedom as fully warranted, with or without the aid of deceit. Both they and their husbands are comic figures, serving to ridicule women's lustfulness and men's inability to control it.

Feminine wiles are sometimes justified, both in Germany and in England, especially if used to repel sexual assaults. Typically, a chaste woman, solicited by a lecher, turns the tables on him and gives him his just deserts. In one tale from the *Cent Nouvelles Nouvelles*, taken up by jest-books in both countries and appearing also in street literature, the woman pretends to accede to his desires but has the man's wife take her place in the dark. The lover, having enjoyed his fun, allows his servant or apprentice a share also, thus unknowingly cuckolding himself.[38] In the English ballads the female protagonist, usually a maid resisting the advances of an authoritative male, earns high praise by her actions, while the wife is delighted with her adventure. A German song pamphlet on this theme makes the moral slightly more ambiguous:

also kam er doppelt zum schaden /	And thus he suffered double pain:
der Weber mit der Frawen sein /	The weaver with his wife
mit schand vnd Laster beladen	Covered in vice and shame.

The weaver's wife shares her husband's punishment, suffering disgrace for her enjoyment of the journeyman's embraces:

Er gfiel der Weberin gar wol / es nam sie frembd der sachen.	He pleased the weaver's wife full well.
Daß jhr Man so hortig waß / kein sach thet jhr gefallen baß.[39]	She thought it passing strange Her husband should so nimble be; No greater pleasure e'er had she.

The central theme of all versions is mockery of the man's lustful folly; the wife's great appreciation of the substitute lover adds to the husband's absurdity and so to the fun. Other wily women serve similarly as instruments of a humorous justice, punishing lascivious men with financial loss, humiliation, or physical discomfort.[40] The foolishness of the men's lechery makes women fitting avengers, subjecting the sinners to ridicule for being bested by a female—and in the English versions, a female of low social status as well—in addition to the shame of exposure.

For women who profit from their sexual charms, the German literature offers almost none of the limited tolerance granted to the beautiful in England. Only Judith, a favorite heroine for sixteenth-century German authors, appears fully justified in turning her beauty to advantage. Her seduction and beheading of Holofernes received admiring tributes in songs by Hans Sachs and others, and she held her place in standard lists of virtuous women in the seventeenth century. With Bethulia helplessly besieged by Holofernes and his army, the godly and well-respected widow Judith undertakes to save her city. Dressing in her most costly and seductive clothes, she insinuates herself into Holofernes' favor. Within a few days he invites her to a drinking party, and when the captain falls asleep, she cuts off his head and spirits it back into the city. In the morning the attackers are dismayed and the town victorious, and all praise God for aiding and inspiring Judith's actions. Her popularity cannot but strike the modern reader as curious, since her deeds accord so ill with the behavior ordinarily prescribed for women—and correspond closely, in fact, with the female behaviors usually denounced as hateful and devilish. The poets who sing her praises explicitly recognize her use of feminine wiles and seduction but betray little sense of any discordancy. An Augsburg song from the 1530s relates Judith's actions to those of all coquettes, concluding that:

Die frewlin hand so klugen list	Such clever wiles do women have
Kain mann so starck so weysz auch ist	That any man on earth, though brave
so hailig auch auff erden /	Or wise or even holy,
Winckt jm ain fraw mit ainem blick	A woman with a look can yet
Bald hat sy jn an jrem strick mag jm doch offt nit werden.[41]	Entrap him slily in her net Tho' she's oft not his wholly.

Hans Sachs, in a *Meisterlied* on Judith, tries to allegorize the tale by suggesting that Holofernes represents the Devil, who is destroyed by the woman's seed. Elsewhere he lamely offers Judith's story as an example to teach women temperance, since it is Holofernes' drunkenness that allows her to kill him.[42] The general consensus, however, is that God's seemingly incongruous use of a woman as instrument of his vengeance makes his power all the more wondrous. A woman can be expected to use deceit and seduction to gain her ends; the marvel is that God by his inspiration can turn these methods to the service of good. To this end he actively enhances her power:

Gott gab auch jrer schöne zu	God granted that her beauty blest
Des fürsten hertz mocht han kain ru	Would give the prince's heart no rest;
thett stettigs nach jr sinnen.[43]	It dwelt upon her always.

Sachs has her praise God for saving his people "Durch eines schwachen weybes hand [by a weak woman's hand],"[44] and another moralist points out that for Holofernes' arrogance:

Ist er mit spott /	So has he borne
gestrafft von Gott /	God's wrath and scorn
das jm von einer Frawen /	That by a woman baited,
Judith genandt /	Called Judith, and
mit jrer hand /	By her own hand,
den Kopff wardt abgehawen.[45]	He was decapitated.

Her lowly female status makes God's primacy all the clearer. Just as clearly, only a special, divine dispensation can justify her use of wiles and charms to bring a male under her power.

Women who accentuate their sexuality by such brazen behavior as dancing, primping, and overdressing draw stern denunciations from moralizing songwriters, who complain that they "bietens den jungen Gesellen an [offer themselves to young men]" or "bieten sich selber feil [put themselves up for sale]"[46] and are likely to come to shame. If one of them becomes pregnant, she will go where no one knows her, get someone else to take care of the baby, and palm herself off as virgin on an unsuspecting young man "durch ihr betrug vnd list [by her deceit and wiles]."[47] Still worse are those who use sex to gain control over a man and make a fool of him, so that "was jn die metz haist das muß er thun [he must do whatever the strumpet tells him]."[48] The "schone Bulerin [beautiful harlot]" of a dialogue by Hans Sachs uses beauty, wiles, flattery, and illusion to milk her victims of their goods. She gloats:

Trenck sie mit gifft aus meyner Schaln /	When they drink poison from my cup
So müssen sie das Gloch bezaln /	They've always got to pony up.
Vnter meyn Füssen ich sie hab.[49]	I tread them underneath my feet.

Unscrupulous women can carry their influence over their lovers even further, inducing them to commit crimes for their mistresses' sake. In a song *Von der Frawen von der Weissenburg* [Of the Lady of the Weissenburg], a woman urges her lover to murder her husband, and love of her overcomes his scruples:

Ir Bul gedacht im Hertzen /	At heart then thought her lover,
weh mir hie vnnd auch dort /	Woe ever is my meed
es bringt mir leid vnd schmertzen /	And sorrow will me cover If I should do this deed.
würd ich stifften das Mord.	But love of woman stronger
Doch thet jhn vberwinden /	So overcame his will,
der Frawen lieb so groß /	His hands delayed no longer
Das er mit seinen henden vnschuldig blut vergoß.[50]	The guiltless blood to spill.

Another unfaithful wife, a "Künigin auß Lamparden [Queen of Lombardy]," conceives a deadly hatred for her husband when she learns that he has killed her father and had his skull made into a goblet, then mocked her by suggesting that she drink from it. Though she has some justification for her anger, the song condemns her as a "trewloß Fraw on alle ehre [faithless woman void of honor]" when she presses her lover to kill her husband. The lover is reluctant, but "Den Ritter thet der frawen lieb hart dringen [love of the woman pressed the knight hard]." After the murder the pair absconds with plenty of treasure and marries, but their happiness proves fleeting. The woman falls into her old adulterous ways after several years and eventually plots to kill this husband in turn. When he finds she has poisoned his wine, he forces her to drink also, so that both perish. The author advises women to learn from this bad example not to act according to their own will but to remain subject to men:

Das ist eym Weyb die gröste Ehr /	A woman's honor is the best When she will follow man's behest
wo sie folgt mannes weyß vnd lehr /	And ways of evil wives detest.
vnd ist von bösen weybern ferr.[51]	

By subsuming murder, theft, and adultery under the general heading of insubordination, the moral represents any claim to independent action as akin to crime.

The most sinister and powerful women are also the most exotic. The extremely popular song of Tannhäuser, based on medieval legend, dates from early in the sixteenth century and was often reprinted into the seventeenth. The knightly hero succumbs to the charms of beauty in "fraw Venus berg [the mount of Lady Venus]." Feeling repentant, Tannhäuser wishes to leave in pursuit of salvation:

Nun gebt mir vrlaub frewlein
zart /
Von ewrem stolzen leybe.

Her Danheuser nicht redet
also /
. . . . .
So gehen wir in ein kämmerlein /
Vnd spilen der edlen minne.

Gebrauch jch nun ein frembdes
weib /
Mich dunckt in meynem sinne /
Fraw Venus edle Frawe zart /
Ir seyt ein Teuffelinne.[52]

Now let me go, o lady fair,
And leave your body proud.

Sir Tannhauser, don't talk that
way
. . . . .
Let's go into a chamber now
And play love's noble game.

Should I with a strange woman
lie,
Within my heart I see,
O Venus, noble lady fair,
You must a devil be.

Finally allowed to go, he travels to Rome but can gain no absolution from the pope, and so returns in despair to Venus and eternal separation from God. Only later does God give a sign that he would have been forgiven. Even more destructive is Hans Sachs's Cleopatra, in *Drey schoner Hißtorij / Von dreyen Heidenischen mörderischen Frawen* [Three fine tales of three heathen, murderous women]. After committing incest with her brother and murdering him, she seduces Julius Caesar, then has another brother drowned so that she can rule alone. Her insidious power can prompt men to commit her crimes for her:

Anthonium sy auch pethört /
Das er trieb mit jr pulerey /
Vberrett jn durch
schmeychlerey /
Das er zu todt jr Schwester
schlug.[53]

She then bewitched Antony
So that her lover he became;
With flattery him overcame
So that he struck her sister dead.

Finally, after failing to seduce the conquering Octavian, the "geitzig vnkewsch Morderinn [lustful, unchaste murderess]" kills herself in despair.

While England also generally looked to exotic tales for its most frightful villainesses, English popular literature of the seventeenth century sometimes treats the scheming siren's utter subjection of her male victim—to the point where she practically forces him into crime—as a fact of everyday life. A 1635 ballad on a series of murders committed by Thomas Sherwood and Elizabeth Evans tells how Sherwood came of honest farming stock,

> But weary of that honest life,
>   to London he did hye:
> Where to his dismall wofull Fate,
> He chose a Queane for his copesmate.
> O murder, lust and murder,
>   is the foule sinke of sin.
>
> One Canbery Besse in Turnball-street,
>   on him did cast an eye,
> And prayed him to giue her some drinke,
>   as he was passing by:
> O too too soone he gaue consent,
> And for the same doth now repent.
> O murder, ...
>
> For by alluring tempting bates,
>   she sotted so his minde,
> That vnto any villany,
>   fierce Sherwood was inclind,
> His coyne all spent he must haue more,
> For to content his filthy (Whoore).[54]

A pamphlet reporting on the same crimes warns against harlots, urging men "not to bee seduced, or blind-fold led, as hee was by such bewitching Creatures, to irrevocable ruine."[55] The gallows confessions of many murderers and thieves lay the blame squarely on wanton women behind the scenes. In *An Excellent Ballad of George Barnwel, An Apprentice of London, who was undone by a Strumpet*, Barnwell relates how he was lured into crime by a designing woman, on whom he spent the money he stole from his master. When this source is exhausted, he decides to set upon his rich uncle: " 'E're I will live in lack' (quoth he) 'And have no coyn for thee, / I'le rob the churl and murder him!' 'Why should you not?' (quoth she)." After he kills the uncle, she denounces him to the authorities, but both are apprehended and condemned. Barnwell warns: "Take heed of Harlots then, and their inticing trains, / For by that means I have been brought, to hang alive in chains."[56] Yet another condemned man, in *Whitney's Dying Letter To his Mistris that betray'd him: With her Answer*, concludes:

> Beware how Whores your secrets gain,
> Their subtle charms deride;
> They to the Gallous bring more Men,
> Then all the World beside.[57]

His mistress answers remorsefully and kills herself, acknowledging herself guilty of causing his downfall. The early seventeenth-century murderer Henry Adlington laments that "wine and women wrought my wo"; and a similar fate befalls John Spenser, "a Chesshire Gallant," in the 1620s.[58] Robert Guy, author of *A warning for all good fellowes to take heede of Punckes inticements*, comments:

> Besides I haue seene to my griefe,
> many good fellowes
> By their base wicked meanes,
> brought to the Gallowes,
> And they themselues cunningly,
> has scaped cleare.[59]

Such topical denunciations of whores complement and reinforce the moralizing repetitions of traditional antistrumpet lore, as in the often-reprinted *Solomon's Sentences*, a collection of wise counsels for the young man: "Their foule inticement bringeth death, / And poyson commeth from their breath."[60] Mothers warn their sons, "good fellows" their friends, and sages the foolish.

This preoccupation with the power of whores has little parallel in the popular literature of Germany in either century. Some of the difference is undoubtedly attributable to the peculiar social conditions prevailing in London; unlike the smaller German cities, which could probably achieve somewhat more effective control of their population of prostitutes, the burgeoning English metropolis offered scope for more bold and untrammeled sexual enterprise. Prostitutes in German towns had long plied their trade under strict government supervision, though in the sixteenth century they were losing their official status, as proponents of the Reformation campaigned against them. The widespread closing of brothels and erratic attempts to rid the towns of immorality made prostitutes' livelihood and social position increasingly precarious. English prostitution after the mid-sixteenth century was illicit but ineffectively controlled. Here too the public stews were closed and the women intermittently harassed, but their numbers undoubtedly overwhelmed the government's punitive resources. The notorious wealth of a few prominent seventeenth-century courtesans also made the ill-gotten luxury of the wanton more glaringly visible. Whatever its basis in social reality—and it seems likely that English prostitutes had achieved a greater degree of independence and influence than their German counterparts—this focus on harlots and their power significantly colors the overall picture of women presented to the reader or hearer of popular literature.[61]

Complaints about the machinations of whores concentrate most on the damage they cause their victims. Authors almost invariably cite financial ruin, sometimes complicated by criminality if the man resorts to thievery to supply his lady with luxuries. Others warn of disease for unwary frequenters of "common cracks" or of vaguer general tendencies toward death and damnation; but these dangers lag far behind the overriding concern for loss of wealth. The more highly placed courtesans despoil their customers by demanding costly presents, while humbler practitioners resort to picking pockets; but the motive, result, and moral are the same. The strumpet's life is condemned as much for its ease, idleness, and freedom as for its devotion to lust. Battening on unearned wealth—for the services she provides are regarded as pleasure, not work—she achieves an irresponsible independence. Her patrons appear less as buyers bargaining for a desired commodity than as dupes whom she swindles with a false show of love.

The whore is often pictured as freed from all bonds of labor and subjection, a living denial of the norms of moral and social behavior; and attainment of this freedom is often seen as her motive for entering the trade. *The Country Lass, Who left her Spinning-Wheel for a more pleasant Employment*, announces to her mother that she no longer needs to work, since she finds wantonness a far more lucrative occupation. Her mother rebukes her and warns of shame to come; but "Sweet fac'd Jenny" retorts that her mother has no right to complain, since her exertions allow her "My self Like a Lady here to maintain." She gains both money and indulgence of her sexual desires:

> Then I never shall be poor,
>   But have Gold and Silver store,
>   whoever loses I'm sure to win;
>   The young Squire will come e'ery day,
>   And for his Pastime will freely pay:
>   my Spinning and Carding is not worth a Farthing,
>   I'll fling both my Rock and my Reel away.
>
> Virgin Treasure I'll use at pleasure,
>   why shou'd not young Lasses make use of their own?
>   I have been tormented sore,
>   Seventeen long years and more,
>   while I was forced to lye alone.[62]

If she becomes pregnant, she can always marry her old lover and use him to cover her fault.

In *The Ranting Whores Resolution*, a "Lady of pleasure" similarly celebrates her life of ease and delight:

> In freedom and joyes
> I'le spend all my dayes,
> For there is no greater blessing,
>   Than musick and meat,
>   Good wine and the feat,
> And nothing to pay for the dressing.

She favors only men of means, abandoning them when their supplies run low:

> If once they get poor,
> No Money, no Whore,
> And yet they shall wait on my leisure,
>   I only fulfill
>   My fancy and will,
> Which shews me a Lady of pleasure.[63]

Similarly, a "New Vampt Gentlewoman" boasts that she lives like a lady:

> There is never a pretty fine
>   vapouring young Maid,
> That once served Cupid
>   but still loves the Trade:
> I am not ty'd onely
>   to one Man alone,

> By Natures maintenance
>> I live of my own.
>>> . . . . .
>
> Thus by Gulls, & by Gallants,
>> my profit comes in;
> I had rather do any thing
>> Then sit and Spin.

This in spite of the risk of venereal disease: "Though at last I chance to dye, / Cupids blind Marter."[64]

To sustain themselves in idleness and pleasure, the whores of these texts employ all manner of guile and treachery. Many ballads express indignation at the insincerity of harlots' endearments and their haste to abandon an impoverished lover. The authors seem offended less by the woman's sale of herself than by the fact that paying her once or treating her with gifts does not buy the man her lasting fidelity. As the "Ranting Whore" reveals her methods:

> I call him my Love
> My Jewel, my Dove,
> And swear by my reputation,
>> That I never did know
>> What Love was till now,
> Though I have had men beyond measure.
>> With such tricks as these
>> All Coxcombes I please.[65]

only to drop them when their money runs out. In *A Caueat or Warning*, a young man who has been ruined by such a woman recounts his experience for the edification of others:

> Shee'l stroke your cheeks shee'l stroke your chin,
> Shee'le fling her armes about you,
> And shee'le protest with vowes and oaths,
>> She cannot liue without you:
> Sheele sigh and sob if that you say,
> Youle come to her no more:
> And Gallants all by this my fall,
>> take heed trust not a whore.
>>> . . . . .
> Sheele sit alone with you and sweare,
> By God that did her make,

> While breath within her body is,
>   shee will not you forsake:
> Shee'le let you toy, and stroake and kisse,
> Shee'le let you doe much more.

But when she has effected the complete waste of a man's fortune, she will abandon him to prison without a thought.

> For if you still will follow whores,
>   they will deuoure you all:
> Your quoine, your states, your health and friends,
> Then turne you out of doore.[66]

The Two-Penny Whore recounts the misfortune of a "Lusty young Shaver, a vapouring Gallant, / That vainly had spent and consum'd his estate, / In Taverns and Ale-houses wasting his talent." Finding himself with only twopence left, he seeks out a harlot of old acquaintance to spend it on. "All in her Silks and bravery adorned," she haughtily rebuffs him, eliciting an impassioned complaint:

> O how canst thou slight me,
> And then could so closely hugg me in thy Lap.
> It was for my Money, and not for my Person,
> That you did my company so much adore:
>   . . . . .
> How often with oaths, & with great protestation,
> Ingaged you have to be faithful to me:
> In weal or in woe I should nere be forsaken,
> And now all my Coyn's gone, I slighted must be:
> But yet here's two-pence left, prethee now take it,
> And let us do once as we have done before:
> Quoth she I nere did for two-pence, & therefore
> Be packing, & hunt out your two-penny whore.

At length she agrees to sleep with him, taking the twopence and extending credit for the rest. For the author, however, this charitable gesture only aggravates her offense:

> And thus you may see the condition of wantons,
> And in what a wanton condition they are,
> Before they will leave off their lustful occasions,
> If they cannot get money, they trust their ware.
> They'l keep a man company while his Coyn lasteth

And never forsake him until he be poor:
And then much ado he shall have with his wanton,
For one single Job to set on the Score.[67]

The whore's disingenuous behavior is rarely viewed as a response to male demand. Rather, it appears as a spontaneous outpouring of her malice: she takes delight in deluding men to serve her own pleasure. Occasionally, however, she can expose male complicity in vice. Knowing the weaknesses of men, she can defend herself with an "impudence" unthinkable for modest and respectable women. In *The Bridewel Whores Resolution*, an imprisoned prostitute flaunts her freedom from officially established moral scruples, even as she unmasks male hypocrisy:

> Methinks it should Justice please,
>> that we should make use of our own.
>
> An old Man came to me last night,
>> and call'd me lascivious Jade;
> I told him he was in the right,
>> for wantonness was my trade.

This answer pleases him so well that he promises to return the next day with money, to remove her from prison and make her his joy. The other whores in Bridewell relate their wrongs and sufferings, complaining that they are punished with whippings while men shamelessly importune women "to act what they'd have us do." One points out:

> Those joys they forbid us to take,
>> in a corner they'l use with delight;
> What justice does bid us forsake,
>> by the Bye is enjoy'd e'ry Night.[68]

Similarly, in *Whipping Cheare*, the harlots note,

> If the London Prentises,
> And other good men of fashion:
> Would but refraine our companies,
> Then woe to our occupation.[69]

In such pieces as these, which purport to take the strumpets' point of view, the women serve as mouthpieces for satirists' humorous attacks on vice.

While wanton "gentlewomen" form the upper crust of harlotry, the English ballads represent such women's luxury as accessible to any fair and willing young maid. Though they reflect many gradations of class and wealth among loose women, from the lowly "beggar-wench" to the duchess of Portsmouth, ballads and pamphlets often deny the significance of these differences, asserting that all whores are of the same breed. A poor Worcestershire lass can live richly in London:

> I scorne to thinke of poverty,
>   or wanting food or cloathing;
> Ile be maintayned gallantly,
>   and all my life want nothing;
> A frolicke minde Ile alwayes beare,
>   my poverty shall not appeare.[70]

This conflation of classes, perhaps more than any other single aspect of popular literature's portrayal, underlines the fact that these descriptions, for all their first-person attribution, stem from outside the world of the women themselves. Despite the famous anecdote of Nell Gwyn's self-description as "the Protestant whore," there was a vast social gulf between the genteel "lady of pleasure" and the common prostitute—a gulf which it would hardly be in the lady's interests to ignore. Many of the "whores" portrayed in ballads are not prostitutes at all but kept mistresses—or, as some authors portray them, women who pretend to be loving mistresses but in fact are ready to sell themselves to anyone for money. In harping on the women's economic motivation, the authors undoubtedly put their finger on a key to women's involvement in such relationships; but while recognizing that the alternative might be to "sit and spin" (at pitifully low wages) or to live in poverty "wanting food or cloathing," authors seem to consider economic need a motive even worse than lust and the women's purported idleness at least as bad as their wantonness. Some of the authors' horror of idleness and identification of female leisure with lewdness may be a reaction to the decline of women's employment during the seventeenth century—a decline which among the prosperous created an increasing class of leisured women, and among the less fortunate left many women with scant means of earning a livelihood. In the popular literature women with time on their hands are halfway to whoredom, whether as the loose-minded wives "Idlesby" and "Doelittle" of a mid-century pamphlet or as whores in earnest.

The fickleness of loose women clearly serves in these pieces as matter for mirth as well as condemnation; male authors lampoon the women's pretenses even as they expose the folly of those who trust them. At the same time, these works reflect an attitude that firmly resists a view of such sexual encounters as mere economic transactions. The woman is seen as offering, implicitly or explicitly, more than she delivers, and thus as cheating her victim of an affection he views as rightfully his. By retaining emotional and economic autonomy, she shatters the pleasant illusion that sexual relations with her will conform, for all their irregularity, to the norm of female subordination and faithfulness to the man who has "had" her. Still, for all their indignation at the harlots' deceit, authors are fascinated by such women's freedom. The whores' supposed detachment from social bonds and blending of all classes feed a fantasy of escape from the real world into one of irresponsible sexuality—an escape which the texts set up as a female option but which serves a male imagination.

Set against the prominent place accorded harlots in the English literature, their German sisters seem relatively weak, shadowy creatures. The few prostitutes or wanton mistresses who appear are maintained by their patrons and sometimes treat them as dupes, but their power is slight compared to that of their English counterparts. Though Sachs's "schone Bulerin" gloats over her conquests, she has little company.[71] In the German songs strumpets achieve no social ascendancy, although women who follow immodest and immoral foreign-inspired fashions are accused of being "Huren." The activities of German whores remain, as far as street literature is concerned, barely visible.[72]

Young German women sometimes are shown gaining both sexually and economically from illicit encounters, in ways that recall the exploits of the English "sweet-faced Jenny." An early sixteenth-century song of a hunter tells how he catches his prey in the forest, and the two enjoy the delights of love. When she returns home her mother scolds her, but the girl has chosen her own pleasure and is not to be intimidated:

Sy sprach mein liebe mutter /   She said, "Now my dear mother,
laß ab von deinem zorn /   Leave off thy anger's storm.
ich bring den küen futter /   I bring the cows their fodder;
mich stach ein hagen dorn /   I've been pricked by a thorn.
ich waiß ein freyen Jeger /   I know a hunter carefree
er erfrewt mich mit seim horn.[73]   Who delights me with his horn."

Another song similarly pictures a young girl blithely telling her mother about the pleasure she gets from her lover, assuring her that he will be true and will provide them with money.[74] Like the hunter's song, this piece offers a male fantasy of a scene played between women; the closing declares the singer to be a "Landsknecht [soldier]," and the emphasis is clearly on the power the lover earns by his sexual performance. Again as in the hunter's song, the man also holds economic power over the girl, who is evidently of a lower social class. The girl claims independence from her mother but only to become dependent on the man; unlike her English counterparts, she does not devise plans to exploit men for her own purposes.

"Whoredom," of course, overlaps with simple fornication, and both countries enjoyed depictions of illicit encounters. In England the complaints of helpless pregnant maidens abandoned by their lovers form a sharp contrast to the first-person songs of "whores" and point to the illusory quality of much of the latter's power. Indeed, the dividing line between the whores and abandoned maidens is less the taking of money for sex than the ability to embark on an independent life without social respectability. Of course, the two elements are closely intertwined, since it is only the whore's illicit means of support that makes her independent life economically possible. Some abandoned maids avoid whoredom and ruin by marrying other men, in which case their doings are treated humorously, as a variation on the theme of cuckoldry. In German texts the maiden's straying brings on no extremes of carefree independence or solitary suffering. She usually retains ties either with her family or with her seducer. The pregnant girls of the German literature usually can count on sympathetic aid from their families, while the English generally find only scorn and abuse and therefore seek to hide the truth from their families as well as from others. The English girls are alone and abandoned, and several are depicted as dying in despair, either from suicide or from childbirth. This is partly a reflection of the harsh legal treatment of bastardy in England, where even families could be prosecuted by church courts for "harboring" their pregnant daughters.[75] English songs presenting first-person laments of girls who have lost their honor are heavily laced with satire, often adopting a country setting to underline the naïveté, folly, or earthiness of their subjects. The rustic element also suggests urban criticism of rural mores, particularly of the custom of sexual relations between betrothed couples, which had been widely tolerated in both countries but was increasingly attacked. Though Germany, too, was moving toward stricter regulation of extramarital sexuality in this period, the situations depicted there are less stark than in England even in the seventeenth century. Studies by social historians indicate that the number of illegitimate births remained low in Germany until the eighteenth century, while England experienced at least a temporary upsurge in the late sixteenth and early seventeenth centuries, as premarital intimacies failed to lead to the expected marriage.[76] Both countries suffered from economic dislocation in the late sixteenth century, but the contrast suggests that traditional forms of courtship and marriage were preserved longer in Germany.

In the ballads trusting a young man who promises marriage is often condemned as foolish, and girls are warned that there is nothing to prevent men from leaving them in the lurch. The "lovely Northerne Lasse" laments in the earlier seventeenth century that she was seduced and abandoned by a false shepherd. Her family offers no comfort:

> When once I felt my belly swell,
> no longer might I abide;
> My mother put me out of doores,
> and bang'd me backe and side.

Fortunately a young man hears her complaint and offers to marry her. Later in the century, in a more serious treatment, the *Fair Maid of Dunsmore*, a shepherdess seduced by a lord, is similarly rejected by her family: "Instead of giving her relief, / Her friends do prosecute their hate." Alone and in disgrace, she stabs herself, whereupon her lover is stricken with remorse and vows to pine until he dies. In another, often-reprinted ballad, a well-born lady is lured by promises of marriage but forsaken by her lover when she becomes pregnant. Hiding her condition from her parents, she gives birth alone and dies in the process along with her child, and her false lover kills himself.[77] All these pieces blame the false lovers and warn young women against yielding to lovers' solicitations. They clearly point out the women's powerlessness: only by dying are they sometimes able to take indirect revenge on their seducers.

In Germany, too, girls are given no recourse against faithless lovers, but they are not nearly so isolated. Even girls who have run away with men are shown returning home, to get help either from their mothers with childbirth or from brothers in hiding their shame and arranging a good marriage. One unfortunate girl elopes with a soldier who abuses her; when she tells him of her pregnancy in hopes of averting his blows, he sends her back to her mother:

Da sie zu jhrer Fraw Mutter kam /	When she came to her mother,
gar schön ward sie empfangen /	Most kindly was she greeted:
sey Gott will kom mein Tochter	"You're welcome home my
zu Hauß /	daughter;
wo hast dich lassen betriegen[?][78]	How have you been betrayed?"

In a sixteenth-century song, a king's daughter refuses to worry about who will support her bastard child if she should become pregnant:

Geh ich mit einem Kindelein /	If I should have a baby small,
darum ist mir nicht leide /	That doesn't trouble me;
ich hab dort heim ein Vatter	At home I have a father rich
reich	Who'll help me raise my little
der hilfft mir ziehen mein	child;
Kindelein /	Thus will it nurtured be.
damit wirdt es erzogen.[79]	

Or, girls who have run off with soldiers or beggars stay with their seducers, miserable but not isolated.[80] A girl who finds herself pregnant consults with her mother about how to proceed or gets help from her mother in hiding her condition from her father.[81] The lone female figure of English texts is a rarity here.

While women often are shown making purposeful use of their sexuality, both literatures also frequently depict them as subject to the power of their bodies. Pregnancy, only rarely and indirectly a source of advantage for women, makes them highly vulnerable—whether to desertion by the child's father or to visitations from the Devil and his minions. Though women, as consenting sexual partners, have some control over the onset of this condition, they are seen as helpless once it is established; and while the changeability of their bodies can inspire either pity or ridicule, it very seldom adds to their prestige for the authors of popular literature. In the German literature mothers can expect some consideration, based on the gratitude of children for their nurturance, but this amounts to small compensation for the dangers they face when pregnant. In both countries, of course, pregnancy presented real risks to a woman's health and/or respectability, but the literature often goes beyond this to enlarge on the possibilities of social shame and occult disaster.

The changes wrought by pregnancy—independent as they are of the woman's wishes—are seen as an aspect of her weakness, and the language used to describe pregnancy often emphasizes the involuntary and undig-

nified quality of her condition. In England women giving birth are jestingly said to "fall in pieces," and a girl who has given birth is "broken" or
"crackt," while German songs humorously compare pregnancy (or its
cause) to being bitten by a dog or gored by a steer—language that
portrays the pregnant woman as a passive victim, damaged by violence.[82]
An English maid who becomes pregnant loses her health and strength,
feels "cruell gripings," and helplessly watches her "belly swell." In childbirth itself she looks forward to "woful pangs" and "groninge."[83] If she is
unmarried, popular texts of both countries often either ridicule or pity her
efforts to conceal her condition and avoid shame.

To be sure, a pregnant wife occasionally is depicted in both countries
as gaining privileges because of her condition—getting her husband to
coddle her, cater to her whims, and do all the heavy work.[84] But here also
she is "wanton sick," and her demands are seen as unfair attempts to take
advantage of her own weakness. A man who indulges her desire for extra
rest or dainty treats is a figure of fun, in "bondage to a curst Wife." Aside
from these few pieces that satirize pregnant women's malingering, women
appear in both literatures as pursuing their normal round of activities
into late pregnancy. The condition might offer women some protection
against violence, as assault on a pregnant woman is frowned upon, and it is
clearly expected that husbands should refrain from beating their wives out
of consideration for the future children, at least in late pregnancy; but in
popular literature this rule generally appears only to be breached, and the
emphasis falls instead on the special dangers pregnant women face.

Though pregnancy was, of course, a common and expected state for
women and far more frequent than in the postcontraceptive age, popular
literature's treatment of it is far from matter-of-fact. Nor, on the other
hand, is there much trace of admiration for the everyday yet seemingly
miraculous phenomenon of birth. Rather, the predominant strains of
mockery or fear suggest unease at the tendency of female bodies to slip
out of control, along with a concern, especially in England, to keep the ill
effects of such slippage from spreading beyond women themselves. Pregnancy here is viewed as very much a female affair, with the implication
that men would not have it any other way. The disorderly aspects of
sexuality and reproduction are firmly relegated to the female sphere.

Still, the repercussions of women's physical disorderliness often escape these bounds. For the women of the German texts especially, the
dangers of pregnancy go beyond physiology and social mores: their sex

makes them the passive receptacles of occult influences that can do harm or good either to themselves or to others. Especially in the late sixteenth and early seventeenth centuries, the German world appears as fraught with mysterious and unpredictable powers for both sexes, far more than the relatively pedestrian English scene. These forces attack people from without or from within: a supernatural rain of blood suddenly engulfs the land, or a devil-inspired frenzy leads parents, for no apparent reason, to murder all their children. The bodies of women, with the changes wrought by maternity, are particularly subject to such influences. German pamphlets tell dreadful tales of the evil uses to which malefactors can put pregnant women and mother's milk. In addition, pregnancy can have supernatural results, a phenomenon common to both countries but more pronounced in Germany, with monstrous births bringing either suffering and shame or, less often, vindication for the mother.

From the 1570s through the early seventeenth century, German pamphlets relate various versions of a shameless husband's sale of his pregnant wife to bloodthirsty murderers. These songs usually do not trouble to explain why criminals would pay to obtain a pregnant victim. The audience is assumed to know that bands of murderers, in league with the Devil, can use the bodies of male fetuses to protect themselves against arrest or to perform other acts of malicious sorcery. News pamphlets on the arrest and condemnation of murderers often report their confession to large—sometimes fantastic—numbers of killings, usually including several pregnant women. The practice of eliciting confessions by means of torture in Germany undoubtedly exaggerated the number of crimes. Such gruesome deeds as disemboweling the women and eating the infants' flesh are reported to aid the villains in their witchcraft. A murderer confesses in a 1603 pamphlet that he belongs to a band of 200 sworn to wreak havoc all over Germany. He admits to eighty murders, among them five pregnant women

die er lebendig geschniden auff / die Frucht von jhnen genommen.	Whom he disembowelled alive; The fruit from them he took
Und gebraucht zu der Zauberey / Menschen vnd Vieh gar mancherley / dar mit gebracht vmbs leben.[85]	And used to do his sorcery. Both beasts and people many he Has thereby done to death.

The women remain passive in the face of both violence and the magic of their physical processes, and the magic can be put to sinister uses against others. Sometimes the women are rescued through God's providence by good men who happen by; then their condition turns to good, often culminating in the birth of male twins. Women's milk can possess occult powers also: a 1599 report from Dresden tells how two Jews attempt to buy milk from a pregnant woman, claiming that they need it for medicinal purposes. On the advice of her husband, she gives them cow's milk instead, which spoils their plan to kill thousands of people by witchcraft.[86] The women themselves have little control over the magical qualities harbored by their bodies.

Germany and England both produced reports of monstrous births, but in Germany these reports seem to be more concerned with demonic forces that can seize and pervert the fetus. In both countries such prodigies are commonly seen as a general warning to the community at large; but women are sometimes blamed for bringing on unnatural births themselves. Popular ballads in England sometimes see these phenomena as divine punishments for arrogant pride or premarital sex.[87] When blame is assigned for the disaster in Germany, its commonest cause is invocation of the Devil; expectant mothers are warned not to name him, but the curses of others can harm even the innocent. The curse of a godless husband can doom the wife to a monstrous birth, followed by her death.[88] When a careless mother angrily tells her child to eat its food in the Devil's name, Satan is able to kill it.[89] In a report from 1623, a monstrous birth produces three devilish creatures who torture their mother for six weeks, after which they carry her off to hell. The author comments:

Dise Geschicht abscheulich /	This history so frightful
ist wol ein Spiegel klar /	Provides a mirror true
all denen Weibern grewlich /	To all those women spiteful
welliche jmmer dar /	Who with the devil do
den Teuffel haben in dem Mund /	Their mouths at all times freely fill.
wehe den Müttern vntrewlich /	Dire punishment is rightful
zu aller zeit vnd stund.[90]	For faithless mothers still.

The Devil, of course, is always ready to devour, and God to punish, blasphemers; but such mysterious occasions as births provide special opportunities for supernatural intervention.[91] Such wonders are not always seen as signs of the mother's sin, however; and in a few cases German women gain respect through miraculous births. One poor pregnant woman, repulsed by a rich woman when she begs for alms, calls on God for aid and deliverance. In the hospital, after great suffering, she gives birth to three wondrous children; they prophesy dire punishments from God for the people's sins, then die.[92] Another poor woman, giving birth to a deformed child alone in a field, is visited by a heavenly lady in white who explains God's purpose in sending this wonder. Having learned the meaning of its various deformities, with their predictions of war and pestilence and their warnings against pride and sin, the mother amazes the town with news of her vision.[93]

The power of motherhood receives far greater emphasis in the German texts than in the English, even as German children receive far more attention. In Catholic areas, the cult of the Virgin Mary exalts the idea of motherhood. Songs call on her to gain mercy for sinners by appealing to Christ's filial love:

zeig Jhm deine Brüste /	Thy breasts to him display
die er offt mit Luste /	Which in his earthly day
in seines Lebens Friste /	In such a happy way
gesogen hat.[94]	He often sucked.

Other women also use the image of the mother's breast to gain sympathy. In a song printed several times during the seventeenth century, a young woman locked in a castle begs the watchman to admit her noble young lover. He hesitates because of the danger, but she pleads:

O Wächter laß dein Zorn /	O Watchman, leave thy wrath,
du kränckest mir mein Hertz /	thou mak'st me sick at heart.
gedenck das dich hat geboren /	Remember a woman hath
ein Weib mit grossem schmertz /	borne thee with pain and smart.
laß mich der Brüst geniessen /	O help me for the sake
die du gesogen hast /	of the breasts that gave thee
thu du mir das Thor	suck!
auffschliessen.[95]	Open for me the gate!

While English mothers appear giving wise counsel to their grown children or taking advantage of pregnancy to gain their husbands' indulgence, English works generally lack this strong appeal to the special tie between mother and child. German mothers sometimes appear influencing their children decisively for good or ill: inciting a son to murder his impoverished fiancée[96] or helping one to endure martyrdom in the name of true religion. The mother of seven godly brothers, after watching six of them killed, is told by the tyrant responsible to save the youngest by dissuading him from his faith:

Derhalben sprach sy jn freündtlich an	And so to him she kindly spoke In parent's loving wise;
mit vätterlicher sprache,	So that the king her meaning
Das sie der König möcht verstan,	took
redt solchs gar wolbedachte:	These words she did devise:
mein Son, erbarm dich jetzund mein,	Have pity on me now, my son, For that I during nine months
die ich dich han der Monat neün	long
vnder meim hertzen tragen;	Beneath my heart thee bore;
Drey jar an meinen brüsten gsäugt,	Three years thee suckled at my breast
biß auff die stund erzogen;	And raised thee to this hour.
Volgst mir, so ist mein hertz erfreuwt.[97]	If thou obey'st my heart's at rest.

She then urges him to look only to heaven and follow his brothers. Even in crime women can retain their maternal ties. One German witch supports her son in his poaching by means of a demonic charm; but when the Devil demands the blood of her three-year-old grandson, she rebels against him and loses her powers.[98]

Though women's sex gives them certain privileges and powers, German texts depict women as more dependent than do the English. Maternal influence, relying on the love or pity of others and effective only for those with competent and compliant sons, offers little scope for independent activity. The English characters, too, in their use of seduction, need cooperation from the men they want to influence; but they more often are imagined as taking the initiative and using their victims for their own purposes. On the other hand, as victims in their turn, they parody their own independence, as they are unaided as well as uncontrolled. German wives, through adultery, are shown gaining a limited freedom but do not thereby disturb the restrictive framework of marriage and society. Their liberty depends on secrecy, and their cleverness aims to remain hidden. While straying English wives are shown gadding to playhouses and taverns with their gallants, the women of the German texts stay home plotting ways of letting lovers into their bedrooms without their husbands' knowledge. The English authors often disparage or ridicule their women's aggressive behavior; like the German, they generally prefer passivity, and the figure of a sexually unrestrained woman is everywhere an antiheroine at best. Nevertheless the English women's demands, whether for sexual satisfaction or household authority, often dominate the scene. Such vivid female voices could have encouraged some women to conceive of themselves as active and in control, but the chief aim in both countries was probably the opposite: to discourage female self-assertion by tarring it with the brush of sexual deviance.

The different inflections of sex and power in English and German texts underline the ways in which thinking about sexuality is culturally constructed. The German valuation of maternity meshes with a more general German concern for intergenerational relations, just as England's conceptions of sexuality intertwine with its individualism. In both countries the treatment of the power of sexuality appears highly ambiguous for women: as the embodiments of sexual attraction they hold power over men, but they remain subject to their own bodies; and sexual activity outside marriage, whether pursued for power or not, is shown to carry grave risks. The greater sexual restraint of many German characters may be due partly to more effective censorship in Germany, but also in part to a different conception of sexuality, as a natural but sinful desire rather than a tool for individualistic self-promotion. The English treatment of sex as power should be read not as a reflection of social attitudes toward sexual practice but as a cultural fantasy of freedom from social constraints. In German texts sex can draw both men and women into ruin if not properly channeled, and women are only slightly more successful at manipulating it than men. The English texts deal quite differently with both power and vulnerability in female sexuality, elaborating each into an extreme portrayal of a woman cut off from social ties: the whore on the one hand, the abandoned maiden on the other.

8.

Women and Violence:
Tragedy and Comedy

 In both England and Germany the violence of street literature—whether humorous, horrific, realistic, or stylized—plays a crucial role in determining the place and power it accords to women. Though this violence has been touched on in other chapters, it merits separate discussion, for it was a key element in ideas about gender relations and social hierarchy, as well as in the conventions of popular literature itself. The literary violence offers no direct reflection of social behavior but rather underlines the importance of violence as a concept defining the boundaries of social interaction. Violence was in one sense a violation of boundaries—a crossing of the line between one individual and another, an assault on the bodily territory of the other. In this it parallels sexual contact, and the two were often linked in the imagery of popular culture. At the same time, however, it was a powerful means of reimposing boundaries, punishing the violator of norms and restoring order.

Violence serves in these texts not merely as a tool to enforce one's will in particular instances but as a more permanent sign of status. Just as law and custom accorded to superiors the prerogative of violent discipline of inferiors—to husband of wife, master of servant, parents of children—the wielders of violence in popular literature are placing themselves above their victims. The imaginary violence serves both to enforce sexual hierarchy and to challenge that hierarchy when its proper male representatives prove unworthy of their status. Comic violence, one of the favorite devices of street literature, is nearly always inflicted on a transgressor of social norms. Women fall victim to this sanction as scolding wives or sexual offenders, but popular literature also often allows them to reverse the established order and punish men for faults that range from sexual disorderliness to pusillanimity. This comic license granted to women makes them unusual among subordinate social groups: it is, with few exceptions, not funny for a servant to assault a master, a child to beat a parent, a beggar to molest a landowner or merchant; but a woman in arms, unless she causes some tragedy, is usually a subject for mirth. The comedy of female violence relies not only on the simple inversion of weak and strong, high and low, but also on the symbolic links between sexual relations and violence, links which heighten both the tension and the humor of confrontation between the sexes. In serious depictions of violence, on the other hand, women's aggression is often seen as unnatural, while violence against unoffending women is made to appear even more appalling than similar attacks on men. In societies where women's contact with violence theoretically should have been limited to receiving discipline from husbands or fathers and imposing it on children and servants, female involvement in unauthorized violence, whether active or passive, was a disorderly crossing of boundaries which upset the conventions of social order.

While violence plays similar roles in the popular literatures of England and Germany, the political realities of the two countries shaped widely differing social contexts for their literary violence. The contrast appears most sharply in the simplest type of violence to trace, that of war. While England enjoyed nearly constant internal peace during the sixteenth century, Germany suffered the bloody Peasants' War of 1525 and religious war among its principalities in the 1540s and 1550s. In the seventeenth century the gap widened; despite the upheaval of its civil war, nothing in England could compare with the devastation wrought in Germany by the rapacious armies of the Thirty Years' War. A whole generation's constant experience and expectation of pillage and cruelty must profoundly affect its attitudes and behavior; yet such impact remains difficult to assess, particularly since it is for the period during and after the Thirty Years' War that German popular literature becomes sparse. Much evidence suggests a greater tolerance for violence in Germany than in England even before the Thirty Years' War: not only moralists' and jurists' readier endorsement of wife beating but also the constant reports

of gruesome crimes and punishments create the strong impression of a
more violent society. In this the early modern popular literature matches
the later German folklore studied by Robert Darnton.[1] Indeed, Germany's decentralized political organization made regulation of violence
more difficult, especially in rural areas. However, though the levels of
violence depicted and accepted in the two countries often differed, the
patterns and purposes of violence in the two literatures often parallel each
other—but with variations that raise questions about attitudes toward
violence and women and their place in each culture's conceptions of its
world.

The transgressions by which the characters of popular literature
incur the penalty of humorous violence vary with sex and situation. For
men sexual foibles are commonly punished by violence from males or
females, or both. Their tormenters range from injured husbands to irate
tavern keepers, and they are left to the mercy of any who care to punish
them. Married men and clerics who fall into such sins are especially low. A
husband's failure to conform to the rules of sexual morality places him in a
class of persons justly subject to violence and, in the comic world of
popular literature, frees his wife from the ordinary constraints on her
behavior. Violent reprisals against such a culprit are seen as laughable in
themselves but as all the more fitting and uproarious when imposed by his
wronged subordinate. In Germany such comic derogation of male authority also follows from drunkenness, in England from sexual inadequacy. In
all cases the man has shown himself unworthy of the masculine honor he
bears and thus is subject to the humiliating reversal that places the woman
on top.

This humorous view dominates accounts of domestic female violence in England, except for reports of crimes in which women actually
kill someone. German authors also generally chuckle at women's violence,
but some writers on marriage soberly complain of the mutual violence
that plagues married life: unruly wives, to them, are no laughing matter.
Several quote Jesus Syrach's praise of good women and execration of bad
ones; citing his authority, they assert that a shrewish wife so torments her
husband "Das er sich thut vergessen [that he forgets himself]" and violence follows:

Der Man bricht Töpff vnd Glas /   If he breaks glass and pan,
Die Fraw auch gleicher maß /   The wife will match her man,

sie leben alle stunde	So that they're living ever
wie Katzen vnd auch Hunde /	Like cats and dogs together:
mit Schelten / Schlagen vnd	Scolding early and brawling late
rauffen /	Until at last they separate.
daß sie von einander lauffen.[2]	

Hans Sachs, in *Die Zwölff Eygenschafft eines boßhafftigen weybs* [The twelve qualities of a vicious woman], presents a husband's complaint about his wife's multitude of sins. If the man reproves her for such failings as drinking, bad housekeeping, immodesty, and quarrelsomeness, she scolds so terribly that he is driven to violence:

Und ist im maul so resch vnd munter,	And her mouth it is so quick and bright
Das jch mit worten gar lig vnter /	That I am with words defeated quite,
Denn ist die Gall mir vberlauffn,	So that I do with anger boil
Das jch jr thu ein kappen kauffn.[3]	Till I with fists her vict'ry spoil.

With this they fight like cats, the woman scratching, biting, and finally driving him out of the house with a knife. Though the enumeration of her dozen faults, like the description of a bad woman's nine animal hides, is meant to be amusingly ingenious, the woman herself seems designed to elicit more disgust than laughter. Her violence, like the blood-drawing scratches of other defensive wives in the German literature, reflects a messy, furious, yet ultimately fruitless defiance, far removed from the comical insolence of English wives who kick their husbands out of bed or bash them with ladles.

For women the standard failing that invites violent reprisal is wifely disobedience, and man's unquestioned right to punish such behavior scarcely requires the mask of comedy. German wives repeatedly are advised that patience and obedience will spare them their husbands' blows; pious tracts and scurrilous broadsheets join in advancing the same message. In England the "Patient Man's" complaint that his wife scolds ceaselessly and "Then if I chance to heaue my hand, / straight-way she'le 'murder!' cry" shows a casual assumption of the male prerogative.[4] In both countries also the law sanctioned husbands' traditional rights of discipline. Even when gentler moralists, particularly in England, deprecate the use of violence in upholding domestic rule, they generally deny not the right but its expediency; and they often reserve beating as a method to be resorted to when all else fails. The German texts continue to appeal to readers' enjoyment of violence against upstart wives into the seventeenth century, while the English shift their emphasis to comic reversal of this standard picture.

Unlike husbands, wives in popular literature are seldom beaten for sexual straying—perhaps because their misbehavior need not reach the extreme of adultery to merit violent punishment. Though they do not always bother to depict it, however, both literatures agree that women guilty of sexual disorderliness deserve violent treatment.[5] The English literature often represents prostitutes as an immoral and debased group which invites physical abuse. In real life, of course, prostitutes risked institutionalized violence for plying their trade. In England they could be whipped publicly through the streets or sent to Bridewell prison for beating and forced labor.[6] The whores of London were also persecuted by the city's apprentices, who periodically destroyed their houses and furniture.[7] Violent treatment of a prostitute could be seen as no more than her due. An anti-Catholic rhyme of 1641 puts the Roman church in the harlot's place and demands that she be whipped:

> Loe here's an Antidote which you will free
> From that vilde strumpet of impiety,
>
> . . . . .
>
> And macerate the bulke of that base slut,
> With all the crew of th'Antichristian cut;
> A whip, a whip to mortifie her skin,
> And lash her soundly like an arrant queane,
> From place to place, and so signe her a passe
> To Rome from whence she came, with all her trash.[8]

Given their social definition as objects of violence, the prostitutes of popular literature are perhaps more remarkable for their usual freedom from violence than for their occasional subjection to it. *A pleasant new Songe of a iouiall [jovial] Tinker*, a ballad from the early seventeenth century, tells of a tippling knave who "when he was drunke, would beat his Punck / and make her pawne her Cloathes"; but he also beats his wife and daughter in his drunken fits.[9] Wives complain that they are treated no better than whores and insist on their right to more respectful usage,[10] but the perpetrators of violence and their literary creators often ignore such distinctions. A prose broadside of 1681 humorously recounts the antics of "Whipping Tom," a mysterious character who lurks about the streets of

London; he seizes passing women, beats their backsides, and then vanishes. He is said to frequent Fleet Street, the Strand, and other areas known for lewd activities; accosted by a "town miss," he "so swinged her Tail, that 'tis thought, she will not be capable of her Trade for some considerable time." His victims are not confined to professional strumpets, however: he reportedly has frightened a pregnant gentlewoman so that she miscarried and died in childbed. The account, printed "for the benefit of such Husbands as are troubled with gadding Wives," treats all women as potential game for the fabulous marauder.[11] A woman who steps out of line by "gadding" is as vulnerable as the sexual offender.

Most comic violence involving women is reserved for the domestic sphere, but in England women also venture into the public domain to receive or inflict violent punishments. In Germany a seventeenth-century broadside shows women with whips leading a group of men in chains; the scene represents men's enslavement by pretty faces.[12] But this elaborate engraving, with its youths of fashion and wealth, probably had a limited audience; and unruly women otherwise generally attack men at home. In England women often burst these bounds. In some cases the heroines serve as comic props for making fun of absurd male behaviors or to point jokes about the incongruity of female adoption of male-style violence; but some also gain admiration for their vigor and courage.

The late seventeenth century was particularly amused by the exploits of strapping young maids against their male enemies. Several ballads of the 1690s facetiously pit stout London lasses against fainthearted tailors. "Couragious Betty of Chick-Lane" conquers two at once: "She bang'd 'em, and bruis'd 'em, and bitterly us'd 'em," threatening to press them into the king's service.[13] Six other frolicsome maids dress as seamen to impress fourteen more tailors: "They thought to resist, but Joan with her fist, / She thumpt them about till the Taylors they Piß[t.]"[14] The tailors are furious when they learn of the imposture, for

> Said Will, "Had I known Nan, Bridget, and Jone
> Had been the pressmasters, they soon should have flown,
> For, calling my wife, she'd 'a' ended the strife;
> But for my own part I ne'er fought in my life—
>   I'm a Taylor."[15]

Here the comic reversal of female violence is used to ridicule a group seen as cowardly and effeminate.

A similar subjection to female beating falls to the lot of "Slippery Will," who has courted many women but never married them. Regretting his inconstancy, he goes to his old loves, but they all send him packing, with increasing violence. Mary

> fetcht a spit and ran at me,
> Thinking to end my life;
> She used me most cruelly,
> And at me drew her knife.

Finally Nan

> at me did raile and chide,
> And swore she would beat me blind;
> She took her distaffe in her hand,
> And laid on me very sore;
> I thought it was no boot to stand,
> But got me out of doore.[16]

"Kentish Dick," in another ballad of the late seventeenth century, faces a more serious threat, though he is never caught by his female enemies. This lusty coachman has gotten many maids pregnant but refuses to marry them, and his abused lovers stalk him with dire intent:

> some says, their is seven,
> and others eleven,
> At this very time,
> with child by this spark;
> Who does waddle about,
> For to find the knave out.
>   . . . . .
> We'll geld him, says one,
> of nutmegs we'll free him,
> if ever we see him,
> Or he'll over-run
> all maids of the town:
> Let's sever from him,
> That unruly limb,
> which did us degrade.[17]

The threat or commission of such outrages by women, particularly women weighted and hampered by pregnancy, creates an absurd scenario which either mocks the man's subjection to vengeful women (when they are successful) or winks at his elusiveness (when they are not). In both these pieces the man's nonviolent sexual assault, wounding the women in their emotions and social standing (to say nothing of possible long-term effects on their bodies), leads them to seek revenge by seizing the male weapon of phallic violence. Attacking with knife and distaff, the ex-sweethearts achieve at least a symbolic castration of Slippery Will, though the opponents of Kentish Dick are thwarted in their more explicit objective. As in the scenes of domestic strife, women's violence casts them in a role traditionally reserved for men and often emasculates their opponents, but only to dissolve the feminine threat in laughter—for just as only a ludicrous male succumbs to female violence, only a discordant woman, laughably at war with her own social being, attempts to exercise it.

Other pieces toy with the notions of sex and violence without posing direct contests. Several mid-seventeenth-century English ballads celebrate the military adventures of such valiant lasses as "The Gallant She-Souldier" and "The famous Woman Drummer." The heroines of these pieces are married to soldiers, and conjugal devotion leads them to follow their mates into battle. Dressed as men, they take part in all the duties and pastimes of military life; and the authors describe their accomplishments with much amusement and a great deal of sexual innuendo:

> In every place where she did come, she shew'd herself so valiant;
> And few men might compare with her, her actions were so gallant;
> She manage could her sword full well, and to advance a pike, sir;
> But for the beating of a Drum, you seldome saw the like, sir.
>
> . . . . .
>
> She beat with three men at one time, and won of them a wager;
> And had not one strange chance befell, she would have been Drum-
> Major.[18]

She becomes pregnant and surprises everyone by giving birth to a son. Her counterpart shows similar vigor:

> For exercising of her Armes,
>   good skill indeed had she,
> And knowne to be as active
>   as any one could be;
> For firing of a Musket
>   or beating of a Drum

> She might compare assuredly
> with any one that come.
>
> . . . . .
>
> For other manly practices,
> she gain'd the Love of all
> For Leaping, and for Running,
> or wrestling of a fall,
> For Cudgells or for Cuffing,
> if that occasion were,
> There's hardly one of ten Men
> that might with her compare.[19]

And her adventures have the same end. The ballads take care to assure readers that it is the women's soldier-husbands who have fathered their children. The similarity of the two pieces suggests imitation. One of them reports the woman's name and address in East Smithfield; they may both be tongue-in-cheek embellishments of a real incident, but other pieces appeared later on similar themes.[20] For the authors, a woman who combines soldierly violence with pregnancy irresistibly implies a sexual joke in which violence, or indeed any vigorous activity, bears a salacious double meaning.

English authors occasionally drop this leering attitude to give more favorable treatment to women who use violence. "Long Meg of Westminster," heroine of a pamphlet reprinted several times between 1582 and 1650, is depicted as both admirable and humorous in her self-assertion. She takes on a vigorous public role but virtuously accepts domestic sexual hierarchy. Cudgeling extortionate cart drivers and cowardly gentlemen, she makes herself beloved throughout London. When she and some friends are set upon by thieves, she bests two at once: "Doe your worst, quoth shee: now lasses pray for me: with that she buckled with these two sturdy knaves, and hurt the one sore, and beat down the other, that they intreated her upon their knees to save their lives." She agrees to spare them, but only on condition that they swear never to attack any company that includes a woman, poor or helpless people, children, or any distressed persons. They comply and go off "full of grief that a woman had given them the foyle." She later joins the army in war against the French and acquits herself so valiantly that Henry VIII rewards her with a pension. After the wars she returns to Westminster and marries "a proper tall man, and a Souldier, who used her very well, and she returned him all obedience, coveting nothing but his content, which he perceiving loved her very well." Though unrestrained in her use of violence for the public good, Meg has fully learned the duties of a wife. On hearing of her former exploits, her husband challenges her to fight it out with cudgels: "She replyed nothing, but held down her head, whereupon he gave her three or four blowes, and she in all submission fell down upon her knees, desiring him to hold his hands and pardon her. Why, quoth he, why take you not the stick? Husband quoth she, whatsoever I have done to others, it behooveth me to be obedient to you, and never shall it be said, though I can cudgell a knave that wrongs me, that Long Meg shall be her Husbands master, and therefore use me as you please; at these words they grew friends, and never quarrelled any more."[21]

Though domestic violence is beyond the scope of tolerance, other women similarly gain admiration for valor in the field. A ballad of the late sixteenth century, reprinted through the late seventeenth, celebrates the deeds of Mary Ambree. Avenging the death of her lover in battle, she takes arms at Gaunt against the enemies of England:

> Then took she her Sword and her Target in hand;
> And called all those that would be of her band,
> To wait on her person there came thousands three,
> Was not this a brave bonny lass Mary Ambree?
> . . . . .
> The Sky then she filled with smoak of her Shot,
> And her Enemies bodies with Bullets so hot,
> For one of her own Men a Score killed she.[22]

When she reveals herself as a woman, her enemies honor her so much that the prince of Parma wants her for his bride. Patriotically refusing to marry a foreigner, she returns to England. A ballad of the mid-seventeenth-century, *The valiant Commander with his resolute Lady*, similarly extols the wife of the Cavalier defending Chester. On seeing the danger, she romantically dons male attire to fight beside her love.[23] In another ballad Maid Marian even fights Robin Hood without detracting from her character. Separated from her lover, she disguises herself as a page and goes to seek him. They fail to recognize each other and fight till both are wounded. Robin admires her prowess and asks her to join his band, leading to an affectionate reunion.[24]

The German street literature shows almost none of this romantic

celebration of violence used by women for a good cause. Only Judith, by a
special act of God, gains unqualified approval. Otherwise the view of
female violence, even in the service of virtue, is guarded at best. A broadside of 1573 reports the exploits of Margaret von Kennow of Harlem, who
led the town's women in armed resistance to the Spanish siege. The
author shows a peculiar mixture of amusement and anxiety: after jesting at
the spectacle of violent women, he offers nervous explanations of why
their activity was (barely) permissible in this emergency, even though such
feminine presumption is ordinarily pernicious. Tongue-in-cheek, the
piece warns men who say that women carry swords in their mouths that
"Hauptmännin Gret [Captain Greta]" might make them eat their words:

Duckt euch jr Männer die diß sagen /	Take cover, you men who such things say
Vnd vorthin meh die Weiber schlagen.	Or who dare strike women from this day;
Dan jetz die Weiber anderst werden	For women today are changing fast
(Weil sich doch endert alls auff Erden)	(As nothing on earth stays like the past):
Sie fülen jetzund jr vermögen /	Now first they can feel their power swell,
Vnd das jhn auch wol steht der Degen.[25]	And find that the sword suits them as well.

The Spaniards, to their shame, drove the women to this pass by their lust
and atrocities. The author fears that this dangerous precedent could
tempt women to overstep their proper bounds and threaten men's rightful
rule; but since they only acted in this extremity for the protection of their
homes and honor, their actions are laudable.

A less troubled, though by no means approving, view emerges from a
Meisterlied of *Die weiber Amastanas* or Amazons. It recounts the history of
these fearsome women, how they avenge the defeat of their husbands and
resolve thenceforth not to marry but to rule themselves. For reproductive
purposes they visit men once a year, but they send male children away and
raise their daughters to warlike exercises, burning off their right breasts so
that they can fight better. Thus they establish a great empire:

Sie haben zwungen Leut vnd Land	O'er land and folk they took command

In Europa vnd Asia	In Europe and Asia as well;
Theten Ephesis bawen	Ephesis town they founded.
Sie wurden aller Welt bekandt	Their name was known in every
Vnd allem Volck erschröcklich	land:
da	All people feared these women
Diese streitbare Frawen	fell,
Haben regieret hundert Jar	Their warlike fame resounded.
Vnd reicht noch auff vns	A hundred years did they hold
jmmerdar	sway,
Das die Weib herrschen ohn	And reach still down to us today,
vnterlass	So that women rule us evermore
Wir Mann sitzen geschwogen.[26]	While we men sit dumbly by.

Like many *Meisterlieder*, this one takes its theme from another author (the Roman historian Justin) and turns it rather prosaically into song, but adds a conclusion which domesticates the story. The Amazons' history seems matter-of-factly accepted until the final comparison with contemporary life makes a joke of a female rule sustained by violence.[27] Violent heroines did appear in seventeenth-century German novels, and Grimmelshausen created an extreme example of female disorderliness in the violent and lascivious Courage, who (unlike Long Meg of Westminster) shows little hesitation about cudgeling her husband; but these themes found little echo in the literature of the streets.[28] At least at the broad social levels of the street literature audience, Germany shared neither the Englishmen's admiration for female violence nor their confidence in its harmlessness.

Though women's violence in these texts is usually directed against men, there are also comic possibilities in violent squabbles between women. This sort of scene is almost invariably humorous, but it is not common in either country and is particularly rare in England. Scenes between women seldom aroused male authors' interest. In the mid-sixteenth century Hans Sachs published a *Kampffgesprech zwischen einer frawen vnd ihrer hausmeit* [Quarrel between a woman and her housemaid], a dialogue in which the two antagonists accuse each other of the stereo-typical faults of maid and mistress: the maid is lazy, the mistress unreason-ably demanding, the maid gluttonous, the mistress stingy. The charges escalate into imputations of adultery and fornication, and finally the two women come to blows. Watching this battle, Sachs's persona can hardly contain his amusement: "Des mocht jch mir wol lachen aussen [It made me want to laugh out loud]."[29] A satirical pamphlet from 1621 recounts another encounter between mistress and maid. When the former accuses her husband of sleeping with the servant, the latter "sprach du leugst wie ein Hex vnd Hür [said, thou lyest like a witch and whore]" and erupts into violence:

Die Magt schlug dFrawen gar zu platz /	The maid did soundly her mistress bat,
vnd krätzten einanderen wie ein Katz /	Each scratched the other like a cat,
raufften herumb ein andern krumb.[30]	Scuffled about till both were lame.

At least two seventeenth-century German broadsides present humorous pictures of a group of disheveled women fighting over a pair of men's breeches. Brandishing broomsticks and keys and tearing each other's hair, the women illustrate female lust and are meant as a rebuke to proud and unchaste women.[31]

In England this sort of feminine brawling seems limited to a late seventeenth-century ballad in which Alice and Betrice, two women of less than respectable mien, trade insults. After calling each other "stinking Quean," "fulsome Trot," and so forth, they finally descend to blows.[32] Even scolding matches are highly unusual. A late seventeenth-century ballad pairs two "Cracks of the Town" in an exchange of taunts about their trade,[33] but otherwise English authors seem unimpressed by the comic qualities of battles between women. Ballads occasionally refer to jealous wives who slit the noses of their husbands' paramours,[34] but such exploits form no central part of the action. Aside from a few violent crimes committed against other women,[35] English viragoes reserve their fury primarily for male targets.

A more common joke in both countries than battles between women was the confrontation between a hardy shrew and the Devil, or even a host of devils, an especially favored theme for German broadsides. The women invariably overwhelm their enemies, leaving the demons to pity the earth-bound husbands, who cannot flee to hell for refuge. The women's victories are sometimes achieved without violence, by their scolding tongues alone, but they do not shrink from physical assaults; as one boasts, "a shrew doth never fear." Though one might expect that beating the Devil would be considered a good deed, the feat is treated as a triumph of greater evil over lesser; only by her excessive malignancy can the shrew prevail. Her violence against the Devil is linked with her domestic disruptiveness, and the description of her conquest with a denunciation of her behavior to her husband. Her pairing with devils emphasizes the unnatural and sinful quality of her insubordination. Still, the condemnation and ridicule cannot quite suppress her heroic qualities. The shrew's courage and vigor provide an excuse for male failure to tame her and an image of power for women. As it happens, however, these devil-taming shrews are not those who have gained the most complete domestic authority. They perpetually act contrary to their husbands' wishes and torment them with scolding, but they are not fully in command. The women who use masterful violence against their husbands apparently no longer bother themselves with demons. Conquest of the Devil, who here appears as a cowardly and comic figure, is actually a lesser feat than triumph over a man. This fact is underlined by some German depictions in which the devils' sexual identity is quite ambiguous: they have pendulous breasts and animal features, making them more like beasts or women than men, and thus perhaps fit opponents for violent women.[36]

When popular literature depicts violence against women, it sometimes uses the same comic treatment accorded feminine violence. In conjugal affairs especially this approach predominates, but outside this realm violence against women is often treated more seriously. While unruly wives or harlots are exposed to violence that is perceived as entertainingly appropriate, the infliction of unauthorized and unjust violence on women often arouses greater horror than unjust violence against men. The German literature dwells particularly on the heinousness of attacks on pregnant women. Most of the women reported as murdered in sixteenth-century German news pamphlets are in this condition, making the crimes particularly atrocious, especially in cases where a husband kills his wife. In England also, though pregnancy is less common in literary murder victims, it aggravates the crime.[37] Reports of wartime atrocities enlarge on the outrages committed against women and children, describing rapes, mutilations, and tortures. In the earlier sixteenth century German pamphlets complain of such outrages by the Turks and later in the century recount similar deeds by the Spaniards in Holland:

O Gott, der grossen pin!	O God, the agony!
das manche Mutter must sehen	That many mothers had to see
an jhren Tochtern schon,	Their daughters fair defiled;

daß sie [sie] musten lassen schmehen
vor jhren augen thun.
Auch theten sie sie schenden
an jrer Mutter schoß,
hieben jhn ab füß vnd hende;
O Gott, deß jamers gros;
das mancher Mutter jr hertze
zersprungen möchte sin
vor wee vnd grossem schmertzen.[38]

Were forced to let them ravished be
Before their very eyes.
Thus did they rape and shame them
E'en in their mothers' sight,
Hack off their limbs and maim them;
O God, the dreadful plight!
That many a mother's tender heart
Might break itself in two
For woe and grievous smart.

Here not only the violence against women but also the sympathetic pain of loving mothers inspire the author's pity and indignation. The English texts had fewer nearby wars to report on than the German, but their descriptions of carnage are similar: Catholic soldiers are said to have killed Protestants without mercy, "tearing little sucking infants limb from limb before their mothers faces, and dashing their brains out against the rocks; and afterwards ripping up the bowels of the mothers, cutting off their breasts," and other indescribable crimes.[39]

Much of the horror inspired by violence against women was related to women's reproductive functions, but both "factual" and fictional accounts also sometimes view their flesh as especially tender and its violation as especially pitiable. The *Andächtiger Ruff Von dem H. Leben vnd Marterkampff / der glorwürdigen Jungfrawen Sanct Barbara* [Reverent song of the holy life and martyrdom of the illustrious maid Saint Barbara] of 1613 describes the tortures imposed on her by anti-Christian authorities:

Die Kleider namen sie von jer /
Schlagen auff sie / wie auff ein Thier.

Mit Neruen oder Ochsen Zehn /
Jhr junger Leib / der zart vnd schön.
Ward wüst zerhacket vnd zerfetzt.[40]

From off her they the clothes did strip
And like a beast they did her whip

With many a cruel rod and thong:
Her body tender, fine, and young
Was pitifully hacked and torn.

Margaret Miles has pointed to the sexual voyeurism of such "religious pornography," with its graphic depictions of tortures inflicted on naked female martyrs.[41] Such treatments appeared in various genres of art and literature during the period. The martyr's nakedness underlined her helplessness and victimization but also made her an erotic object for the male viewer. At the same time, such images impressed on female viewers a sense of their vulnerability and need for male protection against male violence. Also, more subliminally, they reinforced women's sense that their bodies harbored a dangerous eroticism which was independent of their will.

Even without literal nakedness, depictions of helpless women subjected to male violence could serve similar purposes. Another sufferer for religion, Anne Askew, tells in a ballad of her errors and fate, praying:

> Strengthen me, good Lord, thy truth to stand,
>   for the bloody butchers have me at their will,
> With their slaughter knives ready drawn in their hands,
>   my simple Carcass to devour and kill.[42]

Though the woodcut pictures Askew as a humbly dressed penitent kneeling in prayer, the language places her body at the will of devouring, knife-wielding males. A seventeenth-century ballad, *The Spanish Virgin*, calls on its hearers to weep for the heroine's fate:

> All tender hearts that ake to hear
>   of those that suffer wrong,
> All you that never shed a tear,
>   give ear unto my song.

A cruel Spanish lady, jealous of one of her maids, has her cast into a deep dungeon filled with huge snakes:

> Amongst this ravenous poisonous crew,
>   this fair one innocent,
> Was cast her murderers to view,
>   who straight did her torment.[43]

The imagining of women, particularly young and beautiful women, exposed to the threat of violence is used to arouse both titillation and pity. It enhances the drama of such songs as that of Adelger, a German seducer and murderer whose twelfth beautiful victim is rescued by her brother at the last moment,[44] and of Saint George, who saves the lovely virgin Sabrina from the dragon that would devour her.[45] The image of woman as suffering victim evoked, as it still does, a special pathos.

The sexual overtones of such literary violence were matched by the violent overtones of some literary sexuality. Sexual encounters are described in martial metaphors, and the lines between peaceful sexual couplings and rapes sometimes become blurred. Of course, rape was deplored, both as yet another pernicious effect of lust and as a crime of lawless, shameless, violent men. But the indignation aroused by accounts of actual rapes often disappears in pieces that merely toy with the idea of rape. The sense of seriousness and horror was more lively in the German literature, where rape was a more common theme than in English works. The latter frequently treat the notion lightly, breaking into execrations only when faced with the most egregious crimes. Like the idea of domestic violence, the idea of sex as violence was often a joke; the enjoyment of ribald naughtiness could outweigh the element of violence so that the latter was made to appear incidental, merely an amusing sidelight of the view of woman as object and sex as broad, male-centered comedy.

The image of sex as a game played at women's expense emerges in both countries in the language used to describe sex and its complications. An early seventeenth-century German song makes light of the situation of a girl who has slept with her lover and become pregnant:

Und hat dich denn ein Hündlein
    gebissen /
es hat dich doch nicht gar
    zerrissen /
es hat dich lassen leben.[46]

And has then a little dog thee bit,
Thou hast not been torn apart by
    it,
It's surely left thee living.

In another German song a maid tells her mother she is going to tie up the bull, but really goes to lie with her lover. The mother, worried that it has taken so long, says, "Nun biß Gott willkommen mein Annelein / hat dich der stier nit gstaissen [Now welcome home, my Annelein, / Thank God the steer's not gored thee]."[47] But when her daughter proves to be pregnant, she has the bull butchered.

Playful treatment of the notion of sex as violence affects the language used to describe sexual encounters in England, also. In some cases metaphors of battle engage the principals in a more or less equal contest. The late seventeenth-century ballad of *The City Caper* obscenely describes the encounter between a prostitute and her customer as a naval skirmish between a pirate ship and a merchantman. She salutes him and they fall to:

> The battel between them now warmer was grown,
> And the grapling Irons were mutually thrown,

> She gave him her broad-side of kisses so strong,
> There was no hope left of his holding out long:
>
> . . . . .
>
> From prow unto poop he did grope her all o're,
> And finding her Gun to be full Cannon bore,
> For his Amunition he swore was as large,
> And threatned to give her forthwith a due charge.[48]

He sails off proud of his exploit, but she gives as good as she got, for she rifles his cargo of watch, gold, and jewels, and she leaves him diseased as well.

In other cases the woman presents a more passive object for male assault. Several ballads make a jest of rape and women's resistance to it, as in *The Dumb Lady: Or, No, no, not I; I'le Answer,* a ballad of the 1680s. Here the lady connives at a pretense of rape. Finding that she will answer nothing but no, the lover eventually learns to ask the right questions, for

> their was so little distance
> and so yielding a defence
> That he found all her resistance
> was but only complesence,
> Now said he you must surrender
> if I force you will [you] cry?
> All she said for to defend her,
> Was indeed my dear not I.

Their intercourse is presented as a sustained conflict:

> Hard it was at the first Sally
> for to say which side would beat,
> Tho' poor Willey oft did Rally
> he as often did retreat:
> But what most deserv'd my wonder
> Willey he for all his Art,
> Tho' he kept poor Nanny under
> was the first desir'd to part.[49]

Such bawdy songs treat force as a legitimate tool in sexual persuasion and women's reluctance as a mere facade. In a similar scene from a German song, the speaker approaches a housemaid and toys with her despite her repulses:

ich macht wie vor /	I persevered
bis das ich zwar /	Until I steered
das maydlein ins bethlein drange.	The maiden into the bed.
Sie wert sich seer /	She fought me though,
ruckt hin vnd her /	Jerked to and fro:
für war ich wird schier schreyen /	"I'm about to scream, It's true!
ich zerr vnnd reyß /	I'll tear and fight
vnd kratz vnd beyß /	And scratch and bite!
was wölt jr mich nun zeyhen /	What would you now make me
. . . . .	do?
ich schrey ich schrey /	. . . . .
kem mein fraw herbey /	I'll scream and cry!
jr würdt recht auß geputzet.[50]	Came my mistress by
	She'd know what to do with you."

But when he returns the next day, she greets him joyfully, and they return to their former pastime.

Two ballads of the English Restoration go still further in facetious treatment of rape, postponing the woman's acquiescence until after the fact. In *The Coy Shepherdess*, Amintas presses the unwilling Phillis to grant him her love, persisting despite all her denials:

> She cry'd Pish nay fye for shame
>   in faith you shall not do it
> But the youth her overcame
>   and eagerly fell to it.
>
> Thus she strived all in vain,
> Whilst she felt a pleasing pain,
> Yet he by no means would refrain,
>   but kindly did imbrace her,
> He kist his love, and told her plain
>   he never would disgrace her.

This jocularly brutal celebration of male potency presents its violence as a purely sexual act and transforms the woman's resentment of violence into lack of sexual satisfaction:

> In great rage she flung away,
> Tumbling ore the new made hay;
> Whilst he asham'd and breathless lay
>   although he then displeas'd her

> He rally'd and renew'd the fray,
> and manfully appeas'd her.[51]

The song presents men's ability to provide that "pleasing pain" as a source of irresistible power over women and depicts women as willing victims: their show of resistance is seen as a mask for their true attitudes of passive submission and sexual desire.

In a similar incident, "The Swimming Lady" of 1664 unwittingly arouses the lust of a young lad who secretly watches her naked bathing. He dives in and catches her, and then:

> He gat her ore, upon the shore,
>   And then, and then, and then;
> As Adam did old Eve injoy,
>   You may guess what I mean;
>
>   . . . . .
>
> With watry eyes, she pants, and cryes
>   I am utterly undone.[52]

But the lover faithfully promises to wed her immediately and thus erase any possible harm that might come of his action. Such pieces humorously treat sex as a natural form of violence which all women must undergo and which, in the end, they are expected to enjoy and accept.

Yet such farcical rapes were uncommon in both literatures, appearing in isolated pieces of uncertain popularity. In the English street literature serious accounts of rapes were rarer still, although two lost ballads on the rape of Lucretia appear in the Stationers' registers for the sixteenth century.[53] In Germany several songs lament the fates of Lucretia and her fellow victims of violent male lust. The women's heroic defense of their honor, or desperate sorrow at its loss, draws the authors' admiration and sympathy. A sixteenth-century song on Lucretia, by Ludwig Binder, tells how Sextus took his unsuspecting hostess by surprise:

Wie groß so was der frawen schmertz /	How great the grief within her breast!
dielinck handt legt er auff jr hertz /	With his left hand her heart he pressed;
Er truckt sie das was ir keyn schertz /	Indeed it was for her no jest:
ein bloß schwert het er in seiner rechten hande.	A naked sword had he in his strong right hand.

Unable to gain his will through violence alone, he threatens to kill both her and her servant and lay them together in her bed, thus destroying her honor:

Damit zwang er der frawen ab /	So he did from this woman steal
jr ehr als jch vernummen hab /	Her honor, as the tales reveal,
das sie sich in sein willen gab /	So that she to his will did yield.
die fraw gedacht / o wee der grossen schanden.[54]	The woman thought, alas for this great disgrace.

Overcome with shame, she tells her family of the wrong done her and then kills herself to preserve her good name. In a manner typical of German popular moralists, Binder uses this dramatic tale to point a moral that seems limp and unapt by comparison: women should prize honor above earthly goods and avoid opening their houses to strange men.

Another song celebrates a noblewoman who, faced with an armed rapist, jumps out the window and

endt jr leben in Keuscher zier /	Ended her life in virtue pure
vnd ward also dem notzwinger entgangen.	And so at last escaped the ravisher.
Dabey betracht ein keusches Biderweibe /	So should a wife who values chastity
das sie für jr Ehr setz auch jren leibe /	Thus stake her life for honor's purity,
das jhr Nam wirdig inn gedechtnus bleibe.[55]	So that she'll live in worthy memory.

While Binder skirts the problem of his apparent endorsement of suicide, Hans Sachs, similarly praising Lucretia and other women who sacrificed themselves for honor's sake, takes the issue up. It makes him somewhat uncomfortable; but "Wiewol die nit gar löblich send / Die an sich selb legten jhr hend [Though they have doubtful claim to praise / Who 'gainst themselves their hands would raise],"[56] the high motives of faithfulness and preservation of honor make them laudable anyway. For these women the horror of rape lay not in physical violence but in damage to a chastity which, despite its intangibility, depended wholly on the physical act; innocence was no protection against dishonor. Offered a choice between sex and violence, the virtuous woman must choose the latter.

Though, or perhaps because, such victims of a fate worse than death were in a hopeless situation, marked by a shame which could end only with their lives, the authors sympathetically imagine their sufferings and invite the audience to do the same. In the often-reprinted song of *Das Fräulein von Britania*, the lovely and virtuous maid of Brittany, on her way to marry the emperor, is waylaid by the French king, who forces her to wed him despite the fact that he already has a wife. She insists on preserving her plighted honor, but to no avail, and "man sach vil heißer trehern / auß iren euglin gen [Then many hot tears were seen / To flow from out her eyes]."[57] This sympathy can be extended even to a heroine who has behaved somewhat improperly herself. The virtuous maiden Allda has lived piously and resolved to embrace chastity, but suddenly she falls in love: "Daruon die fromme Tochter / Verlor vernunfft vnd witz [And thus the pious daughter / Did sense and reason lose]." Inveigled by the young man, who promises honorable marriage, she agrees to elope, only to be raped in a lonely wood:

Wol in ein grünen Walde /	In a forest green indeed
Da nam er jr jhr Ehr.	Did he her honor take.
Sie halff kein weren vnd klage /	No aid could bring her woeful plea,
Jr weinen war vmb sust /	Her tears no pity wake.
Trewloß ward da der Knabe /	Cruelly and faithlessly
Mit mutwill büßt er sein lust.	The youth his lust did slake.

He would leave her to return home in dishonor, but she begs him to finish his work and kill her:

Ach gwer mich der letzten bitte /	One last request, I pray thee, Here with thy hand me kill!
Tödt mich mit deiner Hand /	O with thy sword repay me
Nimbs Schwerdt zal mir damitte /	The honor thou didst steal.
Mein Ehr / dein gstolen pfand.	

He grants her wish, stabbing her and leaving her body to the wild beasts:

Also geben den lohne /	Thus secret love and marriage
Bulschafft vnd heymliche Ehe /	Ever give their wages ill:
. . . . .	. . . . .
Sie gerathen nimmermehe.[58]	Such things never turn out well.

Allda, despite her admirable qualities, suffers God's punishment for her transgression. Like Lucretia, however, she remains a heroine to be admired and pitied; emphasizing the women's tears and distress, these pieces call on the imagination of the audience, especially the female audience, to identify with the victim. These accounts are seen as useful examples for virtuous women, teaching them that their sex makes them especially subject to both violence and shame. For these authors women's unique vulnerability is a terrible but indefeasible fact, one which holds important lessons for all women.

The surviving English street literature shows much less interest in rape or its victims. The Lucretia theme did feature in poetry and drama, showing sympathy for her plight among authors and audiences, although Ian Donaldson has noted an early modern decline in her popularity with the shift from a culture of shame to one of guilt.[59] It is unfortunate that the ballad treatments have not survived. Rape appears in a few topical reports that dwell more on the depraved perpetrators than on the suffering victims and address their warning messages to men rather than women. A ballad of 1667 reports on a lustful wretch who with the help of two bawds has raped a ten-year-old girl. She is plied with wine "And then deliver'd up to One, / Was more a Devil than a Man." His two accomplices are justly executed, but the chief author of this "filthy Deed" has regrettably escaped.[60] Another reprobate uses drink to overcome an older virtuous maid, who soon dies in despair. Her widowed mother lays on the villain a curse which miraculously destroys him.[61] The tragedy and pathos that captured the imagination of German authors—the deep admiration for the women's self-sacrificing love of honor and pity for their helpless despair—found little echo in English popular texts.

The differing views of rape in Germany and England stem in part, of course, from the differing genres and contexts in which it appeared. In Germany it formed a theme for moralists who, in search of edifying examples for women, fixed on these pathetic but heroically self-destructive victims. In England the authors of lascivious amusements, seeking to extend their enjoyment of male pleasure and power, passed the bounds of violence. The emotive sympathy of the German literature for rape victims went far beyond its cold esteem for a heroine like Judith who required no pity. Most heroines of the German popular press were martyrs of one sort or another, but these women were particularly notable for their painful, admirable recognition of their own pollution. Violence, sexuality, and a social code of chastity combined to strip them of all power except for their ability to bring down death on themselves, thus ridding themselves of shameful consciousness and the world of their shameful presence. Women, so often seen as the source of a dangerous sexuality, are treated in these texts as the passive receptacles of a sexual attraction that draws on them violence and defilement; all the poison of sex is turned against such heroines, adding a special poignancy to their status as weak, suffering females.

If German sexual fears focus mainly on sin and pollution, the writers and heroes of English texts seem obsessed with potency. Female sexuality threatens less to drag men into animality than to deprive them of their own sexual powers. The fantasy of rape, with a triumphant male potency seizing its own satisfaction and giving the woman hers in spite of herself, is the obverse of the many scenes of adulterous wives lording it over their helplessly unsexed cuckolds. As female sexuality presents a challenge that overpowers men who prove inadequate, so men who rise to the challenge can expect to have women at their command. Having magnified the powers of the female body, the English imagination here reduces women to pure body; whatever they might say they want, the men's unanswerable virility gives the women what they really want and thus fulfills the only claim they have a right to make. The women's enjoyment of the sexual violence done them, though sometimes postponed till after the fact, is crucial to the outlook of these pieces, just as the women's desperate shame is to the German. Both place the women in an attitude of powerless humiliation in the face of male violence, and both depict the woman's body as a thing beyond her control: the German to heighten fears of sexual defilement, the English to exalt the male potency that so much of English popular literature calls into question.

In jest and earnest, fancy and fact, popular literature links women's relationship to violence closely with their sexuality and its tensions. Both the amusement caused by women's usurpation of violence and the emotion aroused by violent attacks on tender women draw on sexual overtones for their effect. At the same time, the differing concerns of Germany and England often focus their attentions on different aspects of violence and provide different triggers for mirth or pathos. Though both enjoy the inversion of normality that places women on top, the German literature places stricter limits than the English on the lengths that such an inversion can be allowed to reach. German wives beat their husbands but seldom push their sway to the point of claiming the humble fealty ordinarily expected of a wife. Similarly, the few viragoes of public life in the German songs and tales are disarmed by a humor that equates them with mere quarreling females—the same shrews whose rule is constantly condemned but whose actual power, as depicted in popular literature, proves so slight and fleeting. In German domestic strife a comedy that recruits violence on the side of hierarchy to quash disruptive elements is more potent and popular than complete reversal of the sexual order.

The English literature, on the other hand, not only allows women to gain substantial power by pummeling their husbands but also enjoys the notion of female vigor and combativeness in the public sphere. Fighting women are marshaled in support of good causes and are admired, though often only in jest, for their prowess. Preoccupied with relationships of individual prestige and self-assertion, English authors readily admit women into the competition. At the same time, the English literature brings to the issues of female aggression and victimization a conscious and radical eroticism. English authors often imagine relations between the sexes as personal contests in which battles of will and force overlie and represent a basic carnal competition. Such an outlook either frees the women of literature from social restraints or reduces them to purely physical objects to be used and abused at men's pleasure.

For the German literature, in contrast to England's individualism and erotic consciousness, preservation of communal order and familial integrity are the overriding concerns. Even triumphantly violent women often appear not as individuals but as allegorical embodiments of a social evil, "Siemann" or the "böse Rauch." While the English literature, especially in the later seventeenth century, sets rambunctious maidens loose in its streets and taverns, the German seldom lets women stray from the domestic fold. Even the women who fight with devils or other women are viewed in terms of their behavior within the household. In the German view of a precarious human order hedged about with supernatural forces, women represented both familial stability and mysterious reproductive processes, both the preservation of social purity and a sexuality which neither sex could fully control. Assaults on innocent women, threatening social continuity or staining the community with sexual pollution, here seemed particularly appalling. Differing English and German perceptions of social meaning and human needs informed their contrasting visions of violence and its relation to women.

9.

Women and Crime:
A Return to the Family

In the popular texts of both England and Germany, reports of crime formed a distinct genre, developing their own standard themes and modes of presentation. Professing to carry edifying moral examples to masses who might otherwise be tempted into criminal behavior, authors and publishers made capital of their audience's taste for sensationalism and gore. The authors and audience of popular literature took little interest in nonviolent forms of crime, and the crime reports of both countries focus their attention on violent acts—particularly murders—followed by violent punishments. In addition to their role as cheap entertainment, however, such pieces subject acts of violent, irrational, or supernatural disorder to the patterns and categories of a socially accepted view of the world. While they might not always succeed in making such events understandable, they cast them in familiar and culturally intelligible terms.

It is in the realm of crime literature that differing degrees of violence in Germany and England are most insistently registered. While both countries could enjoy the spectacle of gruesome murder, the German pamphlets make the English scene appear tame. Unlike the English, few of the culprits featured in the German literature limit themselves to a single murder. In German pamphlets murderers, tortured into the confession of almost miraculous numbers of killings, repeatedly recount enormities that English authors and criminals apparently have not imagined.[1] The hideousness of the crimes is matched only by that of the punishments. Murderers in the English literature are usually hanged or, in the case of women who have killed their husbands, burned—scenes sometimes depicted with apparent relish of the sufferers' dying screams. Though these are no easy deaths, the torments and mutilations inflicted in Germany, and scrupulously recorded by authors anxious to deter any who might be inclined to crime, surpass them by far. One need not assume that ballads and pamphlets describe a representative sample of crimes and punishments to be struck by the greater violence of German society and imagination.

With their system of inquisitorial justice, including the regular use of judicial torture, German authorities had much more effective means of extracting confessions than those of England, where torture was officially prohibited. The effects of judicial torture in multiplying confessions of witchcraft are well known, but the street literature accounts suggest that it exaggerated "real" crimes as well. Though the criminals themselves often appear to be authentic, there is commonly no suggestion of actual dead bodies to verify claims of mass or serial murder. Particularly dubious are the standard admissions of multiple killers that they have disemboweled pregnant women. Presumably if such crimes had really occurred with any regularity there would be at least some reports of bodies without known killers, rather than always vice versa. Local crimes such as those within families tend to offer more substantiating evidence; but here, too, the stylized patterns, and a few obvious fabrications, make suspicion appropriate.

Many of the crime accounts of both countries provide circumstantial details to authenticate the stories, and most appear to be based on actual crimes, or at least on actual trials and executions. In England, particularly, texts published in London could hardly fabricate an execution at nearby Smithfield, though reports of more distant events could be looser. In Germany, the more decentralized publication and distribution made invention less detectable. In both countries some of these purportedly factual accounts report implausible or impossible events, and some are clearly reworkings of previously published material or folkloric themes. Even for the accounts based on fact, however, the narrative is a literary creation. This is especially clear for the many first-person last goodnights in England, which were freely invented even in cases where the actual criminals clearly said nothing of the kind. But it applies also to more sober third-person accounts, which selected, organized, explained, and embellished. For purposes of analyzing popular culture, what matters is not so much the sifting of fact from fiction as the interpretation of the cultural images that were presented to the English and German audiences of crime literature.

Accounts of crimes usually follow both logical and chronological order, recounting the crime, its discovery, the criminal's condemnation and/or confession, and the execution. Most authors add pious or moralistic reflections. Other reports depart from this standard structure to shift their main focus from the crime to the criminal: here the confession, repentance, and God-fearing death of the condemned are given center stage. The crime may be related from the prisoner's point of view or may only be touched on obliquely as a basis for the protagonist's remorse. This confessional device, rare in Germany, is common especially in English broadside ballads, which often present a first-person valediction from the repentant sinner. Having plumbed the depths of sin and by God's grace recognized their error, such malefactors are seen as uniquely fitted to issue warnings and admonitions from the scaffold. Even divines trusted in the wholesome effect of such witnesses in imparting the fear of God to listeners who, with their emotions roused by the tragic contemplation of both crime and punishment, would be readier than usual to take godly words to heart. Though the translation into popular literature might weaken or distort the desired effect, authors could claim for their reports of crimes, confessions, and executions the same deterrent justification that applied to public executions.

This popular genre of gallows confession suggests an attitude toward criminals far removed from that of modern society, in which criminals are seldom seen as appropriate advisers for the public. For early modern Europe the criminal was a sinner who had fallen more dreadfully into temptation than most and therefore deserved harsh earthly punishment; but as a human soul, even a murderer or witch could be included in the benefits of Christ's sacrifice and redemption. With their direct experience of the wages of sin, they could repent and warn others against similar mistakes. This monitory role of converted sinners meshed more comfortably with Protestant than with Catholic ideals, as it blended ideas of the individual's direct encounter with God, redemption by faith rather than works, and the legitimacy of lay teaching. It was in Protestant England that the theme gained real popularity, though last-minute conversions appear occasionally in German pieces also. Such salvation was available to both sexes, and in the popular texts women if anything take fuller advantage of it than men—in keeping with the prevalent notion that women tended to extremes of either good or evil. Despite the crimes that led him or her to the scaffold, the convict might, if repentant, both look forward to heaven and address religious lessons to the public on earth. The English texts particularly exploit this last possibility, sometimes lending to contrite criminals a wisdom and saintliness that make their moral status peculiarly ambiguous; but both literatures are alive to the hope of redemption for criminals and see no incongruity in imagining them in heaven.[2]

German accounts often give vivid descriptions of crimes and the circumstances surrounding them, but seldom delve far into the workings of the criminal mind. The Devil's agency provides the commonest and apparently most satisfying explanation for the outbreak of criminal violence in both men and women. This appeal to the Devil was strongest in the years around 1600, which were also the peak years for German crime reporting. English reports of murders, on the other hand, often concentrate their attention on the criminal's state of mind both before and after the crime. Analyzing the various steps, motives, and circumstances that led up to the tragedy, they seek to make the deed comprehensible as well as reprehensible. Though they often blame the temptations of the Devil, they also examine the character of criminals of both sexes, and Satan usually appears more as adjunct than as motivator. It is possible that the need to convince a jury of a criminal's guilt—as opposed to the inquisitorial procedure of obtaining a confession through the use of torture as practiced on the Continent—may have helped foster this concern with motivation. In the English street literature, authors denounce murderers, but the English style of presenting psychological analysis or repentant confessions encourages imaginative identification with the culprits. The confessions, especially, often give them a voice in the judgment passed on them, help shape the audience's perception of their crimes, and engage public sympathy for their spiritual pain if not for their deserved earthly punishment.

In neither country do authors hesitate to feature female criminals as well as males in their accounts, and women are given a larger place in the popular literature of crime than their proportion among criminals would have warranted. Among murderers of spouses in England, for example, women outnumber men in the literature before 1650, whereas J. S. Cockburn found the proportion in the records of three Elizabethan counties to be strongly skewed in the other direction.[3] Crimes were

commonly selected for notice because they seemed especially shocking, and women's crimes may often have seemed more novel and startling than men's. The fact that crime reports frequently appeared in clusters, with a sudden rash of spouse murders or infanticides preceded and followed by relative calm, suggests that fashion also played a role in crime reporting, or that publicity may sometimes have served to inspire rather than deter. It is often difficult to determine what induced authors to choose particular villains or villainesses as themes for their works, however, and extraneous factors could be as decisive as the nature of the crime. In England criminals from London were probably more likely to gain literary notoriety than others, and publicity in both countries must often have depended on the accidental presence or absence of a journalistically inclined witness.

Authors of both countries sometimes tie crimes committed by women into a larger pattern of female disorderliness. Traditions of misogyny came easily to hand, with examples of female foibles ranging from the seduction of Eve to the vanities of court ladies. Gentler critics merely refer to women's frailty, and some even see this as an extenuating circumstance. Other authors, expecting women when good to be almost angelic, find their turning to evil especially horrific. While it is not surprising that such widespread cultural clichés surfaced in the crime literature, it is just as remarkable that they were often ignored. Treatments of crimes by women closely parallel treatments of crimes by men, and in each country women's offenses, confessions, and punishments share many basic features with those of their male counterparts. It is usually in connection with primarily female crimes, such as witchcraft and infanticide, that misogynistic explanations appear. Even in these cases, however, femininity is not always seen as decisive, and factors applicable to both sexes— greed, resentment, hatred, the Devil's inspiration—figure prominently. Rhetoric might distinguish women as strangely different, but the actual depictions of their actions tie them firmly to their cultures' conceptions of human and criminal nature in general.

In both literatures most crimes involving women are family-related. The two countries differ widely, however, in the forms of familial crime publicized. In the German literature such conflict usually takes the form of mass murder involving violence between parents and children. Occasionally a man or woman strikes out at a single relative; but more often husbands, wives, mothers, fathers, sons, daughters fly into a frenzy and butcher the entire family, or as much of it as they find within reach. Even in cases of infanticide by unmarried women, the culprit has commonly disposed of several bastards before her depravity finally comes to light. In England, by contrast, the key focus of deadly familial violence is the married couple. Wives often kill their husbands, and husbands sometimes kill their wives, but their rage dissipates when it has dispatched the conjugal foe. Some women kill their children; but for unwed mothers this appears as a single hidden crime, and wives who kill their children often do it to strike at their husbands. I have found only two cases among the English sources of either husband or wife killing both spouse and children—and one is an account of a foreign atrocity. In contrast, ten such episodes appear in the German literature. Altogether over twenty German accounts tell of killings of more than one family member by another, as against seven among the English sources, and two of the latter deal with French and Italian poisoners.[4]

English authors denounce the killing of either husband or wife as an unnatural crime, but a woman's murder of her lord arouses special horror. Like the murder of one's master, husband murder was classed as petty treason in English law, so that women convicted of this offense suffered burning instead of the milder hanging prescribed for ordinary homicides. Not surprisingly, authors of pamphlets and ballads often dwell on the element of sinful rebellion that aggravates the deed. Husband murder was an especially common theme in the literature from 1590 to 1630, with an average of two or three pamphlets and ballads a decade, some of them dealing with the same crimes. Wife murder, on the other hand, rarely appeared until late in the seventeenth century, perhaps because until then it did not seem heinous enough to inspire balladists and pamphleteers. The cases of wife killing that did gain early attention generally featured aggravating circumstances such as exceptional brutality; the killing alone was not enough.[5]

The popularity of husband murder seems to have coincided with a time of special ferment in the ordering of relations between the sexes. David Underdown and Susan Amussen both have recently noted a preoccupation with female rebellion in the later sixteenth and earlier seventeenth centuries, and have linked this with changes in social and economic structures. Christina Larner has pointed to this period as one of a new criminalization of women: while courts had long attributed women's actions to the influence of fathers or husbands, they were now being held accountable, with an upsurge in prosecutions for infanticide, witchcraft, and sexual offenses. Larner has attributed these changes to the new religious ideologies of the early modern period, which gave women full spiritual responsibility without negating older conceptions of their inferiority. Such changes in attitudes toward women influenced the general tenor of popular literature as well as the current vogues in crime. Suzanne Hull, for example, found an upsurge in literature directed to women during the latter part of the sixteenth century; and works arguing their merits and demerits (such as Swetnam's *Araignment Of Lewde, idle, froward, and vnconstant women*) went into multiple editions in the first decades of the seventeenth.[6] By the mid-seventeenth century English popular literature seems to have adopted a view more tolerant of female power than before: shrews are left untamed, wives reclaim their erring husbands, married couples are expected to love each other, and the killing of a wife seems as dreadful and unnatural as the killing of a husband.

Accounts of husband murder vary widely in their attitude toward the culprit, according to both the temperament of the author and the circumstances of the crime and its aftermath. While some condemn the wife in violent language, others take a milder view, dwelling on the pressures and circumstances that led her to such an extremity. About half of the reports of this crime (seven of fifteen) cast the narrative in first-person confessional form, giving the guilty wife direct access to the public ear. This is a higher proportion than among wife murderers (five of fifteen) and a much higher proportion than among female criminals in general (fourteen of forty-five), suggesting the dramatic power that authors sensed in these women's situation. *The wofull lamentacon of mrs. Anne Saunders, which she wrote with her own hand, being prisoner in newgate, Justly condemned to death,* presents her sorrowful reflections on a murder committed in 1573. She tells how she connived with her lover and others at the murder of her husband; now she regrets her sinful life, declaring her wretched fate to be well deserved. Still she calls on the audience's pity for her losses, especially the loss of her dear children:

> Let tender mothers judge
>   and gushe out teares with me,
> When as the[y] wey my inward doubt
>   and eke my anguishe se[e].

She blames her accomplices for leading her astray but blames herself as well:

> O righteous god, thou knowest
> their councell wrought me ill;
> And yet, Anne Saunders, woe to the[e]
> that leanedst so muche thertill![7]

Allured by Satan, she allowed him to rule, but her faith in Christ's salvation consoles her in the face of death; she is confident that despite her shameful death, God will raise her to eternal bliss.

Adulterous love is the commonest cause of premeditated husband murder in the English literature (nine of eleven cases), while the German literature hardly recognizes this as a motive outside the world of fiction. English popular literature sometimes takes a surprisingly lenient view of such lustful plotting. In one famous case of 1591, the subject of several ballads and at least one pamphlet, Mrs. Page conspires with her lover to have her husband killed. The ballads show her grieving and repenting her crime, but also blaming her greedy parents for compelling her to marry the rich Page despite her passion for George Strangwidge:

> With sighs and sobs I did them often move
> I might not wed, whereas I could not love
>
> . . . . .
>
> I was their child, and bound for to obey,
> Yet not to wed Where I no love could lay.[8]

A more sober pamphlet account similarly traces the crime's origin to her parents' error: "although she had setled her affection altogether vpon Strangwidge, yet through the perswasion of her freendes though sore against her will, she was married to M. Padge of Plimouth, notwithstanding that she had protested neuer to loue ye man with her hart, nor neuer to remoue her affection setled vpon the said Stranguidge."[9] The ballad by Thomas Deloney vividly portrays the unwilling wife's emotion and resentment:

> Because perforce I was made Page's wife.
> My closen eyes could not his sight abide;
> My tender youth did lothe his aged side;
> Scant could I taste the meat whereon he fed;
> My legs did lothe to lodge within his bed.[10]

She can repent her crime but never her love, and in another ballad even insists that her bond with Strangwidge has divine sanction:

If faith and troth a perfect pledge might be,
I had beene wife unto no man but he.

. . . . .

Farewell, sweet George, my loving, faithfull friend!
Needes must I laud and love thee to the end;
And albeit that Page possest thy due,
In sight of God thou wast my Husband true.[11]

Like many condemned criminals, she faces death with a firm assurance of Christ's salvation, looking forward to heaven.

The crime remains heinous, but the straying sinner can hope for sympathy from the public as well as from God. One strange pamphlet, printed in 1604, almost makes a heroine of the poisoner Elizabeth Caldwell. Dedicated to a lady who, like Caldwell, was of gentle birth, this piece probably was aimed at an audience above that of ballads and humbler pamphlets; but it only carried to an extreme a sympathy for malefactors common to many criminals' last good-nights. Caldwell, a virtuous young woman married to a husband who often leaves her alone without sufficient provision, is eventually seduced after long resistance. With much difficulty also, her lover and an old woman persuade her to feed her husband ratsbane. The poison kills a child but not her husband. Perhaps the ill success of her venture, combined with her good breeding, makes Caldwell seem more forgivable; but she also repents heartily and spends all her time in prison religiously, trying to convert others with the example of her fate. The penitent's letter to her husband, urging him to reform his life, explains her newfound right to admonish others about the need for repentance: "None can better speake of it, for none better knowes it then my selfe, my sorrowfull hart hath smarted for it, and my soule hath beene sick to the gates of hell, and of death to finde it: and to haue it, is more precious then all the world." She reminds him of his neglect, which the Devil exploited to subvert her, and warns of God's wrath if he persists in sin. The author, reflecting on her fall and repentance, depicts her as the instrument of God: "Thus the deceitfull deuill, who hath sometimes permission from God to attempt the very righteous, (as Iob) was now an instrument to her sorrow, but her feeling faith the more increased, and no doubt to her comfort, though in our eyes terrible: for indeede so it ought, beeing sent from God as an example to thousands. For where so many liue, one or two pickt out by the hand of God, must serue as an example to the rest, to keepe thousands in feare of Gods wrath, and the worlds terror."[12]

Such seemingly incongruous glorifications of criminals remain rare, however, and they are matched by indignant fulminations. A pamphlet of 1583 tells of a woman who, by the Devil's suggestion, falls in love with her servant. After living long in adultery, she urges the servant to kill her husband, which he unwillingly does: "Oh most horrible and wicked Womon, a woman, nay a deuill: stop your eares you chaste & graue matrones, whome Gods feare, dutie, true looue to your Husbands, and vertue of your selues hath so beautified as nothing can be more odious vnto you, then ye such a gracelesse strumpet should be found, so much to dishonor your noble sexe." She is condemned and burned, and "her wretched carkas was soone dissolued into ashes." Even in this case, however, the author traces the origins and development of the motives that led to violent crime: "Often times they would carnally acquaint them selues together, till lust had gotten so much power of the Woman: as she began altogether to loathe and dislike her Husband."[13] The husband, forewarned by neighbors, should have sent the servant away; but his wife persuaded him not to. Not the Devil alone, nor even the woman's vicious character, but the combination of these with her circumstances and adulterous relationship is seen as paving the way to murder.

The first decades of the seventeenth century saw reports of several husband murders, most of them arising not from lustful premeditation but from violent domestic quarrels. Though fictional popular literature presents conjugal battles as cause for mirth, the crime reports treat their potentially fatal end as incontrovertible evidence of the need for female submission in marriage. Alice David confesses in *The vnnaturall Wife*, a 1628 ballad, that she was married to a respectable locksmith,

> And well he liued by his Art,
>   though oft I him vbbraide;
> And oftentimes would chide and braule,
> And many ill names would him call:
>   oh murther,
>   most inhumane,
> To spill my Husbands blood.[14]

Her scolding ends in tragedy one night when she and her husband argue over a shilling that she refuses to give him. The Devil here plays a more prominent role than in most English murder ballads, becoming the source of an evil will that the criminal herself will not acknowledge. As she recounts in another ballad on the murder:

> words betwixt vs then did passe,
>   as words to harsh I gaue,
> And as the Diuell would as then,
>   I did both sweare and raue.

While they strive for the money, she draws her knife and stabs him:

> But cursed hand, and fatall knife
>   and wicked was that houre,
> When as my God did giue me ore
>   vnto his hellish power.[15]

She warns all wives to shun her errors, "Lest like to me, you burne in fire. . . ." Instead, they should submit peacefully to their husbands' rule:

> Good wiues and bad, example take,
>   at this my cursed fall,
> And Maidens that shall husbands haue,
>   I warning am to all:
> Your Husbands are your Lords & heads,
>   you ought them to obey,
> Grant loue betwixt each man and wife,
>   vnto the Lord I pray.[16]

In the following year, 1629, Katherine Francis was burned for the same crime, and the balladist Martin Parker set his account to the same tune as *The vnnaturall Wife*, adding the refrain:

> Oh women,
>   Murderous women,
> whereon are your minds?

This tune had served before for a ballad against female vanity, exclaiming against topknots with the refrain, "Oh women, monstrous women. . . ." The 1620s had seen the publication of many works arguing women's merits and demerits, and Parker drew on this background, together with public memory of recent murderesses, to tie criminal violence by women into the wider debate:

> Those women that in blood delight,
>   Are ruled by the Deuill,
> Else how can th' wife her husband kill,
> Or th' Mother her owne childs blood spill.

The balladist clearly hoped to enhance the sales appeal of his work by combining familiar themes and melody in a novel form. At the same time, such pieces depict women as a distinct type of beings, to be characterized as especially murderous, monstrous, or virtuous. This view drew its strength from both literary and cultural stereotypes; but it did not prevent authors from depicting female criminals, like male criminals, as sinful but intelligible human beings.

Despite his rhetorical delight in the castigation of women as bloodthirsty devils, Parker's account of the crime adds a more circumstantial explanation. The couple had long lived "at houshold iarres":

> Like Cat and Dog they still agree'd;
> Each small offence did anger breed:
>
> . . . . .
>
> She oftentimes would beat him sore,
>   and many a wound she gaue him,
> Yet hee'd not liue from her therefore,
>   to stay ill fate would haue him.

She hates him, and finally she stabs him in the midst of a drunken quarrel:

> She long had thirsted for his blood,
>   (euen by her owne confession)
> And now her promise she made good,
>   so heauen gaue permission
> To Satan, who then lent her power
> And strength to do't that bloody houre.[17]

Like many other spouse murderers in popular literature, she makes no attempt at flight or concealment but goes to a neighbor and tells what she has done. Though the lesson taught by her evil example is addressed to all women, her hatred and the "ill fate" of the couple's individual circumstances lead to the crime. Satan gives ready assistance but is not the prime mover of either female or male aggression.

While the vogue of reports on murderous wives seems to have petered out by the mid-seventeenth century, accounts of wife murder became more common. Until late in the century, wife murder attracted little interest unless spiced with unusually atrocious or astonishing features. A pamphlet of 1654 by Laurence Price details two especially gory murders of virtuous wives by raging husbands: one hacks his wife up with a cleaver "that the like was never seen, and that her bloud ran all about the

Roome," while the other inflicts over thirty stab wounds, neither with any apparent provocation.[18] A ballad of the 1660s features another extraordinary wife killer, who strikes his wife a deadly blow while drunk, then forswears the deed and is killed by the Devil. In the catalogue of his crimes recited by a messenger of God, the culminating murder seems a mere aggravation of his earlier sins:

> Thy full delight was drunkenness,
> And leud Women, O cursed sin,
> Blasphemous Oathes, and Curses vile
> A long time thou hast wallowed in:
>
> Thy Neighbours thou would'st set at strife
> And always griping on the Poor;
> Beside thou hast murdered thy Wife,
> Alack what salve will cure thy sore.[19]

Very few pieces on wife murder appear to have been printed in the sixteenth century, but the later seventeenth century brought a substantial cluster. This imbalance in the popular literature probably bears little relationship to the real incidence of such crimes. Yet the English press and popular audience apparently found murderous wives especially interesting in the late sixteenth and early seventeenth centuries, only shifting their attention to wife murderers in the later seventeenth. Some of the difference is probably due to imitation of successful ballads on celebrated cases like that of Mrs. Page or Arden of Feversham; but the shifting popularity of the contrasting themes still suggests a change in the audience's sensitivity to the dangers of male or female disorderliness in marriage.

The authors of accounts of wife murder take as moralistic a view as writers on husband murder; once again marital discord is the enemy, and authors draw lessons for all from the errors of the few. The motives common among the murderesses, discordant marital relations and adultery, hold also for the men, but the elaboration of these themes takes a different course. The accounts convey less sense of amazement than those dealing with the same crime by women. The morals drawn from such accounts aim at restraining disorderly husbands, but some shift a portion of the responsibility from the male culprit to a witting or unwitting female instigator. The Devil also appears as an occasional accomplice, as he does among husband killers.

One early pamphlet report turns wife murder into a lesson directed primarily at shrewish wives. The murder, which occurred in 1604, is described as committed by a wheelwright who "was maried to a yong woman that liued in good name, and in good report amongst her neighbours, yet was she not vnfurnished of that fault which is too common to many women, that is, shee was milde and gentle in all her speeches and gestures to her neighbors and strangers, but to her husband shee was an other manner of woman, for all, or the most parte of her wordes to him were sharpe, bitter, and biting, especially when they were alone." The pamphleteer evidently takes this account of her private behavior from the husband; the wife was obviously no longer available for comment, but the author does not question the man's version. After killing her, the murderer shows no remorse, "saying he had doone God and the world good seruice, in sending so vnquiet a creature out of it." In palliation of her fault, the author notes that her husband spent freely on his pleasures and left the family in want: "And beside, he would oftentimes be ouer gone with drinke, at which times hee woulde not sticke . . . to beate and abuse his wife, rayling at her." One night when her husband has come home late from drinking, she speaks her mind at length; when she refuses to hold her tongue at his bidding, he first strikes her with his fist, then deliberately kills her with two blows of a staff. He burns part of her body in an attempt to conceal his misdeed, but is apprehended and condemned. In an afterword to the reader, the author shows far more concern for regulating the behavior of wives than that of husbands, devoting less than five lines of admonition to men as against eleven to women. His warning to husbands urges them not to offend their wives as this one had, "for if the hatred of a woman be once rooted in her heart, tis no way to be dissolued, but by death." Wives should be mild and modest to their husbands, "lest they driue them to vnmanly cruelty."[20]

At the end of the seventeenth century, the ballad of *The Murtherer Justly Condemned* takes a far different view of a similar crime, though one in which the husband is less cold-blooded. The song offers the story of George Feast:

> Tis of a vile Butcher which with bloody Knife,
> Without all compassion did murther his wife,
> In Leaden-Hall Market, who came to reclaim,
> Him from his Debauchrys and life of ill fame.

He has been long absent carousing, neglecting both his business and his wife, "Which put her in passion, that streightway she went, / To know by this usuage what to her he meant." When she finds him she voices her anger, and the ballad sanctions this as his due; but the scene ends in bloodshed:

> Though justly reproved, yet so Angry he grew,
> That at her with violence his Knife he then threw;
> But that little Harming, I Tremble to tell ye,
> He took it and Struck it full Deep in her Belly,
> At which she Shriek'd and Cry'd out, Oh! I'm Dead
> But he sought not to Fly, o're-come with the Dread.

After his condemnation he repents treating his wife so,

> Whom often, tis plain, he before had abus'd
> Because she would tell him of his wicked life,
> And give him good Counsel like a loving wife.

His fate is a warning to all rash men to "govern their passions that bring them to shame."[21]

Like their earlier female counterparts, the murderous husbands of the 1680s and 1690s are often depicted expressing repentance in their own words and urging others to avoid their vices. Like the women, too, they are often led astray by adultery; and several seek to share the responsibility for their crime with the lewd women who have shared their pleasures. John Chambers, who hired a servant to kill his wife, blames harlots for his downfall. At his execution he calls to onlookers,

> Wishing that they by him might warning take,
> And all lewd Womens Company forsake,
> For they alone, alas! has Ruin'd me.

Edmund Allen makes the same claim in the 1690s.[22] The attempt to share the blame with others is a standard feature of criminals' farewell songs; but while the women can only chide individual seducers, the men can point to a tradition of evil women and their poisonous power.

While the rage of English family members thus spends itself on their individual partners, the German erupts more often between parents and children or between one bedeviled individual and the entire household. Such incidents were reported in both centuries, with peaks in the last two decades of the sixteenth century and in the 1620s. These multiple killings are also bloodier than the English, with hatchets the commonest weapons and dismemberment not unusual. Men seem to outnumber women as the principal actors in these accounts, but not by much. The men are generally husbands and fathers, while among women daughters (and servants) can be as ruthless as wives. Domestic rampages are regularly attributed to the machinations of the Devil, who is always on the watch to fan anger into fury. Often there are indications of additional motives, but usually without the close scrutiny of the criminal's mind so dear to English authors. The criminals are depicted as surrendering to violent urges that, once unleashed, are uncontrollable—but that generally concentrate their attacks on the immediate family. The elements of unpredictable irrationality and unnatural attack on those who should be nearest and dearest, combined with moralistic warnings about the prowling Devil, draw a picture of the perilous insecurity of human life and virtue, protected only by the grace of God from unspeakable horror.

The men's motives for these murders, as in England, often match the causes of less tragic marital discord in popular literature. One butcher and father of six children wastes all his goods on drink, stays at the alehouse all day, and fights with his family every night. His wife's virtuous reproaches only make him worse, and one day in 1599 he finally kills them all with a meat cleaver. Another wastrel similarly answers his wife's complaints of his irresponsible neglect with violence in 1607: undeterred by her advanced pregnancy, he stabs her and then kills their five children. His thirst for blood unslaked, as "Der bös Geist jn besessen hat [the evil spirit possessed him]," he goes to his mother's house and kills her, then to the alehouse to kill the alewife and five children, and finally to his brother-in-law's house, where he slaughters the whole family: altogether twenty-four killings in a single night. Yet another godless roisterer of 1616, sought out by his pregnant wife at an alehouse where he has stayed for more than two days, beats and curses her so that she and the child die three days later.[23]

In other cases, although the family's troubles may not be traceable to drink, it is also economic tensions that lie behind the outbreak of violence. In 1585 a wealthy innkeeper and factor for several merchants, finding his accounts short, begins abusing his servants. When his pregnant wife objects, he strikes and kills her, and then, "als bey dem alle natürliche angeborne blutstrew verloschen [as if all natural, innate blood loyalty was extinguished in him]," his son. "Weiln aber der leidige Teüfel / . . . [ihn] einmal in sein Netz vnd Garn gebracht / war seines mördens vnd würgens noch kein end [But since the dreadful Devil . . . had once caught him in his net and snare, there was still no end to his murdering and strangling]," and he kills his two younger children and three servants. In another case of 1623, a rich miser hoards up food and denies all help to the poor; but his god-fearing wife rebukes him, and in hard times she supplies the needy with grain and other food. When he learns of this, her husband flies into a rage: "das hat jhr Mann vernommen / vnd thet alß wolt er von sinnen kommen / vnd trawet Gott gar nicht. / Der Teuffel hat jhn besessen [Her husband learned of this and acted as if he would lose his senses and had no faith in God at all. The devil possessed him]." The Devil promises him money if he kills his wife, so he cuts her throat and on receiving the Devil's payment goes on to murder his six children. In 1621 a rich baker, having gambled away a hefty sum, wishes he could get more money from the Devil, who promptly appears and demands his soul in return. After taking the money and losing it at dice, he runs home madly: "gantz toll vnd vnsinnig er war / der Teuffel hett jhn bsessen gar [completely mad and crazed was he / the Devil possessed him utterly]." He kills his three sons with his sword, his wife and daughters with a hatchet. When apprehended he confesses that the Devil possessed him and that he deserves death.[24]

Accounts of these family killings dwell particularly on the fate of the innocent, helpless children, and their pleas for mercy are described with the utmost pathos. The children are "schön vnd zart [pretty and tender],"[25] and their naïveté in the face of horrific violence is meant to touch the hearts of hearers. Many authors directly recount their speeches to enraged parents. When one father kills his eldest son, the youngest "schry mit grossem schmertz [cried most grievously]":

Ach / ach hertzlieber Vatter mein /
Last mich länger ewr Söhnlein sein /
nembt mir das Leben nicht /
ich wil euch allzeit gehorsamb sein /
worinn jhr werd bedörffen mein.[26]

Beloved father mine, I pray,
Your little son please let me stay.
O do not take my life,
And I will always you obey
In all that you may ask or say.

But "Der Mörder kein erbarmung hett [the murderer had no pity]," pulls him out of bed, and cuts off his head. Some children show consciousness of the economic burden they place on their parents and try to remove this cause of resentment, but to no avail. Once again it is the youngest who begs:

ach Vatter laß mich leben /	O father, let me live!
jhr solt mir weder Essen noch trincken /	No longer needst thou food or drink
Kein Brodt in die Schul mehr geben.	Or bread for school me give.
	He heeded not at all the same,
Das namb er gar zu Hertzen nicht /	The wicked villain void of shame:
der Ehr vergessen Bößewicht / gar nichts gieng jhm zu Hertzen.[27]	Nothing could touch his heart.

By thus recreating the most touching scenes they could imagine, the authors underline the inhuman cold-bloodedness of the raging murderers. A demonic madness has seized them, a madness which their heedless sin has invited and whose eerie compulsion detracts nothing from their guilt.

While English pieces usually examine motivations and backgrounds with some care, descriptions of the devilish rage of German mass murderers can leave the issues of cause and motivation obscure. Where the English seek psychologically plausible explanations, the German authors foster a disquieting sense of universal vulnerability to the Devil's sudden, internal attack. At least three pamphlet accounts of 1596–97 tell of a godless woman, a carpenter's wife:

Wie sie der Teuffel auch besaß /	And how the devil her possessed,
lies jhr kein ruh ohn vnterlaß /	Relentlessly gave her no rest,
Sie gieng mit schwerem Leibe.	While she with child was heavy.
Nicht dacht sie an Gottes Gebot /	God's law she had forgotten quite,
sie schalt vnd fluchet früe vnd spat /	She cursed and shouted day and night:
man fant nit [j]hres gleichen /	None with her could compare.
Eua Lagmin ward sie genant /	Eva Lagmin was this wife's name;
sie lebt in grosser Sünd vnd Schand /	She ever lived in sin and shame,
der Teuffel thet sie erschleichen.	And thus the Devil did her snare.

She is pregnant with her fourth child and has a good husband, but the Devil induces her to kill them all. She pours hot pitch into her husband's mouth while he sleeps, wrings the neck of the youngest child, stabs the second despite its cries and pleas, and splits the head of the four-year-old with an axe. Still her frenzy is not spent:

Ehe sie in jhrem Grimm erdacht /	Before she in her rage took thought
der Teuffel jhr ein Strick bald bracht /	A rope the Devil quickly brought
Sie solt sich selbs erhencken /	That she herself might hang.
Den nam das verzweiffelte Weib /	The desperate woman took the cord
Erdruckt die Frucht in jhrem Leib /	And crushed the fruit her body bore,
Darnach thet sie sich hencken.	Then after hanged herself.

The news of this catastrophe nearly drives her relatives to despair. Her terrible story holds a lesson for other pregnant women, whom the Devil is also seeking to devour:

Bitt Gott jhr Schwangern Frawen all /	Pray God, you pregnant women all,
Das euch Gott behüt vors Teufels Fall /	That God you guard from the Devil's thrall.
thut nicht schelten vnd Fluchen.[28]	O do not scold and curse!

Avoiding the cursing and scolding that could lead them into the Devil's clutches, they should turn instead to prayer for God's protection from such a dreadful fate.

One of the most horrific, and also one of the earliest, of these mass child murders is committed by a mother and immortalized in a pamphlet of 1551 by a Lutheran pastor, Burckhard Waldis. This woman, apparently of humble station, one day hacks her four young children to bits while her husband is out working during the day. No reason is assigned for her sudden fury, except for the insidious agency of the ever-vigilant Devil. A large, grisly woodcut reinforces the chilling effect of the account. The woman is depicted with her hatchet raised in the act of decapitating a child, surrounded by bloody, mutilated fragments of those she has already killed. Like many of the other young victims of such crimes, her son begs for life in affecting terms designed to reflect the child's homely and simple perception of the world:

Er sprach hertz liebste mutter mein /
Verschon mein doch vnd laß dir sagen
Ich wil dir all das wasser tragen
Das dir den winter thut von nöten /
Verschon mein doch wölst mich nit tödten.

Da halff keyn bitt es war vmb sunst /
Ihrn willen schafft des Teuffels kunst /
Sie schlug vff jn gleich nach der schwer /
Als obs eyn frisches krautheupt wer.

He said, "O dearest mother mine,
Spare me, I'll do whate'er thou'lt say:
I'll carry for thee from today
The water the whole winter through.
O please don't kill me! Spare me, do!"

But no plea helped, it was in vain;
The Devil did her will maintain.
She struck him with the self-same dread
As if it were a cabbage head.

The startling juxtaposition of the commonplace concerns of household and childhood with so cruel and bloody an event posits an unseen evil lurking beneath the calm of everyday human life. The pamphlet's conclusion drives this point home, seeing the story as a warning to all Christians that they must never relax their guard against the Devil:

Wir sind gar elend leut auff erden /
Wann wir von Gott verlassen werden /
So sündigen wir all augenblick /
Vnd ligen in des Teuffels strick /
Der vns stets seines willens plagt.

We here on earth are wretched sure
When God leaves us alone and poor;
Then every moment do we sin,
And lie within the Devil's gin,
Who plagues us ever as he will.

This ghastly tale might indeed be extraordinary; but its cause, the Devil's ceaseless promotion of sin, is a constant of earthly life.

The woman in this account, whose name is never given, slits her own throat once the children are dead; but the wound is not immediately fatal.

It takes her nine days to die, during which time she is blessed with true repentance for what she has done:

Da gab der ewig Gott sein segen /	Th'eternal God then lent his grace,
Da sie durch Gottes wort gelert /	That by God's word improved was she,
Das sie sich seliglich bekert /	And then converted blessedly,
Mit ernst thet sich zu Gott ergeben.[29]	And earnestly did yield her soul to God.

Despite her depravity, the wretched murderer is embraced in the same system of sin, temptation, judgment, and salvation as the rest of humanity; and the Lutheran author credits her conversion to the virtue of God's word. Her terrible rampage makes her a terrible sinner, but still at base a sinner like other sinners.

The murderer, however violent, could seem a mere passive instrument in the Devil's hands. A pamphlet of 1598 reports the murder of a husband and children by wife and servant, who together plan to run off with all the husband's goods. The victim has grown rich from the proceeds of the cloister he manages in the Netherlands, and with his wife and four children he lives a pleasant life:

Sie lebten in Frewd vnd Wollust groß	They lived in joy and pleasure great
Sechs gantzer Jar merckt eben /	For six whole years, note well:
Letstlich enstund groß angst vnd not.	At last arose great grief and dread.

Despite his large income he oppresses his workers and milks the poor, for which God finally punishes him:

Das draus erfolgt groß Hertzenleid /	So from this did great suffering flow
An jhm vnd seinen Kindern /	For him and for his children,
Deßgleichen an dem Weib.	And for his wife also.

The woman, "auß falschem Hertz vnd Mut [out of a false heart and mind]," connives with the servant at murder and theft. After the servant has killed and buried the husband, the woman strangles three of her children. The third, a five-year-old girl, joins many other young victims in advancing a pitiful plea:

Weinet bitterlich in der gestalt /	In fact she cried most bitterly
Vnd thet zur Muter sagen.	And said unto her mother,
Ach liebe Muter thu mirs nit /	"O mother dear, don't do to me
Wie dem Philipp dort hinden /	As you did to Philip there!"
. . . . .	. . . . .
Aber sie war verblendet /	But she was wholly blinded.
Der Teuffel hett sie besessen	The Devil had her quite
gar /	possessed:
Zu dem selbigen male /	As with the other children,
Kein erbarmung bey jr nicht	There was no pity in her breast.
war.30	

As the woman is about to kill the fourth child, however, her heart suddenly fails her; stricken with what she has done, she faints. But the villainous servant pitilessly finishes the job.

Several pieces use mass child murder by parents to point a different lesson, that of the social evils of uncharitable greed. Impoverished parents, in despair at being refused food for their children, lose their senses and put an end to their charges. The featured parent is usually, but not always, a mother; and while the scenes depicted share much with other accounts of familial crime, this tragedy brought on by poverty was elaborated into a recurrent tale with mythic overtones. Such reports were printed several times in the late sixteenth and early seventeenth centuries, with variations but the same basic plot. An early specimen, from 1573, tells of a father much like other child murderers: his wasteful improvidence has led to poverty, his youngest child pleads unsuccessfully for mercy, and after the crime he is justly executed. Other elements, however, add a new dimension: he has vainly begged his hard-hearted sister for bread, and it is his despair at the sight of his hungry children that gives the Devil an opening. When he kills the children, his sister's bread turns to stone.31

In other cases it is women who turn on their families, and unlike male child murderers, they sometimes commit suicide as well. Mothers who have killed their children are the only criminals who kill themselves in either German or English crime literature, though even in such cases suicides are a minority (two of seven in England, five of sixteen in Germany). The impoverished women in the German literature are often seen more as victims than as villains, and the blame for their fates is cast on the miserly rich who have pitilessly turned them away. A pamphlet of 1580 tells of a poor widow in Brabant who is spurned by a greedy nobleman and returns home with nothing to give her starving children:

Die Fraw sah jre Kinder an /	She looked upon her children
die augen theten jr vbergan /	small
in dem kam sie von sinnen /	And from her eyes the tears did
wol durch des bösen Geistes	fall,
rath.[32]	And thus she lost her senses
	Through counsel of the evil one.

She kills the children and hangs herself. When the nobleman hears of it, he goes to see, but is swallowed up by the ground, a fate he shares with a similar cruel Brabantine landlord of 1591.[33] Another widow, in 1602, appeals to a rich baker to lend her bread, but he cares nothing for the misery of her and her family. That night the children cry so for hunger that at midnight she gets up and wildly drowns them in a well. One of the children begs for life, disclaiming any thoughts of hunger, but she throws them all in and then jumps in herself, crying out for God's judgment against the baker and his greed. The baker's bread, like that of the obdurate sister, turns to stone; and he, having cursed God, is torn limb from limb by a band of demons.[34] The keen sense of both the emotional bond and the economic burden of children is here used to evoke sympathy even for parents whose love, need, and despair drive them to filicide.

Though not as common as the killing of children, parricide also holds a significant place in the German crime texts. Unlike the child murders, these killings are often premeditated, and both male and female children engage in deadly plotting. One son and daughter, learning that their widowed father plans to remarry and thus possibly deprive them of his wealth, spend two years devising various ways to kill him, until one day the son lures him out onto a mountain and the two together knock him off a precipice. Three days later they are arrested; they confess without torture and are executed by beheading.[35] A still darker reprobate is the disobedient daughter Magdalena, who figures in at least two accounts of the later seventeenth century. Scorning her virtuous parents, she fraternizes with a gang of murderers at a nearby inn. After having secretly borne and murdered two illegitimate children, she demands her inheritance; but her father withholds it on the grounds that she is still single. Magdalena leaves in a fury, swearing to kill the old dog, and her murderous friends encourage her to kill him and take his goods. She returns home to a hearty welcome from her parents; but after they have gone to bed she cuts their throats, then murders all her siblings with sword and knife. She and her cohorts are all apprehended, the murderers confessing to over 130 killings. The men are executed on the wheel, while Magdalena and the female innkeeper are burned.[36]

Deadly tensions in the families of the German crime literature are thus concentrated between parents and children, and when authors ascribe an origin to the troubles, economic factors often emerge as central. The father is losing his estate, the children want their parents' or master's wealth, the mother despairs when poverty prevents her from feeding her children. In the English accounts, by contrast, passion and personal animosities play a much more prominent role. English murderers, like the German, may give way to emotional rage, but to a rage directed against an individual object. One woman lashes out at a husband because he beats her, another merely because she has a hasty temper, others out of attachment to an adulterous lover; husbands kill wives under the influence of whores and debauchery, out of sudden anger, or in resentment of their scolding; but the murderous violence is almost always focused and limited. The English also more often engage in murderous practices that require long-term planning, such as the use of poison or the recruitment of accomplices, all in the hope of eliminating the object of their hatred. Several German husbands are castigated for selling their pregnant wives to murderers, a move which also demands some forethought; but their motive is a casual greed sparked by the murderers' offer of gain rather than a settled loathing of their wives. Children might plot to kill their parents or a man to dispatch several wives (with children) in succession, but always, it seems, more from a desire to escape a burdensome situation than to attack a particular personality. One exceptional German woman in the later seventeenth century apparently poisons her husband out of jealousy, but she stands nearly alone in both the nature of her crime and the directly personal exposition of her fate.[37] For all the familial nearness of its targets, the murderous domestic rage of German pamphlets turns more against the social pressures represented by the family and its order than against particular individuals, and it is apt to spill over into multiple killings. The familial killers of the English literature, preoccupied with feelings that bind them to particular spouses or lovers, are generally more regulated even in their fury.

Women held a virtual monopoly of certain types of crimes, such as witchcraft and infanticide, and accounts of these offenses are far more likely than others to ascribe the women's misdeeds to female weakness or malice. Women's natural frailty can even be adduced as a cause for greater pity and sympathy for the criminal, who as a woman lacks the resources to repel temptation. The more usual reaction, however, is horror at the women's unnatural cruelty and susceptibility to the Devil's snares. One English author explicitly remarks on women's tendency to extremes of good and evil, an assumption common to many writers on female crime (as to writers on female nature): "they that are good are really good indeed, and they that are bad are usually extreamly evill."[38]

A pamphlet of 1616, *A pitilesse Mother*, offers the fate of this erring gentlewoman as "a cleare looking Glasse to see a womans weaknes in, how soone and apt she is wonne vnto wickednes, not onely to the bodies ouerthrow, but the soules danger." She is a virtuous woman of good parentage, who "lived in good estimation, well beloued, and much esteemed of all that knewe her, for her modest and seemely carriage, and so might haue continued to her old age, had not this bloody accident committed vpon her owne children blemished the glory of the same." Like that of the gentle husband murderer Elizabeth Caldwell, this murderess's honorable birth makes her fate more pitiful, shocking, and regrettable. The poor woman, in her eagerness for salvation, falls into the hands of bloodthirsty Roman Catholic priests, who convince her that the killing of Protestants is a good deed and that the murder of her young children will save them from heresy. With the help of the Devil, she strangles two children despite their innocent smiles and is about to kill herself; but a maid arrives in time to prevent it. Only after much persuasion by godly preachers is she brought to repent before her execution. "Thus Countrymen of England haue you heard the ruine of a Gentlewoman, who if Popish perswasions had not beene, the world could not haue spotted her with the smallest marke of infamy, but had carried the name of vertue euen vnto her graue."[39]

Another culprit of good family appears in a similarly passive and pitiable light in a pamphlet of 1679. This beautiful young lady was raised by a virtuous mother, but after her mother's death she succumbs to the temptations of corrupt London and becomes pregnant. This is not surprising, for "from the first Fall, our Grand-Mother Eve has entailed such weakness on her succeeding Generations, since Pleasure, Curiosity, Pride and Idleness lay claim to so large a share of our young Ladies Time."

Trying to hide her shame, she gives birth secretly and kills the child; but when its ghost appears and reveals the burial place, searchers discover "a most beautiful Corps, in all things suitable to the Fairest, the most deluded Mother in the World."[40] The pamphlet reports that the "beautiful Unfortunate" has been arrested and now awaits trial. Though the piece examines her motives and circumstances, its emphasis on her feminine weakness and beauty makes her seem almost a passive victim of fate. Here also, as with Elizabeth Caldwell and the woman seduced by popery, gentle birth draws from the pamphlet authors extra sympathy for their subjects.

Like other criminals, infanticides sometimes are given a direct voice in the stories of their fall, a form of presentation which both invites identification and makes the criminal's thoughts and actions the center of attention. The 1634 confession and farewell of a servant, *No naturall Mother, but a Monster*, takes a more down-to-earth (and pejorative) view even as it deals with an antiheroine of lower social level. Martin Parker, the fluent balladist of so many humorous jingles, here lends his talent to her self-analysis. She was brought up well:

> But my vnbridled will
> Did put me forward still,
> From bad to further ill.
>
> . . . . .
>
> My carriage was too wild,
>
> . . . . .
>
> And I was got with child,
>
> . . . . .
>
> The father on't was fled,
> And all my hopes were dead,
> This troubled sore my head,
>   woe worth that folly.

Fearing shame, she decides to conceal the truth; and

> To this bad thought of mine
> The Deuill did incline,
> To any ill designe,
>   he lends assistance.

She hides the baby in some straw, where it smothers; but God reveals her wickedness, for her mistress notes the change in her appearance and extracts a confession. Condemned to be hanged at Tyburn, she addresses a warning to maids in her situation, inviting them to imagine her suffering contrition:

> Sweet Maidens all take heed,
> . . . . .
> Adde not vnto the deed
>   of fornication,
> Murder which of all things,
> The soule and conscience stings.
>
> . . . . .
> Though the first fact be vilde,
> . . . . .
> If you be got with childe,
>   through lawless sporting,
> Be grieu'd for your offence,
> And with true penitence,
> Striue to make recompence,
>   for former vices.

The humanness of her character, her path to sin, and her later suffering contrast with the monstrous and unnatural quality of her crime: even snakes and tigers care for their young, but "can a womans heart, / bloodily, bloodily, / So willingly depart / from her owne baby[?]"[41] Though the penitent is made to conform to stereotypes of both dying criminals and fallen maidens, and to voice a standard moral message, the ballad encourages a lively identification with her situation and inner turmoil. Her weakness is a woman's weakness; but it differs little from the weakness shown by males who similarly fall into temptation, just as her responsibility and punishment are the same.

German infanticides, like most German criminals, receive less personalized treatment than the English; the observer remains firmly outside the perpetrator's mind. Occasionally one is shown falling into a single murder from fear of shame,[42] but more common is the picture of a wholly vicious woman who deliberately commits a whole series of secret infant murders in order to indulge in a life of lust. Sometimes the women combine this type of crime with other killings, so that infanticide is merely part of a larger murderous pattern. Like the English, German authors warn maids not to follow this example, but usually with a general recommendation of virtue and godliness rather than a closer imaginative scrutiny of the motives that might lead a woman to such behavior. Responsibility for their vice lies heavily on the culprits themselves but sometimes is also shared with their parents, who should have raised them with stricter attention to religion and morality. This focus on child rearing, absent in the English literature, is a recurrent theme in Germany, particularly among Protestant authors.

One such undisciplined daughter, of the mid-seventeenth century, has virtuous but indulgent parents. She is her old father's only child, "ein Tochter schön vnd hüpsche / er war jhr viel zu milt [With this fine, pretty daughter / Too mild by far was he]." The parents urge her to rectitude and piety,

aber es war zu fräche /	But she was much too brazen,
darzu all schalckheit voll /	And full of malice too.
das macht sie liessen jhm alles nach /	This made them let her have her will
alles was es gelüstet /	In all that she desired;
drumm kams in schand vnd schmach.	Thus into shame she fell.

When she is fifteen they send her into service in the city. Though she pretends to be pure, she is secretly unchaste:

da hat es lang gebulet:	There long she played the wanton
heimlich es kam nit auß /	In secret, no one knew;
vnd wolt doch stäts die frömste sein /	And vaunted still her honesty.
vnd thet also dergleichen /	And thus she did her sinning
mit trug vnd falschem schein.	Ever deceitfully.

Finding herself pregnant at length, she goes to another house and disposes of the child in a privy. She travels to a place where no one knows her and lives shamelessly for several years, bearing a second child and leaving it to be killed by a hog. With her third pregnancy, however, comes the reckoning: God sends her a monstrous birth as a sign of his wrath. When arrested by the authorities, she soon confesses her seven years of ill-doing and is condemned to have hot oil poured in her mouth and a breast cut off at her execution. This shocking fate is a warning to parents to keep tight reins on their children, "Vnd nemmens vnder dRut / weil sie noch zbucken sind [And take them under the rod / While they can still be bent]."43

A similar strumpet, Catharina of Limburg, accumulates a still greater total of murdered infants. Though her wealthy parents do their best to instill virtue in her, she ignores all their precepts and persists in vice long enough to bear and kill seven bastards. After disposing of four at home, she goes and becomes a prostitute in Mainz. The author of the 1626 broadside describes her secret murders as pitiless and deliberately cruel: to kill the fifth she

gieng wol auff das heimblich gemach /	went into the privy,
wurff drein das Kind mit ganzer macht /	Threw the child in with all her might,
mit grossen Zorn vnd grimmen /	With anger and with fury,
doch hat sies aber verbergen thun.[44]	But still she did all this conceal.

Her turpitude finally comes to light when, having returned to her parents' home and borne twins, she cuts the throat of the first but is betrayed by the cry of the second. Arrested and tortured, she confesses the seven previous killings. Another young woman, also the daughter of a prosperous burgher, is equally brutal. Neighbors tell her father of her pregnancy, but she vigorously denies it, and

so bald das Kind auff die Welt kam /	Soon as the child this world did see
schlug sies todt an einen Baum /	She struck it dead against a tree
und thäts in Stuck zerschneiden.	And cut it up in pieces:
Zu stücklein klein wie Fisch gemein /	To little bits like common fish;
. . . es thät sie nit gereuen.[45]	. . . no pity did she have.

She follows this up by killing her father with a hatchet as he sleeps.

For the very bloodiest offenders, Protestant authors turn to cloisters, where lascivious nuns conspire to hide the fruits of their fornication. A report of 1599 tells of an abbess who has lived in sin with a nearby steward for fourteen years, killing any children that come along:

wann sie ein kind gebären thet	When she a child did chance to bear,
zustucken thets sies verhauwen /	She hacked it into pieces small,
warffs in das wasser tieff.	Threw it in water deep.

The author is aghast at this "Gottloß verrucht frauw / der teüffel thet sie blenden / [Godless, despicable woman / The Devil blinded her]."[46] The other nuns want to conceal her crimes, but God brings them to light, and she is executed with appropriate severity. In another case a whole convent full of nuns uses a young student for their pleasure and murders both him and the children that result from their vice.[47]

The punishments inflicted on such culprits are as ghastly as their crimes. The egregious Catharina has both breasts torn with hot pincers and both hands cut off before she is burned, and her fellow murderesses suffer equally gruesome fates. The addition of extra torments at German executions was graded according to the horror of the crime, with such tortures and mutilations not uncommon for aggravated cases.[48] The German crime accounts create an atmosphere of almost fantastic depravity and bloodiness, which was fed by the judicial torture used to elicit multiple (and often improbable) confessions. For all the injunctions of moralistic authors, this level of atrocity must have limited the extent to which ordinary people could relate the criminals' deeds to the kinds of temptations they faced themselves. On the other hand, the repeated depiction of this bloody plunge into uncontrolled sin, often with no clear motive or with motives not much more sinister than those of ordinary men and women, projected a strong sense of the precariousness of human order, virtue, and reason. The Devil might seize control if given the slightest opening. The gruesome punishments meted out to evildoers were intended to deter others; but as the author of Catharina's history complains, they seemed to have little effect:

kein besserung mehr verhanden ist	No more do sinners mend their lives,
man brauchet nur viel arger list	Each only for more cunning strives;
nach keiner Straff thut man mehr fragen.[49]	Of punishment they think no longer.

The German crime literature conveys a conviction of human helplessness on the verge of a chaos bounded only by constant divine intervention.

This sense of the pervasiveness of irrational and supernatural evil emerges strongly in the literature on witchcraft, a crime which was seen as attacking the whole community and as traceable almost exclusively to women and their league with the Devil. England also produced pamphlets devoted to the trials and executions of witches, but the scale and focus of English witchcraft bounded its threat. Scholars have often noted the contrast between English and Continental witch trials, with small-scale harmful magic on the one hand and massive demonic pacts on the other; in popular literature this contrast parallels the two countries' divergent conceptions of criminal deviance in general. Like attacks on family members in the English literature, witchcraft directs its harm against individual objects. While the German accounts often feature huge gatherings of witches intent on devastating a whole country by storms or poison, followed by executions of dozens or hundreds, the English authors depict witches as a few malicious women venting their personal grudges by devilish means.

A German news sheet of 1588, for example, reports a gathering of 18,000 witches, followed by the burning of 133. A song of 1583 tells how 400 witches in Westphalia join in a dance which causes a dreadful storm, and the author notes that 180 have been burned that year in various cities; such numbers are by no means exceptional.[50] The largest number dealt with in the English literature appears to be the 18 witches of Suffolk in 1645,[51] but typically reports mention only two or three culprits, and the scale of their crimes is comparably small. The malicious Flower witches of 1619, a mother and her two daughters, plague their neighbors by bewitching cattle but reserve their main assault for a single family, that of the earl of Rutland, from whose service one of the daughters has been discharged.[52] Elizabeth Frauncis, of 1556, uses Satan's help to kill a lover who rejects her, abort or kill her unwanted children, and lame the husband with whom she lives in discord. Elizabeth Sawyer confesses in 1621 that she has agreed to serve the Devil out of "malice and enuy, for if any body had angred me in any manner, I would be so reuenged of them, and of their cattell."[53] Again and again the English witches are shown attacking individuals for individual offenses, usually the denial of charity or the scornful treatment of a lowly and needy woman.[54] The author of *The Witches of Northamptonshire* explicitly connects witchcraft with poverty: witches "for the most part, as they are of the meanest, and the basest sort both in birth and breeding, so are they the most vncapable of any instruction to the contrary, and of all good meanes to reclaime them."[55] Other authors similarly emphasize the contrast between the impoverished witches and their "worshipful" victims and apparently see this as aggravating their crimes.[56]

German witches also are shown venting their spleen against those who displease them, and many are poor women who are seen as attacking their neighbors and betters; but often the magnitude of their crimes carries them well beyond the level of personal resentments. "Black Gertrude" bewitches the daughter of a nobleman because his wife refused to give her beer;[57] another witch, the "alte Fritzinne" of 1579 in Dillingen, was arrested on suspicion of witchcraft and released: "Derhalben sie den ergrimmet / vnnd auff einen jeden ein Groll vnd Haß geworffen / Wer sie erzürnet / dem hat sie / durch jre Kunst / vnd Zauberey / vergeben vnnd getödtet / Etliche erlehmet / Geblendet / jr etliche auch den bösen Feind zugebracht / Damit sie denn lange zeit besessen / Vnd vbel geplaget sind worden [Because of this she became enraged and cast her wrath and hatred on everyone. Anyone who angered her, she poisoned and killed by means of her art and sorcery. Several she lamed and blinded, and several also delivered to the evil one, so that they were for a long time possessed and sorely tormented]." In addition to her vengeance against the townspeople, however, she for years has caused terrible storms that are indiscriminate in their damage.[58] Others similarly harm those they hate, but also cause massive famines by spoiling crops, feed poison or human flesh to strangers, and kill or bewitch large numbers of children, men, women, and cattle. One midwife-witch of 1650 is reported as killing more than 200 children, and together with two other witches she conspires to poison thousands of people. The mass meetings of witches are seen as causing even more widespread destruction; at one meeting in 1603, 900 novices were reportedly ordered to kill 900 children that year.[59] The German victims need not directly have offended a witch to suffer from her malice.

In addition to offering them a means of venting their resentment, Satan often is shown taking advantage of greed or need to entice witches with economic inducements, a method which works for him in both countries. One old German crone is approached by the Devil in the shape of a handsome, well-dressed young man who calls himself Junker Hans. If she will be his, he promises three gold gulden daily, instruction in herb lore, and faithful service, "welches jr vnd den jren grossen nutz / fromen / reichthumb vnd gewalt bringen solte / darein entlichen gewilliget / vnt sich mit jm verbunden / mit Leib vnd Seel sein eigen zu sein [which was to bring great benefit, wealth and power to her and hers; to this at last she agreed, and made a pact with him to be his in both body and soul]." Though he fails to keep his word about the money, he brings harmful herbs with which she makes mischief. Another witch in the same pamphlet, "die schwartze Gertraut [black Gertrude]," is bought for only three groschen.[60] The author of a 1610 news sheet asserts that the Devil "mit listen / verheißt jhn Gelt vnd Gut [slyly promises them money and goods]" and thus entices people into witchcraft. A pamphlet of 1627 tells of a man who receives from the Devil twenty talers monthly for twelve years. But the author notes, as a somewhat surprising fact, that rich people become witches, too.[61] Several pieces comment on the spread of witchcraft convictions even to the highest levels of society:

Reiche Leut ohn vnterschied /	Rich people, without favor,
wie auch fürnehme Herren /	Men high and noble also,
sampt dero Weiber sind bereit /	Now with their wives together
verbrennet worden vnd	Have been burned, and more will
werden.[62]	go.

In Germany the pervasive evil goes far beyond the resentments of marginal and dispossessed old women.

Other witches apparently succumb to the temptation of lust. Anna Eberlehrin, whose story appears in a German broadside of 1669, takes her first steps to perdition when she dances at a wedding with the Devil, in the shape of a fashionable young man. She then submits herself to him completely, having sex with him often and using devilish magic to cause widespread injury and death. After her first fall, however, there is no indication of why she wishes to cause harm; once the Devil has gained control, it seems to be his will rather than hers that determines her actions. The author of a 1628 report laments that Christians allow themselves to be deluded by the Devil "Nur schendlichen wollusts wegen / so sie mit dem Teuffel pflegen / der sie doch nur betrieget [only on account of shameful lust, which they practice with the Devil, who merely betrays them]." Many of the English pieces also recount the copulation of witches with the Devil, sometimes seeing this as part of their motive. Elizabeth Weed confesses in a pamphlet of 1646 that the Devil provided her with a manlike spirit to lie with her "when and as often as she desired," which he did "very often."[63]

For all these various motives, however, the adoption of witchcraft involved an element which authors of both countries found difficult to explain. Nothing seemed sufficient to account for the witches' antihuman activities but either a mysteriously hateful disposition or a complete subjection to demonic influence. English authors ascribe to witches a perverse hatred of humanity. A ballad of the late seventeenth century tells how the victims of witchcraft cry loudly for relief:

> But all's in vain, no rest at all they find,
> For why? all Witches to cruelty are enclin'd,
> And do delight to hear sad dying groans,
> And such laments as wou'd pierce Marble Stones.[64]

A pamphlet of 1592, *A Most Wicked worke of a wretched Witch*, notes the dreadful spite of witches. A farm laborer offends a witch by calling her one, and from that day her wrath turns against him. A month later he meets her by chance, "and giuing hir the time of the daye, like a peruerse woman, like a perillous waspe, like a pestiferous witch, incensed with hate at the sight of him [she] held downe hir head, not daigning to speake."[65] Witches are seen as a breed apart, poisoning their hearts with hellish malice to the utter perversion of normal human sympathies. The old Fritzinne of Dillingen similarly hates everyone,[66] and other German witches appear as driven into their crimes by the Devil; once they have fallen into his clutches, his demands seem to determine their malicious acts, especially for those who are organized into mass meetings.[67]

While Satan appears as the prime mover of all ill-doing in Germany, English witches more often take the initiative in their downfall. English authors commonly emphasize the women's ill character and disorderly lives, qualities that predate and invite their league with the devil. Joan Cunny has lived as her name might suggest: "very lewdly, hauing two lewde Daughters, no better then naughty packs."[68] Elizabeth Stile, in 1579, has been "found by manifest and vndeniable proffes of her honest neighbors to be a leude, malitious, and hurtfull woman to the people and inhabitants thereaboutes." In *A True Relation of the Araignment Of eighteene Witches* (1645), they all "confessed that cruell malice and helbred envie was their chiefe delight, continually a long time before they made their Covenant with the Devill."[69] Yet, though the women's own evil issues the call, the Devil soon takes control and makes them his tools. English authors, like the German, see the real power of witchcraft as vested in Satan alone; the witches are his "inthraled bondslaues."[70] Sometimes the witches claim that their demonic helpers have pushed them further than their own evil will would have gone: one witch's familiar, for example, kills a child when she only wants it slightly nipped;[71] and another witch faithfully attends church for twenty-one years because she "had a desire to be rid of that unhappy burthen which was upon her."[72]

Both English and German authors assume that witches are normally women. Some authors explicitly link witchcraft to the weaknesses or vices of women as a sex, as in a German broadside of 1555, which recalls Satan's original temptation of Eve and explains that the Devil turns his chief attention to the weaker sex: he "helt auch sein alte weyse / er setzet sonderlich dem weiblichen geschlecht hart zü / als dem schwecheren werckzeug / damit er sie von Christo wegreysse / vnd in ewige verdamnuß füre / vnd wie er zü Eua sprach / sie wurden werden wie die Götter / Also bläßt er noch das gifft in der weyber hertzen / lernet sie zaubern / auff das er sie klüg mache / das sie mehr wissen dann andere leüt / vnd also den Göttern gleich werden / damit macht er sie jm anhengig / vnd zü Teüffels dienerin / ja auch zü Teuffels breüten [keeps to his old ways. He presses the female sex especially hard, as the weaker vessel, that he may tear them away from Christ and lead them to eternal damnation; and as he told Eve they would become like gods, so he still pours poison into women's hearts. He teaches them witchcraft, promising to make them clever, that they may know more than other people, and so become like gods. Thus he attaches them to himself and makes them devil's servants, and even devil's brides]."[73] Other authors quote a common proverb: "wie man spricht / was nit kan der Teuffel kan [sic] zu wege bringen / das bringet ein altes Weib zu wegen [As people say, what the devil can't manage, an old woman does]."[74] Authors of both countries sometimes cite the weakness and ignorance of women to explain their susceptibility; but more often they offer no special explanation for the prevalence of women among witches, apparently expecting that readers will take this prevalence for granted. A German report of 1583, for example, notes carefully that three of the forty-seven witches arrested that year at Aschenbruck were men and that their sex did not exclude them from punishment for witchcraft:

darunder waren nun drey Mann / die hat man auch verbrent forthan / thet jren nicht verschonen.[75]	Among them also were three men Who like the rest were burnèd then, Nor were they spared at all.

The motives that authors present as leading witches into their sins— greed, poverty, malice, and lust—are hardly exclusive to women, though misogynists might argue that malice and lust are stronger in women, and though women ran a greater risk of poverty when detached from male support. Often the reasons cited for women's fall into witchcraft do not seem particularly sex-linked. One English author with pretensions to learning asserts in 1619 that "there bee certaine men and women growne in yeares, and ouergrowne with Melancholly and Atheisme, who out of a malicious disposition against their betters, or others thriuing by them; but most times from a heart-burning desire of reuenge," take up witchcraft. Another writes in 1645 that the Devil, having begun with the seduction of Eve, "deceiveth all the world, by whose deceitfull promises and subtill devices (for his own end, and desire of their destruction,) hath insnared and drawne these poore silly creatures, into these horrid and detestable practises, of renouncing God and Christ, and entring into a solemne league and contract with the Devill."[76] Misogynistic fears and assumptions underlying the association of women with witchcraft are thus sometimes made explicit in popular literature, but often authors seem to expect the culprits' sex to raise no questions in readers' minds; women's susceptibility to the Devil's snare of witchcraft was an accepted convention.

The well-known misogynistic commentary of the *Malleus maleficarum*, the influential witch-hunting manual published in 1486 by two German Dominicans, provides many examples linking women's flaws to their affinity for witchcraft. Their summation on the female tendency to this sin: "All witchcraft comes from carnal lust, which is in women insatiable." But the authors of the *Malleus* lay no claim to originality in this regard. Their charges against women are drawn from prior authorities, and many of them are commonplaces. The *Malleus* authors even adduce misogynistic jokes to strengthen their case, citing St. Jerome's story of Socrates and his shrewish wife: after scolding Socrates out of the house, she empties the chamberpot on him, prompting his philosophic comment that he expected rain to follow the thunder.[77] Their use of this tale, a staple of early modern jestbooks, is particularly telling, even jarring, in a work of such serious import for the lives of the hunted. It warns against taking at face value the claims of facetious authors that their antifemale jibes are merely harmless fun. Fun perhaps, but with important consequences intended or unintended, for the jokes formed part of a ready cultural store of misogynistic wisdom which could ease the acceptance of outright attacks on women.

While the predominance of women among the victims of early

modern witch-hunting is obvious, the reasons for it are not. Scholars have noted social, economic, and demographic changes that left women more economically powerless than before.[78] Such changes could foster the perception of women—especially poor, old women—as witches, since they were seen as resentful of their economic situation and likely to seek supernatural revenge. On the other hand, some women probably did resort to magical practices, or a reputation for them, as a source of otherwise unobtainable power. Other scholars have pointed to the focus of witchcraft's harms on domains of female occupation: dairying, brewing, and childbearing were especially vulnerable, with women as witches seen as negating their own nurturant and reproductive roles. As Larner has suggested, the witch-hunt's attack on women was linked both with ancient fears about the mysterious powers of female sexuality and with new conflicts over women's social and ideological roles. Much evidence points to an intensified misogyny during this period, which was closely intertwined with the prosecution of women as witches.[79]

Most of the English accounts of witchcraft appear not in the form of ballads or broadsides but in more lengthy and elaborate pamphlets, sometimes with sprinklings of Latin or dedications to prominent patrons. Prefaces frequently discuss the nature of witchcraft, sometimes affecting a learned style and rhetorical flourishes. The pamphleteers who wrote them clearly felt themselves superior to the rough balladists who catered to the street trade. Henry Goodcole, in a pamphlet of 1621, explains in an apology to readers that he is not attempting a learned disquisition on witchcraft but has been driven into print in the interests of truth: "which in some measure, hath receiued a wound already, by most base and false Ballets, which were sung at the time of our returning from the Witches execution. In them I was ashamed to see and heare such ridiculous fictions of her bewitching Corne on the ground, of a Ferret and an Owle dayly sporting before her, of the bewitched woman brayning her selfe, of the Spirits attending in the Prison: all which I knew to be fitter for an Ale-bench then for a relation of proceeding in Court of Iustice. And thereupon I wonder that such lewde Balletmongers should be suffered to creepe into the Printers presses and peoples eares."[80] A ballad of 1619 on the witchcraft of Margaret Flower and her daughters advertises a book (that is, a pamphlet) on their fate for sale from the same printer.[81] These longer pieces, which far outnumber broadside accounts of witchcraft, clearly sought to address a more serious and elevated audience. The subject of witchcraft seems to have fascinated the educated English even more than the lowly.

Many of the English writers on witchcraft apparently felt it necessary to defend belief in witchcraft before going on to recount their news. Occasional German pieces also express doubts about witches' magical feats, concluding that their nightly flights, metamorphoses, and spells are the Devil's delusions. Hans Sachs, in a 1553 *Gesprech von Fünff Unholden* [Dialogue of five witches]," depicts the old women making extravagant claims of their powers to cause love, impotence, death, or storms, copulate with the Devil, and change themselves into animals at will:

Ist doch lauter betrug vnd lügen;	But this is pure deceit and fraud;
. . . . .	. . . . .
Der Teufel lest ein Weib sich zwingen,	The Devil lets her ply her art To banish faith from a woman's heart.
So ferr ers in vnglaub müg bringen.	
. . . . .	. . . . .
Das wettermachen sie bethort,	The storms these women think they raise
Schlüg sonst gleich wol auch an das ort.	Were bound to strike in any case.
Des Teufels Ee vnd Reuterey	The devil's rides and marriage bed
Ist nur gespenst vnd fantasey.	Are only in the woman's head.
. . . . .	. . . . .
Diß als ist heidnisch vnd ein spot	All this is heathen mockery
Bey den, die nicht glauben in Got.	For those who know no piety.
So du im glauben Gott erkenst,	If thou hast faith in God confessed,
So kan dir schaden kein gespenst.[82]	No devil's fraud can thee molest.

The author of a 1589 pamphlet similarly concludes that a witch who thinks she has traveled bodily through the air while asleep is the victim of the Devil's trickery. Nevertheless, she is guilty of witchcraft in the eyes of the law: "Also sihet man / wie der Teuffel ein Lügner vnd Betrieger ist / vnd wie er / aus Gottes verhengniß / den armen Menschen die Augen jhrer Vernunfft / zuuerblenden pfleget / daß sie meinen / sie können vnnatürliche vnnd vnmügliche ding außrichten / dadurch sie jhres gefallens / den Leuten schaden zufügen / vnnd sich der straff der Obrigkeit entziehen mögen / darein sie doch endlich vnuersehens vnd plötzlich gestürtzt werden [So one sees how the Devil is a liar and deceiver, and how by God's permission he blinds the eyes of these poor people's reason, so that they think they can achieve unnatural and impossible things, and thus as they please can harm people and elude punishment by the authorities; but in the end they are suddenly and unexpectedly cast down]."[83]

Most of the German pieces, however, take the reality of what they report for granted (twenty-six of twenty-eight), while the English pamphlets commonly justify their claims to truth (thirteen of thirty-two). Some of this argumentation is tied to the intellectual pretensions of the English authors: one long pamphlet of 1650, *The strange Witch at Greenwich*, offers a dialogue between "Scepticus" and "Veridicus," filled with learned references and erudite witticisms.[84] Another cites authorities to show that the Devil cannot really transform witches into animals or carry them through the air; but like his German counterpart he concludes that they deserve punishment anyway for crediting and collaborating with Satan's delusions.[85] A pamphlet of 1579 laments that witches are often tolerated both by their neighbors and by local officials, whose slackness allows the Devil to run rampant. Another, of 1652, notes that many people do not believe in witches, but that their existence is proved both by the Bible and by the present account of the devilish deeds of Joan Peterson.[86] Even works with no claims to refinement sometimes recognize the doubts of skeptics and attempt to refute them. *Truth brought to Light,* a ballad of 1662, tells of the terrible crimes of Widow Perry,

> A wicked wretch who brought strange things to pass,
> So wonderful that some will scarce receive,
> These lines for truth nor yet my words beleive [*sic*].

But the authenticity of this account is well attested:

> Let not this seem incredible to any,
> Because it is a thing afirmed by many,
> This is no feigned story, though tis new,
> But as tis very strange tis very true.[87]

While the Devil's main purpose in England is to secure the souls of his deluded slaves, his more ambitious German counterpart uses the witches to effect catastrophes that will drive countless other Christians to despair and damnation. The harms attributed to witches were perversions of the fertility and nurture which women could ordinarily represent. In addition to causing sickness and death, witches often are reported to interfere with sex and reproduction, robbing men of their potency or women of the fruits of pregnancy. One confesses in 1580 that she has bewitched a couple to prevent intercourse, has made a well-known burgher's wife barren by causing five stillbirths, and has deformed the child of another.[88] The "alte Fritzinne" of 1579 has destroyed fetuses and caused havoc among mothers and their infants: "Etliche Sechswöcherin / jre Kinder / von jnen im schlaff weg gebracht vnd viel Sechswöcherin / von jren sinnen gebracht / da sie denn / jre Kinder selbst ertödtet [from several new mothers she took their children away while they were asleep, and many new mothers she brought from their senses, so that they killed their children themselves]."[89] Like the perpetrators of domestic crimes, witches make especially vicious attacks on children. English children are also seen as highly vulnerable to witchcraft; but there the victims or their parents generally have given some particular cause of offense, while in Germany no such explanation is given. A pamphlet of 1583, reporting the burning of 180 witches, singles out for special mention two midwives, one of whom has killed nineteen children and three mothers, the other seven children and five mothers. Another pair of midwife-sorcerers are accused of killing numerous children over the course of twenty-three years.[90] In 1609 twenty witches confess that over thirty years they have killed 568 children, some of them not yet baptized.[91] On a smaller scale, the report of Anna Eberlehrin's crimes notes her murder of "4. vnschuldige vnmündige Kinder [four innocent little children]"; and the destruction of children figures in many other accounts as well.[92] Even the witches themselves sometimes are depicted as conscious of the special evil involved in their crimes against children. At a 1582 witches' dance where the group is about to cause a terrible storm, one softhearted witch hesitates and weeps, explaining to her confederates that "Es betawren sie nur die kleinen Kindlein / vnd das vnschuldige Blut / so durch diß Wetter sollen vmbkommen [she only regretted the little children and the innocent blood that must perish because of this storm]."[93]

In addition to murdering children, German witches contaminate the food of their victims. Several seventeenth-century accounts note the arrest of innkeepers' wives who have substituted rats, snakes, or caterpillars for wholesome human food. One confesses in a pamphlet of 1603 that she has amassed over 600 gulden by serving up such vermin in place of legitimate meat. But there are still worse cases. A ring of witches exposed in 1627 not only has poisoned people by feeding them mice and rats but has cooked six people after killing them.[94] The twenty infant-killing witches of 1609 do not stop with murdering the 568 children: at night they dig up the bodies, and

ein Wirtin in der eile /	In haste then did a hostess
das fleisch gekocht jrn Gesten bald /	The flesh for customers prepare,
solches zu essen geben /	And such for food she gave them;
Mäuß Ratten auch der gstalt.[95]	Mice and rats too were there.

Another group of 900 witches engages in similar evil practices and takes still higher tolls. In the house of a single innkeeper's wife, they kill 500 people in their sleep, cook them, and serve them to guests:

Das Fleisch sie bald gekochet han /	The flesh they cooked without delay
den Gästen geben auff dem Plan /	And this before their guests did lay,
wo sie gleich sind herkommen:	No matter what their breeding.
Wenn sie hat gehabt köstlich Leut /	When noble folk did come to her
hatte sie also bald bereyt /	She straightway made them meals that were
Ottern / Raupen vnd Schlangen.[96]	Of vipers, worms, and serpents.

Unsuspecting travelers, even the wealthy and well-respected, might at any time find themselves poisoned by witches purveying human flesh and other foul meats.

Many of the German witches' evil spells, particularly those concerted by large bands of the Devil's servants, attack the whole community's crops, whether by storms, floods, frost, or supernatural disease. As with the large-scale murders of children, women, and men, such destructive witch-craft goes far beyond the harmful magic that springs from personal malice and resentment. The latter, however frightful and dangerous, has at least an intelligible and limited end. The universal malevolence of these German witches serves no one but the Devil, and its inhumanity strikes at the whole of earthly existence. The life-giving earth becomes sterile, women are made barren, youth is cut off in its first flower, all is poisoned by demonic corruption. To cause these calamities witches sometimes pour out or bury a pot filled with the pestilent materials of their witchcraft: an inverted and debased parody of insemination, sowing death instead of life. The women here doubly repudiate the positive essence of their sex, usurping the male posture in their rape of the earth and destroying fertility.[97]

Though witches provide the clearest instance of the Devil's involvement with earthly evildoers, the German themes of mass destruction and demonic inspiration tie witchcraft closely to wider patterns of crime and crime literature. Pamphlets describing bands of mass murderers offer a striking male analogue to the female witch bands.[98] These men confess to hundreds of killings, always including some pregnant women, since eating the flesh of male fetuses is supposed to make them immune to arrest. Some bands make explicit contracts with the Devil to this effect; and though they murder by conventional violence, their uncanny ability to amass such huge numbers of victims before being caught feeds the fearful consciousness of strange powers at work. In England, by contrast, the witches share with other criminals not their supernatural underpinnings but their individualized focus. Like English familial killers, they are driven by emotion to inflict harm, but for limited and definable ends.

The views of criminal women that emerge from the two literatures show the same contrasts as their differing pictures of crime and disorder in general. In the context of each country's crime, however, the places allotted to German and English women are markedly similar. The authors of each, when confronted with female malefactors, sometimes allude to women's heritage of weakness and temptability; lacking men's solidity of character, women can be expected to drift into extremes of either good or evil. On the other hand, the women of each country are integrated into the patterns of criminal behavior and description that apply to their male compatriots. For English women, this means a focus on crimes directed at particular individuals and a close imaginative scrutiny of background and motivation. The crimes publicized in German accounts more often are directed against groups, particularly familial groups; and the problem of motives is often solved by citing pure devilish inspiration. The German scene, of a community which seems to engulf individuals but is itself almost out of control, contrasts sharply with the English picture, where individualized conflicts, unpredictable but often understandable, flash out briefly against a background of relative calm and order.

Conclusion

10.

Perspectives

 The interpretation of female disorder in street literature demands a full awareness of the uncertain congruences between literature and life. Scholars have noted the paradoxical vigor of literary heroines in the classical world, where most women were immured in domesticity; the early modern contrast, though less stark, is still clear.[1] Just as the many modern depictions of devouring women cannot be taken as evidence that people expect women to act this way, or even that they have direct experience of any who do, the many violent shrews of popular literature should not lead us to conclude that husband battering was the great unreported misdemeanor of early modern society. There were violent and unruly women, as evidenced by the shaming rituals directed against them, but the literary depictions reveal less about the prevalence of the act than about imagined female disorderliness as a component of social mentality.

The literary images served a number of social and psychological uses for both sexes. One of the most obvious is the control of women through their fear of fitting an absurd or dishonorable stereotype: no one wants to be thought a shrew or a fool. Similarly, the works that blamed female misbehavior on unworthy males placed limits on acceptable male behavior. From this point of view, a worsening of an image may suggest that social behavior is not being controlled by milder forms; if women do not fear to be called shrew or men to be called cuckold, then making the image more repulsive or developing a new one may help to reimpose order. Thus the escalating violence of English shrews may suggest some increased license among English women, though not necessarily in the form of the activities shown in street literature. Another clear purpose of the depiction of female unruliness is to express fears about women and about the stability of the patriarchal order—both male fears and the fears of female disorder that may be common to both sexes. Their expression in popular literature could help control these fears through cathartic public disapproval, often with imaginary violence, or through shared laughter.[2] The functions of such images were not all restrictive, however: imagined female freedom could provide an outlet from tensions for men, as Natalie Davis has shown and as appears from the street literature's treatment of English whores. More elusive, though at least as important, is the potential liberating effect for women of the depiction of powerful women, however negatively conceived. Women need not share the dominant cultural devaluation of their role, at least not in the same terms as men: thus in early modern England they had their own views of the relative importance of chastity and submissiveness, and in other cultures they have judged their own concerns to be more significant than men's.[3] Though there is little direct evidence of women's reactions, they need not have conformed to the authors' intentions.

Thus, while authors perhaps aimed only to present warnings to unruly women through their exposure of shrews, or opiates for the female masses in their paeans to virtuously passive heroines, these by no means formed the limits of the literature's effects. The vigor of shrews and other viragoes could evoke grudging admiration even from men. The constant complaints of female domestic mastery, however modest the content of this rule, probably encouraged women to perceive themselves as powerful, within limits that they may have seen as natural or desirable rather than arbitrarily imposed. Such considerations offer hints about some of the more vexing questions of women's history: that is, why and how have women borne with male dominance for so many millennia? For the women of early modern Europe, at any rate, life within patriarchy need not have implied adoption of a slave mentality, despite the brutality with which female rebellion was often quelled in popular literature. Rather, women could have been encouraged to see themselves as mistresses of an alternative, if socially inferior, order, even as they could undermine male rule on a personal level by the use of their personal strengths of intelligence and courage. Thus popular literature could please and entertain women, and even nurture their self-respect, while continuing to serve the larger interests of patriarchal sexual politics.

The early modern changes in women's social status formed a common background to both German and English depictions of disorderly women. While population pressure and market changes combined to decrease women's economic opportunities, the consolidation of public order centered in the state increasingly restricted their activities to a more rigidly defined private sphere. In ideological terms, women were honored as wives but denied most other roles, as Reformation theology offered them spiritual equality within a system of social inferiority. The increased focus on domestic affection, which was to fill the private sphere, encouraged the perception of emotion as a peculiarly female province. For in the public world it was increasingly expected that rational men would suppress their passions, respecting the stricter boundaries being erected both between individuals and between civilized and animal behavior. Of course, women participated in this reformation of manners—in the greater privacy accorded bodily functions as in the increasing social disapproval of violence. But in the realm of cultural conceptions women still embodied disorder, for they represented the unruly drives that disturbed male self-control, the private world that persistently impinged on the public, and the natural world that resisted human attempts to impose its rational will.

The English and German depictions of female power and disorderliness in popular literature share large areas of common ground, but they also differ substantially in their attitudes toward women and gender relations. The greater English enjoyment of independent women stands against the greater German appreciation of passivity, while the English tendency to conflate all women's powers with their sexual prowess contrasts with the German emphasis on piety and intelligence as women's means of gaining influence and renown. Images of women, in turn, intertwined with differing views of the family, human personality, and the supernatural. The English literature shows concern for love between both actual and potential marriage partners, while the German focuses its attention mainly on the proper filling of roles. In the German families depicted, emotional tension and resonance lie more between parents and children than between husband and wife; the English scenes present the reverse. English authors more often explore individuals' motives and character, while German authors tend to concentrate on the external forces affecting them. Similarly, the English world appears largely subject to human influence or control; the threatening and mysterious German world, prey to unpredictable supernatural powers, offers no such reassurance. Such differences between English and German narratives, like their similarities, have roots that reach far into the culture and history of each country, and of European society as well. The attempt to trace them raises fascinating questions about the relationships between cultural attitudes toward women and their wider social context.

The greater acceptance of women's power in English street literature is accompanied by a greater doubt of male omnipotence, a doubt most clearly expressed in the male characters' recurrent worries about cuckoldry and sexual inadequacy. These preoccupations suggest both a more complicated view of sexual relations and a greater readiness to recognize and imagine female feelings. The Englishmen's sexual self-doubt is offset by a sexual bravado which claims complete mastery for men who make the sexual grade. The clash between patriarchal and companionate ideals, stronger in England than in Germany, may have fostered such doubts. The persistent focus on sex and love as determinants of women's independence places limits on their sphere even though it allows them wider latitude than the German literature: not only does the power of a woman depend directly on her relationship with men, but her power remains largely in the realm of play. From rebellion against parents to domestic violence, the English women's self-assertion tends to define itself in relation to a male. The complex English attitude thus asserts both women's importance and their triviality; sex is central to their power struggles, but on the other hand sex is merely an amusing, private game. Clearly, whatever influence the English women gain results less from their physical sexuality (which they share with German women) than from accepted ideas of their right to demand what they want. By reducing this to a purely sexual claim, male authors and audience not only defused women's sexual threat by regarding it as a joke, but also perhaps reassured themselves that sexual relations were perennially unchanging, even at a time when the politics of gender was in ferment.

English street literature's celebration of female power, especially in sexual relations, coincided with the early modern decline in the range of women's economic options. It appears that London wives were effectively excluded from positions of economic power by the mid-sixteenth century, perhaps earlier and more fully than in at least some German towns.[4] If literary misogyny reflects fears of women's economic power, as both Martha Howell and David Underdown speculate, then the lesser misogyny of England might mean that here women, already more thoroughly stripped of economic clout, were perceived as less of a threat.[5] Thus their power could be redefined and assigned to the private sphere. In England the erosion of women's economic role paralleled a growing literary emphasis on their power in the realm of interpersonal relations. Though it retained a bawdy and comic outlook, the street literature's tendency to define women's power in terms of their sexual relations with men may represent one step in the development that would ultimately ensconce women on a pedestal of nonproductive and desexualized prestige.

If the sexual fears of English males in these texts are centered on castration, those of the Germans turn rather to engulfment. Not so much the individual woman but the dangerous forces her sex represents menace both the opposite sex and humanity at large. On the most mundane level, the power of lust, though centered in women, might impel either sex to sin that could undermine the foundations of social order. More disturbing still were the mysteries that linked female bodies with the unseen. The process of generation is seen as especially subject to supernatural interference and serves to unleash unpredictable forces. Curses uttered and sins committed by or against pregnant women are imbued with heightened and deadly effect. The children that women bring forth can represent miraculous warnings from God or scions of the Devil, and both the bodies of fetuses and the milk of mothers can be turned to sinister magical purposes. Though the whole world is seen as resistant to human control, women stand closer than men to the sources of its occult disorder.

The German women themselves are depicted as unable fully to harness the unruly powers they harbor. Sex is turned against them as often as it works for them, and their scope for purposeful manipulation of its power is relatively limited. The women of the German literature are given an indirect source of power and their most effective outlet in dedication to a transcendent ideal of religion or honor. Passive in relation to earthly pursuits, the women who take this path can hope for an escape, not from the sufferings imposed by female sexuality and its dark powers, but possibly from its taint. While the ideal of female sainthood was Catholic in inspiration, it appears to have attracted the admiration of Protestants as well. The self-abnegation of saintly heroines drew universal praise from male authors, who seemed to recognize the capacity for this abnegation

But power in the realm of interpersonal relations is power, given the increasing importance of the world of Shakespeare.

and martyrdom as in some ways a special feminine gift. By turning away from the world, such women gain a spiritual power more significant than the might of their oppressors. If the English authors had touted this saintliness as the key to virtuous female power, it might have been a facile dismissal of women's earthly aspirations; but in the context of a German world so beset with uncanny perils and resistant to human control, the prescription had genuine emotional force. The martyr-heroines, while playing a role appropriate for womanhood, also were embodying an ideal applicable to both sexes. If they could see and act rightly, both women and men would do well to shift their ambitions away from the chaotic, sinful, deceptive world, where individual achievement and control were illusory, and lose themselves in God. While the German women thus are denied the self-assertion attributed to the English characters, those who choose saintly heroism have freed themselves from dependence on individual men by renouncing all that the world can give, even though at the same time they act in accordance with male conceptions of ideal female behavior.

The English focus on relationships between individuals contrasts sharply with the German concern for impersonal forces, and this contrast emerges most clearly in their depictions of familial relationships. In its frequent depiction of love not only as the prelude to wedding but also as a key ingredient in marriage itself, English popular literature belies some historians' assumptions about the emotional barrenness of early modern marriages.[6] Whether or not most spouses really used the endearments common in ballads' depictions of happy marriages, the recurrence of this theme in a literature aimed largely at those preparing for married life must have both shaped and reflected common ideals. There is no reason to suppose, either, that lower-class listeners would have found these ideals less appealing or less practical than their more propertied neighbors. The message of popular literature accords with the finding of Michael Mac-Donald that problems of love and courtship caused a substantial proportion of the mental troubles experienced by English people of relatively humble status around the turn of the seventeenth century.[7]

Such notions as these find little echo in the German literature, where the dutiful filling of marital roles can bring relative felicity, but marriage is scarcely touched by the spark of romance. Yet the German family scenes are charged with emotion, and with a tension which is often concentrated not between marital partners but between generations. The burden of children, their innocent simplicity, and the fateful consequences of improper child rearing receive far greater attention in the German literature than in the English. Not the interaction of two formerly independent individuals but people's relations with their parents and offspring rouse the greatest concern for familial bonds in German authors. The German texts concentrate on communal rather than individualist relations, on generational rather than spousal ties, on blood and status rather than contract. In doing so, they allot women greater respect and influence as mothers than do the English texts, in which women like men tend to be treated as discrete individuals despite their reproductive role. In terms of the "Malthusian" marriage system described by Alan Macfarlane, Germany fits only part of the pattern.[8] While the perception of children as costly is strongly expressed, and marriage is presented as a calculated choice, at least for men, the prime focus on the conjugal couple is missing. If the Malthusian pattern is seen as characteristic of an individualistic society, Germany would seem to have taken only partial steps in that direction; but the contrasts between Germany and England suggest that scholars have perhaps been too quick to assume a single continuum of development in modern Western familial relations.

The familial structures of England and Germany were basically similar in the sixteenth and seventeenth centuries, sharing a pattern common to northwestern Europe. Moralists of both countries, too, painted similar pictures, emphasizing rational rule by the father, submission and competent management by the mother, and respectful obedience from children and servants. In both countries children often were sent at an early age to become servants or apprentices in other households, though this practice may have been more widespread in England. Despite these similarities, the German literature shows a more intense concern for upholding the power and prestige of the father against both women and children, particularly in the works written by Protestants. The same concern appears in German legal changes that intensified the control of parents over children's marriages in the interests of preserving familial property, and that increasingly required women to transact their affairs through a male guardian.[9] The greater German interest in children, in a literature written mainly by men, suggests the possibility of greater attention by German fathers to their children's upbringing. Certainly German moralists hoped to promote such attention, and they constantly reminded their readers of parental duty and the need for discipline and education of children. In England even authors of domestic conduct books seem to have been much less interested in this issue, and writers of popular literature ignored it almost completely. German authors take parenthood more seriously for men as well as women.

The German view of children shared much with its view of women. Children, in their incompletely socialized state, were like women in retaining links with the unseen world. In street literature their bodies can be used for sorcery, they are especially susceptible to spiritual visions, and they are given their most poignant roles as passive victims. At the same time, their utterances reflect a timeless innocence and truth far removed from the reason and unreason of adults. The role of children in English street literature is negligible by comparison. Those between infancy and adolescence are hardly noticed; and those who appear, only to be rocked in their cradles or killed by cruel adults, are scarcely more than props. For this English scene of individuals engaged mainly in the rational pursuit of self-interest, it seems that children had little to say. Not that they were unloved: authors of both countries take for granted the deep affection of parents for their children. But perhaps the German outlook, with its intense awareness of subrational and irrational influences, retained an ear for messages it saw as childlike, for prattle that the English literature had banished to an invisible nursery. German authors show a keen awareness of the qualities that differentiate children from adults and imply that adults should listen to their words.[10] It is true, of course, that the children usually appear only to be slaughtered—a backhanded compliment to parental affection. But it is the view of children as tender and special that makes these scenes so poignant, and the heavy investment in children went along with a counting of their cost. The strong German concern for children, contrasted with its relative lack of concern for spousal relations—and the reverse in England—raises serious questions about the prevailing assumption among historians that companionate marriage and child-centered affections go hand-in-hand in the development of "modern" familial sensibilities. In street literature, at any rate, the two appear quite distinct, even at times opposed.

The social ideals of English and German authors both demanded a society ruled by reason, but their conceptions of this quality differed greatly. For the German literature society is cemented by a social reason which enforces strict adherence to prescribed rules and roles; individuals exercise reason through obedience to these rules. For the English, on the other hand, reason is an attribute which individuals of both sexes use in determining and expressing their will. English authors pay far more attention to their characters' inner motivation, creating a basis for imaginative identification and suggesting that both individuals' actions and the world around them respond to conscious efforts at control. For the German characters reality is both more fixed and more unstable: social divisions and the roles that people have to fill are strictly laid out, but demonic influences can interrupt the expected flow of life at any time. English authors, less worried by the prospect of uncanny phenomena, perhaps could afford a less rigid social outlook than the Germans, who—particularly in the years around 1600—seem to have felt a constant need to shore up the structure of human society against the surrounding chaos. This pervasive German anxiety about dangers lurking behind the visible world meshed with its fears of female sexuality in ways that must have helped fuel the German witch-hunting fervor: women, representing a wide range of incomprehensible powers, participated in a threat not just to individuals but to the whole fabric of human existence.

While these differences emerge clearly from a study of the two sets of street texts, their origins and development are more difficult to trace. Part of the difference between the pictures presented by German and English authors stems from the chronological gap in the distribution of their street literature. For Germany a much greater number of sources date from the sixteenth century than from the seventeenth, while for England the reverse is true. For example, the German fears of demonic activity and enjoyment of severe and harmful violence against shrews were evidently shared more by the England of the sixteenth century than by that of the seventeenth; conversely, the English preoccupation with sex may have been closer to German concerns of the seventeenth century than of the sixteenth. And the preference for male victories in marital strife belongs more to the sixteenth century than to the seventeenth. Still, this chronological difference does not account either for the magnitude of the contrasts or for the elements and developments in each country that seem to have no counterpart in the other. Moreover, one of the most striking differences—that in the depiction of familial relationships—emerges from crime literature, the genre with the greatest chronological congruence between German and English sources.

One clear contributing factor to the German sense of instability and threat appears in the contrasting political structures of the two countries.

While Tudor and Stuart England was gaining in centralization and was ruled by a common system of law, the individual German governments each fought to maintain an order whose fragility was emphasized by the conflicting jurisdictions around it. This sense of a lawless exterior world was especially powerful for cities and towns, whose careful regulation of their internal affairs contrasted sharply with the less controlled countryside where robbers, murderers, and witches might roam. Periodic warfare, with the release into the community of men trained to plunder, heightened the dangers outside the walls.

The two countries had markedly different legal systems—a relatively uniform common law in England, marked by jury trials and greater protection for the accused, as against the increasing dominance of Roman law principles in Germany, with the promotion of inquisitorial methods and judicial torture. These differences greatly affected both the treatment of criminals and the picture of them presented in popular literature. Roman law significantly influenced civil law on the Continent as well, affecting property and inheritance rights, with ambiguous results for women. While Roman inheritance rules were more egalitarian than many local laws, the Roman conception of patriarchal authority could foster increased subjection of wives and their property to husbands. Further, since Roman rules were assimilated rather than adopted wholesale, localities might pick and choose. Merry Wiesner has found that in Germany, Roman principles favorable to women were often ignored, while those that furthered male dominance were applied. Macfarlane has adduced the absence of Roman law as a possible general explanation for England's cultural divergence from the Continent, but it seems unable to bear the full weight of the contrasts. Family law proved most resistant of all legal spheres to the inroads of Roman principles on prior custom.[11] Furthermore, since the incursions of Roman law were still in process, and still contested, in the sixteenth century, it seems unlikely that it could have exerted a decisive influence on cultural conceptions of family and gender.[12]

Like the threat of physical danger, economic dangers also loomed larger for the German authors than for the English—despite the fact that the German street literature was more expensive and thus addressed a somewhat higher class of readers. Though average real wages of workers in England and Germany may have been roughly comparable during the sixteenth and seventeenth centuries, central Europe was more vulnerable to periodic crises and famines, in addition to the economic insecurity that could follow from war and crime.[13] Thus in the English ballads about families threatened with poverty, the difficulties are overcome by loving cooperation and industriousness, while the German songs present a much less hopeful picture: worthless husbands continue to leave their children and wives without bread, parents are driven by hunger and despair into doing away with their children, and the children themselves are depicted as clearly conscious of the economic burden they pose. The precariousness of German life included economic and physical as well as supernatural threats.

The Reformation involved both a revaluation of conjugal life and a theology which focused its attention on the individual soul. While both England and Germany experienced this religious change, their conceptions of marriage and the individual were hardly drawn together in parallel development. The English literature's growth of individualism and introspection stands against the German preoccupation with social cohesion; and though seventeenth-century German developments are difficult to trace from popular literature, there is little hint of a move in the English directions. For England, the Puritan movement has been credited with fostering both ideals of companionate marriage and a focus on the individual mind and character. Yet while it is conceivable that Puritanism had some indirect influence on popular literature, it is unlikely that ballads and chapbooks, forms of entertainment scorned by Puritans, would have become imbued with distinctively Puritan ideas. It is much more likely that both Puritans and balladists were expressing a broader cultural development. For Germany, similarly, Reformation ideology seems to have been less than decisive in shaping the worldview presented by street literature. Reformation ideals of marriage appear in pamphlets written by moralists, but dramatic depictions of married life fail to embody them. The emphasis on the rearing of children accorded with reformers' notions of godly discipline, but its appearance mainly in the context of tragedy and horror undercut any faith in its effectiveness. In the late sixteenth century the literature conveyed a sense of mysterious danger and impending doom which paralleled the apocalyptic thinking of many Protestants;[14] yet the threat seems to have been no weaker for works printed in Catholic areas.

In discussing the impact of the Reformation on women, Natalie Davis has argued persuasively that the Protestant gender order can be seen as more assimilationist—treating women as basically similar to men though at a lower level—while the Catholic view was more pluralistic, assigning separate spheres for male and female endeavor. Though Davis is discussing French Calvinists, assimilationist elements appear at least in theory to apply to Lutheranism and Anglicanism as well: the promotion of universal Bible reading, the abolition of separate female religious orders, lay participation in worship by both sexes.[15] From this point of view, the English social ideology appears congruent with its religious ideology, both envisioning women as slightly inferior men; but in Germany the picture is more complex. Here texts from both confessions adhere to a more pluralistic vision of gender which stresses women's maternal roles and their essential difference from men. Protestant Germany may have experienced significant tension between religious assumptions that the sexes should be basically similar and the deeply held cultural conviction that they were not.

The differences in sensibility reflected in the popular literatures of England and Germany may well have more to do with differences in social mobility than with religious dogma. The English social structure seems to have been much more fluid than the German; at least, contemporaries believed it to be so. Lawrence Stone found the mid-sixteenth to the mid-seventeenth centuries to be a time of unusually high mobility in English society.[16] His recent work has painted a more static picture over the long term, at least at the level of the elite; but it has also established English-men's persistent belief in the prevalence of social mobility.[17] Whatever the absolute numbers involved, the conviction that change in status was both possible and common clearly colored English views of social order. Germany, by contrast, showed a profound suspicion of the crossing of social boundaries. Nobles were not to engage in activities proper to burghers, nor peasants to imitate (or compete with) townsmen; rather, everyone should remain in his (and her) place.[18] This difference was intensified by the gulf between the smaller German cities and the great London metropolis, as the London environment could have fostered greater anonymity, more impersonal and "rational" relationships, and a greater potential for changes in social status. The difference is clearly reflected in street literature, with the German presenting a scene of strictly defined roles and statuses, while in England both virtuous maids and calculating whores are shown stepping overnight from poverty to luxury. Beyond this, however, a readiness to contemplate shifts of status by individuals may be linked with other differences between German and

English outlooks. If individuals' efforts of will and industry could change their social fate, then the world was more amenable to human control; at the same time, the workings of the individual's mind became more important, perhaps even more understandable. In relation to women, such attitudes could foster greater readiness to accept female initiative and to imagine female experience. In the context of broader conceptions of gender and danger, a more optimistic view of human ability to create order may have helped lessen the perceived threat of female disorder.

The greater individualism of English attitudes may come as no great surprise: Macfarlane has argued that individualism in England extends well back into the Middle Ages, with marital ideals and gender order to match.[19] Yet this picture is too static to be satisfying. Despite differences in the expression of sexual tension between England and Germany, it is clear that both countries shared in the general early modern uneasiness about relations between the sexes. Thus, an appeal to England's uniqueness does not answer our questions about the cultural meaning of the disorderly women of early modern popular culture. The development in English depictions suggests a move toward greater individualism during the sixteenth and seventeenth centuries and perhaps can serve as a model of the impact of early individualism on conceptions of gender. The view of familial relationships as essentially contractual defined women's roles as more parallel to those of men and encouraged the focus on companionate marital relationships. At the same time, it tended to devalue women's maternal, nurturant roles and to downplay their associated sources of power. Sex was still seen as their weapon, but with an emphasis on the manipulative, instrumental use of it, especially for economic self-promotion. Women were now expected to fight fair, with fairness defined not according to weapons or tactics but according to the aim toward rational, individualistic ends. The outlook that imagined the powerful, independent whore also created her obverse in the abandoned unwed mother; neither could rely on social or familial support, and both pictures underscore the competitive disadvantage that women faced in a world of individualist economics and individualist sex. The street literature does not prove that English women enjoyed more power than their German counterparts; in economic terms it may even be that the opposite was true. Rather, the English view redefines women's power to make it more consonant with men's, so that the power they do have is conceived in terms closer to theoretical equality.

In German street literature the direction of change is less clear; but it is striking that the earliest heroines, the earliest shrews, and the earliest sirens are all depicted as more active and powerful than their successors. The later sixteenth century in Germany brought a widespread tendency toward resistance to change and a hardening of social controls, as religious authorities sought to impose uniformity and town and countryside fought to stave off economic decline. In this atmosphere it is perhaps not surprising that women's options were not treated expansively. As Steven Ozment has observed in his work on the family, "to the people of Reformation Europe no specter was more fearsome than a society in which the desires of individuals eclipsed their sense of social duty."[20] While English and German moralists in the main would have agreed on this anti-individualist stance, German authors were less willing to suspend it, even in imagination. The picture of early modern Germany's movement toward individualism as drawn by David Sabean, with its emphasis on an ideology imposed from above, differs sharply from the English experience as described by Macfarlane and others, in which individualist conceptions seem embedded in social relations at the local level.[21] The street literature suggests that there was especially strong resistance in Germany to extending individualist conceptions to women. Marital choices and self-promotion are attributed primarily to men; and even the witch figure, who in Sabean's analysis represents a step toward the idea of a consistent, discrete individual, dissolves in street texts into a larger evil independent of her will. For German authors the paramount aim was social cohesion, for whose preservation the power of all individuals must be turned to the service of order. The disorderly woman was too disruptive to be allowed free rein.

Abbreviations and Short Citations

Notes

Bibliography

Index

Abbreviations
and Short Citations

Locations

BL	British Library, London
Bod.	Bodleian Library, Oxford
BSB	Bayrische Staatsbibliothek, Munich
DSB	Deutsche Staatsbibliothek, Berlin
GNM	Germanisches Nationalmuseum, Nuremberg
HAB	Herzog-August Bibliothek, Wolfenbüttel
Lambeth	Lambeth Palace, London
NLS	National Library of Scotland, Edinburgh
Pepys	Pepys Library, Magdalene College, Cambridge
SA	Society of Antiquaries, London
SBPK	Staatsbibliothek Preussischer Kulturbesitz, Berlin
ZB	Zentralbibliothek Zurich

Printed Collections

BB   J. W. Ebsworth, ed. *The Bagford Ballads.* 2 vols. Hertford, Eng.: Ballad Society, 1878.

Euing   *The Euing Collection of English Broadside Ballads* (Glasgow: University of Glasgow Publications, 1971).

PA   Hyder Edward Rollins, ed. *The Pack of Autolycus.* Cambridge, Mass.: Harvard University Press, 1927.

PB   Hyder Edward Rollins, ed. *The Pepys Ballads.* 2 vols. Cambridge, Mass.: Harvard University Press, 1922.

PG   Hyder Edward Rollins, ed. *A Pepysian Garland.* Cambridge, Eng.: Cambridge University Press, 1922.

RB   *The Roxburghe Ballads.* Vols. 1–3 ed. William Chappell; vols. 4–9 ed. J. W. Ebsworth. Hertford, Eng.: Ballad Society, 1872–99.

79 Ballads   *A Collection of Seventy-Nine Black-Letter Ballads and Broadsides, Printed in the Reign of Queen Elizabeth. . . .* London: Joseph Lilly, 1867.

Shirburn   Andrew Clark, ed. *The Shirburn Ballads.* Oxford: Clarendon Press, 1907.

Blümml   Emil Karl Blümml, ed. *Ludwig Uhlands Sammelband fliegender Blätter aus der zweiten Hälfte des 16. Jahrhunderts.* Strassburg: J. H. Ed. Heitz, 1911.

Brednich   Rolf Wilhelm Brednich. *Die Liedpublizistik im Flugblatt des 15. bis 17. Jahrhunderts.* 2 vols. Baden-Baden: Verlag Valentin Koerner, 1974–75.

Brückner   Wolfgang Brückner. *Populäre Druckgraphik Europas: Deutschland vom 15. bis zum 20. Jahrhunderts.* Munich: Georg D. W. Callwey, 1969.

Coupe   William A. Coupe. *The German Illustrated Broadsheet in the Seventeenth Century.* Baden-Baden: Verlag Librarie Heitz, 1966.

Goetze   Edmund Goetze, ed. *Sämtliche Fabeln und Schwänke von Hans Sachs.* Vols. 1 and 2. Halle: Max Niemeyer, 1893.

Liliencron   Rochus von Liliencron. *Die historischen Volkslieder der Deutschen vom 13. bis 16. Jahrhundert.* Leipzig, 1865; rept. Hildesheim: Georg Olms Verlagsbuchhandlung, 1966.

Wäscher   Hermann Wäscher. *Das deutsche illustrierte Flugblatt.* Dresden: Verlag der Kunst, 1955.

Miscellaneous

brs.   Broadside
16c   Sixteenth century
17c   Seventeenth century

Notes

2. Gender and Disorder in Early Modern Europe

1. I use *patriarchy* as a useful shorthand term for early modern male dominance, with no implication that social power was exclusively in the hands of fathers. Cf. Ezell, *Patriarch's Wife*.

2. See Ortner, "Is Female to Male as Nature Is to Culture?" For critiques and elaborations of this idea, see McCormack and Strathern, *Nature, Culture, and Gender*.

3. See Douglas, *Purity and Danger*, esp. pp. 94–113.

4. See Beauvoir, *The Second Sex*.

5. See Rogers, *Troublesome Helpmate*; Hays, *Dangerous Sex*.

6. Davis, *Society and Culture in Early Modern France*, 124–51; see also Davis, " 'Women's History' in Transition."

7. See Amussen, *An Ordered Society*; Underdown, "Taming of the Scold"; Roper, *Holy Household*; Mary Elizabeth Perry, *Gender and Disorder in Early Modern Seville* (Princeton, N.J., 1990).

8. On the historical analysis of gender, see Scott, "Gender: A Useful Category of Historical Analysis." Following Scott, I use the term *gender* to refer to the socially constructed elaboration of sex roles; but I resist the use of *gender* as a simple substitute for *sex*, which threatens to become a euphemism that obscures more than it enlightens.

9. Clark, *Working Life of Women in the Seventeenth Century*; Bücher, *Die Frauenfrage im Mittelalter*.

10. Howell, *Women, Production, and Patriarchy in Late Medieval Cities*; Wiesner, *Working Women in Renaissance Germany*; Davis, "Women in the Crafts in Sixteenth-Century Lyon"; Howell, "Women, the Family Economy, and the Structures of Market Production"; Cahn, *Industry of Devotion*.

11. Wiesner, *Working Women in Renaissance Germany*, 4–5; on women's work in Germany, see also Maschke, *Die Familie in der deutschen Stadt des späten Mittelalters*, 35–41.

12. See Wiesner, *Working Women in Renaissance Germany*; Clark, *Working Life of Women in the Seventeenth Century*; Willen, "Women in the Public Sphere in Early Modern England," 562–64.

13. Emmanuel Le Roy Ladurie, *The Peasants of Languedoc*, trans. John Day (Urbana, Ill., 1974), 110–12.

14. See Cahn, *Industry of Devotion*, 204–5n.

15. See Macfarlane, *Marriage and Love in England*, 264; Lawrence Stone, *The Crisis of the Aristocracy, 1558–1641*, abridged ed. (London, 1967), 290.

16. On this development in Italy, see Christiane Klapisch-Zuber, *Women, Family, and Ritual in Renaissance Italy*, trans. Lydia Cochrane (Chicago, 1985), 214–16.

17. See Herlihy, *Medieval Households*, 100–101. Of course, other factors, such as demographics and general economic structure, also play a role. For additional studies of European dowry, see Marion A. Kaplan, ed., *The Marriage Bargain: Women and Dowries in European History* (New York, 1985).

18. See Herlihy, *Women in Medieval Society*; Herlihy, "Life Expectancies for Women in Medieval Society"; cf. Ennen, *Medieval Woman*, 161–63.

19. See Hajnal, "European Marriage Patterns in Perspective"; Mitterauer and Sieder, *European Family*, 35–37.

20. Laslett, *World We Have Lost*, 81–106; Flandrin, *Families in Former Times*, 50–92; McLaren, "Marital Fertility and Lactation"; Dülmen, *Kultur und Alltag*, 23–38.

21. See Flandrin, *Families in Former Times*; Mitterauer and Sieder, *European Family*.

22. Stone, *Family, Sex, and Marriage*; also exaggerated is Shorter, *Making of the Modern Family*.

23. See, e.g., Wrightson, *English Society*, 89–118; Houlbrooke, *English Family*; Pollock, *Forgotten Children*; MacDonald, *Mystical Bedlam*, 75–85, 88–105; Ozment, *When Fathers Ruled* and *Magdalena and Balthasar*.

24. See Macfarlane, *Marriage and Love in England*.

25. Ozment, *When Fathers Ruled* and *Magdalena and Balthasar*.

26. Roper, *Holy Household*.

27. See Davies, "The Sacred Condition of Equality."

28. See Stone, "The Rise of the Nuclear Family in Early Modern England," 53–54; M. Weber, *Ehefrau und Mutter*, 283.

29. See Thomas, "Women and the Civil War Sects"; Mack, "Women as Prophets."

30. See Davis, "City Women and Religious Change," in *Society and Culture in Early Modern France*, 65–95; Roper, *Holy Household*, 206–51.

31. Larner, "Crimen Exceptum"; Larner, *Enemies of God*, 100–102; Monter, "Protestant Wives, Catholic Saints, and the Devil's Handmaid." See also Coudert, "Myth of the Improved Status of Protestant Women."

32. See Larner, *Enemies of God*, 25; Jean Delumeau, *Catholicism between Luther and Voltaire* (London, 1977).

33. Flandrin, *Families in Former Times*, 127–29.

34. See ibid., 180–84; Otis, *Prostitution in Medieval Society*; Roper, *Holy Household*, 89–131.

35. Miles, *Carnal Knowing*, 127–35.

36. See Thomas, "The Double Standard"; Klaits, *Servants of Satan*. On the fear of women and their sexuality, see Delumeau, *La peur en Occident*, 305–45.

37. See Stone, "Interpersonal Violence in English Society."

38. Burke, *Popular Culture in Early Modern Europe*, 207–43; see also Delumeau, *Catholicism between Luther and Voltaire*; Stallybrass and White, *Politics and Poetics of Transgression*.

39. See Otis, *Prostitution in Medieval Society*; Wiesner, "Women's Defense of Their Public Role."

40. See Kelly, "The Social Relation of the Sexes" and "Did Women Have a Renaissance?" in *Women, History, and Theory*, 1–50.

41. See Elias, *Civilizing Process*; Honegger, *Die Hexen der Neuzeit*, 1–151. Hans Peter Duerr has pointed out that there is no such thing as uncivilized human society, the supposed starting point of this development; but the issue here is Europeans' perceptions of the process. See Duerr, *Der Mythos vom Zivilisationsprozeß: Nacktheit und Scham* (Frankfurt am Main, 1988).

42. See Honegger, *Die Hexen der Neuzeit*; Bovenschen, "Die aktuelle Hexe, die historische Hexe, und der Hexenmythos."

43. Roger Finlay and Beatrice Shearer, "Population Growth and Suburban Expansion," in *London, 1500–1700: The Making of the Metropolis*, ed. A. L. Beier and Roger Finlay (London, 1986), 39.

44. Wrigley, "A Simple Model of London's Importance," 51.

45. Powell, *English Domestic Relations, 1487–1653*, 174–75; Hogrefe, *Tudor Women*, 8–9.

46. See, e.g., M. Weber, *Ehefrau und Mutter*, 233.

47. Ibid., 239; Koebner, "Die Eheauffassung des ausgehenden deutschen Mittelalters," 161.

48. For the extraordinary latitude allowed to German husbands, see M. Weber, *Ehefrau und Mutter*, 216.

49. See Kelso, *Doctrine for the Lady of the Renaissance*, 83–87; Koebner, "Die Eheauffassung des ausgehenden deutschen Mittelalters," 162–69.

50. For such writings directed to English women, see Hull, *Chaste, Silent, and Obedient*; Kelso, *Doctrine for the Lady of the Renaissance*.

51. Koebner, "Die Eheauffassung des ausgehenden deutschen Mittelalters," 282.

52. On sexual fears in witch-hunting, see Klaits, *Servants of Satan*, 48–85.

53. See Levack, *Witch-Hunt in Early Modern Europe*, 124–28, 182–84.

54. See Cohn, *Europe's Inner Demons;* Muchembled, *Culture populaire et culture des élites;* Kieckhefer, *European Witch Trials.*

55. Thomas, *Religion and the Decline of Magic*, 520–26, 568–69; Macfarlane, *Witchcraft in Tudor and Stuart England*, 161; Midelfort, *Witch Hunting in Southwestern Germany*, 184–85; Larner, *Enemies of God*, 100–102.

56. Stone, *Family, Sex, and Marriage*, 189–91, 272–74.

57. See Carlson, "Marriage and the English Reformation," 341–416; Macfarlane, *Marriage and Love in England*, 294–98.

58. See Roper, *Holy Household*, 159–60.

59. See Robisheaux, *Rural Society and the Search for Order*, 106–15; Dülmen, *Kultur und Alltag*, 136–39.

60. See Macfarlane, *Marriage and Love in England* and *Origins of Individualism.*

3. The Literature of the Streets

1. For a discussion of the problem of these "mediators" in interpreting popular culture, see Burke, *Popular Culture in Early Modern Europe*, 65–77.

2. Rollins, "Black-Letter Broadside Ballad," 321; see also Roth, *Die neuen Zeitungen*, 74; Brednich, 1:136.

3. For a stimulating analysis of women's responses to popular modern texts, see Janice A. Radway, *Reading the Romance: Women, Patriarchy, and Popular Literature* (Chapel Hill, N.C., 1984).

4. See Würzbach, *Rise of the English Street Ballad*, 54–64.

5. Rollins, "Black-Letter Broadside Ballad," 296.

6. Altick, *English Common Reader*, 22; *Tarltons Jests* [c. 1590?, 1611, 1638], in Hazlitt, *Shakespeare Jest-Books* 2:232.

7. Rogers, *History of Agriculture and Prices in England* 5:664–69. See also Phelps Brown and Hopkins, "Seven Centuries of Building Wages" and "Seven Centuries of the Prices of Consumables."

8. See Cook, *Privileged Playgoers*, 228–36.

9. See Wright, *Songs and Ballads;* Würzbach, *Rise of the English Street Ballad*, 253.

10. Rollins, "Black-Letter Broadside Ballad," 277. See also Würzbach, *Rise of the English Street Ballad*, 262, 279.

11. S. F., *Death in a New Dress: Or Sportive Funeral Elegies* . . . (1656), 8 fols., A4 (BL).

12. See Rollins, *Analytical Index*, v.

13. Rollins, "Black-Letter Broadside Ballad," 321.

14. See, for example, Henry Goodcole, *The wonderfull discouerie of Elizabeth Sawyer a Witch, late of Edmonton* . . . (1621), 14 fols., A3v (BL); Würzbach, *Rise of the English Street Ballad*, 242–52.

15. Thomas Nashe, *The Anatomie of Absurditie*, quoted in Würzbach, *Rise of the English Street Ballad*, 258.

16. See Rollins, "Martin Parker" and "William Elderton"; Esdaile, "Autolycus' Pack"; Mann, *Works of Thomas Deloney*, vii–xiv.

17. See Rollins, "Black-Letter Broadside Ballad," 260.

18. Ibid., 296–304.

19. See, e.g., Gerald E. Bentley, *The Jacobean and Caroline Stage* (Oxford, 1968), 6:135.

20. Chaucer Junior, pseud., *Canterbury Tales* . . . (1687), 12 fols. (Pepys).

21. Cressy, *Literacy and the Social Order*, 72, 176. Cressy expresses his figures as percentages of illiteracy. On the audience for seventeenth-century chapbooks, particularly in rural areas, see also Spufford, *Small Books and Pleasant Histories*, 19–75.

22. See Cressy, *Literacy and the Social Order*, 20–25; Spufford, *Small Books and Pleasant Histories*, 22.

23. Roth, *Die neuen Zeitungen*, 74–78. Control seems to have become more strict toward the end of the sixteenth century.

24. Schottenloher, *Flugblatt und Zeitung*, 147.

25. *Ein Schön New Geistlich Lied / so wider das vnfletige Schandt Huren liedlein / das Jagts jm zu gemacht ist worden / so man jetzundt gar gemein pfleget zu singen* . . . (1569), 4 fols., A2–A2v (BL).

26. Roth, *Die neuen Zeitungen*, 68–69.

27. Brednich, 1:75.

28. Ecker, *Einblattdrucke von den Anfängen bis 1555* 1:50; B. Weber, *Wunderzeichen und Winkeldrucker*, 25–30.

29. Coupe, 14, 19; Krieg, *Materialien zu einer Entwicklungsgeschichte der Bücher-Preise*, 23.

30. Krieg, *Materialien zu einer Entwicklungsgeschichte der Bücher-Preise*, 17, 21.

31. Pribram, *Materialien zur Geschichte der Preise und Löhne in Öster-reich* 1:641–42, 570.

32. Elsas, *Umriss einer Geschichte der Preise und Löhne in Deutschland* 1:22–23, 73–74.

33. See Coupe, 13.

34. Barbara Münchheym, *Ein new Lied. Von der Gottseligen wie auch Heiligen Frawen Sanct Ita* . . . (Rorschach am Bodensee, 1614), 8 fols. (BL).

35. Krieg, *Materialien zu einer Entwicklungsgeschichte der Bücher-Preise*, 82.

36. See Engelsing, *Analphabetentum und Lektüre*, 34–36; Becker-Cantarino, *Der Lange Weg zur Mündigkeit*, 152, 161–64.

37. Strauss, *Luther's House of Learning*, 200; see also Engelsing, *Analphabetentum und Lektüre*, 39. For a recent study that finds substantial literacy among peasants in seventeenth-century Mecklenburg, see Jochen Richter, "Zur Schriftkundigkeit mecklenburgischen Bauern im 17. Jahrhundert," *Jahrbuch für Wirtschaftsgeschichte* 1981 (3): 79–102.

38. It should be noted, however, that the designation of Cologne was sometimes spurious; see Weller, *Die falschen und fingirten Druckorte*, v.

39. See Würzbach, *Rise of the English Street Ballad*, 25–26. Würzbach may underestimate the social status of the ballad public. See also Ecker, *Einblattdrucke von den Anfängen bis 1555* 1:102–9.

40. See, e.g., *The Complete Fairy Tales of the Brothers Grimm*, trans. Jack Zipes (Toronto, 1987); Böhme, *Altdeutsches Liederbuch*; Francis James Child, ed., *The English and Scottish Popular Ballads*, 2 vols. (New York, 1962).

41. Goedeke, *Grundrisz zur Geschichte der deutschen Dichtung* 2:24.

42. *A Woman's Work is never done* [1629, 1650s], *RB* 3:301–6.

43. L. W., *The Maidens sad complaint for want of a Husband* [mid-17c], brs. (Douce Ballads 2:145, Bod.).

44. *The Virgins A.B.C.* [c. 1684], in *Euing*, no. 369; *The Young-Mans A.B.C.* (1684), in *Euing*, no. 407; Cuntz Haß, *Du junger man merck vnd versteh / Vnd wilt du greyffen zu der Ehe . . .* (Nuremberg, [2d half 16c]), 8 fols. (SBPK Yg 5456).

45. On the differences between oral literature and other genres, see Frye, *Anatomy of Criticism*, 243–51; for a genre study with extensive analysis of oral performance and its effects on ballad texts, see Würzbach, *Rise of the English Street Ballad*.

46. See Rollins, *Analytical Index*. The loss has been especially great among sixteenth-century titles.

47. See ibid. My English sources include 72 items from the sixteenth century, but the registers list 136 relevant ballads which are no longer extant.

48. Wehse, *Schwanklied und Flugblatt in Großbritannien*, 44.

49. Brednich, 1:16–17.

4. Woman as Protagonist: Virtue and Disorder

1. In its medieval courtly lyrics Germany produced many female-voiced songs, but this tradition seems not to have flourished in later street literature. On the courtly genre, see Plummer, *Vox Feminae*.

2. Schotter, "Woman's Song in Medieval Latin," 29–30.

3. Interestingly, the few German female-voiced songs include two of this type: *Valet-Lied A.M.T.G.D. Wegen durch Gifft Ertödteten Ehmanns Peinlich leidenden Sünderin* (1665) (BL), and *Wunderbarliche vnnd seltzame Geschicht / so sich hat zugetragen / In der Keyserlichen Freyen Reychstatt Nörlingen / Von einem Weybsbild / die sich für ein Manns person außgeben hat . . . mit jhrem rechten Tauffnammen Eua Balbiererin von Glotz . . .* (Basel, 1566) (ZB; another ed. 1566).

4. *A Woman's Work is never done* [1629, 1650s], *RB* 3:301–6.

5. See, e.g., Ludwig Binder, *Diß lied sagt von Lucretia . . .* (Nuremberg, [c. 1560?]) (BL): Hans Sachs, *Dreyerley klagred dreyer Weibsbild / Lucrecie / Thisbes / vnd Virginie* (1554) (BL); Sachs, *Die neun getrewen Hayden . . .* (Nuremberg, 1553) (BL); *Susanna Lied. Von der Gottsfürchtigen vnnd Keuschen Frawen Susanna . . .* (1615) (DSB Yd 7853.24); *A Looking Glass for Ladies* [1670s], *RB* 6:553–55; *A most pleasant Ballad of Patient Grissell* [16c, 1624, 1675], *RB* 2:268–74.

6. Hans Schirenbrandt, *Ein hüpsch news Lied / von der frommen vnd Gotsförchtigen Frawen Susanna* (Augsburg, [c. 1560]), 7 fols., A4v (BL; another ed.: Augsburg, c. 1600).

7. *An excellent Ballad Intituled: The Constancy of Susanna* [1563, 1592, 1624, 1675], *RB* 1:190–96.

8. In some classical sources the parent nurtured is the mother; see *Notes and Queries,* 4th ser., 2 (1868): 277.

9. *Zwey schöne herliche Meisterlieder. 1 Auß dem Cento Nouella. . . . 2. Von der grossen Trew der Edlen Tugendsammen Frawen . . .* (n.d.), 4 fols. (BL).

10. *A worthy example of a Vertuous Wife, who fed her Father with her own milk* [1596, 1624, 1675], *RB* 8:4–6.

11. Hans Sachs, *Die zwölff durch leuchtige Weyber des alten Testaments . . .* (Augsburg, 1596), 8 fols. (BL; other eds.: Nuremberg, 1553, c. 1553).

12. See Sachs, *Die neun getrewen Hayden* (1553).

13. *Newe Zeytung. Von einem Megdlein das entzuckt ist gewest / vnd was wunderbarliche Rede es gethan hat / geschehen zu Freyberg in Meyssen im Jar. M.D.LX.* (Nuremberg, 1560), 4 fols., A2v–A3 (SBPK).

14. Ph. Z., *New Zeitung Geschehen in Der Stadt Magdeburgck . . . von einem megdlein Von Acht Jahren . . .* (Magdeburg, 1577) (BL; another ed.: n.p., 1577).

15. *Drey Warhafftige Newe Zeittung. Die Erste von Einem Meidlein von achtzehen jaren* (Ursel, 1594), 4 fols. (BL). See also *Drey Erschröckenliche newe Zeitungen. Die Erste: Warhafftige vnnd zuvor vnerhörte newe Zeitung / so sich im Böhmerwaldt / in einem Wirtzhauß zum Stock begeben . . . 1609 . . .* (Prague[?], 1609[?]) (ZB); *Warhafftige Newe Zeitung von einem Töchterlein / welches siben Jahr alt gewesen . . .* (Augsburg, 1618) (BL); *Eine warhafftige Newe Zeitung / welche sich begeben vnnd zugetragen hat im Land zu Meissen / in einer Stadt Schaffstet genant / mit eines Bürgers Tochter . . .* (Leipzig, 1616) (DSB Yd 7851.13); *Dreyerlei. Denckwürtige vnd warhafftige . . . Zeytung auß*

Prag / . . . *Warhafftige Propheceyung* / *eines Scheffers Töchterlein* . . . (1581) (SBPK); *Prophezeyhung* / *eines armen Bawren Tochter in Preussen* . . . (Danzig[?], 1580) (SBPK).

16. L[aurence] P[rice], *A Wonderful Prophecy* [1656, 1680s], *RB* 8:81–84 (2 other eds.).

17. *The Godly Maid of Leicester* [1675, 1680s], *RB* 8:86–89.

18. *The Sorrowful Mother; Or, The Pious Daughter's Last Farewel* [1680s–90s?], *RB* 8:90–92.

19. *Drey Geistliche Lieder* / *Das Erste* / *Susanna keusch vnd zart* / . . . *Das Ander* / *Von Sanct Dorothea* / (1668), 4 fols., A2v (BL; other eds.: Augsburg, 1636, Nuremberg, c. 1600).

20. *Andächtiger Ruff Von dem H. Leben vnd Marterkampff* / *der glorwürdigen Jungfrawen Sanct Barbara* (Ingolstatt, 1613), 10 fols. (BL).

21. *Ein hübsch new Geistlich Lied von der H. Jungkfrauwen vnd Märterin S. Catharina* (Freiburg, 1607), 8 fols., A4 (BL).

22. *Andächtiger Rueff* / *Von dem H. Leben vnd Marterkampff* / *der glorwürdigen Jungkfrawen S. Catharina* . . . (Augsburg, 1631), 34 pp., 13 (BL). See also *Drey schöne Neue Geistliche Lieder* / *Das Erste: Von S. Catharina* . . . (Augsburg, [17c]), 4 fols. (BL; another ed.: Augsburg, c. 1640).

23. Münchheym, *Ein new Lied. Von der Gottseligen wie auch Heiligen Frawen Sanct Ita* (1614), A4v, A7v.

24. On the adoption of a religious voice by early women writers in England, see Beilin, *Redeeming Eve*, xx–xxii, 49–50.

25. On the cult of Mary and its significance, see Warner, *Alone of All Her Sex*.

26. *Ein schöne Litaney* / *Von der Allerseligsten Jungfraw und Mutter Gottes Maria* . . . (1686), 4 fols., A4 (BL).

27. See Garth, "Saint Mary Magdalene."

28. *Ein schön Geistliches Lied* / *Von der Heyligen Büsserin* / *Maria Magdalena. Seyt gladen ihr jung Cavalier* . . . (Augsburg, [c. 1650?]), 4 fols., A2, A2v–A3 (BL). See also *S. Maria Magdalena* (Augsburg, [c. 1650?]), brs. (BL).

29. See Münchheym, *Ein new Lied. Von der Gottseligen wie auch Heiligen Frawen Sanct Ita* (1614), A7v.

30. *Ein neüw Lied* / *von einer Jungfrawen die mit dem bösen geist besessen was* . . . [c. 1559], 4 fols., A1v, A2, A3 (ZB; 3 other eds. c. 1559).

31. Sebastian Khueller, *Kurtze Vnnd warhafftige Historia* / *von einer Junckfrawen* / *welche mit etlich vnd dreissig bösen Geistern leibhafftig besessen* / *vnd . . . erlödiget worden* (Munich, [1540?]), 7 fols., B1 (HAB).

32. *Wonderful News from Buckinghamshire. Or, A Perfect Relation How a young Maid hath been for Twelve years and upwards possest with the Devil* . . . (1677), 8 pp. (BL).

33. *The Distressed Gentlewoman* [c. 1691?], *PA*, 226–28.

34. *A strange and true Relation Of A Young Woman possest with the*

Devill. By name Joyce Dovey . . . (1647), in Foster, *Reprints of English Books, 1475–1700,* no. 35, p. 5.

35. *Der Alexander von Metz . . .* [c. 1550?], 8 fols. (BL; other eds.: Bamberg, 1493, Erfurt, 1495, Nuremberg, 1515, 1521, Zurich, c. 1545, and n.p., 1613).

36. See Martin Mayr, *Ain Schön lied / von ainem Ritter auß der Steyrmarck / genant Trinumitas / vnd von aines Künigs Tochter auß Dennmarck / genant Floredebel* (Augsburg, [2d half 16c]), 8 fols. (BL; other eds.: Nuremberg, 1507, c. 1510, 1532, c. 1600, Zurich, c. 1545, Bremen, c. 1581, Basel, 1582, c. 1610).

37. *The first part of the Marchant's Daughter of Bristow* [1595, 1624, 1675], *RB* 2:86–95.

38. *The Valiant Virgin* [1670s?], *RB* 7:546–48.

39. *The true Mayde of the South* [1st half 17c], *RB* 2:626–32; *An Admirable New Northern Story* [2d half 17c], *RB* 1:24–29. On the extensive literature dealing with such themes, see Dugaw, *Warrior Women and Popular Balladry.*

40. See chap. 8 below.

41. *A new Ballad of bold Robin Hood* [2d half 17c], *RB* 2:440–48.

42. J. P., *A Fairing for Maids* [1639, 1656], *RB* 8:676–77.

43. Tobias Bowne, *Tobias' Observation* [1687], *RB* 7:155–56.

44. L[aurence?] P[rice?], *The Batchelor's Feast* [1636], *RB* 1:46–51. See also *The Batchelor's Triumph, RB* 3:427–29; *Clod's Caroll, RB* 1:201–6.

45. *Drey Schöne Newe Kurtzweilige Lieder zum erstenmahl in Druck außgangen. Das Erste. Von einer Jungfraw / die dreyzehen Freyer gehabt . . .* (1658), 4 fols., A2–A2v (GNM).

46. *Zwey schöne newe lieder / Das erst / Winter. . . . Das ander Lied sagt von eines Kauffmans döchterlein . . .* [16c], in Blümml, no. 52(2).

47. *Zwey schöne newe Meyster Lieder: Das Erst: Wie drey Frawen vber jhre Mäyd klagen / . . . Das ander / die faulen Haußmeyd . . .* (1611), 4 fols. (BL).

48. See *Ein schön Geistliches Lied / Von der Heyligen Büsserin / Maria Magdalena* [c. 1650?].

5. The Locus of Power: Marital Order

1. Kelso, *Doctrine for the Lady of the Renaissance,* 83–87; Stone, *Family, Sex, and Marriage,* 325–26; Koebner, "Die Eheauffassung des ausgehenden deutschen Mittelalters," 162–69, 279; Moser-Rath, "Das streitsüchtige Eheweib"; *Der frawen Spiegel in wellichem spiegel sich das weyblich byld / jung oder altt beschauwen oder lernen / zu ge brauchen / die woltat gegen irem eelichen gemahel* [1520?] (BL).

2. Dülmen, *Kultur und Alltag,* 45–46.

3. Jegel, "Altnürnberger Zensur," 61.

4. *Zwey Hüpsche lieder / Das erst / Nach allen Creaturen / gfalt mir nit mee . . .* (Bern, 1564), in Blümml, no. 51(1) (another ed.: Zurich, c. 1545).

5. *Zwey Schöne Newe Lieder / wie man ein Braut Geystlich ansingen soll* (Straubing, [1560s]), 4 fols., A2 (DSB Yd 7831.51).

6. *Ein lied vom Ehestand . . .* [16c], brs. (DSB Yd 7803.5).

7. *Spiegel einer Christlichen vnd friedsamen Haußhaltung* (Nuremberg, [c. 1650]), brs. (BL).

8. Sachs, *Die neun getrewen Hayden* (1553).

9. *Der Alexander von Metz* [c. 1550?], A8v. See also the similar "Der Graf von Rom," in Böhme, *Altdeutsches Liederbuch*, 38–42.

10. *Susanna Lied. Von der Gottsfürchtigen vnnd Keuschen Frawen Susanna* (1615), A1v.

11. *Ein lied von einem eelichen volck . . .* [early 16c], brs. (DSB Yd 7801.2).

12. *Ein schön newes Lied / ob eim jungen Gesellen ein Weyb zu nemen sey oder nit / . . .* (Augsburg, [1603?]), 4 fols. (BL; another ed. c. 1560).

13. Hans Sachs, *Der Buler Artzney. Mehr die Neun Geschmeck inn dem Ehelichen standt* (Nuremberg, [mid-16c]), 10 fols., A4, B1v–B2 (BL).

14. *The Bride's Good-morrow* [16c, 1624], *RB* 1:63–64.

15. Thomas Deloney, "A Song in Praise of a Single Life" [late 16c], in *Garland of Good-Will*, 48.

16. *The Poor Man's Counsellor; Or, The Marryed-man's Guide* [1670s], *RB* 8:103–4.

17. *The Wonderful Praise of a Good Husband* [1685–88], *RB* 7:147–48.

18. Thomas Deloney, *The most rare and excellent History of the Dutchesse of Suffolke's Calamity* [16c, 1624, 1675], *RB* 1:291–92.

19. *The valiant Commander with his resolute Lady* [1640s?, 1670s], *RB* 6:281–83.

20. *The Maid's Comfort* [mid-17c], *RB* 8:cxxix*–cxxxi*.

21. *A constant Wife, a kinde Wife, A louing Wife, and a fine Wife, Which giues content vnto mans life* [1631, 1656, 1675], *PB* 2:202–6.

22. *The Benefit of Marriage* [1663–64], in *Euing*, no. 18.

23. *The Housholder's New-Yeere's Gift* [1598, mid-17c], *RB* 1:128.

24. *The Chearful Husband: or, The Despairing Wife* [late 17c], *RB* 3:514–17.

25. M[artin] P[arker], *Robin and Kate; or, A bad husband converted by a good wife* [1634], *RB* 2:413–18.

26. *A new Ballad, Containing a communication between the carefull Wife and the comfortable Hus[band,] touching the common cares and charges of House-hold* [mid-17c], *RB* 1:122–25; *A Dainty new Dialogue between Henry and Elizabeth* [late 17c], *RB* 3:663–66; *The Carefull Wife's Good Counsel* [late 17c], *RB* 3:478–80.

27. J[ohn] Wade, *A Good Wife is a Portion every day* (1673), *RB* 6:332–35; text here follows the original in BL.

28. *Ein schön new Lied von ainem man der seinem weyb auff einem brieff*

schrieb was sie thon oder lassen sol / vnd wie ehs Im gieng [c. 1550], 4 fols., A2 (BL). On the recommendation of feminine wiles to coax a husband into virtue, see Ozment, *When Fathers Ruled,* 70.

29. *Ein schön new Lied / wie ein fraw jren Mann strafft / vnd weret jm er sol nit zum wein geen* . . . [c. 1550], 4 fols., A2 (BL; other eds. c. 1560, c. 1580[?]).

30. *Ein schön new Lied von ainem man der seinem weyb auff einem brieff schrieb* [c. 1550], A1v, A2.

31. *The Woman to the Plow, And the Man to the Hen-Roost* [1629, 1675, 1680s], *RB* 7:185–87. This exchange of tasks, a common theme in folklore, appeared also in German jestbooks; see Moser-Rath, "*Lustige Gesellschaft,*" 11, 119.

32. *The Knight and the Beggar-Wench* [1658], in *Euing,* no. 155.

33. *The Biter Bitten* [1680s], *RB* 3:445–48.

34. *The Taylor's Lamentation* (1685), *RB* 7:474.

35. *Zwey Schone newe Lieder / genanndt der Rolandt / von der Männer vnd Weyber vntrew* [16c], 6 fols., A4v, A5 (DSB Yd 7850.17).

36. Hans Sachs, *Der Lose Mann* (Nuremberg, 1556) (BL); see also *Zwey Schöner newer Lieder / das erste / Es het ein Fraw ein losen Man* . . . (Nuremberg, [2d half 16c]) DSB Yd 8571).

37. *Drey Warhafftige Newe Zeittung. Die Erste von Einem Meidlein von achtzehen jaren* (1594).

38. Münchheym, *Ein new Lied. Von der Gottseligen wie auch Heiligen Frawen Sanct Ita* (1614).

39. See chap. 7 below.

40. *A most pleasant Ballad of Patient Grissel* [16c, 1624, 1675], *RB* 2:268–74; *The Antient, True, and Admirable History of Patient Grisel, A Poore Mans Daughter in France: Shewing, How Maides, by her example, in their good behauiour may marrie rich Hvsbands* . . . (1619), 16 fols (BL).

41. *Constance of Cleveland* [1603, 1624, 1650s], *RB* 6:572–75.

42. M[artin] P[arker], *A Hee-Diuell* [1630], *PG,* 332–36.

43. M[artin] P[arker], *The Married-womans Case* [c. 1630], *PB* 2:170–73.

44. *The Married wives complaint. Or, The hasty Bride Repents her bargain* [later 17c], brs. (Douce Ballads 2:144b, Bod.).

45. Hans Sachs, "Die 7 clagenden Weiber" [1550s] and "Die 7 clagenden mender" [1550s], in Goetze, 1:34–43.

6. *Marital Disorder*

1. Hans Sachs, "Der Narrenfresser" [c. 1560], in Goetze, 1:11–16 (2 eds.).

2. *Freundlicher / wolthätiger / freygebiger Auffzug / Deß Herrn Uber-Sie / von vnd zu Miltenhausen* . . . (1617), in Wäscher, no. 89.

3. *Pasquils Iests, Mixed with Mother Bunches Merriments . . .* (1604), 24 fols., D1 (BL; other eds. 1609, 1629, 1635, c. 1650, 1669).

4. Moser-Rath, *"Lustige Gesellschaft,"* 117.

5. M[artin] P[arker], *A Banquet for Soueraigne Husbands* (1629), PG, 328–31.

6. See below.

7. M[artin] P[arker], *A Banquet for Soueraigne Husbands,* PG, 331.

8. Ed. Ford, *[. . .], or, A merry discourse 'twixt him and his Ioane* [1st half 17c], *RB* 1:251.

9. *Ein schön new Lied / wie ein fraw jren Mann strafft / vnd weret jm er sol nit zum wein geen* [c. 1550], A3v.

10. See Ingram, "Ridings, Rough Music, and Mocking Rhymes in Early Modern England"; Dieterich, "Eselritt und Dachabdecken"; Hermann Heidrich, "Grenzübergänge. Das Haus und die Volkskultur in der frühen Neuzeit." See also the illustration to *Halfe a dozen of Good Wives: All for a penny* [1634], *RB* 1:451; reproduced on p. vi.

11. Amussen, "Gender, Family, and the Social Order," 208. See also Sharpe, *Defamation and Sexual Slander.*

12. Hans Sachs, *Von den neun Häuten der bösen Weiber* [mid-16c], in Wäscher, no. 8; *Here Begynneth the Scole house of women . . .* (1560) (BL).

13. *Ein new Lied von eynem bösen weib . . .* (Nuremberg, [c. 1530]; facs. rept. Zwickau, 1913, ed. Götze), fol. A2v.

14. M[artin] P[arker], *Have among you! good women* [1634], *RB* 1:434–40.

15. Robert Guy, *The witty Westerne Lasse* [1631, 1640?], *RB* 3:46–51.

16. "Es het ein edelman ein weib" (1610), in Böhme, *Altdeutsches Liederbuch,* 130–31. Frequent reuse of the tune attests to this song's popularity. ·

17. See "Es ist ein elende Sach Umb ein verdachtes Weib" [c. 1630s], in Ditfurth, *Deutsche Volks- und Gesellschaftslieder,* 11–12; "Der Bettler" [15c, c. 1530, 1582], in Böhme, *Altdeutsches Liederbuch,* 128–29.

18. S. S., *The Joviall Crew, Or, The Devill turn'd Ranter . . .* (1651), 15 pp., 4 (BL).

19. *Ein new lied gemacht von einem stoltzen meydlein* [16c], brs. (DSB 7801.41).

20. Hans Sachs, *Die Zwölff Eygenschafft eines boßhafftigen weybs* (Nuremberg, 1553), in Goetze, 1:20–29 (2 eds.).

21. Haß, *Du junger man merck vnd versteh Vnd wilt du greyffen zu der Ehe* [2d half 16c], A5v.

22. *All is ours and our Husbands; Or, The Country Hostesses Vindication* [c. 1680s], *RB* 3:379–82.

23. S[amuel] R[owlands], *A Crew of kind Gossips, all met to be merrie: Complayning of their Husbands, with their Husbands answeres in their owne defence . . .* (1613), 19 fols., B3v (BL).

24. In my English sources on marital discord, there are 40 female

victories to 10 male; in German texts, 13 female to 21 male. The patterns change across time, with the proportion of female victories increasing in both countries: for sixteenth-century England, the figures are 6 female wins to 4 male; for the seventeenth century, 34 female to 6 male; for sixteenth-century Germany, 4 female to 17 male; for seventeenth-century Germany, 8 female to 4 male. These figures overstate the changes somewhat, since they include only the first issue of a text, not subsequent reprintings. Cf. Capp, "Popular Literature," 215.

25. *Any thing for a quiet life; Or the Married mans bondage to a curst Wife* [1st half 17c], *PB* 2:18–21.

26. M[artin] P[arker], *Keep a good tongue in your head* [1634], *RB* 3:236–42.

27. M[artin] P[arker], *Hold your hands, honest Men* [1634], *RB* 3:242–48.

28. Arthur Halliarg, *The Cruell Shrow: Or, The Patient Man's Woe* [1st half 17c], *RB* 1:94–98.

29. *The Dumb Maid: or the Young Gallant Trappan'd* [c. 1678?], *RB* 4:357–59 (also in *Euing*).

30. Hans Sachs, "Ein recept vur der weiber klappersuecht" [mid-16c], in Goetze, 1:368–70.

31. Hans Sachs, *Von den neun Häuten der bösen Weiber* [mid-16c], in Wäscher, no. 8 (also in Goetze, 1:164–69; other eds.: Nuremberg, 1553, c. 1553, 1554, 1555, 1640, 1710, Regensburg, 1680).

32. *Kurtze Beschreibung von denen neun Häuten der bösen Weiber, / wie solche die Männer auf manierliche Art abziehen, und ein recht frommes Weib / daraus machen können* (Regensburg, 1680), in Wäscher, no. 84.

33. Goetze, 1:167.

34. *Ein Schön New Lied / Von einem Körblemacher* (Nuremberg, [2d half 16c]), 3 fols., A2, A2v (DSB Yd 8436; another ed.: Hamburg, c. 1585).

35. *Ein schimpflicher Spruch / von einem Korbmacher vnnd seiner Frawen . . .* (1570), 4 fols., A3v–A4 (BL).

36. T. Rider, *A merie newe Ballad intituled, the Pinnyng of the Basket* [2d half 16c], 79 *Ballads*, 105–11.

37. Brietzmann, *Die böse Frau in der deutschen Litteratur des Mittelalters*, 182.

38. "Ein Tagweyß / wie man die bösen weyber schlahen sol," in *Ein kurtzweylig Lied / von eynem liederlichen man vnd seynem weyb . . .* (Nuremberg, [c. 1550?]), 4 fols., A3, A3v, A4 (BL; another ed. in Brietzmann, *Die böse Frau in der deutschen Litteratur des Mittelalters*, 182–83).

39. *Offt Probiertes und Bewährtes Recept oder Artzney für die bösse Kranckheit der unartigen Weiber* (Nuremberg, [c. 1650]), brs. (HAB; another ed. in SBPK).

40. *Ein köstlich gutes bewertes Recept / vor die Männer / so böse Weiber haben* [c. 1620?], brs. (GNM).

41. "A New Yeeres guift for shrews" [1620], in *Catalogue of Prints and Drawings in the British Museum*, Division 1, no. 89.

42. *The Wife lapped in Morels skin; or, The Taming of a Shrew* [16c], in Utterson, *Select Pieces of Early Popular Poetry* 2:173–221. On this text, see also Woodbridge, *Women and the English Renaissance*, 201–4; Woodbridge, "New Light on *The Wife Lapped in Morel's Skin* and *The Proud Wife's Paternoster*."

43. *Mercurius Fumigosus, or the Smoking Nocturnall* . . . (1655), no. 34, p. 267 (BL).

44. See Moser-Rath, "*Lustige Gesellschaft*," 405, 455–56.

45. Henry Sponer, "My jornay lat as I dyd take" [1550s], in Wright, *Songs and Ballads*, 97–101.

46. "Ballet. By west off late as I dyd walke" [c. 1578], in Böddeker, "Englische Lieder und Balladen aus dem 16. Jahrhundert," 220.

47. *The Batchelor's Delight* [1st half 17c], *RB* 3:423–26.

48. *Poor Anthony's Complaint* [1680s], in *Euing*, no. 275.

49. *The Married Mans complaint Who took a Shrow instead of a Saint* [mid-17c], brs. (Douce Ballads 2:150a, Bod.).

50. *The West Country Weaver* [late 17c?], *RB* 7:22–23.

51. See, e.g., *Von Einem Bößen Weib, welche sich auff einer breytten Heydten mit den Teüffeln geschlagen* . . . ("Rumpelskirchen," [17c]), brs. (HAB; another ed. in SBPK); *A Pleasant new Ballad you here may behold, How the Devill, though subtle, was gul'd by a Scold* [1630, 1656], *RB* 2:366–71.

52. *Das lied ist genant der böß rauch In der flamm weiß* [1st half 16c], brs. (DSB Yd 7801.53).

53. *Drey schöne Newe Weltliche Lieder. Das Erste. Von dreyen Weibern / so zum Weine gewesen / &c.* [17c], 4 fols., A2 (DSB Ye 1770).

54. *Ein kurtzweylig Lied / von eynem liederlichen man vnd seynem weyb* [c. 1550?]), A1v, A2–A2v, A3 (another ed. mid-16c).

55. *Drey schön neue Weltliche Lieder. Das erste: Ist ein Streitt / zwischen einem bösen Weib / vnd einem versoffnen Mann* . . . (Augsburg, [c. 1640?]), 4 fols., A1v, A2, A2v (DSB Ye 1746; other eds. 1580s, 1647, 1658).

7. Sex and Power

1. *True Love Exalted: Or, A Dialogue between a Courteous young knight of the City of London and a Searge-Weaver's Daughter of Devonshire* [c. 1690?], *RB* 6:93–95; text here follows the original in BL.

2. *The West-Country Lawyer; Or, The Witty Maid's Good Fortune* [early 1690s?], *RB* 7:428.

3. *The Antient, True, and Admirable History of Patient Grisel, A Poore Mans Daughter in France: Shewing, How Maides, by her example, in their good behauiour may marrie rich Hvsbands* . . . (1619). See also *The Rarest Ballad*

that ever was seen, of the Blind Begger's Daughter of Bednal-Green [16c, 1675], *RB* 1:37–46.

4. *The Beautiful Shepherdess of Arcadia* [16c, 1624, 1656], *RB* 3:449–55.

5. For a popular exception in the chivalric mode, however, see Mayr, *Ain Schön lied / von ainem Ritter auß der Steyrmarck / genant Trinumitas / vnd von aines Künigs Tochter auß Dennmarck / genant Floredebel* [2d half 16c]. Here it is the man's attractiveness rather than the woman's that rouses desire and leads eventually to marriage.

6. Such fears did find a place in lengthier works; see Moser-Rath, "*Lustige Gesellschaft*," 119. For an unusual example of male sexual inadequacy as a cause of female marital rule in a German broadside, see Müller, *Eheglück und Liebesjoch*, 102.

7. *Der Weltlich Joseph* (Basel, 1566), in Blümml, no. 37 (other eds.: c. 1545, Augsburg, c. 1635, n.d., Basel, c. 1610, Freiburg, 1660; also in BL under title *Ein hüpsch new Lied / von dem Gotsförchtigen Joseph . . .*).

8. Martin Schlacht, *Ein schön news Lied: Von der Königin von Franckreich / vnd von jrer falschen Buhlschafft . . .* (Augsburg, [c. 1590s]), 8 fols., A2v–A3, A3v (BL; other eds.: Nuremberg, c. 1520, Straubing, c. 1580, Basel, 1605).

9. *Neweroffneter Ernsthaffter / hochstraffwürdiger vnd vnverbrüchlicher Männerbefehlich . . .* (Nuremberg, [c. 1650]), brs. (HAB).

10. *A Ditty delightfull of mother Watkins ale* [pre-1592], *79 Ballads*, 251–55.

11. *Loves Power* [c. 1685?], *RB* 7:445; text here follows original in BL.

12. *Enfield Common: Or, The Young Damsel Cured Of The Green Sickness By a Lusty Gallant . . .* [late 17c], brs. (Osterley Park Ballads, BL). For a less successful man, see *A Pleasant New Ballad: Being a Merry Discourse between a Country Lass and a young Taylor* [late 17c], *RB* 3:604–6.

13. *The Doting Old Dad* [1680s], *RB* 4:412–13.

14. See, e.g., *Ein schön new Lied / von einem alten Man vnd einem jungen Fräwlein* [1620?], 4 fols. (BL); *Den Hanenreitern* [c. 1640], brs. (GNM).

15. For a German example from the novel, however, see Grimmelshausen, *Courage*. Also, for a German counterpart to *Watkins ale*, see "Frau Fischerin," in Böhme, *Altdeutsches Liederbuch*, 124–25.

16. [Walter Pope?], *The Forc'd Marriage; Or, Unfortunate Celia* [1670s], *RB* 8:190–91 (also in *Euing*, Bod.); text here follows the original in BL.

17. *The Lamentation of Chloris for the Unkindness of her Shepherd* [c. 1680], *RB* 6:131–32 (also in *Euing*, Pepys); text here follows the original in BL.

18. *The Parliament of Women* (1646), 12 fols., A3v, A6v (BL; another ed. late 17c).

19. M[artin] P[arker], *Household Talke* [1st third 17c], *RB* 1:441–46.

20. *A mery balade, how a wife entreated her husband to have her owne wyll* [pre-1571], 79 *Ballads*, 130.

21. *Who would not be a Cuckold* [early 17c], in Rollins, *Old English Ballads*, 196.

22. *Cuckold's Haven, Or, The marry'd man's miserie* [1638], *RB* 1:148–53.

23. *My Wife will be my Master* [c. 1640?, 1681, c. 1685], *RB* 7:188–89.

24. *Mirth for Citizens: Or, A Comedy for the Country* [1670s?, 1680s], *RB* 8:699–700; text here follows the original in BL.

25. *The Cuckold's Complaint: Or, The Turbulent Wives severe Cruelty* [c. 1690], *RB* 7:431; text here follows the original in Pepys.

26. On this, see also Jardine, *Still Harping on Daughters*, 121–24.

27. On early modern views of the disorderly female body, see Davis, *Society and Culture in Early Modern France*, 124–25.

28. Amussen, *An Ordered Society*, 118–22.

29. Ingram, "Ridings, Rough Music, and Mocking Rhymes in Early Modern England," 176–77.

30. Kahn, *Man's Estate*, 12–14.

31. For discussions of these tensions, see Underdown, "Taming of the Scold"; Amussen, "Gender, Family and the Social Order"; Stone, "The Rise of the Nuclear Family in Early Modern England."

32. *Zwey Schöne Meister Lieder / Das erst / Von listen weibern . . .* [16c], 3 fols. (DSB Yd 8421).

33. *Von einer Keyserin Wie sie jr Ehe brach / dardurch dem Keyser ein Horn wuchs an seiner Stiern . . .* (Straubing, 1561), 4 fols., A2, A4 (DSB Yd 7831.67; another ed.: Nuremberg, c. 1550).

34. *The Sack-Full of Newes* (1673), in Hazlitt, *Shakespeare Jest-Books* 2:164–87 (other eds. 1557, 1582, 1587, 1685). This tale, from fabliaux tradition, was also common in late seventeenth-century German jest-books; see Moser-Rath, "*Lustige Gesellschaft*," 127.

35. For a German example of this, see G. N., *Ein newes lied / Ein Burger ist gesessen / zu Thübing* [Nuremberg], [c. 1530], 4 fols. (DSB Yd 7821.31); here the husband was paid off, however.

36. *Touch and Go; or, the French Taylor finely Trappann'd* [c. 1665], *RB* 7:486.

37. *The Bull's Feather* [c. 1675], *RB* 3:418–20.

38. See *The Unfortunate Miller* [c. 1685], *BB* 2:530–33; *The Wanton Vintner and the Subtile Damosel* [1680s], *RB* 8:479–80; *The Crafty Maid of the West* [c. 1672], *RB* 8:626–28; *The Westminster Frolick* [c. 1685], *RB* 8:477–78; Moser-Rath, "*Lustige Gesellschaft*," 128.

39. Hans Amma, *Zwey schöne Newe Lieder. Das Erste / ist eine Propheceyhung. . . . Das Ander Liedt Von einem Weber . . .* (Prague[?], 1603[?]), 4 fols., A4 (HAB).

40. See, e.g., *The Biter Bitten* [c. 1685], *RB* 3:445–48; *The Witty Maid*

of the West [c. 1685], *RB* 7:426–27; *Ein hüpsch New Lied / Vonn einer Stoltzen Müllerin . . .* [c. 1590s?] (BL).

41. *Ain hübsch New Lied / von der Judit . . .* (Augsburg, [c. 1532?]), 4 fols., A4, A3v (GNM).

42. Hans Sachs, *Ein schön Meyster Lied / Von der Gottsförchtigen Frawen Judith . . .* (Leipzig, 1607), 5 fols., A4v (BL; other eds.: Nuremberg, 1554, c. 1555; n.p., 1607); Sachs, *Die zwölff durch leuchtige Weyber des alten Testaments* (1596).

43. *Ain hübsch New Lied / von der Judit* [c. 1532?], A3.

44. Hans Sachs, *Die Judit mit Holoferne . . .* (Nuremberg, 1554), 4 fols., A4 (BL).

45. "O Mensch hast du nit genommen war," in *Zwey Schöne Gaistliche Lieder. Das Erst: Die Gnad kompt oben her* [c. 1620?], 4 fols., A3v (BL).

46. *Newe Zeitung / in Gesangs weiß / Von der Statt Genff . . .* (Basel, 1590), 4 fols., A4v (BL); *Ein Schön new Lied / von den Jungen Gesellen / vnd den Jungfrawen . . .* (Ulm, [c. 1600]), in Blümml, no. 60.

47. *Ein Schön new Lied / von den Jungen Gesellen / vnd den Jungfrawen* [c. 1600], in Blümml, no. 60.

48. Niclas Wolgemut, *Das ist das new Teutsch Hurübel . . .* [c. 1520?], 4 fols., A4 (BL).

49. Hans Sachs, *Ein Gesprech eyner Bulerin vnd eines ligenden Narren vnter jhren Füssen* (Nuremberg, [c. 1553]), 4 fols., A1v (BL).

50. *Ein hübsch lied / Von der Frawen von der Weissenburg* (Nuremberg, [c. 1571–1604]), 4 fols., A2v (DSB Yd 7850.39; other eds.: Nuremberg, c. 1550, n.p., 1557).

51. *Ein schön Liedt / Von eyner Künigin auß Lamparden / Wie grewlich sie jren Ehegemahel vmb das leben hat bracht* (Nuremberg, [2d half 16c]), 4 fols., A2v, A4 (DSB Yd 8081; another ed.: Frankfurt, 1536).

52. *Das Liede von dem edlen Danheuser* (Nuremberg, [c. 1530]; facs. rept. Zwickau, 1912, ed. Clemen), 4 fols., A2v–A3 (many other editions, including Nuremberg, 1515, c. 1560, Leipzig, 1520, Augsburg, c. 1600, Basel, 1612).

53. [Hans Sachs], *Drey schöner Hißtorij / Von dreyen Heidenischen mörderischen Frawen* (Nuremberg, 1540), 4 fols., A3v–A4 (BL; another ed.: Nuremberg, 1553).

54. *Murder upon Murder* [1635], *PG*, 432–36; parentheses in original.

55. H[enry] G[oodcole], *Heavens Speedie Hue and Cry sent after Lust and Murther* (1635), 12 fols., B4v (BL). For another case of women behind crime, see *Three Inhumane Murthers, Committed By one Bloudy Person, upon His Father, his Mother, and his Wife . . .* (1675), 6 pp. (BL).

56. *An Excellent Ballad of George Barnwel* [1624, 1675], *RB* 8:61–66.

57. *Whitney's Dying Letter To his Mistris that betray'd him: With her Answer* (1692), *PB* 6:316–19.

58. *The lamentation of Henrye Adlington* [early 17c], *Shirburn*, 106–8;

Thomas Dickerson, *John Spenser a Chesshire Gallant* [c. 1626], *PG*, 257–62.

59. [Robert Guy], *A warning for all good fellowes to take heede of Punckes inticements* [c. 1625], *PB* 1:263–65.

60. *Solomon's Sentences* [1586, 1675], *RB* 2:538–43.

61. See Maurer, *Geschichte der Städteverfassung in Deutschland* 3:103–16; Roper, *Holy Household*, 89–131; Wiesner, "Paternalism in Practice." On English prostitutes, see Salgado, *Elizabethan Underworld*, 52–53; Haselkorn, *Prostitution in Elizabethan and Jacobean Comedy*.

62. *The Country Lass, Who left her Spinning-Wheel for a more pleasant Employment* [late 17c?], brs. (BL).

63. *The Ranting Whores Resolution* [1658, 1672, 1675], *BB* 1:*479–81.

64. *Venus Darling; Or, A New Vampt Gentlewoman* [c. 1670], brs. (Rawlinson Ballads 566(41), Bod.).

65. *The Ranting Whores Resolution, BB* 1:*480.

66. *A Caueat or VVarning. For all sortes of Men both young and olde, to avoid the Company of lewd and wicked Woemen* [c. 1620?], *PB* 1:129–32.

67. *The Two-Penny Whore* [1680s?], in *Euing*, no. 191A (also in BL under title *The Royoters Ruine . . .*).

68. *The Bridewel Whores resolution . . .* [c. 1675], brs. (Rawlinson Ballads 566(98), Bod.).

69. *VVhipping Cheare* [c. 1612], *PG*, 40–43.

70. M[artin] P[arker], *A Fayre Portion for a Fayre Maid* [1633], *RB* 1:364–69.

71. Sachs, *Ein Gesprech eyner Bulerin vnd eines ligenden Narren vnter jhren Füssen* [c. 1553]. For other whores, see *Ein schön newes Lied / von einem Burgersknecht vnd von einer Bettlerin* [1620?] (BL); Hans Folz, *Von zweyer frawen krig* (Nuremberg, [early 16c?]), 8 fols. (SBPK Yg 5216); *Charter Stutzerischen. . . . A La Modo Matressen* [17c], brs. (HAB); Jörg Graff, *Ein new Liede / von pulerey* (Nuremberg, [c. 1530?]), 4 fols. (DSB Yd 7850.36).

72. Whores seem to have been much more prominent in German carnival plays and other drama; see Schmidt, *Die Frau in der deutschen Literatur des 16. Jahrhunderts,* 133–34. Their rarity in street literature may be due partly to incomplete survival of the texts, but still they could hardly have matched the prominence of their counterparts in the English literature.

73. Jörg Graff, *Ein newes lied von einem Jeger* [1st half 16c], brs. (DSB Yd 7801.22).

74. *Drey schöne Newe Lieder das erste / Das Meidlein zu dem Brunnen gieng. . .* [1st half 16c], 4 fols., A3 (DSB Yd 9330; another ed.: Nuremberg, c. 1530).

75. In addition to those cited below, see M[artin] P[arker], *The Bonny Bryer* [c. 1634], *RB* 7:165–67; *The Somersetshire Tragedy; Or, The Wronged Lady's Lamentation, and Untimely Death* [c. 1670s], *RB* 8:117–18; see also Ingram, *Church Courts, Sex, and Marriage in England,* 286–89.

76. Dülmen, *Kultur und Alltag*, 186; Wrightson, "The Nadir of English Illegitimacy in the Seventeenth Century." For evidence that unmarried mothers in eighteenth-century Germany maintained familial contacts, see Ulbrich, "Infanticide in Eighteenth-century Germany," 112.

77. *The lovely Northerne Lasse* [1632], *RB* 1:587–92 (also in *Euing*, Bod.); *The Fair Maid of Dunsmore's Lamentation* [1680s], *RB* 6:767–70 (also in *Euing*, Bod.); *A Lamentable Ballad of the Ladies Fall* [1603, 1624, 1670s], *RB* 6:764–65.

78. *Zwey Schöne newe Lieder. Das erste: Ich wolt gern singen* . . . [17c], 4 fols., A1v (DSB Yd 7850.23); see also "Es het ein Schwab ein töchterlein" [c. 1530], in Böhme, *Altdeutsches Liederbuch*, 133–34.

79. *Drey schöne Lieder / Das Erste / Ich hab dich lieb* . . . *Das Dritte / Es war ein mal ein junger Knab / er freyt eins* . . . (Nuremberg, [c. 1550?]), 4 fols., A3v (BL).

80. *Zwey Schöne newe Lieder. Das erste: Ich wolt gern singen* [17c?]; *Ein hüpsch New Lied / Schürtz dich Gredlein* . . . (Augsburg, [c. 1560]), 4 fols. (BL; 3 other eds.).

81. *Drey schöne newe Weltliche Lieder. Das Erste / Weh! das ich armer Jung-Gesell*. . . . *Das Ander: Es war ein Jungfraw zart / es trägt an jhrem Bäuchlein so hart* ([Nuremberg?], 1663), 4 fols. (BL); Jacob Wartz [?], *Ein schön news Liedt / Vonn einem Edlen Jüngling auß Armenia* . . . (Augsburg, 1610), 8 fols. (BL); *Eigene Schuldbekäntnüß Einer So genandten vnd vermeinten Jungfraw Aderlässerin* [c. 1650], in Wäscher, no. 87. See also Jörg Graff, *Ein new lied gemacht im thon als man singt von dem Künig von franckreych vnd der stat Tollen* [pre-1542], brs. (DSB Yd 7801.69).

82. *The Female Warrior* [1680s?], *BB* 1:329; R[ichard] C[limsall], *The praise of London* [1632, 1634], *PB* 2:223; *The Blind eats many a Flye: Or, The Broken Damsel made Whole* [1680s], brs. (BL); (*Hey Hoe, for a Husband,*) or, *The Parliament of Maides* . . . (1647), 6 pp., 3 (BL); *Vier Hüpsche Weltliche Lieder*. . . . *4. Ich ritt eins mals zu Braunschweig auß* (1611), 4 fols., A4 (BL); *Ein Schöns Newes Lied / Der Braune Stier genandt* (n.d.), 4 fols. (BL).

83. *A Lamentable Ballad of the Ladies Fall*, *RB* 6:764–65; *A Loue-sick maids song, lately beguild, By a run-away Louer that left her with Childe* [c. 1615?], *PB* 1:91; Robert Guy, *The witty Westerne Lasse* [1631, 1640], *RB* 3:48; *Deplorable News from Southwark* . . . [1660s?], brs. (Book of Fortune Ballads, BL); *The lovely Northerne Lasse*, *RB* 1:589; *A pretye songe* [c. 1590], *Shirburn*, 339.

84. *Any thing for a quiet life; Or the Married mans bondage to a curst Wife* [c. 1620s?], *PB* 2:18–21; Hans Sachs, "Die neünerley verwandlüng in dem elichen stant" [1559], in Goetze, 1:350–52; *Zwey schön newe Lieder / Erstlich: Wie die Männer jhre Weiber halten sollen / daß sie lang schön bleiben* . . . (Augsburg, [c. 1640?]) (DSB Ye 1743).

85. *Ein Gründtliche auch warhafftige vnd erschlöckliche* [sic] *newe Zeitung / von sechs Mördern* . . . (Ulmitz[?], 1603), 4 fols., A1v (DSB Ye 5571). See also *Zwey erschreckliche Newe Lieder / Das erste von einem Kinde / das*

geborn ist in Yfland / . . . *Das ander von einem Manne / der seine Fraw verkaufft / welche schwanger gieng* (1580), 4 fols. (DSB Ye 4529); *Drey gantz Neue Anmüthige Gesänger / Das Erste: Ein erbärmliche Geschicht. . . . Das Dritte: Von einem Schäffer / welcher sein schwangers Weib zweyen Mördern verkaufft hat* [c. 1600?], 4 fols., A3v–A4 (BL); *Drey newer zeyttung. Ein erschröckliche vnd erbärmliche geschicht / so sich ein meilwegs von der Statt Bremen . . . zugetragen / wie daselbst ein Mann sein schwanger Weib verkaufft . . .* (1579), 4 fols. (BSB); *Zween Erschreckliche geschicht / Gesangs weise. Die Erste / von einem Wirt im Allgergaw / Bastian Schönmundt genandt . . .* (1596), 4 fols. (DSB Ye 5141).

86. *Newe Zeitung: Welcher gestalt / zween falsche Juden / durch Zauberey zuwegen gebracht / daß vil tausend Stück Vihe hingefallen vnd gestorben ist . . .* (Dresden, 1599), 4 fols. (HAB; another ed.: Vienna, 1599).

87. See, e.g., *The Lamenting Lady* [c. 1620], *PG*, 124–31; *Pride's Fall* [1608?, 1656, 1675], *RB* 8:20–22; *The true reporte of the forme and shape of a monstrous Childe . . . 1562, 79 Ballads*, 27–30.

88. See, e.g., *Abreissung eines vngestalten Kinds . . .* [1578], in Wäscher, no. 78; *Ein schreckliche Geschicht von einem grawsamen Kindt / welches geboren worden zu Arnhem im Gelderland* (Cologne, 1576), 4 fols. (BL; 2 other eds.); *Zwo Warhafftige vnd traurige newe Zeitung / sampt einem Klaglied. Welche in dem Franken Land geschehen . . .* (Rottenburg, 1624), 4 fols. (BL); *Ein wahrhafftige Newe Zeitung. Von einem Ehrvergeßnen Mann / der sein Schwanger Weib / durch das leidige Spilen vnnd Vollsauffen / das Kindt in Mutterleib verfluchet hat . . .* (Cologne [?], 1638), 4 fols. (DSB Ye 6956). For an English example of a curse of a godless husband, see S. Clark, *Elizabethan Pamphleteers*, 104.

89. *Ein warhafftige erschröckliche Newe Zeytung / . . . im Flecken Treber bey / Geraw / . . . wie daselbst der Teuffel einem reichen Burger sein rechtes Kind abgewechselt . . .* (Oppenheim, 1618), 4 fols. (BL).

90. *Zwo warhafftige vnd erschröckliche newe Zeitungen. Die erste . . . in der Statt Feldkirch eines Hauptmanns Weib seines Namens Bernhardt Schmid . . .* (Hohen Ens, 1623), 4 fols., A3 (HAB). The author does not mention any cursing by the particular woman afflicted here.

91. For a case of demonic intervention in an English childbirth, see L. P., *Strange and wonderfull news of a woman which Lived neer unto the Famous City of London, who had her head torn off from her Body by the Divell . . .* [17c], brs. (Book of Fortune Ballads, BL). See also *The Snare of the Devill Discovered: Or, A True and perfect Relation of the sad and deplorable Condition of Lydia the Wife of John Rogers House-Carpenter . . .* (1658), 12 pp. (BL).

92. *Zwo warhafftige vnd reschröcklich* [sic] *newe Zeitung. Die Erste / . . . wie ein Armes Weib drey Kinder geboren . . .* (Aschaffenburg, 1629), brs., in Brednich, no. 103.

93. *Zwey Warhafftige newe Zeitung / Von einer schrecklichen Mißgeburt . . .* (Stettin, 1628), 4 fols. (HAB).

94. *Ein schöne Litaney / Von der Allerseligsten Jungfraw und Mutter Gottes Maria . . .* (1686), A4.

95. *Ein schöne Tageweis: Von Einem Frawelein auff einer Burg / vnd von einem jungen Knaben* (1664), 4 fols., A2v (BL; also in DSB Yd 7821.3; another ed.: Basel, 1608).

96. *Zwey überaus schöne Lieder. Das Erste: Von einer erschröcklichen Mord-Geschicht . . .* [1st half 17c?], 4 fols. (DSB Yd 7855(7)).

97. *Ein Hüpsch new Geistlich Lied / gezogen auß dem andern Buch Machaberoum . . .* (Basel, 1572), in Blümml, no. 11 (another ed.: Rotenburg, c. 1600).

98. *Zäuberische Zeitung / Wie eine Hexin durch Teuffelszkunst jren Sohn mit sonderlichen Aberglaubischen dingen zum Wildschiessen behülfflich gewesen . . .* (Cologne, 1589), 6 fols. (HAB).

8. Women and Violence: Tragedy and Comedy

1. See Robert Darnton, *The Great Cat Massacre and Other Episodes in French Cultural History* (New York, 1984), 46–51.

2. *Eine warhafftige geschicht / Von einen vngerathenen Sohn. . . . Das Ander / wie man sich in dem Ehestande verhalten sol . . .* (Alten Stettin, [c. 1601]), 4 fols., A3v (DSB Yd 7852.21). See also *Ein schön New Geistlich Leid* [sic] */ wider das schandliedlein / so man jetzund pflegen zu singen / Mein Man der wil in Krieg ziehen . . .* (n.d.), 4 fols. (DSB Hymn. 7539).

3. Hans Sachs, *Die Zwölff Eygenschafft eines boßhafftigen weybs* (Nuremberg, 1553), 8 fols., B1v (BL; rept. in Goetze, 1:20–29; 1 other ed.).

4. See Arthur Halliarg, *The Cruell Shrow: Or, the Patient Man's Woe* [1st half 17c], *RB* 1:96.

5. See, e.g., *The Sack-Full of Newes* (1673), in Hazlitt, *Shakespeare Jest-Books* 2:169–71.

6. Salgado, *Elizabethan Underworld*, 52. On German prostitutes, see Maurer, *Geschichte der Städteverfassung in Deutschland* 3:103–16.

7. See *The Whores Petition To the London Prentices, The Prentices Answer to the Whores Petition,* and *The Citizens Reply To the Whores Petition, and Prentices Answer* (1668), brs. (Bagford Ballads, vol. 3, nos. 46–48, BL).

8. A. B., *A Canterbury Tale, Translated Out of Chaucers old English . . .* (1641), 4 fols., A4v (BL).

9. *A pleasant new Songe of a iouiall Tinker* [1616?, 1630, 1661], *PB* 1:104–8.

10. See, e.g., *A Match at a Venture* [c. 1680s], *RB* 7:138–40.

11. *Whipping Tom Brought to light, and exposed to View . . .* (1681), brs. (NLS). This character apparently had an earlier incarnation in 1591, whose attacks may have been directed against men; see Rollins, *Analytical Index,* 14.

12. *Der Arglistige Blockschleiffer* (Cologne, [3d quarter 17c]), brs., in Brückner, no. 84.

13. *Couragious Betty of Chick-Lane* [1690s], *RB* 3:641–44.

14. *The Maidens Frollick* [1690s], *RB* 3:401–4; text here follows original in BL.

15. *An Answer to the Maidens Frollick* [1690s], *RB* 3:405–7.

16. *Slippery Will* [c. 1700?], *RB* 2:503–8.

17. *Kentish Dick* [late 17c], in *Euing*, no. 148.

18. L[aurence] P[rice], *The famous Woman Drummer* [1650s], *RB* 7:730–32. Drum-beating was also a sexual pun.

19. *The Gallant She-Souldier* [1650s], *RB* 7:728–29; text here follows original in BL.

20. See *The Maiden Warrier* [c. 1689?], *RB* 7:736–39; *The Female Warrior* [1680s], *BB* 1:326–29.

21. *The Life and Pranks of Long Meg of Westminster* [c. 1650], 12 fols., A8v, B1, B2v–B3 (BL; another ed. 1582).

22. *The Valarous Acts performed at Gaunt, By the brave Bonny Lass Mary Ambree* [c. 1590?, 1629, 1675], *BB* 1:311–15.

23. *The valiant Commander with his resolute Lady* [1640s?, 1670s], *RB* 6:281–83.

24. S. S., *A Famous Battle between Robin Hood, and Maid Marian; declaring their Love, Life, and Liberty* (n.d.), brs. (Wood 401(21), Bod.).

25. *Newe Anbildung Der Weitbeschreiten / Hertzhafften Hildin vnd Frawen Margret von Kennow . . .* (1573), brs. (BL).

26. *Schöner newer Meister Lieder zwey. Das erst. Die weiber Amastanas In dem gülden thon Marmers . . .* (Leipzig, [17c]), 4 fols., A2v (DSB Yd 7852.25).

27. For a discussion of English satires that similarly trivialize the supposed female rule of Amazons, see Nussbaum, *Brink of All We Hate*, 43–48.

28. See Grimmelshausen, *Courage*, 32–39, 119.

29. Hans Sachs, "Kampffgesprech zwischen einer frawen vnd ihrer hausmeit" (Nuremberg, 1553, 2 eds.), in Goetze, 1:52–58.

30. *Wunder vber alle Wunder / Was massen Herr Rudolph Schweitzer . . .* (1621), 4 fols., A3 (BL).

31. See, e.g., *Satyrisches Gesicht / zu Nichtburg in Vtopia durch den blinden Cupidinem entdeckt: Wie sich nemlich sieben böse Weiber vmb ein paar stinckende Manns Buxen geschlagen / . . .* [17c], brs. (HAB); *Beschreibung vnd Figur der zukünfftigen bösen vnd Manntheuren Zeit: Nemlich / daß sich Sieben Weiber vmb ein par Mannshosen schlagen werden . . .* [17c], brs. (GNM).

32. *A new Dialogue between Alice and Betrice* [1680s], *BB* 1:68–70.

33. *The Unthankful Servant: Or, A Scolding Match between Two Cracks of the Town . . .* (n.d.), brs. (Osterley Park Ballads, BL; also in Pepys).

34. See, e.g., M[artin] P[arker], *Have among you! good Women* [1634],

RB 1:434–40; M[artin] P[arker], *Well met, Neighbour* [1630s–1640s], *RB* 3:98–103.

35. E.g., *The Patient Wife betrayed*, in *Euing*, no. 289; *The lamentable fall of Queen Elnor*, *RB* 2:67–73; *A true Relation of one Susan Higges*, *RB* 2:632–38; *The Whipster of Woodstreet*, *PB* 6:31–33.

36. *A Pleasant new Ballad you here may behold, How the Devill, though subtle, was gul'd by a Scold* [1st half 17c, 1636, 1656], *RB* 2:366–71; *Unerhörte / seltzame / auch Wunderbarliche newe Zeitung v. e. bös. Weib / welche sich auff einer breiten Heyd m. den Teuffeln geschlagen . . .* (1609), in Coupe, no. 24; *Das über den Teüffel Triumphirende Weib* [2d half 17c], in Brückner, no. 75; *Von Einem Bößen Weib, welche sich auff einer breytten Heydten mit den Teüffeln geschlagen . . .* ("Rumpelskirchen," [17c]), brs. (HAB; another ed. in SBPK).

37. In German accounts about half of the women killed by their husbands are reportedly pregnant, as against about one-third in English texts. The proportion of pregnant victims rises much higher for Germany if multiple killings are included: the figures then become 64 pregnant to 7 not pregnant (largely because pregnant victims were singled out for mention in cases of multiple murder).

38. *Warhafftige beschreibung von der gewaltigen Belegerung der Statt Harlem in Hollandt . . .* (Ulm, [1573?]), 4 fols., in Blümml, no. 75.

39. *A Dreadful Relation, of the Cruel, Bloudy, and most Inhumane Massacre and Butchery . . .* (1655), brs. (BL). See also "Ein lied, gemacht, wie es im Osterland ergangen ist," "Ein klaglied von den grausamen wütrischen und tyrannischen handlungen, so der Türk . . . geübt . . .," and "Das Lied von Dole," in Liliencron, 3:602–4, 578–80, ix–xi.

40. *Andächtiger Ruff Von dem H. Leben vnd Marterkampff / der glorwurdigen Jungfrawen Sanct Barbara . . .* (1613), A6.

41. Miles, *Carnal Knowing*, 156–57.

42. *An Askew*, *RB* 1:29–34. She died in 1546; the ballad was reprinted in 1675 (Rollins, *Analytical Index*).

43. *The Spanish Virgin; Or, The Effects of Jealousie* [c. 1660–80], *PB* 3:197–201.

44. *Ein gar schon new Lied / vom Adelger* (Augsburg, [c. 1560s]), 4 fols. (BL).

45. *An excellent Ballad of St. George for England* [1624, 1657, 1675, 1680s–1690s], *RB* 1:379–88.

46. *Vier Hüpsche Weltliche Lieder. . . . 4. Ich ritt eins mals zu Braunschweig auß* (1611), 4 fols., A4 (BL; other eds.: Basel, n.d., Augsburg, c. 1560, n.p., 1613).

47. *Ein Schöns Newes Lied / Der Braune Stier genandt* (n.d.), A3r. See also *Zwey schöne newe Lieder. Das Erst: Die newe Jagt genandt* [1620?], 4 fols. (BL); "Nonnen-Lied" (n.d.), in Ditfurth, *Deutsche Volks- und Gesellschaftslieder*, 23–25.

48. *The City Caper: Or, The Whetstones-Park Privateer* [late 17c], brs. (Douce Ballads 1:26, Bod.; also in BL).

49. *The Dumb Lady: Or, No, no, not I; I'le Answer* [1680s], *RB* 4:352–54; text here follows the original in BL. Cissie Fairchilds has described rural courtship patterns in eighteenth-century France in which rape, perfunctory resistance, and female acquiescence appear almost institutionalized; see Fairchilds, "Female Sexual Attitudes."

50. *Drey schöne lieder / Das erst / So hab ich all mein tag gehört. Das ander / Eins morgens frü* . . . (n.d.), 4 fols. (DSB Yd 7821.17).

51. J. P., *The Coy Shepherdess; Or, Phillis and Amintas* [1660s?], *RB* 3:618–22; punctuation here follows the original in BL.

52. *The Svvimming Lady* . . . (1664), in Brednich, no. 143.

53. Rollins, *Analytical Index*, 49, 94.

54. Binder, *Diß lied sagt von Lucretia* [c. 1560?], A2–A2v.

55. *Zwey Schöne Meister Lieder / Das erst / Von listen weibern* (n.d.), A3v.

56. Sachs, *Die neun getrewen Hayden* (1553), C1–C1v.

57. "Das Fräulein von Britania," in Liliencron, 2:300–302 (pamphlet eds.: Strassburg, late 16c, Basel, 1613).

58. *Allda. Ein erbärmklich Lied / von der züchtigen junck frawen Allda genandt* . . . (Augsburg, [2d half 16c]), 8 fols., A4, A5v, A6v, A7 (DSB Yd 8795; other eds.: Basel, 1607, Ravensburg, 1629).

59. Donaldson, *Rapes of Lucretia*, 33–34.

60. *The Bloody Butcher, And the two wicked and cruel Bawds* . . . (1667), in Euing, no. 20.

61. *A new Ballad, intituled, A Warning to Youth* [early 17c], *RB* 3:35–41.

9. Women and Crime: A Return to the Family

1. For a striking instance of this, see Kunze, *Der Prozeß Pappenheimer.*

2. On the English "last good-night" literature, see Sharpe, "Last Dying Speeches."

3. Cockburn, "The Nature and Incidence of Crime in England, 1559–1625," in Cockburn, *Crime in England,* 57.

4. The contrast is proportionally even greater, since my sources include a total of forty-four German and eighty-two English crime reports (not including witchcraft, and selected for those involving women or families).

5. The sources before 1630 include 12 husband murders and 2 wife murders; after 1630 there are 2 husband murders and 13 wife murders.

6. See Underdown, "Taming of the Scold"; Amussen, "Gender, Family, and the Social Order"; Larner, *Enemies of God,* 101–2; Hull, *Chaste, Silent, and Obedient,* 129–30; Rogers, *Troublesome Helpmate,* 105.

7. *The wofull lamentacon of mrs. Anne Saunders* . . . [1570s?], in Rollins, *Old English Ballads*, 340–48.

8. [Thomas Deloney], *The Lamentation of Master Page's Wife* [1591, 1609, 1624, 1675], *RB* 1:555–58.

9. *Sundrye strange and inhumaine Murthers, lately committed* (1591), 8 fols., B2–B2v (Lambeth).

10. *The Lamentation, RB* 1:556.

11. *The Sorrowfull Complaint of Mistris Page* [1591], *RB* 1:561–63.

12. Gilbert Dugdale, *A True Discourse Of the practises of Elizabeth Caldwell* . . . (1604), 16 fols., C1v, B2–B2v (BL).

13. *A Briefe Discovrse of Two most cruell and bloudie murthers, committed bothe in Worcestershire* . . . [c. 1583], 12 fols., B3, B4v, B2v (BL).

14. *The vnnaturall Wife* (1628), PG, 284–87.

15. *A warning for all desperate VVomen* [1628, 1633], PG, 288–92.

16. *The vnnaturall Wife*, PG, 285; *A warning for all desperate VVomen*, PG, 292.

17. M[artin] P[arker], *A warning for wiues* (1629), PG, 300–304.

18. Laurence Price, *Bloody Actions Performed. Or, A brief and true Relation of three Notorious Murthers, committed by three Bloud-thirsty men,* 2. *upon their own Wives* (1653), 16 pp., 7 (BL).

19. Abraham Miles, *Strange News from Westmoreland* [1663–64], in *Euing*, no. 342.

20. *A briefe and true report of two most cruel, vnnaturall, and inhumane Murders, done in Lincolneshire, by twoo Husbands vpon their Wiues* . . . (1607; rept. East Lansing, Mich., 1945, ed. Foster), 10 fols., B2–B2v, C1, B3, C2.

21. *The Murtherer Justly Condemned* (1697), in *Euing*, no. 223B.

22. *The Bloody-minded Husband; Or, The Cruelty of John Chambers* [late 17c], *PB* 3:203–5; *The Unnatural Husband* (1695), *PB* 7:90–92.

23. *Zwo Warhafftige Newe Zeitung / Die erst / Von einem Mörder / der sein Ehelich Weib / vnnd Sechs Kinder ermördet hat / geschehen inn der berümpten Statt Prüßeln / in der Schlessien* . . . (1599), 4 fols. (DSB Ye 5311); *Warhafftige . . . Zeitung. Von etlichen Jesuwittern. . . . Die ander Zeitung. So sich zu Hall im Ihnthal mit einem Burger* . . . ("Stuckard," 1607), 4 fols., A3v (BL); *Ein warhafftiger / grundtlicher Bericht vnd newe Zeitung: Was sich mit einem vollen Weinschlauch vnd seinem ehelichen Weib / die groß schwanger gewesen* . . . (Erfurt, 1616), 4 fols. (BL).

24. *Warhafftige vnd schröckliche Newe zeitung / von einer Fürnemmen Person / welche durch verfürung deß bösen Feindes / vnd grimmigem zorn / auff ein mal Acht mordt verbracht / . . . zu Wangen in Algäw* . . . (Laugingen, 1585), 4 fols., A2v (SBPK); *Zwo warhafftige trawrige newe Zeitungen. . . . Die erste / Von einem Undervogt zu Bergen* . . . (Freiburg, 1623), 4 fols., A1v (BL); *Warhafftige Zeitung / So niemals erhört /. . . zu Quedelburg in Sachsen mit einem Becken / mit Namen Heinrich Rosenzweig / welcher durch deß Teuffels List vnd Rath sein Weib vnd 6. Kinder jämmerlicher weise vmbge-bracht* . . . (Erfurt, 1621), brs., in Brednich, no. 117. In a similar English

example, a poor man unwittingly takes money from the Devil and heads for his family in a murderous rage; but a charitable neighbor prevents his crime, relieves the family, and sees to his cure. See Ashton, *Century of Ballads*, 84–88.

25. *Ein warhafftiger / grundtlicher Bericht vnd newe Zeitung: Was sich mit einem vollen Weinschlauch vnd seinem ehelichen Weib* (1616).

26. *Warhafftige Zeitung / So niemals erhört / . . . zu Quedelburg in Sachsen* (1621), in Brednich, no. 117.

27. *Zwo Warhafftige Newe Zeitung / Die erst / Von einem Mörder / der sein Ehelich Weib / vnnd Sechs Kinder ermördet hat* (1599), A2v. See also *Warhafftige Beschreibung von einer schröcklichen Mordthat / so geschehen 1652 . . . in der Neisischen Herrschafft . . .* (Neisse, 1653), brs., in Brednich, no. 121; *Drey warhafftige grundtliche Zeitungen / Die erste / Von ettlichen Hexen . . . welche hin vnd wider in Vngern / vnd Teutschland grossen schaden angericht haben . . .* (Freyberg, 1610), 4 fols., A3–A3v (ZB).

28. *Zween Erschreckliche geschicht / Gesangs weise. Die Erste / von einem Wirt im Allgergaw / Bastian Schönmundt genandt / . . . Die Ander / Eine erschreckliche vnd Warhafftige Newe Zeitung / . . . zu Langenberck . . .* (1596), A3v–A4, A4v (see also DSB Ye 5206, 5208).

29. Burckhard Waldis, *Eyne warhafftige vnd gantz erschreckliche historien / Wie eyn weib jre vier kinder tyranniglichen ermordet / vnd sich selbst auch vmbbracht hat / Geschehen zu Weidenhausen bei Eschweh in Hessen . . .* (Marburg, 1551), 4 fols., A2, A4, A3v (BL; other eds.: Strassburg, 1551, Erfurt, 1551).

30. *Drey Warhafftige Newe Zeittungen. Die Erste / Von dem gewaltigen . . . Wetter. . . . Die Ander / auß dem Niderland /* (Cologne, 1598), 4 fols., A2v, A3 (BL).

31. *Newe Zeitung: Ein Warhafftiges newes Lied / vnd erbermliche geschicht / so sich begeben hat zu Liser an der Mosel / . . . daselbs ein Man genent Gülde Hans / . . . welcher fünff seiner leiblichen Kinder vmbbracht hat / . . . im 1573. Jar* (Schweinfurt, [c. 1573]) (BL).

32. *Zwo newe Zeittung / Die Erste / Ein erschröcklich vnd sehr erbärmlich Geschicht / so geschehen ist den letzten Februarij / in diesem Achtzigsten Jar in Braband . . .* (Vienna, 1580), 4 fols., A2 (DSB Ye 4527; another ed. 1580).

33. *Warhafftige newe Zeitung von einer Frawen sampt dreyen Kindern wie sich selbst durch hungers noth erhangen . . .* (Cologne, 1591), brs., in Brednich, no. 60.

34. *Warhafftige / Erbärmliche vnd auch erschröckliche newe Zeytung / so sich Anno 1602. . . . bey Elbing in Preüssen / . . . mit einer armen Wittfrawen . . .* (Danzig, 1602), brs., in Brednich, no. 126.

35. *Newe Warhaffte / Auch Erschröckliche Zeitunge: Wie ein Son vnd Dochter Sampt einer Dienstmagdt / jhren Leiblichen / Natürlichen Vatter / Hauptman Jacob Eliner . . . zu Brägentz am Bodensee jämerlicher . . . weiß Ermördt haben . . .* (Augsburg, 1595), 4 fols. (DSB Ye 5071).

36. *Zwo vnerhörte vnd schröckliche Zeitungen / Die erste / wie daß ein*

Kauffmans Sohn sich an eine Dienstmagd verlobt . . . (1650), brs., in Brednich, no. 120, based on a Dutch edition ("Gedruckt nach der Niederlandischen Copey"). See also *Eigentlicher Bericht und traurige Zeitung / Von unterschiedlichen Wunderzeichen . . .* (1673), 6 fols. (DSB Ye 7681).

37. *Valet-Lied A.M.T.G.D. Wegen durch Gifft Ertödteten Ehmanns Peinlich leidenden Sünderin* (1665).

38. J. S.[?], *A Brief Anatomie of Women . . .* (1653), 6 pp., 5 (BL).

39. *A pittilesse Mother. That most vnnaturally at one time, murthered two of her owne Children. . . .* [Margret Vincent] (1616), 12 fols., A2, A2v, B2 (BL). See also *Bloody Newes from Dover. Being a True Relation Of The great and bloudy Murder, committed by Mary Champion* (*an Anabaptist*) *who cut off her Childs head . . .* (1647), 4 fols. (BL). Like Vincent, Champion is depicted as motivated by religious frenzy.

40. *Strange and Wonderful News From Durham. Or The Virgins Caveat Against Infant-Murther . . .* (1679), 5 pp., 2, 4 (Bod.).

41. M[artin] P[arker], *No naturall Mother, but a Monster* (1634), *PG*, 425–30.

42. *Newe Zeitung: Welcher gestalt zu Prage ein Mann vnd Weib vber Essen vneins worden / sich geschlagen . . .* (1613), 4 fols. (HAB).

43. *Ein ware gschicht vnd newe Zeitung / Von einem falschen Meitlin . . .* [c. 1650?], 4 fols., A2, A2v, A4v (DSB Ye 7266).

44. *Eine Warhafftige vnd erschröckliche Newe Zeittung / Welche sich begeben . . . hat / in der Statt Limburg / mit eines reichen Becken Tochter / mit Nahmen Catharina . . .* (Frankfurt am Main, 1626), brs., in Brednich, no. 118.

45. *Drey gantz Neue Anmüthige Gesänger / Das Erste: Ein erbärmliche Geschicht . . . zu Pißka . . .* [c. 1600?], A1v.

46. *Ein warhafftigen bericht vnd neuwe zeittung von einem kloster . . . von der Aabtissin welche grosse vnzucht getrieben mit einem vogt welche zehen kinder mit im gehabt / vnnd dieselbigen jämerlich ermördt . . .* (Cologne [?], 1599), 4 fols., A2v, A2v–A3 (DSB Ye 5301).

47. *Wunder newe Zeitung / vnd warhaffte Geschicht. Von der Nunnen heiligkeit vnd reinigkeit . . .* (Christlingen [Strassburg?], 1584), 4 fols. (HAB).

48. On German executions, see Dülmen, *Theater des Schreckens.*

49. *Eine Warhafftige vnd erschröckliche Newe Zeittung / Welche sich begeben . . . hat / in der Statt Limburg* (1626), in Brednich, no. 118.

50. *Warhafftige: Newe Zeitung auß dem Land Westuahlen / von der Stat Ossenbruck / wie man da hat auff einen Tag 133. Vnholden verbrendt . . .* (1588), 4 fols. (DSB Ye 4801); *Ein New kläglich Lied / von dem grossen schaden der Vnholden / So sie in Westphalen zu Aschenbrügk / . . . begangen haben / in dem jetztwerenden 1583. Jar / wie auch jrer 180. jemmerlich verbrendt seind worden . . .* (Wesel, 1583), 4 fols. (DSB Ye 4645). See also *Zwo warhafftige vnd erschröckliche Zeitung / Die erst / wie das in Thüringen / auff dem Varenberg der Hexen so vil zusammen kommen seind . . .* (Erfurt,

1612), 4 fols. (ZB); *Zwo Newe Zeittung / Was man für Hexen oder Vnholden verbrendt hat . . .* (Hoff, 1580), 4 fols. (ZB); *Ein Warhafftige vnd gründtliche Beschreibung / Auß dem Bistum Würtz- vnd Bamberg / . . . wie man alda so vil Hexen Mann vnd Weibspersohnen verbrennen laßt . . .* (1627), 2 fols. (HAB).

51. *A True Relation Of the Araignment Of eighteene Witches . . .* [at St. Edmunds-Bury in Suffolk] (1645), 8 pp. (BL).

52. *Damnable Practises of three Lincoln-shire Witches* (1619), *PG*, 96–103.

53. *The Examination and confession of certaine Wytches at Chensforde in the Countie of Essex . . .* (1556; rept. London, 1863–64); Goodcole, *The Wonderfull discouerie of Elizabeth Sawyer a Witch, late of Edmonton* (1621), C2.

54. This pattern in English witchcraft is described by Macfarlane, *Witchcraft in Tudor and Stuart England*, and Thomas, *Religion and the Decline of Magic*.

55. *The Witches of Northamptonshire* (1612), 14 fols., A3 (BL).

56. See, e.g., *Witches Apprehended, Examined and Executed, for notable villanies by them committed both by Land and Water . . .* [Mother Sutton] (1613), 10 fols. (Bod.); *Damnable Practises*, *PG*, 96–103; *A Full and True Relation of the Tryal, Condemnation, and Execution of Ann Foster . . .* (1674), 6 pp. (BL).

57. *Newe Zeitung aus Berneburgk / Schrecklich zu hören vnd zu lesen / Von dreyen alten Teuffels Bulerin / Hexin oder Zauberinnen . . .* (1580), 6 fols. (HAB).

58. Hans Kuntz, *Newe zeitung. Von einer Erschrecklichen That / welche zu Dillingen / von einem Jhesuwider / /* [sic] *vnd einer Hexen / geschehen ist . . .* (Ursel, 1579), 4 fols., A2 (BSB).

59. *Erschreckliche Newe Zeitung / Welche sich begeben vnd zugetragen in diesem 1650. Jahr / bey der Stadt Dillhofen . . .* (Dilhofen[?], 1650), 4 fols. (DSB Ye 7261); *Ein Warhafftige Zeitung. Von etliche Hexen oder Vnholden / welche man kürtzlich im Stifft Mäntz / . . . verbrendt . . .* (Frankfurt[?], 1603), 4 fols. (DSB Ye 5581).

60. *Newe Zeitung aus Berneburgk* (1580), A2v, A4.

61. *Drey warhafftige grundtliche Zeitungen / Die erste / Von ettlichen Hexen . . . welche hin vnd wider in Vngern / vnd Teutschland grossen schaden angericht haben . . .* (1610), A1v; *Ein Warhafftige vnd gründtliche Beschreibung / Auß dem Bistum Würtz- vnd Bamberg* (1627).

62. *Gründliche vnerhörte Zeitung / Von den Teuffels-Zauberern . . .* (Hildesheim, [c. 1628]), 2 fols., A2 (DSB Ye 6445). See also *Gewiser Bericht deß Truten vnnd Hexenbrennens Bambergischen Gebiets . . .* (Schmalkalden, 1628), 2 fols., A2 (GNM); *Warhafftige: Newe Zeittung auß dem Land Westuahlen / von der Stat Ossenbruck / wie man da hat auff einen Tag 133. Vnholden verbrendt . . .* (1588).

63. *Relation Oder Beschreibung so Anno 1669 . . . in . . . Augsburg geschehen . . .* (Augsburg, [c. 1669]), in Wäscher, no. 31; *Gewiser Bericht deß*

Truten vnnd Hexenbrennens (1628), A1v; [John Davenport], *The Witches Of Huntingdon, Their Examinations and Confessions . . .* (1646), 15 pp. (BL).

64. *Witchcraft discovered and punished* [1682], RB 6:706–8.

65. G. B., *A Most Wicked worke of a wretched Witch . . . Wrought on the Person of one Richard Burt . . .* (1592), 6 pp., 3 (Lambeth).

66. Kuntz, *Newe zeitung. Von einer Erschecklichen That* (1579).

67. See, e.g., *Gewiser Bericht deß Truten vnnd Hexenbrennens* (1628); *Gründliche vnerhörte Zeitung / Von den Teuffels-Zauberern* [c. 1628]; *Zwo Newe Zeittung / Was man für Hexen oder Vnholden verbrendt hat* (1580); *Ein Warhafftige Zeitung. Von etliche Hexen oder Vnholden* (1603).

68. *The Apprehension and confession of three notorious Witches. Arreigned and by Iustice condemned and executed at Chelmes-forde, in the County of Essex . . . 1589* [c. 1589], 8 fols., A4 (Lambeth).

69. *A Rehearsall both straung and true, of hainous and horrible actes committed by Elizabeth Stile, Alias Rockingham . . .* [c. 1579], 10 fols., A4 (BL); *A True Relation Of the Araignment Of eighteene Witches* (1645), 4. See also *The Witches of Northamptonshire* (1612).

70. G. B., *A Most Wicked worke of a wretched Witch* (1592). See also *A Rehearsall both straung and true* (1579), A2v–A3.

71. *The Apprehension and confession of three notorious Witches* (1589). See also *Gewiser Bericht deß Truten vnnd Hexenbrennens* (1628).

72. [Davenport], *The Witches Of Huntingdon* (1646).

73. *Ein erschröckliche geschicht . . . von dreyen Zauberin / vnnb zw ayen Mannen . . .* (Nuremberg, 1555), brs., in Wäscher, no. 32.

74. Kuntz, *Newe zeitung. Von einer Erschecklichen That* (1579), A3; see also *Newe Zeitung aus Berneburgk* (1580), B1.

75. *Ein New kläglich Lied / von dem grossen schaden der Vnholden* (1583), A2v.

76. *The Wonderfvl Discoverie of the Witchcrafts of Margaret and Phillip Flower, daughters of Ioan Flower . . .* (1619), 23 fols., B2 (BL); *A true and exact Relation Of the severall Informations, Examinations, and Confessions of the late Witches, arraigned and executed in the County of Essex . . .* (1645), 22 fols., A2 (BL).

77. Kors and Peters, *Witchcraft in Europe,* 127, 123.

78. See, e.g., Thomas, *Religion and the Decline of Magic,* 520–26, 568–69; Macfarlane, *Witchcraft in Tudor and Stuart England,* 161; Midelfort, *Witch Hunting in Southwestern Germany,* 184–85.

79. See Wunder, "Hexenprozesse im Herzogtum Preussen während des 16. Jahrhunderts"; Larner, *Enemies of God,* 92–93, 101–2; see also Klaits, *Servants of Satan.*

80. Goodcole, *The wonderfull discouerie of Elizabeth Sawyer a Witch, late of Edmonton* (1621), A3v.

81. *Damnable Practises of three Lincoln-shire Witches* (1619), PG, 96–103. The pamphlet is *The Wonderfvl Discoverie of the Witchcrafts of Margaret and Phillip Flower* (1619).

82. Hans Sachs, "Wunderlich gesprech von fünff unhulden," in Goetze, 1:46–48; printed in *Die Neun Elenden Wanderer. Mehr ein wunderlich gesprech von Fünff Vnholden* (Nuremberg, 1553).

83. *Zäuberische Zeitung / Wie eine Hexin durch Teuffelszkunst jren Sohn mit sonderlichen Aberglaubischen dingen zum Wildschiessen behülfflich gewesen* (1589), A3.

84. Hieronymus Magomastin, pseud., *The strange Witch at Greenwich* . . . (1650), 28 pp. (BL).

85. *A true and exact Relation Of the severall Informations, Examinations, and Confessions of the late Witches, arraigned and executed in the County of Essex* (1645).

86. *A Rehearsall both straung and true, of hainous and horrible actes committed by Elizabeth Stile, Alias Rockingham* [c. 1579], A2v; *The Witch Of Wapping. Or An Exact and Perfect Relation, of the Life and Devilish Practises of Joan Peterson* . . . (1652), 8 pp. (BL).

87. *Truth brought to Light* [1662], *PA*, 96–100.

88. *Newe Zeitung aus Berneburgk* (1580), A2v–A3.

89. Kuntz, *Newe zeitung. Von einer Erschrecklichen That* (1579), A2v.

90. *Ein New kläglich Lied / von dem grossen schaden der Vnholden* (1583), A3–A3v.

91. *Drey warhafftige grundtliche Zeitungen / Die erste / Von ettlichen Hexen* (1610), A2v.

92. *Relation Oder Beschreibung so Anno 1669* . . . *in* . . . *Augsburg geschehen*, in Wäscher, no. 31. See also *Zwo Newe Zeittung / Was man für Hexen oder Vnholden verbrendt hat* (1580); *Warhafftige / Newe zeittug* [sic] *von der vnerhorten erschrecklichen Straff Gottes / so vber die Stadt Friedeberg in der Newmarckt gelegen* . . . (Frankfurt[?], 1594) (DSB Yd 7852.22); *Erschreckliche Newe Zeitung / Welche sich begeben vnd zugetragen in diesem 1650. Jahr / bey der Stadt Dillhofen* (Dilhofen[?], 1650) (DSB Ye 7261).

93. *Warhaffte vnd glaubwirdige Zeyttung. Von Hundert vnd vier vnd dreyssig Vnholden* . . . (Strassburg, 1583), 4 fols., A3 (BSB).

94. *Ein Warhafftige Zeitung. Von etliche Hexen oder Vnholden / welche man kürtzlich im Stifft Mäntz /* . . . *verbrendt* (1603); *Warhafftige erschröckliche Zeytung vnd Geschicht / So sich begeben* . . . *in der Statt Wanga* . . . (Kempten, 1627), brs., in Brednich, no. 124.

95. *Drey warhafftige grundtliche Zeitungen / Die erste / Von ettlichen Hexen* (1610), A2v.

96. *Zwo warhafftige vnd erschröckliche Zeitung / Die erst / wie das in Thüringen / auff dem Varenberg der Hexen so vil zusammen kommen seind* (1612), A3.

97. See, e.g., *Ein erschröcklich geschicht Vom Tewfel vnd einer vnhulden / beschehen zu Schilta bey Rotweil in der Karwochen* (1533), brs. (ZB). A graphic depiction of such a scene appears in the 1514 drawing *Three Witches* by Hans Baldung Grien: the witches' nudity and lewd postures point to sexual deviance, and the picture underlines their usurpation of the male

role as well as their destruction of the female one. The two dominant witches are shown in vigorous, unrestrained movement; the old witch is not so much wrinkled as muscular and virile, and the two witches on top are posed to suggest deviant rape, as well as an infernal baptism, of the young witch beneath. The three figures together form a phallic image, topped by the pot of witches' brew, a perversion of semen, which one witch is about to pour. The picture appears in Charles W. Talbot, "Baldung and the Female Nude," in *Hans Baldung Grien: Prints and Drawings*, ed. James H. Marrow and Alan Shestack (Chicago, 1981), 19–37, 32. See also Miles, *Carnal Knowing*, 136–37.

98. *Eine warhafftige Newe zeyttung / so sich begeben hat zu Eschwein / wie allda ein mörder ist eingebracht worden / welcher 55. Mord mit seiner eygen Hand verbracht hat* . . . (Coburg, 1597), 4 fols. (BL). See also *Erschröckliche Warhafftige newe Zeittung von etlichen Mördern / wie sie sich dem Teuffel ergeben* . . . (Strassburg, 1583), 4 fols. (BL); *Ein Gründtliche auch warhafftige vnd erschlöckliche* [sic] *newe Zeitung / von sechs Mördern* . . . (Ulmitz[?], 1603), 4 fols. (DSB Ye 5571).

10. Perspectives

1. See, e.g., Emily James Putnam, *The Lady* (Chicago, 1969), xxvii–xxix.

2. See Underdown, "Taming of the Scold."

3. See Amussen, "Gender, Family, and the Social Order," 208; Reiter, "Men and Women in the South of France: Public and Private Domains," in Reiter, *Toward an Anthropology of Women*, 252–82.

4. See Howell, *Women, Production, and Patriarchy in Late Medieval Cities*, 18–19; Rappaport, *Worlds within Worlds*, 36–42.

5. See Howell, *Women, Production, and Patriarchy in Late Medieval Cities*, 182–83; Underdown, "Taming of the Scold."

6. See Stone, *Family, Sex, and Marriage*; Stone argues that the lower orders must have been especially callous about marriage. For critiques of Stone's view, see, e.g., Wrightson, *English Society*, 70–72; Houlbrooke, *English Family*, 14–15; Sharpe, "Plebeian Marriage in Stuart England."

7. MacDonald, *Mystical Bedlam*, 88.

8. See Macfarlane, *Marriage and Love in England*.

9. See Robisheaux, *Rural Society and the Search for Order*, 95–120; Wiesner, "Frail, Weak, and Helpless," 167.

10. For a case of literary representation of baby talk, see Casey, *Susanna Theme in German Literature*, 84–85.

11. Macfarlane, *Marriage and Love in England*, 338–39; Wiesner, "Frail, Weak, and Helpless," 162–63; M. Weber, *Ehefrau und Mutter*, 240–41.

12. On resistance to Roman law in sixteenth-century Germany, see Strauss, *Law, Resistance, and the State.*

13. Abel, *Massenarmut und Hungerkrisen im vorindustriellen Deutschland,* 63, 39.

14. See Robin Bruce Barnes, *Prophecy and Gnosis: Apocalypticism in the Wake of the German Reformation* (Stanford, Calif., 1988).

15. Davis, *Society and Culture in Early Modern France,* 93–94.

16. Stone, "Social Mobility in England."

17. Stone and Stone, *An Open Elite?*

18. Strauss, *Law, Resistance, and the State,* 112–13; see also Macfarlane, *Marriage and Love in England,* 257.

19. See Macfarlane, *Marriage and Love in England* and *Origins of English Individualism.*

20. Ozment, *When Fathers Ruled,* 177.

21. See Sabean, *Power in the Blood;* Macfarlane, *Marriage and Love in England* and *Origins of Individualism;* MacDonald, *Mystical Bedlam.*

Bibliography

Primary Sources: English

Note: The place of publication is London unless otherwise indicated.

An Account of the Tryal and Examination of Joan Buts, For being a Common Witch and Inchantress. 1682. Brs. NLS.

An Act to prevent the Destroying and Murthering of Bastard Children. 1680. Brs. Guildhall Library, London.

An Answer To the Character of an Exchange-wench: or a Vindication of an Exchange-woman. 1675. 6 pp. BL.

The Antient, True, and Admirable History of Patient Grisel, A Poore Mans Daughter in France: Shewing, How Maides, by her example, in their good behauiour may marrie rich Hvsbands. . . . 1619. 16 fols. BL.

The Ape-Gentle-woman, or the Character of an Exchange-wench. 1675. 6 pp. BL.

The Apprehension and confession of three notorious Witches. Arreigned and by Iustice condemned and executed at Chelmes-forde, in the Countye of Essex . . . 1589. [c. 1589]. 8 fols. Lambeth.

The Araignement & burning of Margaret Ferne-seede. . . . 1608. 7 fols. BL.

Ashton, John, ed. *A Century of Ballads.* 1887.

B., A. *A Canterbury Tale, Translated Out of Chaucers old English. . . .* 1641. 4 fols. BL.

B., G. *A Most Wicked worke of a wretched Witch . . . Wrought on the Person of one Richard Burt. . . .* 1592. 6 pp. Lambeth.

A Banquet Of Jests. Or Change of Cheare. 1639. BL.

The Blind eats many a Flye: Or, The Broken Damsel made Whole. [1680s]. Brs. BL.

Bloody Newes from Dover. Being a True Relation Of The great and bloudy

Murder, committed by Mary Champion (an Anabaptist) who cut off her Childs head. . . . 1647. 4 fols. BL.

Bloudy Newse from the North, and The Ranting Adamites Declaration. . . . 1650. 6 pp. BL.

Böddeker, R., ed. "Englische Lieder und Balladen aus dem 16. Jahrhundert." *Jahrbuch für romanische und englische Sprache und Literatur* 14 (n.s. 2) (1875): 81–105, 210–39, 347–67; 15:92–129.

[Borde, Andrew]. *A ryght pleasaunt and merye Historie, of the Mylner of Abyngton.* . . . N.d. 13 fols. Bod.

B[rewer], T[homas]. *Mistres Turners Repentance, Who, about the poysoning of that Ho: Knight Sir Thomas Overbury, Was executed the fourteenth day of Nouember, last.* 1615. Brs. SA.

The Bridewel Whores resolution. . . . [1670s?]. Brs. Rawlinson Ballads 566(98), Bod.

A briefe and true report of two most cruel, vnnaturall, and inhumane Murders, done in Lincolneshire, by twoo Husbands vpon their Wiues. . . . 1607. 10 fols. Rept. in *Tudor and Stuart Texts*, no. 4, ed. Joseph Arnold Foster. East Lansing, Mich., 1945.

A Briefe Discovrse of Two most cruell and bloudie murthers, committed bothe in Worcestershire. . . . [c. 1583]. 12 fols. BL.

A Broad-Sideag ainst [sic] *Marriage Directed to that Inconsiderable Annimal, Called, A Husband.* 1675. Brs. BL.

Bull-Feather Hall: Or, The Antiquity and Dignity of Horns, Amply shown. 1664. 16 pp. BL.

Burdet, W. *A Wonder of Wonders. Being A faithful Narrative and true Relation, of one Anne Green.* . . . 1651. 6 pp. BL.

A Caution to Married Couples: Being a true Relation How a Man in Nightingale-lane Having beat and abused his Wife, Murthered a Tub-man. . . . 1677. 8 pp. BL.

The Character of a Town-Gallant. . . . 1675. BL.

The Character of a Town Misse. 1675. 8 pp. BL.

Chaucer Junior [pseud.]. *Canterbury Tales.* . . . 1687. 12 fols. Pepys.

Child, Francis James, ed. *The English and Scottish Popular Ballads.* 5 vols. New York, 1962.

The Citizens Reply To the Whores Petition, and Prentices Answer. 1668. Brs. Bagford Ballads, BL.

The City Caper: Or, The Whetstones-Park Privateer. [Late 17c]. Brs. Douce Ballads, 1:26, Bod.

Clark, Andrew, ed. *The Shirburn Ballads.* Oxford, 1907.

A Collection of Rare and Curious Tracts. Great Totham, Essex, 1837.

A Collection of Seventy-Nine Black-Letter Ballads and Broadsides, Printed in the Reign of Queen Elizabeth. . . . 1867.

Collmann, Herbert L., ed. *Ballads and Broadsides, chiefly of the Elizabethan Period.* Oxford, 1912.

The Country Lass, Who left her Spinning-Wheel for a more pleasant Employ-ment. [Late 17c?]. Brs. BL.

Cruel and Barbarous News From Cheapside in London: Being a True and Faithful Relation Of an horid Fact, acted by an unhuman Mistriss upon the body of her Apprentice. . . . 1676. 5 pp. Bod.

The Cruel French Lady. . . . 1673. 8 pp. Bod.

[Davenport, John]. *The Witches Of Huntingdon, Their Examinations and Confessions.* . . . 1646. 15 pp. BL.

Deloney, Thomas. *The Garland of Good-Will.* Ed. James Henry Dixon. 1851.

————. *The Works of Thomas Deloney.* Ed. Francis O. Mann. Oxford, 1912.

Deplorable News from Southwark. . . . [17c]. Brs. Book of Fortune Ballads, BL.

The Description of a Town Miss. Or, A Looking-Glass for all Confident Ladies. [1670s]. Brs. BL.

A Description of the Sect called the Familie of Love. . . . 1641. 6 pp. BL.

A Detection of damnable driftes, practized by three Witches arraigned at Chelm-isforde in Essex. . . . 1579. 10 fols. BL.

A Dialogue Between Mistris Macquerella, a Suburb Bawd. . . . 1650. 6 fols. BL.

A Dialogue between the D. of C. and the D. of P. at their meeting in Paris, With the Ghost of Jane Shore. N.d. 2 fols. NLS.

A Discoverie of Six women preachers, in Middlesex, Kent, Cambridgshire, and Salisbury. . . . 1641. 5 pp. BL.

The Divell a Married Man: or, The Divell hath met with his Match. N.d. 8 pp. BL.

The Downefall of Temporizing Poets, unlicenst printers, upstart Booksellers, trotting Mercuries, and bawling Hawkers. . . . 1641. 5 pp. BL.

A Dreadful Relation, of the Cruel, Bloudy, and most Inhumane Massacre and Butchery. . . . 1655. Brs. BL.

Dugdale, Gilbert. *A True Discourse Of the practises of Elizabeth Caldwell.* . . . 1604. 16 fols. BL.

Ebsworth, J. W., ed. *The Bagford Ballads.* 2 vols. Hertford, Eng., 1878.

Enfield Common: Or, The Young Damsel Cured Of The Green Sickness By a Lusty Gallant. . . . [Late 17c]. Brs. Osterley Park Ballads, BL.

The Euing Collection of English Broadside Ballads. Glasgow, 1971.

An Exact Relation of the Barbarous Murder Committed on Lawrence Corddel A Butcher. . . . 1661. 5 pp. Bod.

An excellent New Song, called, The Intreagues of Love. . . . N.d. Brs. Osterley Park Ballads, BL.

The Examination and confession of certaine Wytches at Chensforde in the Countie of Essex. . . . 1556. Rept. Philobiblon Society, *Miscellanies* 8 (1863–64).

F., H. *A Prodigious & Tragicall History of the Arraignment, Tryall, Confession, and Condemnation of six Witches at Maidstone, in Kent.* . . . 1652. 11 pp. BL.

F., S. *Death in a New Dress: Or Sportive Funeral Elegies.* . . . 1656. 8 fols. BL.

The Famous & renowned History of Morindos a King of Spaine; Who maryed with Miracola a Spanish Witch. . . . 1609. 23 fols. Bod.

Father a Child that's none of my own, Being The Seamans Complaint, Who took a Whore instead of a Saint. [Late 17c]. Brs. Douce Ballads 1:77a, Bod.

The Fifth and last Part Of The Wandring whore. . . . 1661. 16 pp. Bod.

Fill Gut, & Pinch belly: One being Fat with eating good Men, the other Leane for want of good Women. [1620]. Brs. SA.

Foord, Ed. *Wine and Women: Or A briefe Description of the common courtesie of a Curtezan.* . . . 1647. 31 pp. BL.

Fore-Warn'd, Fore-Arm'd: Or, A Caveat to Batchelors, In The Character of a Bad Woman. Brs. 1684. BL.

The French Intelligencer, no. 21 (1652). 8 pp. BL.

French Occurrences . . . , no. 13 (1652). 4 fols. BL.

A Full and True Relation of the Tryal, Condemnation, and Execution of Ann Foster. . . . 1674. 6 pp. BL.

Furnivall, Frederick J., ed. *Captain Cox, his Ballads and Books; or, Robert Laneham's Letter.* Hertford, 1890.

A General Summons for those belonging to the Hen-Peck'd Frigate, To appear at Cuckolds-Point, on the 18th. of this Instant October. [17c]. Brs. Osterley Park Ballads, BL.

God's Strange and terrible Judgment In Oxford-shire. . . . 1677. 8 pp. Bod.

G[oodcole], H[enry]. *Heavens Speedie Hue and Cry sent after Lust and Murther.* 1635. 12 fols. BL.

Goodcole, Henry. *The wonderfull discouerie of Elizabeth Sawyer a Witch, late of Edmonton.* . . . 1621. 14 fols. BL.

The Gossips Braule, or The Women weare the Breeches. A Mock Comedy. 1655. 8 pp. BL.

The Gossips Feast or, Morrall Tales. . . . 1647. 13 pp. BL.

H., I. *A Strange Wonder or a Wonder in a Woman.* . . . 1642. 4 fols. BL.

Haec-Vir: Or The Womanish-Man. . . . N.d. 11 fols. BL.

Halliwell, James Orchard, ed. *The Tale of The Smyth and his Dame; and The Booke of Robin Conscience.* . . . Brixton Hill, 1848.

The Harleian Miscellany: or, a Collection of Scarce, Curious, and Entertaining Pamphlets and Tracts . . . 1 (1744).

Hazlitt, W. Carew, ed. *Shakespeare Jest-Books.* 1864.

Here begynneth a dialogue betwene the comen Secretary and Jelowsy touchynge the vnstableness of harlottes. [16c]. 4 fols. BL.

Here Begynneth the Scole house of women. . . . 1560. 16 fols. BL.

(Hey Hoe, for a Husband), or, The Parliament of Maides. . . . 1647. 6 pp. BL.

Hic Mulier: Or, The Man-Woman. . . . N.d. 9 fols. BL.

The High-way Hector. . . . N.d. Brs. BL.

The History Of The Life and Death Of Pope Joane. . . . 1663. 16 pp. Bod.

Hopkins, Mathew. *The Discovery of Witches. . . .* 1647. Rept. in *A Collection of Rare and Curious Tracts.* Great Totham, Essex, 1837.

The Horrible Murther of a young Boy of three yeres of age, whose sister had her tongue cut out . . . [Annis Dell]. 1606. 10 pp. BL.

Horrid News from St. Martins: or, Unheard of Murder and Poyson. Being A true Relation how a Girl not full Sixteen years of age, Murdered her own Mother. . . . 1677. 8 pp. BL.

The Humble Petition of Many Thousands Of Wives and Matrons of the City of London. . . . 1643. 8 pp. BL.

Joans Victory Over her Fellow-Servants. N.d. Brs. BL.

John the Glover, and Jane his Servant. N.d. Brs. Douce Ballads 1:103b, Bod.

Jolly Coach-Man: Or, The Buxome Taylors Wifes Late folly. 1685. Brs. BL.

A Letter From the Dutch. of Portsmouth To Madam Gwyn. . . . 1682. Brs. NLS.

A Letter sent by the Maydens of London, to the vertuous Matrones & Mistresses of the same. 1567. 14 fols. Lambeth.

The Life And Death Of Mrs. Mary Frith. Commonly Called Mal Cut purse. . . . 1662. 173 pp. BL.

The Life and Pranks of Long Meg of Westminster. [c. 1650]. 12 fols. BL.

The London Jilts Lamentation. . . . [1680s]. Brs. Douce Ballads 1:116a, Bod.

Madam Gwins Answer To The Dutchess Of Portsmouths Letter. [1682]. Brs. NLS.

Magomastin, Hieronymus [pseud.]. *The strange Witch at Greenwich. . . .* 1650. 28 pp. BL.

The Maids answer to the Batchelors Ballad. . . . [1680s]. Brs. Douce Ballads 2:147a, Bod.

The Married Mans complaint Who took a Shrow instead of a Saint. [Mid-17c]. Brs. Douce Ballads 2:150a, Bod.

The Married wives complaint. Or, The hasty Bride Repents her bargain. [Later 17c]. Brs. Douce Ballads 2:144b, Bod.

Mary of Nimmegen. [c. 1518–19]. Rept. Cambridge, Mass., 1932.

Mercurius Avlicvs. Aug. 27 [1643]. 16 pp. BL.

Mercurius Civicus. Londons Intelligencer . . . , no. 18 (1643). 8 pp. BL.

Mercurius Democritus, Or, A True and Perfect Nocturnall . . . , no. 2 (1652). 8 pp. BL.

Mercurius Fumigosus, or the Smoking Nocturnall . . . , nos. 34 and 35 (1655). 4 fols. BL.

Merrie Conceited Iests: Of George Peele Gentleman. . . . 1627. 30 pp. BL.

The Merry Dutch Miller: And New Invented Windmill. Wherewith he undertaketh to grind all Sorts of Women. . . . 1672. 8 fols. BL.

The Merry Gossips Vindication, To the Groats worth of good Councel Declaration. [Late 17c]. BL.

The Midwife Unmask'd: Or, The Popish Design Of Mrs Cellier's Meal-Tub. . . . 1680. 4 fols. BL.

A Miraculous Cure For Witchcraft Or Strange News from the Blew-Boar in Holburn. N.d. Brs. BL.

Misomastropus [pseud.]. *The Bawds Tryal and Execution: Also, A short Account of her whole Life & Travels.* 1679. 6 pp. BL.

Mistris Turners Farewell to all women. [1614]. Brs. Bod.

The Modish Whore. . . . 1675. Brs. Douce Ballads 2:158, Bod.

A Monstrous Birth: Or, A True Relation Of . . . a woman dwelling at Wetwan in Yorke-shire: And How the Devil kept her Company. 1657. 4 fols. BL.

A Most Certain, Strange, and true Discovery of a Witch. 1643. 7 pp. BL.

The Most Crvell And Bloody Mvrther committed by an Inkeepers Wife, called Annis Dell, and her Sonne George Dell. . . . 1606. 12 fols. BL.

Muld Sacke: Or The Apologie of Hic Mulier. . . . 1620. 15 fols. BL.

The Murderous Midwife, with her Roasted Punishment. . . . 1673. 6 pp. Guildhall Library, London.

Murther, Murther. Or, A bloody Relation how Anne Hamton, dwelling in Westminster nigh London, by poyson murthered her deare husband. . . . 1641. 6 pp. BL.

Murther will out, Or, A True and Faithful Relation of an Horrible Murther committed Thirty Three Years ago, by an unnatural Mother, upon the body of her own Child about a Year Old. . . . 1675. 6 pp. BL.

[Nevile, Henry.] *The Ladies, A Second Time, Assembled In Parliament.* 1647. 12 pp. BL.

[———.] *The Ladies Parliament.* [1647]. 10 fols. BL.

[———.] *Newes from the New Exchange, or the Commonwealth of Ladies.* . . . 1650. 22 pp. BL.

[———.] *The Parliament of Ladies.* 1647. 16 pp. BL.

A New and True Ballad of the Poet's Complaint: Or, a new Song to a new Tune, of a Young Wench living in Holbourn, with a full discription of the notable Tricks put upon her by two Cornuted Suitors. [1670s]. Brs. BL.

A New balet entituled howe to Wyue Well. [1561?] Brs. SA.

Newes From Perin in Cornwall: Of A most Bloody and vn-exampled Murther very lately committed by a Father on his owne Sonne . . . at the Instigation of a mercilesse Step-mother. . . . 1618. Rept. in *Reprints of English Books, 1475–1700,* ed. Joseph Arnold Foster, no. 36. East Lansing, Mich., 1945.

Newes from Scotland, Declaring the Damnable life and death of Doctor Fian. . . . 1597. 16 fols. Lambeth.

News from Old Gravel-lane: Or, a True and Perfect Relation of a Woman That is Tormented with the Devil. 1675. 6 pp. BL.

"A New Yeeres guift for shrews." [1620]. In *Catalogue of Prints and Drawings in the British Museum.* Division 1. Political and Personal Satires, no. 89.

The Night-walkers Declaration. . . . 1676. 8 pp. BL.

A notable and prodigious Historie of a Mayden, who for sundry yeeres neither eateth, drinketh, nor sleepeth, neyther auoydeth any excrements, and yet liueth. 1589. BL.

Now Or Never: Or, A New Parliament of Women. . . . 1656. 4 fols. BL.

P., L. *The Merry Mans Resolution.* . . . N.d. Brs. BL.

———. *Strange and wonderfull news of a woman which Lived neer unto the Famous City of London, who had her head torn off from her Body by the Divell.* . . . [17c]. Brs. Book of Fortune Ballads, BL.

The Parliament of Women. 1646. 12 fols. BL.

Pasquils Iests, Mixed with Mother Bunches Merriments. . . . 1604. 24 fols. BL.

A Perfect Account Of The daily Intelligence from the Armies in England, Scotland, and Ireland . . . , no. 67 (1652). 8 pp. BL.

A pittilesse Mother. That most vnnaturally at one time, murthered two of her owne Children . . . [*Margret Vincent*]. 1616. 12 fols. BL.

A Pleasant Discourse Of A Young Gentle-woman to her Husband The Quaker. N.d. Brs. BL.

The Pleasant History of Tom Ladle. . . . [17c]. 23 pp. Pepys.

The Poor Whores Complaint to the Apprentices of London, &c. 1672. Brs. Bagford Ballads, BL.

The Popes Letter, To Maddam Cellier. . . . 1680. 2 fols. BL.

The Prentices Answer to the Whores Petition. 1668. Brs. Bagford Ballads, BL.

Price, Laurence. *Bloody Actions Performed. Or, A brief and true Relation of three Notorious Murthers, committed by three Bloud-thirsty men, 2. upon their own Wives.* 1653. 16 pp. BL.

———. *A Map of Merry Conceites.* 1656. 8 fols. BL.

P[rice?], L[aurence?]. *The Vertuous Wife is the glory of her Husband.* . . . 1667. 21 pp. BL.

P[rice], L[aurence]. *The Witch of the Woodlands: or, the Coblers New Translation.* [c. 1670?]. 22 pp. BL.

The Proude Wyues Pater noster. . . . 1560. 12 fols. BL.

The Ranters Monster: Being a true Relation of one Mary Adams. . . . 1652. Rept. in *Reprints of English Books, 1475–1700,* ed. Joseph Arnold Foster, no. 34. East Lansing, Mich., 1940.

A Rehearsall both straung and true, of hainous and horrible actes committed by Elizabeth Stile, Alias Rockingham. . . . [c. 1579]. 10 fols. BL.

A Relation of the Devill Balams Departure Out of the Body of the Mother-Prioresse of the Vrsuline Nuns of Loudun. 1636. 12 fols. BL.

A Remonstrance Of The Shee-Citizens of London. . . . 1647. 6 pp. BL.

Rollins, Hyder Edward, ed. *Old English Ballads.* Cambridge, 1920.

———, ed. *The Pack of Autolycus.* Cambridge, Mass., 1927.

———, ed. *The Pepys Ballads.* 2 vols. Cambridge, Mass., 1922.

———, ed. *A Pepysian Garland.* Cambridge, 1922.

R[owlands], S[amuel]. *A Crew of kind Gossips, all met to be merrie: Complayning of their Husbands, with their Husbands answeres in their owne defence.* 1613. 19 fols. BL.

————. *Democritus, Or Doctor Merry-man his Medicines, against Melancholy humors.* [1607]. 24 fols. BL.

[————]. *Well met Gossip: Or, Tis merrie when Gossips meete.* 1619. 14 fols. BL.

The Roxburghe Ballads. Vols. 1–3 ed. William Chappell; vols. 4–9 ed. J. W. Ebsworth. Hertford, Eng., 1872–99.

S., J.[?] *A Brief Anatomie of Women.* . . . 1653. 6 pp. BL.

S., S. *A Famous Battle between Robin Hood, and Maid Marian; declaring their Love, Life, and Liberty.* N.d. Brs. Wood Collection 401(21), Bod.

S., S. *The Joviall Crew, Or, The Devill turn'd Ranter.* . . . 1651. 15 pp. BL.

A Sad and Sorrowfull Relation of Laurence Cauthorn, Butcher. . . . 1661. Brs. Bod.

The Saint turn'd Curtezan. . . . [1681]. Brs. Wood Collection, Bod.

A Satyr against Whoring. In Answer to a Satyr against Marriage. 1682. Brs. NLS.

A Scourge for Poor Robin; Or, The Exact Picture of a Bad Husband. . . . 1678. 8 pp. BL.

The Seven Women Confessors, Or a Discovery of the Seuen white Divels which liued at Queen-street in Coven-Garden. . . . 1642. 4 fols. BL.

The seuerall Notorious and lewd Cousnages of Iohn West, and Alice West, falsely called the King and Queene of Fayries. . . . 1613. 11 fols. Bod.

Signes and wonders from Heaven. . . . N.d. 5 pp. BL.

The Sisters of the Scabards Holiday. 1641. 5 pp. BL.

Skelton, John. "The Tunning of Elinour Rumming." In *The Complete Poems of John Skelton Laureate,* ed. Philip Henderson, 112–30. 1948.

Smith, Walter. *The Wydow Edyth: Twelue mery gestys of one called Edyth, the lyeing wydow whiche still lyueth.* 1525. Rept. in *Shakespeare Jest-Books,* ed. W. Carew Hazlitt, 3:28. 1864.

The Snare of the Devill Discovered: Or, A True and perfect Relations of the sad and deplorable Condition of Lydia the Wife of John Rogers House-Carpenter. . . . 1658. 12 pp. BL.

Sowernam, Ester. *Ester hath hang'd Haman: or An Answere to a lewd Pamphlet, entituled, The Arraignment of Women.* 1617. 53 pp. Rept. 1807. BL.

A Spirit Moving In The Women-Preachers: Or, Certaine Quaeres, Vented and put forth unto this affronted, brazen-faced, strange, new Feminine Brood. . . . 1646. 8 pp. BL.

Strange & Terrible Newes from Cambridge, Being a true Relation of the Quakers bewitching of Mary Philips. . . . 1659. 8 pp. BL.

A strange and true Relation Of A Young Woman possest with the Devill. By name Joyce Dovey. . . . 1647. Rept. in *Reprints of English Books, 1475–1700,* ed. Joseph Arnold Foster, no. 35. East Lansing, Mich., 1940.

The Strange and Wonderful History of Mother Shipton. . . . [Late 17c]. 21 pp. Pepys.

Strange and Wonderful News From Durham. Or The Virgins Caveat Against Infant-Murther. . . . 1679. 5 pp. Bod.

Strange Newes from Scotland, or, A strange Relation of a terrible and prodigious Monster. . . . 1647. 5 pp. BL.

A Strange Report of Sixe most notorious Witches, who by their diuelish practises murdred aboue the number of foure hundred small Children . . . Manchen in high Germanie. 1601. 6 fols. Bod.

[Stubbes, Philip]. *A Christal Glasse for Christian women.* 1591. 12 fols. BL.

Sundrye strange and inhumaine Murthers, lately committed. 1591. 8 fols. Lambeth.

[Swetnam, Joseph]. *The Araignment Of Lewde, idle, froward, and vnconstant women.* . . . 1615. 64 pp. Rept. 1807.

Syr Eglamoure of Artoys. N.d. 20 fols. BL.

T., I. *The Iust Down[fall of] Ambition, Adultery, and Murder.* [1612?]. 12 fols. BL.

The Taming of a Shrew. . . . N.d. Brs. Wood Collection, Bod.

Taylor, John. *A Common Whore With all these Graces Grac'd.* . . . 1622. 16 fols. BL.

Thorowgood, G. *Pray be not Angry: Or, The Women's New Law.* . . . 1656. 4 fols. BL.

Three Inhumane Murthers, Committed By one Bloudy Person, upon His Father, his Mother, and his Wife. . . . 1675. 6 pp. BL.

The Town-Misses Declaration and Apology. . . . 1675. BL.

Treason and Murther: Or, The Bloody Father-in-Law. 1674. 8 pp. BL.

A True Account of the late most doleful, and lamentable Tragedy of old Maddam Gwinn. . . . N.d. 4 fols. BL.

A true and exact Relation Of the severall Informations, Examinations, and Confessions of the late Witches, arraigned and executed in the County of Essex. . . . 1645. 22 fols. BL.

A true and most Dreadfull discourse of a woman possessed with the Deuill. . . . 1584. 8 fols. BL.

The True Confession of Margret Clark. . . . 1680. 6 pp. BL.

A true Discourse. Declaring the damnable life and death of one Stubbe Peeter. . . . 1590. Rept. in *Reprints of English Books, 1475–1700*, ed. Joseph Arnold Foster, no. 33.

A True Discourse of A cruell fact committed by a Gentlewoman . . . [Anna de Boyse]. 1599. 12 pp. BL.

A True Relation Of the Araignment Of eighteene Witches . . . [at St. Edmunds-Bury in Suffolk]. 1645. 8 pp. BL.

A true Relation Of the most Horrid and Barbarous murders committed by Abigail Hill of St. Olaves Southwark, on the persons of foure Infants. . . . 1658. 14 pp. BL.

The trueth of the most wicked and secret murthering of Iohn Brewen, Goldsmith of London, committed by his owne wife, through the prouocation of one Iohn Parker, whom she loued. . . . 1594. 6 pp. Lambeth.

The Tryal and Examination Of Mrs. Joan Peterson . . . for her supposed Witchcraft. . . . 1652. 8 pp. BL.

The Tryal Of Elizabeth Cellier, The Popish Midwife. . . . 1680. 4 pp. BL.

A Tryal of skill, performed by a poor decayed Gentlewoman, Who cheated a rich Grasier of Sevenscore pound, and left him a Child to keep. [1680s]. Brs. BL.

Two horrible and inhumane Murders done in Li[n]colnshire, by two Husbands vpon their Wiues. . . . 1607. 10 fols. Rept. in *Tudor and Stuart Texts,* ed. Joseph Arnold Foster, no. 4.

Two most vnnaturall and bloodie Murthers: The one by Maister Cauerley. . . . 1605. 28 pp.

The Unconscionable Gallant: Or, The Beautiful Lady's Misfortune. N.d. Brs. Osterley Park Ballads, BL.

The Unfortunate Concubines: The History of Fair Rosamond, Mistress to Henry the Second; And Jane Shore, Concubine to Edward the fourth; Kings of England. [Late 17c?]. 8 pp. NLS.

The Unthankful Servant: Or, A Scolding Match between Two Cracks of the Town. . . . N.d. Brs. Osterley Park Ballads, BL.

[Utterson, E. V.], ed. *Select Pieces of Early Popular Poetry: Re-published Principally from Early Printed Copies, in the Black Letter.* 2 vols. 1817.

Venus Darling; Or, A New Vampt Gentlewoman. [c. 1670]. Brs. Rawlinson Ballads 566(41), Bod.

A Vindication of a Marriage Life: In Answer to the Broadside against Marriage. 1675[?]. Brs. BL.

W., L. *The Maidens sad complaint for want of a Husband.* [Mid-17c]. Brs. Douce Ballads 2:145, Bod.

The Wandring-Whores Complaint for want of Trading. 1663. 6 pp. Bod.

Warning for Servants: And a Caution to Protestants. Or, the Case of Margret Clark, Lately Executed for Firing her Masters House in Southwark. 1680. 32 pp. BL.

Wentworth, Anne. *A Vindication of Anne Wentworth.* . . . 1677. 22 pp. BL.

Whipping Tom Brought to light, and exposed to View. . . . 1681. Brs. NLS.

The Whores Petition To the London Prentices. 1668. Brs. Bagford Ballads, BL.

The Wife lapped in Morels skin; or, The Taming of a Shrew. [Late 16c]. Rept. in *Select Pieces of Early Popular Poetry,* ed. E. V. Utterson, 2:173–221. 1817.

[Winstanley, William]. *Poor Robin's True Character of a Scold: Or, the Shrews Looking-glass.* 1678. 8 pp. BL.

Witches Apprehended, Examined and Executed, for notable villanies by them committed both by Land and Water . . . [Mother Sutton]. 1613. 10 fols. Bod.

The Witches of Northamptonshire. 1612. 14 fols. BL.

The Witch Of Wapping. Or An Exact and Perfect Relation, of the Life and Devilish Practises of Joan Peterson. . . . 1652. 8 pp. BL.

The Woman's Victory. . . . [Late 17c]. Brs. BL.

The Womens Complaint Against their Bad Husbands, Or the good Fellows Anatomized by their Wives. 1676. 6 pp. BL.

The Womens Fegari[es,] Shewing The great endeavours they have used for obtain[ing] of the Breeches. [1675?]. 6 pp. BL.

Women Will Have their Will: Or, Give Christmas his Due. 1648. 16 pp. BL.

The Wonderful Discoverie of the Witchcrafts of Margaret and Phillip Flower, daughters of Ioan Flower. . . . 1619. 23 fols. BL.

Wonderful News from Buckinghamshire. Or, A Perfect Relation How a young Maid hath been for Twelve years and upwards possest with the Devil. . . . 1677. 8 pp. BL.

Wright, Thomas, ed. *Songs and Ballads, with other Short Poems, Chiefly of the Reign of Philip and Mary.* 1860.

Primary Sources: German

Note: No place of publication is known for many of these sources.

Ach wie ist mir mein leib. . . . [c. 1640–1650?]. Brs. GNM.

Alexander, Dorothy, and Walter L. Strauss, eds. *The German Single-Leaf Woodcut 1600–1700: A Pictorial Catalogue.* 2 vols. New York, 1977.

Der Alexander von Metz. . . . [c. 1550?]. 8 fols. BL.

Alhier hütte sich ein Idere Fraw / Dem langen Schwetzen nicht vertraw. [c. 1640–50]. Brs. GNM.

Alhier hütt sich ein Jder Mann / Und reitz das Weib zum Zorn nicht an. [c. 1640–50]. Brs. GNM.

Allda. Ein erbärmklich Lied / von der züchtigen junck frawen Allda genandt. . . . Augsburg, [2d half 16c]. 8 fols. DSB Yd 8795.

Amma, Hans. *Zwey schöne Newe Lieder. Das Erste / ist eine Propheceyhung. . . . Das Ander Liedt Von einem Weber. . . .* Prague[?], 1603[?]. 4 fols. HAB.

Andächtiger Rueff / Von dem H. Leben vnd Marterkampff / der glorwürdigen Jungkfrawen S. Catharina. . . . Augsburg, 1631. 34 pp. BL.

Andächtiger Ruff Von dem H. Leben vnd Marterkampff / der glorwurdigen Jungfrawen Sanct Barbara. Ingolstatt, 1613. 10 fols. BL.

Beschreibung vnd Figur der zukünfftigen bösen vnd Manntheuren Zeit: Nemlich / daß sich Sieben Weiber vmb ein par Mannshosen schlagen werden. . . . [1st half 17c]. Brs. GNM.

Beuteler, Paul. *Der Beschertzte und Beschimffte Bockes-Beutel.* 1645. 4 fols. BL.

Binder, Ludwig. *Diß lied sagt von Lucretia. . . .* Nuremberg, [c. 1560?]. 4 fols. BL.

Blümml, Emil Karl, ed. *Ludwig Uhlands Sammelband fliegender Blätter aus der zweiten Hälfte des 16. Jahrhunderts.* Strassburg, 1911.

Böhme, Franz M., ed. *Altdeutsches Liederbuch. Volkslieder der Deutschen nach Wort und Weise aus dem 12. bis zum 17. Jahrhundert.* Leipzig, 1877.

Bolte, Johannes. "Doktor Siemann und Doktor Kolbmann, zwei Bilderbogen des 16. Jahrhunderts." *Zeitschrift des Vereins für Volkskunde* 12 (1902): 296–307.

Der bösen weiber Zuchtschul. . . . [Erfurt?], [c. 1530?]. 12 fols. BL.

Brückner, Wolfgang. *Populäre Druckgraphik Europas: Deutschland vom 15. bis zum 20. Jahrhunderts.* Munich, 1969.

Charter Stutzerischen. . . . A La Modo Matressen. [17c]. Brs. HAB.

Cockelius, Jacobus. *Erschreckliche / vnerhöte* [sic] *Newe zeittung / welche sich newlch* [sic] *in diesem M.D.LXII. Jare zu Dressigk . . . zugetragen. . . .* 1562. 2 fols. BL.

Cudius, Hans. *Newezeitung. Vnd ware geschicht / dieses 76. Jars geschehen im Breißgaw / wie man . . . 55. vnhulden gefangen vnd verbrent hat. . . .* 1576. 4 fols. BL.

Ditfurth, Franz Wilhelm Freiherr von, ed. *Deutsche Volks- und Gesellschaftslieder des 17. und 18. Jahrhunderts.* Nordlingen, 1872.

———. *Einhundertundzehn Volks- und Gesellschaftslieder des 16., 17. und 18. Jahrhunderts.* Stuttgart, 1875.

———. *Volks- und Gesellschaftslieder des 16., 17. und 18. Jahrhunderts.* Stuttgart, 1875.

———. *Zweiundfünfzig ungedruckte Balladen des 16., 17. und 18. Jahrhunderts.* Stuttgart, 1874.

Dreyerlei. Denckwürdige vnd warhafftige . . . Zeytung auß Prag / . . . . Warhafftige Propheceyung / eines Scheffers Töchterlein. . . . 1581. 4 fols. SBPK.

Drey Erschröckenliche newe Zeitungen. Die Erste: Warhafftige vnnd zuvor vnerhörte newe Zeitung / so sich im Böhmerwaldt / in einem Wirtzhauß zum Stock begeben . . . 1609. . . . Prague[?], 1609[?]. 4 fols. ZB.

Drey gantz Neue Anmüthige Gesänger / Das Erste: Ein erbärmliche Geschicht . . . zu Pißka. . . . Das Dritte: Von einem Schäffer / welcher sein schwangers Weib zweyen Mördern verkaufft hat. [c. 1600?]. 4 fols. BL.

Drey Geistliche Lieder / Das Erste / Susanna keusch vnd zart / . . . Das Ander / Von Sanct Dorothea / 1668. 4 fols. BL.

Drey hübsche lieder / Das erst / Es het ein Byder mann ein weyb. . . . Nuremberg, [mid-16c?]. 4 fols. DSB Yd 7821.36.

Drey newe Lieder / Das Erst / Ich het mir ein meidlein außerkorn. . . . Nuremberg, [c. 1560?]. 4 fols. BL.

Drey newer zeyttung. Ein erschröckliche vnd erbärmliche geschicht / so sich ein meilwegs von der Statt Bremen . . . zugetragen / wie daselbst ein Mann sein schwanger Weib verkaufft. . . . 1579. 4 fols. BSB.

Drey schöne Lieder / Das Erst / Die weyber mit den Flöhen. . . . Nuremberg, [c. 1530?]. 4 fols. DSB Yd 7821.7.

Drey schöne Lieder / Das Erste / Ich hab dich lieb . . . Das Dritte / Es war ein mal ein junger Knab / er freyt eins. . . . Nuremberg, [c. 1550?]. 4 fols. BL.

Drey schöne lieder / Das erst / So hab ich all mein tag gehört. Das ander / Eins morgens frü. N.d. 4 fols. DSB Yd 7821.17.

Drey schöne Neue Geistliche Lieder / Das Erste: Von S. Catharina. . . . Augsburg, n.d. [17c]. 4 fols. BL.

Drey schöne neue Weltliche Lieder / Das Erste: Ey so gehts uns Menscher. . . . 1696. 4 fols. BL.

Drey Schöne Newe Kurtzweilige Lieder zum erstenmahl in Druck außgangen. Das Erste. Von einer Jungfraw / die dreyzehen Freyer gehabt. . . . 1658. 4 fols. GNM.

Drey schöne Newe Lieder das erste / Das Meidlein zu dem Brunnen gieng. . . . [1st half 16c]. 4 fols. DSB Yd 9330.

Drey Schöne Newe Lieder / Das Erste / Ein schön New Weinachten Liedt. . . . Erfurt, 1613. 4 fols. DSB Yd 7853.16.

Drey schöne Newe Weltliche Lieder. Das Erste. Von dreyen Weibern / so zum Weine gewesen / &c. [17c]. 4 fols. DSB Ye 1770.

Drey schöne newe Weltliche Lieder. Das Erste / Weh! das ich armer Jung-Gesell. . . . *Das Ander: Es war ein Jungfraw zart / es trägt an jhrem Bäuchlein so hart.* [Nuremberg?], 1663. 4 fols. BL.

Drey schöner / Newe weltlicher Lieder. Das erste. Wer sol dann trösten mich. . . . *Das ander. Ich weiß ein Mägdlein stincket vnd faul.* . . . Cologne, 1603. 4 fols. DSB Yd 7850.26.

Drey schöne Weltliche Lieder / von Samson dem Held. . . . [c. 1550?]. 4 fols. BL.

Drey schön neue Weltliche Lieder. Das erste: Ist ein Streitt / zwischen einem bösen Weib / vnd einem versoffnen Mann. . . . Augsburg, [c. 1640?]. 4 fols. DSB Ye 1746.

Drey warhafftige grundtliche Zeitungen / Die erste / Von ettlichen Hexen . . . *welche hin vnd wider in Vngern / vnd Teutschland grossen schaden angericht haben.* . . . Freyberg, 1610. 4 fols. ZB.

Drey Warhafftige Newe Zeitung. Die Erste von Einem Meidlein von achtzehen jaren. Ursel, 1594. 4 fols. BL.

Drey Warhafftige Newe Zeittungen. Die Erste / Von dem gewaltigen . . . *Wetter.* . . . *Die Ander / auß dem Niderland.* Cologne, 1598. 4 fols. BL.

Drey warhafftige vnd zuuor vnerhörte / erschröckliche newe Zeyttungen: Die erste: von einer wundergeschicht / so sich mit einem Breutigam vnd Braut. . . . Augsburg, 1607. 4 fols. ZB.

Drey Weltliche Newe Lieder. Das Erste / Von der Fortuna. . . . *Das Ander. Schön Jungfraw halt mirs zu gut.* . . . 1646. 4 fols. HAB.

Eigentlicher Bericht und traurige Zeitung / Von unterschiedlichen Wunderzeichen. . . . 1673. 6 fols. DSB Ye 7681.

Eigentliche vnd warhaffte beschreibung / Welcher massen Fraw Giliberta / eines Burgers Tochter von Meintz / zu Rom zu einem Papst erwehlet. . . . 1609. Brs. BL.

Eigentliche und warhafftige Vorstellung des abscheulichen Verfahrens eines Persianers. 1671. Brs. GNM.

Erk, Ludwig, ed. *Deutscher Liederhort.* 2d ed. 2 vols. Leipzig, 1925.

Erschreckliche Newe Zeitung / Welche sich begeben vnd zugetragen in diesem 1650. Jahr / bey der Stadt Dillhofen. . . . Dilhofen[?], 1650. 4 fols. DSB Ye 7261.

Erschreckliche / Warhafftige / Newe Zeitung / so inn der Marggraffschafft Baden geschehen. . . . Erfurt, 1581. 4 fols. BL.

Erschröckliche Warhafftige newe Zeittung von etlichen Mördern / wie sie sich dem Teuffel ergeben. . . . Strassburg, 1583. 4 fols. BL.

Ein erschröcklich geschicht Vom Tewfel vnd einer vnhulden / beschehen zu Schilta bey Rotweil in der Karwochen. 1533. Brs. ZB.

Fehr, Hans. *Massenkunst im 16. Jahrhundert.* Berlin, 1924.

Folz, Hans. *Von zweyer frawen krig.* Nuremberg, [early 16c?]. 8 fols. SBPK Yg 5216.

Frag vnd Antwort / König Salomonis / vnd Marcolphi. Frankfurt am Main, n.d. 24 fols. SBPK Yf 7864.8.

Der frawen Spiegel in wellichem spiegel sich das weyblich byld / jung oder altt beschauwen oder lernen / zu ge brauchen / die woltat gegen irem eelichen gemahel. [1520?]. 9 fols. BL.

Fünff schöne newe weltliche Lieder. Das Erste. Einmals scheint mir die sonne. . . . *Das Dritte: Liliana Schäfferin.* 1663. 4 fols. BL.

Gänßfeldt, Märten von [pseud.]. *Weiber noth / Welche Ein Lutherisch-Evangelische Matron jhrem lieben Herrn vnd Ehegatten auff Den Regenspurgischen Reichstag vorgestellt.* . . . Newhausen, 1653. 21 pp. BSB.

Ein gar schon new Lied / vom Adelger. Augsburg, [c. 1560s]. 4 fols. BL.

Ein gar trawriges Lied. Von einem Studenten / welcher im Jahr 1608. zu Franckfort an der Oder / sich mit einer Jungfrawen verehlichet. . . . 1630. 4 fols. BL.

Gemeiner Weiber Mandat. 1641. Brs. GNM.

Gewiser Bericht deß Truten vnnd Hexenbrennens Bambergischen Gebiets. . . . Schmalkalden, 1628. 2 fols. GNM.

Goedeke, Karl, and Julius Tittman, eds. *Liederbuch aus dem sechzehnten Jahrhundert.* Vol. 1 of *Deutsche Dichter des sechzehnten Jahrhunderts.* Leipzig, 1867. Rept. 1974.

Graff, Jörg. *Ein newes lied von einem Jeger.* [1st half 16c]. Brs. DSB Yd 7801.22.

———. *Ein newes lied von eyner vischerin / wie sie hat gestifft vier mort.* . . . Nuremberg, [c. 1530]. 4 fols. DSB Yd 7821.12.

———. *Ein new lied gemacht im thon als man singt von dem Künig von franckreych vnd der stat Tollen.* [Pre-1542]. Brs. DSB Yd 7801.69.

———. *Ein new Liede / von pulerey.* Nuremberg, [c. 1530?]. 4 fols. DSB Yd 7850.36.

Grimmelshausen, Hans Jacob Christoffel von. *Courage, the Adventuress and the False Messiah.* Trans. Hans Speier. Princeton, N.J., 1964.

Gründliche vnerhörte Zeitung / Von den Teuffels-Zauberern. . . . Hildesheim, [c. 1628]. 2 fols. DSB Ye 6445.

Ein Gründtliche auch warhafftige vnd erschlöckliche [sic] *newe Zeitung / von sechs Mördern.* . . . Ulmitz[?], 1603. 4 fols. DSB Ye 5571.

Grund- vnd probierliche Beschreibung / Argument vnd Schluß-Articul . . . *Belangend die Frag / Ob die Weiber Menschen sein / oder nicht?* 1643. 13 fols. HAB.

Gülden Ave Maria Das ist / Ein Schöner Englischer Gruß / darin die Gebererin Gottes vielen Historien der Heyligen Schrifft verglichen wird. . . . Paderborn, 1618. 4 fols. BL.

H., N. *Ein Christlicher Abentreien / vom Leben Vnd ampt Johannis des Tauffers / für Christliche / züchtige Jungfrawlein.* 1554. 6 fols. BL.

Der Hanenreitern. . . . c. 1640. Brs. GNM.

Der Hanrey. c. 1640. Brs. GNM.

Harms, Wolfgang, ed. *Die Sammlung der Herzog August Bibliothek in Wolfenbüttel.* Vol. 2. Munich, 1980.

——, and Cornelia Kemp, eds. *Die Sammlungen der Hessischen Landes- und Hochschulbibliothek in Darmstadt. Kommentierte Ausgabe.* Tübingen, 1987.

Hartmann, August, ed. *Historische Volkslieder und Zeitgedichte vom sechzehnten bis neunzehnten Jahrhundert.* 3 vols. Munich, 1907–13.

Haß, Cuntz. *Du junger man merck vnd versteh / Vnd wilt du greyffen zu der Ehe.* . . . Nuremberg, [2d half 16c]. 8 fols. SBPK Yg 5456.

Herber, Caspar. *Erschröckliche neuwe Zeittung. Vonn einem Mörder Christman genant.* . . . Mentz, 1581. 4 fols. BL.

Des holdseligen Frauenzimmers Kindbeth-Gespräch. . . . Nuremberg, [c. 1650]. Brs. GNM.

Holla / Holla / Newe Zeytung / der Teuffel ist gestorben. Vienna, 1609. Brs. GNM.

Hort an new schrecklich abenthewr . . . *vnholden.* . . . N.d. Brs. HAB.

Ein hubsches Lied / wie zu Plonig ein Christen eynes Juden Tochter schwanger macht. . . . Nuremberg, [c. 1560?]. 8 fols. DSB Yd 8242.

Ein hübsch lied / Von der Frawen von der Weissenburg. Nuremberg, [c. 1571–1604]. 4 fols. DSB Yd 7850.39.

Ein hübsch new Geistlich Lied von der H. Jungkfrauwen vnd Märterin S. Catharina. Freiburg, 1607. 8 fols. BL.

Ein hübsch new lied von dem Henßlein beckenknecht. Ein ander new Lied / von der Mayerin töchterlein. Nuremberg, [1st half 16c]. 4 fols. DSB Yd 9463.

Ain hübsch New Lied / von der Judit. . . . Augsburg, [c. 1532?]. 4 fols. GNM.

Ein hübsch new lied / von eyner stoltzen haußmaid. Nuremberg, [c. 1545?]. 4 fols. BL.

Ein hübsch new Lied / von eyner wirtin vnd eim Pfaffen. Nuremberg, [c. 1530]. 4 fols. BL. Rept. in *Zwickauer Facsimiledrucke,* no. 20, ed. Johannes Bolte. Zwickau, 1913.

Ein hüpsch new Liede: genandt das Vogel gesang. . . . Augsburg, [1560s]. 4 fols. BL.

Ein hüpsch New Lied / Schürtz dich Gredlein. . . . Augsburg, [c. 1560]. 4 fols. BL.

Ein hüpsch New Lied / Vonn einer Stoltzen Müllerin. . . . [c. 1590s?]. 4 fols. BL.

Ein hüpsch news Lied / von der frommen vnd Gotsförchtigen Frawen Susanna. Augsburg, [c. 1560]. 7 fols. BL.

Jetz die Henn will sein der Haan. . . . [c. 1640–50?]. Brs. GNM.

Josephs Historia. . . . N.d. 8 fols. DSB Yd 7853.43.

Der Jungfrauen Narrenseil. Nuremberg, [c. 1650]. Brs. BL.

Der kanne gevallerschen vnd Weinsuchtiger Weiber vergadderungs anschlag. [1656?]. Brs. BL.

Kauffungen, Joannes. *Eyn schon new lied / von dem heiligen Ehstandt.* . . . Marburg, 1550. 4 fols. DSB Hymn. 6301.

Khueller, Sebastian. *Kurtze Vnnd warhafftige Historia / von einer Junckfrawen / welche mit etlich vnd dreissig bösen Geistern leibhafftig besessen / vnd . . . erlödiget worden.* Munich, [1540?]. 7 fols. HAB.

Kors, Alan C., and Edward Peters, comps. *Witchcraft in Europe, 1100–1700: A Documentary History.* Philadelphia, 1972.

Ein köstlich gutes bewertes Recept / vor die Männer / so böse Weiber haben. [c. 1620?]. Brs. GNM.

Köstlich und hoch-nothwendiger Weiber-Meß-Krahm / Das ist: Ein Gespräch von dem Weiber-Regiment. . . . [2d half 17c?]. 16 fols. HAB.

Kuntz, Hans. *Newe zeitung. Von einer Erschrecklichen That / welche zu Dillingen / von einem Jhesuwider / / [sic] vnd einer Hexen / geschehen ist.* . . . Ursel, 1579. 4 fols. BSB.

Kurtze Beschreibung von denen neun Häuten der bösen Weiber. . . . [2d half 17c]. Brs. GNM.

Ein kurtzweylig Lied / von eynem liederlichen man vnd seynem weyb. . . . Nuremberg, [c. 1550?]. 4 fols. BL.

Die Landtsknechts Hür. [1st half 16c]. Brs. GNM.

Das Liede von dem edlen Danheuser. Nuremberg, [c. 1530]. 4 fols. Rept. in *Zwickauer Facsimiledrucke,* no. 8, ed. O. Clemen. Zwickau, 1912.

Das lied ist genant der böß rauch In der flamm weiß. [1st half 16c]. Brs. DSB Yd 7801.53.

Ein lied vom Ehestand. . . . [16c]. Brs. DSB Yd 7803.5.

Ein lied von einem eelichen volck. . . . [early 16c]. Brs. DSB Yd 7801.2.

Ein Lied von einer faulen Diernen. [c. 1590s]. 4 fols. BL.

Liliencron, Rochus von. *Die historischen Volkslieder der Deutschen vom 13. bis 16. Jahrhundert.* Leipzig, 1865. Rept. Hildesheim, 1966.

Linck, Hieronimus. *Ein schön New Geistlich Leid [sic] / wider das schandliedlein / so man jetzund pflegen zu singen / Mein Man der wil in Krieg ziehen.* . . . N.d. 4 fols. DSB Hymn. 7539.

Mayr, Martin. *Ain Schön lied / von ainem Ritter auß der Steyrmarck / genant*

Trinumitas / vnd von aines Künigs Tochter auß Dennmarck / genant Floredebel. Augsburg, [2d half 16c]. 8 fols. BL.

Münchheym, Barbara. *Ein new Lied. Von der Gottseligen wie auch Heiligen Frawen Sanct Ita. . . .* Rorschach am Bodensee, 1614. 8 fols. BL.

N., G. *Ein newes lied / Ein Burger ist gesessen / zu Thübing. . . .* [Nuremberg], [c. 1530?]. 4 fols. DSB Yd 7821.31.

Neue Zeitung. Ein Rahtschluß der Dienst Mägde. . . . Nuremberg, [c. 1650]. Brs. HAB.

Ein neüw Lied / von einer Jungfrawen die mit dem bösen geist besessen was. . . . [c. 1559]. 4 fols. ZB.

Newe Anbildung Der Weitbeschreiten / Hertzhafften Hildin vnd Frawen Margret von Kennow. . . . 1573. Brs. BL.

Neweroffneter Ernsthaffter / hochstraffwürdiger vnd vnverbrüchlicher Männerbefehlich. . . . Nuremberg, [c. 1650]. Brs. HAB.

Newe Warhaffte / Auch Erschröckliche Zeitunge: Wie ein Son vnd Dochter Sampt einer Dienstmagdt / jhren Leiblichen / Natürlichen Vatter / Hauptman Jacob Eliner . . . zu Brägentz am Bodensee jämerlicher . . . weiß Ermördt haben. . . . Augsburg, 1595. 4 fols. DSB Ye 5071.

Newe Zeitung: Ein Warhafftiges newes Lied / vnd erbermliche geschicht / so sich begeben hat zu Liser an der Mosel / . . . daselbs ein Man genent gülde Hans / . . . welcher fünff seiner leiblichen Kinder vmbbracht hat / . . . im 1573. Jar. Schweinfurt, [c. 1573]. BL.

Newe Zeittung / Vnd wahre Geschicht / dises Lxxvj Jars geschehen im Breißgaw / wie man . . . 136. Vnholden gefangen / vnd verbrendt hat. . . . 1576. 4 fols. ZB.

Newe Zeitung aus Berneburgk / Schrecklich zu hören vnd zu lesen / Von dreyen alten Teuffels Bulerin / Hexin oder Zauberinnen. . . . 1580. 6 fols. HAB.

Newe Zeitung auß Calecut vnd Calabria. "Rumpelskirchen," 1609. Brs. GNM.

Newe Zeitung / in Gesangs weiß / Von der Statt Genff. . . . Basel, 1590. 4 fols. BL.

Newe Zeitung: Welcher gestalt zu Prage ein Mann vnd Weib vber Essen vneins worden / sich geschlagen. . . . 1613. 4 fols. HAB.

Newe Zeitung: Welcher gestalt / zween falsche Juden / durch Zauberey zuwegen gebracht / daß vil tausend Stück Vihe hingefallen vnd gestorben ist. . . . Dresden, 1599. 4 fols. HAB.

Newe zeitung: Wie wunderbarlich Gott / den vnmenschlichen vnd vom Teuffel zugerichten grossen Bauch / an der Jungfrawen zu Eszlingen / offenbaret hat. . . . Erfurt, 1551. 4 fols. SBPK Flugschr. 1550–4.

Newe Zeitung. Wunderliche vnnd Erschreckliche geschicht von einer Jungfrawen. . . . 1615. 4 fols. HAB.

Newe Zeytung. Von einem Megdlein das entzuckt ist gewest / vnd was wunderbarliche Rede es gethan hat / geschehen zu Freyberg in Meyssen im Jar. M.D.LX. Nuremberg, 1560. 4 fols. SBPK.

Ein New kläglich Lied / von dem grossen schaden der Vnholden / So sie in

Westphalen zu Aschenbrügk / . . . begangen haben / in dem jetztwerenden 1583. Jar / wie auch jrer 180. jemmerlich verbrendt seind worden. . . . Wesel, 1583. 4 fols. DSB Ye 4645.

Ein new lied gemacht von einem stoltzen meydlein. . . . [16c]. Brs. DSB Yd 7801.41.

Ein new Lied / von aines Ritters Tochter. . . . Augsburg, [c. 1550?]. 8 fols. BL.

Ein new lied von einem alten weib vnd einem jungen man. . . . N.d. Brs. DSB Yd 7801.33.

Ein new Lied von eynem bösen weib. . . . Nuremberg, [c. 1530]. Rept. in *Zwickauer Facsimiledrucke,* no. 18, ed. Alfred Götze. Zwickau, 1913.

"Nun schweigt. Ich will eüch hören lon." [16c]. Untitled brs. DSB Yd 7801.56.

Offt Probiertes und Bewährtes Recept oder Artzney für die bösse Kranckheit der unartigen Weiber. Nuremberg, [c. 1650]. Brs. HAB.

Päminger, Leonart. *Ein schön kurtzweilig / vnd nutzes Hochzeit Gesprech / vierer Ehefrawen. . . .* 1574. BL.

Prophezeyhung / eines armen Bawren Tochter in Preussen. . . . Danzig[?], 1580. 6 fols. SBPK.

Röhrich, Lutz, and Rolf Wilhelm Brednich, eds. *Deutsche Volkslieder.* 2 vols. Düsseldorf, 1965–67.

Sachs, Hans. *Der Buler Artzney. Mehr die Neun Geschmeck inn dem Ehelichen standt.* Nuremberg, [mid-16c]. 10 fols. BL.

[———]. *Drey schöner Hißtorij / Von dreyen Heidenischen mörderischen Frawen.* Nuremberg, 1540. 4 fols. BL.

———. *Dreyerley klagred dreyer Weibsbild / Lucrecie / Thisbes / vnd Virginie.* 1554. 4 fols. BL.

———. *Ein Gesprech eyner Bulerin vnd eines ligenden Narren vnter jhren Füssen.* Nuremberg, [c. 1553]. 4 fols. BL.

———. *Die Judit mit Holoferne. . . .* Nuremberg, 1554. 4 fols. BL.

———. *Der Lose Mann.* Nuremberg, 1556. 8 fols. BL.

———. *Die neun getrewen Hayden. . . .* Nuremberg, 1553. 12 fols. BL.

———. *Sämtliche Fabeln und Schwänke von Hans Sachs.* Ed. Edmund Goetze. Vols. 1 and 2. Halle, 1893.

———. *Ein schön Meyster Lied / Von der Gottsförchtigen Frawen Judith. . . .* Leipzig, 1607. 5 fols. BL.

———. *Die zwölff durch leuchtige Weyber des alten Testaments. . . .* Augsburg, 1596. 8 fols. BL.

———. *Die Zwölff Eygenschafft eines boßhafftigen weybs.* Nuremberg, 1553. 8 fols. BL.

[———?]. *Ein new Lied / von aines Ritters Tochter / der jr Buhl an jren Armen starb. . . .* Augsburg, [c. 1550?]. 8 fols. BL.

[———?]. *Ein Schön Lied / Von Nöten ist / das ich jetzt trag gedult. . . .* [16c]. 4 fols. BL.

S. Maria Magdalena. Augsburg, [c. 1650?]. Brs. BL.

Satyrisches Gesicht / zu Nichtburg in Vtopia durch den blinden Cupidinem entdeckt: Wie sich nemlich sieben böse Weiber vmb ein paar stinckende Manns Buxen geschlagen. . . . [17c]. Brs. HAB.

Scheible, Johann, ed. *Die fliegenden Blätter des XVI. und XVII. Jahrhunderts.* Stuttgart, 1850. Rept. Hildesheim, 1972.

Ein schimpflicher Spruch / von einem Korbmacher vnnd seiner Frawen. . . . 1570. 4 fols. BL.

Schirenbrandt, Hans. *Ein hüpsch news Lied / von der frommen vnd Gotsförchtigen Frawen Susanna.* Augsburg, [c. 1560]. 7 fols. BL.

Schlacht, Martin. *Ein schön news Lied: Von der Königin von Franckreich / vnd von jrer falschen Buhlschafft.* . . . Augsburg, [c. 1590s]. 8 fols. BL.

Schmidt, Niclaus. *Von den zehen Teufeln oder Lastern / damit die bösen vnartigen Weiber besessen sind.* . . . Leipzig, 1557. 23 fols. BL.

Ein schöne Litaney / Von der Allerseligsten Jungfraw und Mutter Gottes Maria / 1686. 4 fols. BL.

Schöner lieder zwey / das erst / Zucht eer vnd lob. . . . N.d. 4 fols. DSB Yd 9559.

Schöner newer Meister Lieder zwey. Das erst. Die weiber Amastanas. . . . Leipzig, [17c]. 4 fols. DSB Yd 7852.25.

Ein schöne Tageweis: Von Einem Frawelein auff einer Burg / vnd von einem jungen Knaben. 1664. 4 fols. BL.

Ein schöne Tageweiß / gantz kläglich zulesen oder zusingen. . . . [c. 1600?]. 8 fols. BL.

Schöne, Walter. *Die deutsche Zeitung des siebzehnten Jahrhunderts in Abbildungen.* Leipzig, 1940.

Ein schön Geistliches Lied / Von der Heyligen Büsserin / Maria Magdalena. Seyt gladen ihr jung Cavalier. . . . Augsburg, [c. 1650?]. 4 fols. BL.

Ein schön Geistlich Lied / Von vnser lieben Frawen. . . . Constance am Bodensee, 1619. 4 fols. BL.

Ein schön Liedt / Von eyner Künigin auß Lamparden / Wie grewlich sie jren Ehegemahel vmb das leben hat bracht. Nuremberg, [2d half 16c]. 4 fols. DSB Yd 8081.

Ein schon lied weltlich zu singen. Ich stund an einem morgen. N.d. Brs. DSB Yd 7801.38.

Ein schön newes Lied / ob eim jungen Gesellen ein Weyb zu nemen sey oder nit / . . . . Augsburg, [1603?]. 4 fols. BL.

Ein schön newes Lied / von einem Burgersknecht vnd von einer Bettlerin. [1620?]. BL.

Ein schön new Geistlich lied / Ich gieng ein mal spaciren. . . . Regensburg, [1560s?]. 4 fols. DSB Yd 7831.12.

Ein Schön New Geistlich Lied / so wider das vnfletige Schandt Huren liedlein / das Jagts jm zu gemacht ist worden / so man jetzundt gar gemein pfleget zu singen. . . . 1569. 4 fols. BL.

Ein schön New Geistlich Leid [sic] */ wider das schandliedlein / so man jetzund pflegen zu singen / Mein Man der wil in Krieg ziehen.* . . . N.d. 4 fols. DSB Hymn. 7539.

Ein schön new Lied / von einem alten Man vnd einem jungen Fräwlein. [1620?]. 4 fols. BL.

Ein Schön New Lied / Von einem Körblemacher. Nuremberg, [2d half 16c]. 3 fols. DSB Yd 8436.

Ein schön new Lied von ainem man der seinem weyb auff einem brieff schrieb was sie thon oder lassen sol / vnd wie ehs Im gieng. [c. 1550]. 4 fols. BL.

Ein Schön New Lied / von jetziger Junckfrawen Tracht / Hoffart vnd pracht. 1584. 4 fols. BSB.

Ein schön new Lied / von zweien Junckfrawen vom Adel / zu Delden drey meil von Deuenter verbrant. . . . Nuremberg, [1544?]. 4 fols. BL.

Ein schön new Lied / wie ein fraw jren Mann strafft / vnd weret jm er sol nit zum wein geen. . . . [c. 1550]. 4 fols. BL.

Ein schön News Lied / von der Edlen Keyserin. Augsburg, [c. 1560?]. 4 fols. BL.

Ein schöns Lied / Ich hab ein Weyb bey Achtzig Jaren. [1620?]. 4 fols. BL.

Ein schöns Lied / von der alten Schwiger / vnd jrer Schnur. . . . [c. 1560?]. 4 fols. BL.

Ein Schöns Newes Lied / Der Braune Stier genandt. N.d. 4 fols. BL.

Ein schreckliche Geschicht von einem grawsamen Kindt / welches geboren worden zu Arnhem im Gelderland. Cologne, 1576. 4 fols. BL.

Schubart, Adam. *Haußteuffel / das ist / Der Meister Sieman / Wie die bösen Weiber jre fromme Männer / vnd wie die bösen leichtfertigen Buben / jre fromme Weiber plagen.* . . . Frankfurt a. M., 1568. 45 fols. BL.

Secht an jhr liebe Freundt den erschröcklichen Mann / genandt der Narrenfresser. . . . [1st half 17c]. Brs. GNM.

Spiegel Der Keuschheit Oder Ein Bewehrte Artzney Die Fleischliche Lust Zvvertreiben. [c. 1600]. Brs. GNM.

Spiegel einer Christlichen vnd friedsamen Haußhaltung / Nuremberg, [c. 1650]. Brs. BL.

Strauss, Walter L., ed. *The German Single-Leaf Woodcut, 1550–1600.* New York, 1975.

Susanna Lied. Von der Gottsfürchtigen vnnd Keuschen Frawen Susanna. . . . 1615. 4 fols. DSB Yd 7853.24.

Teutscher Frantzoß. Das ist: Ein newes Allamodo Gsang. . . . Innsbruck, 1637. 8 fols. BL.

Die Teütsch Frantzösin. Das ist Ein newes Allamodo Gsang / Von der Abentheürischen / Wunder närrischen / Allamodischen Weiberzier. . . . Innsbruck, 1637. 8 fols. BL.

Valet-Lied A.M.T.G.D. Wegen durch Gifft Ertödteten Ehmanns Peinlich leidenden Sünderin. 1665. 4 fols. BL.

Vier Hüpsche Weltliche Lieder. 1. Vom Fitz vnnd Federle. . . . 4. Ich ritt eins mals zu Braunschweig auß. 1611. 4 fols. BL.

Vier wahre Zeitungen. Die Erste Ein Trost Lied König Friderichs. . . . Erfurt, 1625. 4 fols. ZB.

Ein vnerhörte seltzame wunderbahrliche Newe Zeitung / Von zweyen bösen

Weibern / welche sich auff einer breiten Heyden mit dem Teuffel ge-schlagen. . . . "Rumpelskirchen," [c. 1610?]. Brs. GNM.

Von bruder Rauschen. . . . Nuremberg, n.d. 16 fols. SBPK Yf 7864.10.

Von dem trawrigen ende Guiscardi vnd Sigismunde des Künigs von Salern Tochter / ein gar erbermbkliche History. Strassburg, [16c]. 16 fols. SBPK Yf 7864.9.

Von Einem Bößen Weib, welche sich auff einer breytten Heydten mit den Teüffeln geschlagen. . . . "Rumpelskirchen," [17c]. Brs. HAB.

Von einer Keyserin Wie sie jr Ehe brach / dardurch dem Keyser ein Horn wuchs an seiner Stiern. . . . Straubing, 1561. 4 fols. DSB Yd 7831.67.

Von Sibilla weyssagung Vnd von König Salomonis weyßheyt. . . . [16c?]. 16 fols. BL.

Wackernagel, Philipp, ed. *Das deutsche Kirchenlied von der ältesten Zeit bis zu Anfang des XVII. Jahrhunderts.* Vols. 3–5. Leipzig, 1870–77.

Waldis, Burckhard. *Eyne warhafftige vnd gantz erschreckliche historien / Wie eyn weib jre vier kinder tyranniglichen ermordet / vnd sich selbst auch vmbbracht hat / Geschehen zu Weidenhausen bei Eschweh in Hessen.* . . . Marburg, 1551. 4 fols. BL.

Ein ware gschicht vnd newe Zeitung / Von einem falschen Meitlin. . . . N.d. [c. 1650?]. 4 fols. DSB Ye 7266.

Ein wahrhafftige Newe Zeitung. Von einem Ehrvergeßnen Mann / der sein Schwanger Weib / durch das leidige Spilen vnnd Vollsauffen / das Kindt in Mutterleib verfluchet hat. . . . Cologne [?], 1638. 4 fols. DSB Ye 6956.

Warhaffte vnd glaubwirdige Zeyttung. Von Hundert vnd vier vnd dreyssig Vnholden. . . . Strassburg, 1583. 4 fols. BSB.

Warhafftige Beschreibung / Von einer Jungfrawen / die . . . sechs gantzer Jahr / keiner Speiß noch Tranck genossen. . . . Bern, 1607. Brs. GNM.

Ein warhafftige erschröckliche Newe Zeytung / . . . im Flecken Treber bey / Geraw / . . . wie daselbst der Teuffel einem reichen Burger sein rechtes Kind abgewechselt. . . . Oppenheim, 1618. 4 fols. BL.

Ein Warhafftige / erschröckliche / vnd vnerhörte newe zeittung / so sich im Land zu Vngern / von Ottergezicht vnd Eidexen. . . . Worms, 1550. 4 fols. SBPK Flugschr. 1550–3.

Eine warhafftige geschicht / Von einen vngerathenen Sohn / welcher seinen Vater vnd Mutter / geschlagen vnd ausgejaget hat / . . . Das Ander / wie man sich in dem Ehestande verhalten sol. . . . Alten Stettin, [c. 1601]. 4 fols. DSB Yd 7852.21.

Ein warhafftigen bericht vnd neuwe zeittung von einem kloster . . . von der Aabtissin welche grosse vnzucht getrieben mit einem vogt welche zehen kinder mit im gehabt / vnnd dieselbigen jämerlich ermördt. . . . Cologne[?], 1599. 4 fols. DSB Ye 5301.

Warhafftige / Newe zeittug [sic] von der vnerhorten erschrecklichen Straff Gottes / so vber die Stadt Friedeberg in der Newmarckt gelegen. . . . Frankfurt[?], 1594. 4 fols. DSB Yd 7852.22.

Warhafftige: Newe Zeitung auß dem Land Westuahlen / von der Stat Ossen-

bruck / wie man da hat auff einen Tag 133. Vnholden verbrendt.... 1588. 4 fols. DSB Ye 4801.

Ein warhafftige Newe Zeitung / vnnd gründliche Beschreibung: Welche sich hat begeben . . . in . . . Bern . . . Von einer wolbetagten fürnemmen Jungfrawen.... Bern, 1612. 14 pp. ZB.

Warhafftige Newe Zeitung von einem Töchterlein / welches siben Jahr alt gewesen.... Augsburg, 1618. 4 fols. BL.

Ein Warhafftige Newe Zeitung Von einer Stiefmutter vnd jhrem Stiefkindt.... Magdeburg, 1616. 4 fols. DSB Ye 5955.

Eine warhafftige Newe Zeitung / welche sich begeben vnnd zugetragen hat im Land zu Meissen / in einer Stadt Schaffstet genant / mit eines Bürgers Tochter.... Leipzig, 1616. 4 fols. DSB Yd 7851.13.

Eine warhafftige Newe zeyttung / so sich begeben hat zu Eschwein / wie allda ein mörder ist eingebracht worden / welcher 55. Mord mit seiner eygen Hand verbracht hat.... Coburg, 1597. 4 fols. BL.

Warhafftige Newe zeytung. Vnd ein Traurige Geschicht / in ein Lied verfast / von einer vngezognen Tochter / wie sie ein Kindt vmbgebracht / vnd dasselbig jhrer Magt im Schlaff zugelegt.... Cologne, 1589. 8 fols. DSB Ye 4845.

Ein warhafftiger / grundtlicher Bericht vnd newe Zeitung: Was sich mit einem vollen Weinschlauch vnd seinen ehelichen Weib / die groß schwanger gewesen.... Erfurt, 1616. 4 fols. BL.

Warhafftige vnd Erschreckliche Newe Zeitunge von einer Jungen Diernen / Welche sich dem Teuffel auff sechs Jarlang ergeben / vnd von jhm ehe die zeit verlauffen / weggeführet worden ist.... Dresden, 1582. 4 fols. ZB.

Warhafftige vnd erschröckliche newe Zeitung. Von etlichen Jesuwittern / in . . . München / vnd von einer Burgers Tochter . . . Anno 1607. Stuckard, n.d. BL.

Ein Warhafftige vnd gründtliche Beschreibung / Auß dem Bistum Würtz- vnd Bamberg / . . . wie man alda so vil Hexen Mann vnd Weibspersohnen verbrennen laßt.... 1627. 2 fols. HAB.

Warhafftige vnd schröckliche Newe zeitung / von einer Fürnemmen Person / welche durch verfürung deß bösen Feindes / vnd grimmigem zorn / auff ein mal Acht mordt verbracht / . . . zu Wangen im Algäw.... Laugingen, 1585. 4 fols. SBPK.

Warhafftige vnd zuvor Vnerhörte erschröckliche newe Zeitung: Von einem Mörder / sampt seinem Weyb vnd Tochter.... Constance, 1602. 4 fols. BL.

Ein Warhafftige Zeitung. Von etliche Hexen oder Vnholden / welche man kürtzlich im Stifft Mäntz / . . . verbrendt.... Frankfurt[?], 1603. 4 fols. DSB Ye 5581.

Warhafftige . . . Zeitung. Von etlichen Jesuwittern.... Die ander Zeitung. So sich zu Hall im Ihnthal mit einem Burger.... "Stuckard," 1607. 4 fols. BL.

Warhafftig vnd erschröckliche Geschicht / welche geschehen ist . . . im Land zu Mechelburg. . . . [1570]. Brs. GNM, HAB.

Wartz, Jacob [?]. *Ein schön news Liedt / Vonn einem Edlen Jüngling auß Armenia. . . .* Augsburg, 1610. 8 fols. BL.

Wäscher, Hermann. *Das deutsche illustrierte Flugblatt.* Dresden, 1955.

Weiber-Freund, Cornelius [pseud.]. *Der Männer Zanck-Eisen / Oder Das böse Weiber-Volck . . . Calender . . . MDCLXXXVII. . . .* Nuremberg, 1687. 15 fols. GNM.

Der Weiber Krieg wider den Bapst. . . . 1590. 6 fols. HAB.

Wenck, Balthes. *Von den bosen weyben wie man die ziehen sol. . . .* Nuremberg, [1540s]. 3 fols. DSB Yd 8371.

Wilt auff erden selig leben So solt das liedlein nit begeben. . . . N.d. Brs. DSB Yd 7801.28.

Wolgemut, Niclas. *Das ist das new Teutsch Hurübel. . . .* [c. 1520?]. 4 fols. BL.

Wunderbarliche vnnd seltzame Geschicht / so sich hat zugetragen / In der Keyserlichen Freyen Reychstatt Nörlingen / Von einem Weybsbild / die sich für ein Manns person außgeben hat . . . mit jhrem rechten Tauffnammen Eua Balbiererin von Glotz. . . . Basel, 1566. 6 fols. ZB.

Ein Wunderbarlich vnd vnerhörtes Mirackel / Welches sich warhafftig zugetragen hat bey der Statt Remis . . . von einer jungen Magdt / welche vnschuldig zum Todt verurtheilt. . . . Cologne, 1589. 4 fols. SBPK Flugs. 1589–9.

Wunder newe Zeitung / vnd warhaffte Geschicht. Von der Nunnen heiligkeit vnd reinigkeit. . . . Christlingen [Strassburg?], 1584. 4 fols. HAB.

Wunder vber alle Wunder / Was massen Herr Rudolph Schweitzer. . . . 1621. 4 fols. BL.

Z., Ph. *New Zeitung Geschehen in Der Stadt Magdeburgck . . . von einem megdlein Von Acht Jahren.* Magdeburg, 1577. BL.

Zäuberische Zeitung / Wie eine Hexin durch Teuffelszkunst jren Sohn mit sonderlichen Aberglaubischen dingen zum Wildschiessen behülfflich gewesen. . . . Cologne, 1589. 6 fols. HAB.

Zur Zeitvertreibung / Kurtzweiliger Aderlaß. . . . 1666. Brs. HAB.

Zween Erschreckliche geschicht / Gesangs weise. Die Erste / von einem Wirt im Allgergaw / Bastian Schönmundt genandt / . . . Die Ander / Eine erschreckliche vnd Warhafftige Newe Zeitung / . . . zu Langenberck. . . . 1596. 4 fols. DSB Ye 5141.

Zwey erschreckliche Newe Lieder / Das erste von einem Kinde / das geborn ist in Yßland / . . . Das ander von einem Manne / der seine Fraw verkaufft / welche schwanger gieng. 1580. 4 fols. DSB Ye 4529.

Zwey newe lieder / Das Erste / Künig ein herr ob allem reych. Nuremberg, [1540?]. 4 fols. BL.

Zwey Schöne Gaistliche Lieder. Das Erst: Die Gnad kompt oben her. . . . [c. 1620?]. 4 fols. BL.

Zwey schöne herliche Meisterlieder. 1. Auß dem Cento Nouella. . . . 2. Von der grossen Trew der Edlen Tugendsammen Frawen. . . . N.d. 4 fols. BL.

Zwey schöne lieder / Das erst von dem pracht etlicher Jungfrawen vnd Mägde. N.d. 4 fols. DSB Ye 341.

Zwey Schöne Meister Lieder / Das erst / Von listen weibern. . . . [16c]. 3 fols. DSB Yd 8421.

Zwey schöne neue Geistliche Lieder / Das erste: O seelige Mutter / voller Gnaden vnd Güte. . . . Augsburg, [2d half 17c]. 4 fols. BL.

Zwey Schöne Newe Lieder. Das Erste: Als Hertzog Heinrich von Braunsch- weyg. . . . Das ander Lied. Ein schön Maister Gesang Von der Melusina. . . . Augsburg, 1603. 4 fols. BL.

Zwey schöne newe Lieder. Das Erst: Die newe Jagt genandt. [1620?]. 4 fols. BL.

Zwey schöne Newe Lieder / Das Erste / Einer Politischen Damen Bildniß und Lob. . . . 1654. 4 fols. GNM.

Zwey Schöne newe Lieder. Das erste: Ich wolt gern singen. . . . [17c?]. 4 fols. DSB Yd 7850.23.

Zwey Schone newe Lieder / genanndt der Rolandt / von der Männer vnd Weyber vntrew. [16c]. 6 fols. DSB Yd 7850.17.

Zwey Schöne Newe Lieder / wie man ein Braut Geystlich ansingen soll. Straub- ing, [1560s]. 4 fols. DSB Yd 7831.51.

Zwey schöne newe Meyster Lieder: Das Erst: Wie drey Frawen vber jhre Mäyd klagen / . . . Das ander / die faulen Haußmeyd. 1611. 4 fols. BL.

Zwey Schöne newe Weltliche Lieder / Das Erste. Ach ich armes Mägdlein klage. . . . 1650. 4 fols. GNM.

Zwey schöne newe weltliche Lieder / Das Erste: Die Schwäbische Bawren-Klag / . . . Das Ander: Eines Goldschmids zu Straubingen mit seiner Frawen vnd Haußgesind Vbelhausen. . . . [c. 1580?]. 4 fols. DSB Ye 1761.

Zwey Schöne Newe Weltliche Lieder. Das Erste / Ist ein Streit zwischen einem bösen Weib / vnd einem versoffenen Mann. . . . 1647. 4 fols. BSB.

Zwey Schöner newer Lieder / das erste / Es het ein Fraw ein losen Man. . . . Nuremberg, [2d half 16c]. 4 fols. DSB Yd 8571.

Zwey schön newe Gaistliche Lieder. Das Erste: Von S. Dorothea. . . . Augsburg, 1636. 4 fols. BL.

Zwey schön newe Lieder / Erstlich: Wie die Männer jhre Weiber halten sollen / daß sie lang schön bleiben. . . . Augsburg, [c. 1640?]. 4 fols. DSB Ye 1743.

Zwey schön new Weltlich Lieder welche vormals nie im Druck außgangen. Das erste: Ein Mayer hab ich mir erwehlet. . . . [c. 1640?]. 4 fols. DSB Ye 1758.

Zwey überaus schöne Lieder. Das Erste: Von einer erschröcklichen Mord-Ge- schicht / Welche sich in dem letztern Jahr bey einem Meyerhof zwischen Eberstein und Rheinfels begeben. . . . Der Jugend zur Wahrnung Gesang- sweiß verfaßt. [1st half 17c?]. 4 fols. DSB Yd 7855(7).

Zwey Warhafftige newe Zeitung / Von einer schrecklichen Mißgeburt. . . . Stettin, 1628. 4 fols. HAB.

Zwo erschreckliche / abschewliche / vast vnerhörte / erbarmliche Mordthaten. . . . Strassburg, 1637. 5 fols. HAB.

Zwo newe Zeittung / Die Erste / Ein erschröcklich vnd sehr erbärmlich Geschicht / so geschehen ist den letzten Februarij / in diesem Achtzigsten Jar in Braband. . . . Vienna, 1580. 4 fols. DSB Ye 4527.

Zwo Newe Zeittung / Was man für Hexen oder Vnholden verbrendt hat. . . . Hoff, 1580. 4 fols. ZB.

Zwo Newe Zeitung Die Erste / Was sich zu Lisibon ein Haupstatt in Spannien begeben hat . . . mit einer Abtissen Donna Maria de Meneses genannt. . . . Antdorf, 1591. 4 fols. BL.

Zwo warhafftige / erschreckliche newe Zeitung / Die erste / Von einer Mißgeburt / geschehen in der Stadt Jehna / . . . 1602. . . . Jena, n.d. 4 fols. DSB Yd 7852.15.

Zwo warhafftige newe Zeitung. Die erste / so sich in Newen marckt Brandenburg. . . . Erfurt, 1597. 4 fols. BL.

Zwo warhafftige newe Zeitung / Die Erste / Welche sich begeben . . . hat in der Stadt Braunschweig. . . . Magdeburg, 1605. 4 fols. DSB Yd 7852.23.

Zwo Warhafftige Newe Zeitung / Die erst / Von einem Mörder / der sein Ehelich Weib / vnnd Sechs Kinder ermördet hat / geschehen inn der berümpten Statt Prüßeln / in der Schlessien. . . . 1599. 4 fols. DSB Ye 5311.

Zwo warhafftige trawrige newe Zeitungen. . . . Die erste / Von einem Undervogt zu Bergen. . . . Freiburg, 1623. 4 fols. BL.

Zwo warhafftige vnd erschröckliche newe Zeitungen. Die erste . . . in der Statt Feldkirch eines Hauptmanns Weib seines Namens Bernhardt Schmid. . . . Hohen Ens, 1623. 4 fols. HAB.

Zwo warhafftige vnd erschröckliche Zeitung / Die erst / wie das in Thüringen / auff dem Varenberg der Hexen so vil zusammen kommen seind. . . . Erfurt, 1612. 4 fols. ZB.

Zwo Warhafftige vnd traurige newe Zeitung / sampt einem Klaglied. Welche in dem Franken Land geschehen. . . . Rottenburg, 1624. 4 fols. BL.

Reference Works

Anderson, Charles S. *Augsburg Historical Atlas of Christianity in the Middle Ages and Reformation.* Minneapolis, 1967.

Bahlmann, P. "Noch einige deutsche Zeitungen des XVI. Jahrhunderts." *Zentralblatt für Bibliothekswesen* 7 (1890): 142–44.

Ballou, Patricia K. "Bibliographies for Research on Women." *Signs* 3 (1977): 436–50.

———. *Women: A Bibliography of Bibliographies.* Boston, 1980.

Benzing, Josef. *Die Buchdrucker des 16. und 17. Jahrhunderts im deutschen*

Sprachgebiet. Beiträge zum Buch- und Bibliothekswesen, 12. Wiesbaden, 1963.

Besterman, Theodore. *Early Printed Books to the End of the Sixteenth Century: A Bibliography of Bibliographies.* 2d ed. Geneva, 1961.

Bircher, Martin, ed. *Deutsche Drucke des Barock 1600–1720 in der Herzog August Bibliothek Wolfenbüttel.* Vols. 1–4. Nendeln, 1977–80.

Blagden, Cyprian. "Notes on the Ballad Market." *Papers of the University of Virginia Bibliographical Society* 6 (1954): 161–80.

Bloom, J. Harvey. *English Tracts, Pamphlets, and Printed Sheets: A Bibliography.* 2 vols. London, 1922–23.

Bucher, Otto. *Bibliographie der deutschen Drucke des XVI. Jahrhunderts. I. Dillingen.* Bibliotheca Bibliographica, 5. Ed. Michael O. Krieg. Bad Bocklet, 1960.

Catalog der Stadtbibliothek in Zürich. 7 vols. Zurich, 1864–97.

Duff, E. Gordon. *A Century of the English Book Trade.* London, 1905.

Dunbar, Agnes B. C. *A Dictionary of Saintly Women.* 2 vols. London, 1904–5.

Dünnhaupt, Gerhard. *Bibliographisches Handbuch der Barockliteratur.* Stuttgart, 1980.

Elsas, M. J. *Umriss einer Geschichte der Preise und Löhne in Deutschland.* 2 vols. Leiden, 1936.

Erickson, Carolly, and Kathleen Casey. "Women in the Middle Ages: A Working Bibliography." *Mediaeval Studies* 37 (1975): 340–59.

Fabian, Bernhard. *Die Messkataloge des sechzehnten Jahrhunderts.* Vols. 1–4. Hildesheim, 1972–80.

Fairbanks, Carol. *More Women in Literature: Criticism of the Seventies.* Metuchen, N.J., 1979.

Gaskell, Philip. *A New Introduction to Bibliography.* Oxford, 1974.

Goedeke, Karl. *Grundrisz zur Geschichte der deutschen Dichtung.* 2d ed. Vols. 1–4. Dresden, 1884–91.

Götze, Alfred. *Frühneuhochdeutsches Glossar.* 7th ed. Berlin, 1967.

Halliwell[-Phillips], James Orchard. *A Catalogue of Chap-Books, Garlands, and Popular Histories. . . .* London, 1849.

————. *A Hand-List of the Early English Literature Preserved in the Bodleian Library.* London, 1860.

Hayn, Hugo. *Vier neue Curiositäten-Bibliographeen . . . Amazonen-Litteratur.* Jena, 1905.

————, and Alfred N. Gotendorf, eds. *Bibliotheca Germanorum Erotica et Curiosa.* 3d ed. 9 vols. Munich, 1912–29.

Hazlitt, W. Carew. *Hand-Book to the Popular, Poetical, and Dramatic Literature of Great Britain, From the Invention of Printing to the Restoration.* London, 1867.

[Heyse, Carl Wilhelm Ludwig]. *Bücherschatz der deutschen National-Litteratur des XVI. und XVII. Jahrhunderts.* Berlin, 1854.

Horsley, Ritta Jo. "Women and German Literature: A Bibliography." *Female Studies* 9 (1975): 202–12.

Krieg, Walter. *Materialien zu einer Entwicklungsgeschichte der Bücher-Preise und des Autoren-Honorars vom 15. bis zum 20. Jahrhundert.* Vienna, 1953.

Lemonnyer, J. *Bibliographie des ouvrages relatifs à l'amour, aux femmes, au mariage et des livres facétieux.* . . . 4th ed. 4 vols. Paris, 1894.

McKerrow, R. B., ed. *A Dictionary of Printers and Booksellers in England, Scotland, and Ireland, and of Foreign Printers of English Books, 1557–1640.* London, 1910.

Maltzahn, Wendelin von. *Deutscher Bücherschatz des sechszehnten, siebenzehnten, und achtzehnten bis um die Mitte des neunzehnten Jahrhunderts.* Jena, 1875.

Myers, Carol Fairbanks. *Women in Literature: Criticism of the Seventies.* Metuchen, N.J., 1976.

National Library of Scotland, Edinburgh. *Catalogue of the Lauriston Castle Chapbooks.* Boston, 1964.

Plomer, Henry R. *A Dictionary of the Booksellers and Printers Who Were at Work in England, Scotland, and Ireland from 1641 to 1667.* London, 1907.

————. *A Dictionary of the Printers and Booksellers Who Were at Work in England, Scotland, and Ireland from 1668 to 1725.* London, 1922.

Pollard, A. W., and G. R. Redgrave, comps. *A Short-Title Catalogue of Books Printed in England, Scotland, and Ireland and of English Books Printed Abroad, 1475–1640.* London, 1926.

————. *A Short-Title Catalogue.* . . . 2d ed., rev. W. A. Jackson, F. S. Ferguson, and Katharine F. Pantzer. Vol. 2. London, 1976.

Pribram, Alfred Francis, ed. *Materialien zur Geschichte der Preise und Löhne in Österreich.* Vol. 1. Vienna, 1938.

Rollins, Hyder Edward. *An Analytical Index to the Ballad-Entries (1557–1709) in the Registers of the Company of Stationers in London.* Hatboro, Pa., 1967.

Schmidt, Adolf. "Fünfte Nachlese zu Weller: Die ersten deutschen Zeitungen. Aus der Grossherzoglichen Hofbibliothek in Darmstadt." *Zentralblatt für Bibliothekswesen* 9 (1892): 544–67.

Schottenloher, Karl. *Bibliographie zur deutschen Geschichte im Zeitalter der Glaubensspaltung, 1517–1585.* 2d ed. Vol. 4. Stuttgart, 1957.

Schüling, Hermann. *Bibliographischer Wegweiser zu dem in Deutschland erschienenen Schrifttum des 17. Jahrhunderts.* Giessen, 1964.

Short-Title Catalogue of Books Printed in the German-Speaking Countries and German Books Printed in Other Countries from 1455 to 1600 Now in the British Museum. London, 1962.

Utley, Francis Lee. *The Crooked Rib: An Analytical Index to the Argument about Women in English and Scottish Literature to the End of the Year 1568.* Columbus, Ohio, 1944.

Watson, George, and Ian Willison, eds. *The New Cambridge Bibliography of English Literature*. 5 vols. Cambridge, 1969–77.

Weller, Emil. *Annalen der Poetischen National-Literatur der Deutschen im XVI. und XVII. Jahrhundert*. 1862. Rept. Hildesheim, 1964.

———. *Die falschen und fingirten Druckorte: Repertorium der seit Erfindung der Buchdruckerkunst unter falscher Firma erschienenen deutschen, lateinischen, und französischen Schriften*. Vol. 1. Leipzig, 1864.

———. *Der Volksdichter Hans Sachs und seine Dichtungen: Eine Bibliographie*. Nuremberg, 1868.

———, ed. *Die ersten deutschen Zeitungen*. Stuttgart, 1872.

Wing, Donald, comp. *Short-Title Catalogue of Books Printed in England, Scotland, Ireland, Wales, and British America and of English Books Printed in Other Countries, 1641–1700*. 3 vols. New York, 1945.

Secondary Sources

Abel, Wilhelm. *Agricultural Fluctuations in Europe: From the Thirteenth to the Twentieth Centuries*. Trans. Olive Ordish. New York, 1980.

———. *Massenarmut und Hungerkrisen im vorindustriellen Deutschland*. Göttingen, 1972.

Allen, Richard Martin. "Crime and Punishment in Sixteenth-Century Reutlingen." Ph.D. diss., Univ. of Virginia, 1980.

———. "Hans Sachs's Conception of Women and Marriage." M.A. thesis, Univ. of Virginia, 1974.

Altick, Richard D. *The English Common Reader: A Social History of the Mass Reading Public, 1800–1900*. Chicago and London, 1963.

Amussen, Susan Dwyer. "Gender, Family, and the Social Order, 1560–1725." In *Order and Disorder in Early Modern England*, ed. Fletcher and Stevenson, 196–217.

———. *An Ordered Society: Gender and Class in Early Modern England*. Oxford, 1988.

Anderson, Bonnie S., and Judith P. Zinsser. *A History of Their Own: Women in Europe from Prehistory to the Present*. Vol. 1. New York, 1988.

Barnhill, Sandra Corder. "The Development of the Shrew in British Comedy to 1642." Ph.D. diss., Texas Tech Univ., 1977.

Baskerville, C. R. *The Elizabethen Jig*. Chicago, 1929.

Beattie, J. M. "The Pattern of Crime in England, 1660–1800." *Past and Present* 62 (1974): 47–95.

Beauvoir, Simone de. *The Second Sex*. Trans. and ed. H. M. Parshley. New York, 1974.

Becker-Cantarino, Barbara. *Der Lange Weg zur Mündigkeit: Frau und Literatur (1500–1800)*. Stuttgart, 1987.

———, ed. *Die Frau von der Reformation zur Romantik: Die Situation der*

Frau vor dem Hintergrund der Literatur- und Sozialgeschichte. Modern German Studies, 7. Bonn, 1980.

Beier, A. L. "Social Problems in Elizabethan London." *Journal of Interdisciplinary History* 9 (1978): 203–21.

Beilin, Elaine V. *Redeeming Eve: Women Writers of the English Renaissance.* Princeton, N.J., 1987.

Bellamy, John. *Crime and Public Order in England in the Later Middle Ages.* London, 1973.

Bennett, H. S. *English Books and Readers, 1475 to 1557.* Cambridge, 1952.

———. *English Books and Readers, 1558 to 1603.* Cambridge, 1965.

Berent, Eberhard. "Frauenverehrung und Frauenverachtung in der Dichtung des frühen Barock." In *Studies in Germanic Languages and Literature,* ed. Robert A. Fowkes and Volkmar Sander, 21–34. Reutlingen, 1967.

Beuys, Barbara. *Familienleben in Deutschland: Neue Bilder aus der deutschen Vergangenheit.* Reinbek bei Hamburg, 1984.

Bloch, Ruth H. "Untangling the Roots of Modern Sex Roles: A Survey of Four Centuries of Change." *Signs* 4 (1978): 237–52.

Bollème, Geneviève. *La bibliothèque bleue: littérature populaire en France du XVIIe au XIXe siècle.* Paris, 1971.

Bovenschen, Silvia. "Die aktuelle Hexe, die historische Hexe, und der Hexenmythos. Die Hexe: Subjekt der Naturaneignung und Objekt der Naturbeherrschung." In Gabriele Becker et al., *Aus der zeit der Verzweiflung: Zur Genese und Aktualität des Hexenbildes,* 259–312. Frankfurt am Main, 1977.

Bradford, Gamaliel. *Elizabethan Women.* Ed. Harold Ogden White. Cambridge, Mass., 1936.

Brauner, Sigrid. "Frightened Shrews and Fearless Wives: The Concept of the Witch in Early Modern German Texts (1487–1560)." Ph.D. diss., Univ. of California at Berkeley, 1989.

Brednich, Rolf Wilhelm. *Die Liedpublizistik im Flugblatt des 15. bis 17. Jahrhunderts.* 2 vols. Baden-Baden, 1974–75.

Breslauer, Martin. *Das deutsche Lied geistlich und weltlich bis zum 18. Jahrhundert.* Hildesheim, 1966.

Bridenthal, Renate, Claudia Koonz, and Susan Stuard, eds. *Becoming Visible: Women in European History.* 2d ed. Boston, 1987.

Brietzmann, Franz. *Die böse Frau in der deutschen Litteratur des Mittelalters.* Palaestra 42. Berlin, 1912.

Bronfman, Judith. "The Griselda Legend in English Literature." Ph.D. diss., New York Univ., 1977.

Brückner, Wolfgang, Peter Blickle, and Dieter Breuer, eds. *Literatur und Volk im 17. Jahrhundert: Probleme populärer Kultur in Deutschland.* Wolfenbütteler Arbeiten zur Barockforschung, 13. Wiesbaden, 1985.

Bruyn, Lucy de. *Women and the Devil in Sixteenth-Century Literature.* Tisbury, Eng., 1979.

Bücher, Karl. *Die Frauenfrage im Mittelalter.* Tubingen, 1910.

Bullough, Vern and Bonnie. *Prostitution: An Illustrated Social History.* New York, 1978.

Burke, Peter. *Popular Culture in Early Modern Europe.* New York, 1978.

————. "Popular Culture in Seventeenth-Century London." *London Journal* 3, no. 2 (1977): 143–62.

Cahn, Susan. "Changing Conceptions of Women in Sixteenth and Seventeenth Century England." Ph.D. diss., Univ. of Michigan, 1981.

————. *Industry of Devotion: The Transformation of Women's Work in England, 1500–1660.* New York, 1987.

Camden, C. Carroll. *The Elizabethan Woman.* Houston, 1952.

Capp, Bernard. "Popular Literature." In *Popular Culture in Seventeenth-Century England,* ed. Reay, 198–243.

Carlson, Eric Josef. "Marriage and the English Reformation." Ph.D. diss., Harvard Univ., 1987.

Carroll, Berenice A., ed. *Liberating Women's History: Theoretical and Critical Essays.* Urbana, Ill., 1976.

Casey, Paul F. *The Susanna Theme in German Literature: Variations of the Biblical Drama.* Abhandlungen zur Kunst-, Musik-, und Literaturwissenschaft, 214. Bonn, 1976.

Chandler, Frank W. *The Literature of Roguery.* 1907; rept. New York, 1974.

Charlton, Kenneth. *Education in Renaissance England.* London and Toronto, 1965.

Clark, Alice. *The Working Life of Women in the Seventeenth Century.* 1919; rept. New York, 1968.

Clark, Peter. "The Alehouse and the Alternative Society." In *Puritans and Revolutionaries,* ed. Donald Pennington and Keith Thomas, 47–72. Oxford, 1978.

————, ed. *The European Crisis of the 1590s: Essays in Comparative History.* London, 1985.

————. "The Ownership of Books in England, 1560–1640: The Example of Some Kentish Townsfolk." In *Schooling and Society: Studies in the History of Education,* ed. Lawrence Stone, 95–111. Baltimore and London, 1976.

————, and Paul Slack, eds., *Crisis and Order in English Towns, 1500–1700.* London, 1972.

Clark, Sandra. *The Elizabethan Pamphleteers: Popular Moralistic Pamphlets, 1580–1640.* Rutherford, Madison, Teaneck, N.J., 1983.

Cockburn, J. S., ed. *Crime in England, 1550–1800.* Princeton, N.J., 1977.

Cohn, Norman. *Europe's Inner Demons.* New York, 1975.

Cook, Ann Jennalie. *The Privileged Playgoers of Shakespeare's London, 1576–1642.* Princeton, N.J., 1981.

Coudert, Allison P. "The Myth of the Improved Status of Protestant

Women: The Case of the Witchcraze." In *The Politics of Gender in Early Modern Europe*, ed. Jean R. Brink, Allison P. Coudert, and Maryanne C. Horowitz, 61–89. Sixteenth Century Essays and Studies, 12. Kirksville, Mo., 1989.

Coupe, William A. *The German Illustrated Broadsheet in the Seventeenth Century*. Baden-Baden, 1966.

Cressy, David. *Literacy and the Social Order: Reading and Writing in Tudor and Stuart England*. Cambridge, 1980.

Davies, Kathleen M. "The Sacred Condition of Equality—How Original Were Puritan Doctrines of Marriage?" *Social History* 5 (1977): 563–80.

Davis, Natalie Zemon. *Fiction in the Archives: Pardon Tales and Their Tellers in Sixteenth-Century France*. Stanford, Calif., 1987.

———. *Society and Culture in Early Modern France*. Stanford, Calif., 1975.

———. "Women in the Crafts in Sixteenth-Century Lyon." In *Women and Work in Preindustrial Europe*, ed. Hanawalt, 167–97.

———. " 'Women's History' in Transition: The European Case." *Feminist Studies* 3, no. 3–4 (1976): 83–103.

Delumeau, Jean. *La Peur en Occident (XIVe–XVIIIe siècles): Une cité assiégée*. Paris, 1978.

Deufert, Wilfried. *Narr, Moral, und Gesellschaft: Grundtendenzen im Prosaschwank des 16. Jahrhunderts*. Bern, 1975.

Das deutsche Volkslied: Eine Ausstellung aus 5 Jahrhunderten deutscher Volkskunst. Berlin, 1936.

Dickens, A. G. *The German Nation and Martin Luther*. London, 1974.

Dieterich, Julius Reinhard. "Eselritt und Dachabdecken." *Hessische Blätter für Volkskunde* 1 (1902): 87–112.

Donaldson, Ian. *The Rapes of Lucretia: A Myth and Its Transformations*. Oxford, 1982.

———. *The World Upside-Down: Comedy from Jonson to Fielding*. Oxford, 1970.

Douglas, Mary. *Purity and Danger: An Analysis of Concepts of Pollution and Taboo*. London, 1978.

Dugaw, Dianne. *Warrior Women and Popular Balladry, 1650–1850*. Cambridge, 1989.

Dülmen, Richard van. *Kultur und Alltag in der Frühen Neuzeit*. Vol. 1. Munich, 1990.

———. *Theater des Schreckens: Gerichtspraxis und Strafrituale in der frühen Neuzeit*. Munich, 1985.

———, ed. *Armut, Liebe, Ehre: Studien zur historischen Kulturforschung*. Frankfurt am Main, 1988.

———, ed. *Kultur der einfachen Leute: Bayerisches Volksleben vom 16. bis 19. Jahrhundert*. Munich, 1983.

Dundes, Alan. *Life Is Like a Chicken Coop Ladder: A Portrait of German Culture through Folklore*. New York, 1984.

Eagleton, Terry. *Literary Theory: An Introduction.* Oxford, 1983.

Eaton, Sara J. "Presentations of Women in the English Popular Press." In *Ambiguous Realities: Women in the Middle Ages and Renaissance*, ed. Carole Levin and Jeanie Watson, 165–83. Detroit, 1987.

Ecker, Gisela. *Einblattdrucke von den Anfängen bis 1555: Untersuchungen zu einer Publikationsform literarischer Texte.* Vol. 1. Göppingen, 1981.

Eisenstein, Elizabeth L. *The Printing Press as an Agent of Change: Communications and Cultural Transformations in Early-Modern Europe.* 2 vols. Cambridge, 1979.

Elias, Norbert. *The Civilizing Process: The History of Manners.* Trans. Edmund Jephcott. New York, 1978.

Emmison, F. G. *Elizabethan Life: Disorder.* Chelmsford, 1970.

Engelsing, Rolf. *Analphabetentum und Lektüre: Zur Sozialgeschichte des Lesens in Deutschland zwischen feudaler und industrieller Gesellschaft.* Stuttgart, 1973.

Ennen, Edith. *Frauen im Mittelalter.* 2d ed. Munich, 1985. Translated as *The Medieval Woman.* Trans. Edmund Jephcott. Oxford, 1989.

Erickson, Carolly. *The Medieval Vision: Essays in History and Perception.* New York, 1976.

Esdaile, Arundell. "Autolycus' Pack: The Ballad Journalism of the Sixteenth Century." *Quarterly Review* 218 (1913): 372–91.

Evans, Richard J., ed. *The German Underworld: Deviants and Outcasts in German History.* London and New York, 1988.

Ezell, Margaret J. M. *The Patriarch's Wife: Literary Evidence and the History of the Family.* Chapel Hill, N.C., 1987.

Fairchilds, Cissie. "Female Sexual Attitudes and the Rise of Illegitimacy: A Case Study." *Journal of Interdisciplinary History* 8 (1978): 627–67.

Fehr, Hans. *Massenkunst im 16. Jahrhundert.* Berlin, 1924.

Ferrante, Joan M. *Woman as Image in Medieval Literature from the Twelfth Century to Dante.* New York and London, 1975.

Flandrin, Jean-Louis. *Families in Former Times: Kinship, Household, and Sexuality.* Trans. Richard Southern. Cambridge, 1979.

———. "Repression and Change in the Sexual Life of Young People in Medieval and Early Modern Times. *Journal of Family History* 2 (1977): 196–210.

Fletcher, Anthony, and John Stevenson, eds. *Order and Disorder in Early Modern England.* Cambridge, 1985.

Forster, Robert, and Orest Ranum, eds. *Family and Society: Selections from the Annales: Economies, Sociétés, Civilisations.* Baltimore and London, 1976.

Foucault, Michel. *The History of Sexuality.* Vol. I: An Introduction. Trans. Robert Hurley. New York, 1978.

Fox-Genovese, Elizabeth. "Gender, Class, and Power: Some Theoretical Considerations." *History Teacher* 15 (1982): 255–74.

Friess, Ursula. *Buhlerin und Zauberin: Eine Untersuchung zur deutschen Literatur des 18. Jahrhunderts.* Munich, 1970.

Frye, Northrop. *Anatomy of Criticism: Four Essays.* Princeton, N.J., 1957.

Fuchs, Eduard, and Alfred Kind. *Die Wiebherrschaft in der Geschichte der Menschheit.* Vol. 1. Munich, 1913.

Fussell, G. E. and K. R. *The English Countrywoman: A Farmhouse Social History, A.D. 1500–1900.* New York, 1971.

Gagen, Jean Elisabeth. *The New Woman: Her Emergence in English Drama 1600–1730.* New York, 1954.

Garrett, Clarke. "Women and Witches: Patterns of Analysis." *Signs* 3 (1977): 461–70.

Gartenberg, Patricia. "An Elizabethan Wonder Woman: The Life and Fortunes of Long Meg of Westminster." *Journal of Popular Culture* 17, no. 3 (Winter 1983): 49–58.

Garth, Helen Meredith. "Saint Mary Magdalene in Mediaeval Literature." *Johns Hopkins University Studies in Historical and Political Science* 67 (1950): 339–445.

Gattermann, Hermann. *Die deutsche Frau in den Fastnachtspielen.* Greifswald, 1911.

George, Margaret. *Women in the First Capitalist Society: Experiences in Seventeenth-Century England.* Urbana, Ill., 1988.

Gillis, John R. *For Better, For Worse: British Marriages, 1600 to the Present.* New York and Oxford, 1985.

Goldman, Rachel M. "The Lucretia Legend from Livy to Rojas Zorilla." Ph.D. diss., City Univ. of New York, 1976.

Hajnal, J. "European Marriage Patterns in Perspective." In *Population in History*, ed. D. V. Glass and D. E. C. Eversley, 101–44. London, 1965.

Hallissy, Margaret. *Venomous Woman: Fear of the Female in Literature.* New York, 1987.

Hampe, Theodor. *Crime and Punishment in Germany.* Trans. Malcolm Letts. London, 1929.

Hanawalt, Barbara A. "The Female Felon in Fourteenth-Century England." In *Women in Medieval Society*, ed. Susan Mosher Stuard, 125–40. Philadelphia, 1976.

———. "The Peasant Family and Crime in Fourteenth-Century England." *Journal of British Studies* 13, no. 2 (1974): 1–18.

———, ed. *Women and Work in Preindustrial Europe.* Bloomington, Ind., 1986.

Harper, Edward B. "Fear and the Status of Women." *Southwestern Journal of Anthropology* 25 (1969): 81–95.

Haselkorn, Anne M. *Prostitution in Elizabethan and Jacobean Comedy.* Troy, N.Y., 1983.

Hays, H. R. *The Dangerous Sex: The Myth of Feminine Evil.* London, 1966.

Heidrich, Hermann. "Grenzübergänge. Das Haus und die Volkskultur in der frühen Neuzeit." In *Kultur der Einfachen Leute*, ed. Dülmen, 17–41.

Herford, Charles H. *Studies in the Literary Relations of England and Germany in the Sixteenth Century.* Cambridge, 1886.

Herlihy, David. "Life Expectancies for Women in Medieval Society." In *The Role of Woman in the Middle Ages*, ed. Rosmarie Thee Morewedge, 1–22. Albany, 1975.

———. *Medieval Households.* Cambridge, Mass., 1985.

———. *Women in Medieval Society.* Houston, Tex., 1971.

Hill, Christopher. *The Century of Revolution.* Edinburgh, 1962.

Hobby, Elaine. *Virtue of Necessity: English Women's Writing, 1646–1688.* London, 1988.

Hodgart, M. J. C. *The Ballads.* London, 1950.

Hogrefe, Pearl. *Tudor Women: Commoners and Queens.* Ames, Iowa, 1975.

Honegger, Claudia, ed. *Die Hexen der Neuzeit: Studien zur Sozialgeschichte eines kulturellen Deutungsmusters.* Frankfurt am Main, 1978.

Horsley, Richard A. "Who Were the Witches? The Social Roles of the Accused in the European Witch Trials." *Journal of Interdisciplinary History* 9 (1979): 689–715.

Houlbrooke, Ralph. *Church Courts and the People during the English Reformation, 1520–1570.* Oxford, 1979.

———. *The English Family, 1450–1700.* London and New York, 1984.

Howell, Martha C. *Women, Production, and Patriarchy in Late Medieval Cities.* Chicago, 1986.

———. "Women, the Family Economy, and the Structures of Market Production in Cities of Northern Europe during the Late Middle Ages." In *Women and Work in Preindustrial Europe*, ed. Hanawalt, 198–222.

Hull, Suzanne W. *Chaste, Silent, and Obedient: English Books for Women, 1475–1640.* San Marino, Calif., 1982.

Imhof, Arthur E. *Die verlorenen Welten: Alltagsbewältigung durch unsere Vorfahren—und weshalb wir uns heute so schwer damit tun.* 2d ed. Munich, 1985.

Ingram, Martin. *Church Courts, Sex, and Marriage in England, 1570–1640.* Cambridge, 1987.

———. "Ridings, Rough Music, and Mocking Rhymes in Early Modern England." In *Popular Culture in Seventeenth-Century England*, ed. Reay, 166–97.

Janssen, Johannes. *History of the German People at the Close of the Middle Ages.* Vols. 1, 2, 16. New York, 1966.

Jardine, Lisa. *Still Harping on Daughters: Women and Drama in the Age of Shakespeare.* Sussex, Eng., and Totowa, N.J., 1983.

Jegel, August. "Altnürnberger Zensur vor allem des 16. Jahrhunderts." In *Festschrift Eugen Stollreither*, ed. Fritz Redenbacher, 55–64. Erlangen, 1950.

Jordan, Constance. *Renaissance Feminism: Literary Texts and Political Models*. Ithaca, N.Y., 1990.

Kahn, Coppélia. *Man's Estate: Masculine Identity in Shakespeare*. Berkeley, Calif., 1981.

Kamen, Henry. *The Iron Century: Social Change in Europe, 1550–1660*. New York, 1971.

Kanner, Barbara, ed. *The Women of England from Anglo-Saxon Times to the Present: Interpretive Bibliographical Essays*. Hamden, Conn., 1979.

Karant-Nunn, Susan C. "Continuity and Change: Some Effects of the Reformation on the Women of Zwickau." *Sixteenth Century Journal* 12, no. 2 (1982): 17–42.

Kawerau, Waldemar. "Lob und Schimpf des Ehestandes in der Litteratur des sechzehnten Jahrhunderts." *Preussische Jahrbücher* 69 (1892): 760–81.

Kelly, Joan. *Women, History, and Theory*. Chicago and London, 1984.

Kelso, Ruth. *Doctrine for the Lady of the Renaissance*. Urbana, Ill., 1978.

Kieckhefer, Richard. *European Witch Trials: Their Foundations in Popular and Learned Culture, 1300–1500*. London, 1976.

Klaits, Joseph. *Servants of Satan: The Age of the Witch Hunts*. Bloomington, Ind., 1985.

Klapisch-Zuber, Christiane. *Women, Family, and Ritual in Renaissance Italy*. Trans. Lydia G. Cochrane. Chicago and London, 1985.

Koebner, Richard. "Die Eheauffassung des ausgehenden deutschen Mittelalters." *Archiv für Kulturgeschichte* 9 (1911): 136–98, 278–318.

Kramer, Karl-Sigismund. *Volksleben im Hochstift Bamberg und im Fürstentum Coburg (1500–1800): Eine Volkskunde auf Grund archivalischer Quellen*. Beiträge zur Volkstumsforschung, 15. Wurzburg, 1967.

Kunze, Michael. *Der Prozeß Pappenheimer*. Ebelsbach, 1981. Translated as *High Road to the Stake: A Tale of Witchcraft*. Trans. William E. Yuill. Chicago, 1987.

Lahnstein, Peter. *Das Leben im Barock: Zeugnisse und Berichte, 1640–1740*. Stuttgart, 1974.

Langbein, John H. *Torture and the Law of Proof: Europe and England in the Ancien Régime*. Chicago, 1977.

Lantz, Herman R. "Romantic Love in the Pre-Modern Period: A Sociological Commentary." *Journal of Social History* 15 (1982): 349–70.

Larner, Christina. "Crimen Exceptum." In *Crime and the Law: The Social History of Crime in Western Europe since 1500*, ed. V. A. C. Gatrell, Bruce Lenman, and Geoffrey Parker, 49–75. London, 1980s.

———. *Enemies of God: The Witch-Hunt in Scotland*. Baltimore, 1981.

Laslett, Peter. *The World We Have Lost*. New York, 1965.

Levack, Brian P. *The Witch-Hunt in Early Modern Europe*. London, 1987.

Lewalski, Barbara Kiefer, ed. *Renaissance Genres: Essays on Theory, History, and Interpretation*. Cambridge, Mass., and London, 1986.

Lougee, Carolyn C. *Le Paradis des Femmes: Women, Salons, and Social Stratification in Seventeenth-Century France.* Princeton, N.J., 1976.

McCormack, C., and M. Strathern. *Nature, Culture, and Gender.* Cambridge, 1980.

MacDonald, Michael. *Mystical Bedlam: Madness, Anxiety, and Healing in Seventeenth-Century England.* Cambridge, 1981.

McFarland, Ronald. " 'The Hag Is Astride': Witches in Seventeenth-Century Literature." *Journal of Popular Culture* 11 (1977): 88–97.

Macfarlane, Alan. *Marriage and Love in England: Modes of Reproduction, 1300–1840.* Oxford, 1986.

———. *The Origins of English Individualism.* New York, 1979.

———. *Witchcraft in Tudor and Stuart England.* New York, 1970.

Mack, Phyllis. "Women as Prophets during the English Civil War." *Feminist Studies* 8, no. 1 (Spring 1982): 19–45.

McLaren, Dorothy. "Marital Fertility and Lactation, 1570–1720." In *Women in English Society, 1500–1800,* ed. Prior, 22–53.

Maclean, Ian. *The Renaissance Notion of Woman.* New York, 1980.

Mandrou, Robert. *De la culture populaire aux XVIIe et XVIIIe siècles: La bibliothèque bleue de Troyes.* Stock, 1964.

Marshall, Sherrin, ed. *Women in Reformation and Counter-Reformation Europe: Public and Private Worlds.* Bloomington, Ind., 1989.

Maschke, Erich. *Die Familie in der deutschen Stadt des späten Mittelalters.* Heidelberg, 1980.

———. *Städte und Menschen: Beiträge zur Geschichte der Stadt, der Wirtschaft und Gesellschaft, 1959–1977.* Wiesbaden, 1980.

Mathieson, Barbara O. "Patterns of Misogyny in Jacobean Tragedy." Ph.D. diss., Stanford Univ., 1979.

Maurer, Georg Ludwig von. *Geschichte der Städteverfassung in Deutschland.* Vol. 3. 1870; rept. Aalen, 1962.

Midelfort, H. C. Erik. *Witch Hunting in Southwestern Germany, 1562–1684: The Social and Intellectual Foundations.* Stanford, Calif., 1972.

Miles, Margaret R. *Carnal Knowing: Female Nakedness and Religious Meaning in the Christian West.* Boston, 1989.

———. *Image as Insight: Visual Understanding in Western Christianity and Secular Culture.* Boston, 1985.

Miller, Edwin Haviland. *The Professional Writer in Elizabethan England: A Study of Nondramatic Literature.* Cambridge, Mass., 1959.

Miller, Thomas Fischer. "Mirror for Marriage: Lutheran Views of Marriage and the Family, 1520–1600." Ph.D. diss., Univ. of Virginia, 1981.

Mitchell, W. J. T., ed. *On Narrative.* Chicago and London, 1981.

Mitterauer, Michael. *Ledige Mütter: Zur Geschichte unehelicher Geburten in Europa.* Munich, 1983.

———, and Reinhard Sieder. *The European Family: Patriarchy to Part-*

nership from the Middle Ages to the Present. Trans. Karla Oosterveen and Manfred Hörzinger. Oxford, 1982.

Monter, E. W. "Protestant Wives, Catholic Saints, and the Devil's Handmaid: Women in the Age of Reformations." In *Becoming Visible*, ed. Bridenthal, Koonz, and Stuard, 203–19.

Moore, Cornelia Niekus. *The Maiden's Mirror: Reading Material for German Girls in the Sixteenth and Seventeenth Centuries.* Wolfenbütteler Forschungen, 36. Wiesbaden, 1987.

Morgan, Edmund S. *The Puritan Family: Religion and Domestic Relations in Seventeenth-Century New England.* 2d ed. New York, 1966.

Moser-Rath, Elfriede. "Familienleben im Spiegel der Barockpredigt." *Daphnis: Zeitschrift für Mittlere Deutsche Literatur* 10 (1981): 47–65.

———. "Frauenfeindliche Tendenzen im Witz." *Zeitschrift für Volkskunde* 74 (1978): 40–57.

———. *"Lustige Gesellschaft": Schwank und Witz des 17. und 18. Jahrhunderts in kultur- und sozialgeschichtlichem Kontext.* Stuttgart, 1984.

———. "Das streitsüchtige Eheweib: Erzählformen des 17. Jahrhunderts zum Schwanktyp ATh 1365." *Rheinisches Jahrbuch für Volkskunde* 10 (1959): 40–50.

Moxey, Keith. *Peasants, Warriors, and Wives: Popular Imagery in the Reformation.* Chicago and London, 1989.

Muchembled, Robert. *Culture populaire et culture des élites dans la France moderne.* Paris, 1978.

Müller, Maria E., ed. *Eheglück und Liebesjoch: Bilder von Liebe, Ehe, und Familie in der Literatur des 15. und 16. Jahrhunderts.* Weinheim and Basel, 1988.

Neuburg, Victor E. *Popular Literature: A History and Guide.* London, 1977.

Notestein, Wallace. "The English Woman, 1580–1650." In *Studies in Social History*, ed. J. H. Plumb, 71–107. London, 1955.

Nussbaum, Felicity A. *The Brink of All We Hate: English Satires on Women 1660–1750.* Lexington, Ky., 1984.

O'Faolain, Julia, and Lauro Martines, eds. *Not in God's Image: Women in History from the Greeks to the Victorians.* London, 1973.

Ortner, Sherry B. "Is Female to Male as Nature Is to Culture?" In *Woman, Culture, and Society*, ed. Rosaldo and Lamphere, 67–87.

Otis, Leah L. *Prostitution in Medieval Society: The History of an Urban Institution in Languedoc.* Chicago and London, 1985.

Outhwaite, R. B., ed. *Marriage and Society: Studies in the Social History of Marriage.* New York, 1981.

Ozment, Steven. *Magdalena and Balthasar: An Intimate Portrait of Life in 16th-Century Europe.* New York, 1986.

———. *The Reformation in the Cities.* New Haven and London, 1975.

———. *When Fathers Ruled: Family Life in Reformation Europe.* Cambridge, Mass., 1983.

————, ed. *Reformation Europe: A Guide to Research*. St. Louis, 1982.

Pascal, Roy. *German Literature in the Sixteenth and Seventeenth Centuries*. London, 1968.

Pearson, Lu Emily. *Elizabethan Love Conventions*. New York, 1966.

Perry, Mary Elizabeth. *Gender and Disorder in Early Modern Seville*. Princeton, N.J., 1990.

Phelps Brown, E. H., and Sheila V. Hopkins. "Seven Centuries of Building Wages." *Economica*, n.s. 22 (1955): 195–206.

————. "Seven Centuries of the Prices of Consumables, Compared with Builders' Wage-rates." *Economica*, n.s. 23 (1956): 296–314.

Plant, Marjorie. *The English Book Trade: An Economic History of the Making and Sale of Books*. 2d ed. London, 1965.

Platel, Marguerite. *Vom Volkslied zum Gesellschaftslied: Zur Geschichte des Liedes im 16. und 17. Jahrhundert*. Bern, 1939. Rept. Nendeln/Liechtenstein, 1970.

Plummer, John F., ed. *Vox Feminae: Studies in Medieval Woman's Songs*. Studies in Medieval Culture, 15. Kalamazoo, Mich., 1981.

Pollock, Linda A. *Forgotten Children: Parent-Child Relations from 1500 to 1900*. Cambridge, 1983.

Posern-Klett, Dr. von. "Frauenhäuser und freie Frauen in Sachsen." *Archiv für die sächsische Geschichte* 12 (1874): 63–89.

Powell, Chilton Latham. *English Domestic Relations, 1487–1653*. New York, 1917.

Power, Eileen. *Medieval Women*. Ed. M. M. Postan. Cambridge, 1975.

Pratt, Samuel M. "Jane Shore and the Elizabethans: Some Facts and Speculations." *Texas Studies in Literature and Language* 11 (1970): 1293–1306.

Prior, Mary, ed. *Women in English Society, 1500–1800*. London, 1985.

Quaife, G. R. *Wanton Wenches and Wayward Wives: Peasants and Illicit Sex in Early Seventeenth Century England*. London, 1979.

Rabb, Theodore K. *The Struggle for Stability in Early Modern Europe*. New York, 1975.

Radbruch, Gustav, and Heinrich Gwinner. *Geschichte des Verbrechens: Versuch einer historischen Kriminologie*. Stuttgart, 1951.

Rahmelow, Jan M. "Das Volkslied als publizistisches Medium und historische Quelle." *Jahrbuch für Volksliedforschung* 14 (1969): 11–26.

Rappaport, Steve. *Worlds within Worlds: Structures of Life in Sixteenth-Century London*. Cambridge, 1989.

Reay, Barry, ed. *Popular Culture in Seventeenth-Century England*. New York, 1985.

Reiter, Rayna R., ed. *Toward an Anthropology of Women*. New York, 1975.

Robisheaux, Thomas. *Rural Society and the Search for Order in Early Modern Germany*. Cambridge, 1989.

Rogers, Katharine M. *The Troublesome Helpmate: A History of Misogyny in Literature*. Seattle and London, 1966.

Rogers, James E. Thorold. *A History of Agriculture and Prices in England.* Vol. 5. *1583–1702.* Oxford, 1963.

———. *Six Centuries of Work and Wages: The History of English Labour.* London, 1949.

Rollins, Hyder Edward. "The Black-Letter Broadside Ballad." *Publications of the Modern Language Association of America* 34 (1919): 258–339.

———. "Martin Parker, Ballad-Monger." *Modern Philology* 16 (1919): 449–74.

———. "William Elderton: Elizabethan Actor and Ballad Writer." *Studies in Philology* 171 (1920): 199.

Roper, Lyndal. " 'Going to Church and Street': Weddings in Reformation Augsburg. *Past and Present* 106 (1985): 62–101.

———. *The Holy Household: Women and Morals in Reformation Augsburg.* Oxford, 1989.

Rosaldo, Michelle Zimbalist, and Louise Lamphere, eds. *Woman, Culture, and Society.* Stanford, Calif., 1974.

Roth, Klaus. *Ehebruchschwänke in Liedform: Eine Untersuchung zur deutsch- und englischsprachigen Schwankballade.* Munich, 1977.

Roth, Paul. *Die neuen Zeitungen in Deutschland im 15. und 16. Jahrhundert.* Leipzig, 1914.

Routh, Harold V. "London and the Development of Popular Literature." In *The Cambridge History of English Literature*, ed. A. W. Ward and A. R. Waller, 4:362–415. New York, 1910.

———. "The Progress of Social Literature in Tudor Times." In *The Cambridge History of English Literature*, ed. A. W. Ward and A. R. Waller, 3:93–129. New York, 1909.

Rowbotham, Sheila. *Hidden from History: Rediscovering Women in History from the 17th Century to the Present.* New York, 1974.

Rümelin, Eduard. "Heiratsalter und Fruchtbarkeit der Ehen und ihre Entwicklung seit 1500." In *Württembergische Jahrbücher für Statistik und Landeskunde Jahrgang 1923/24*, 11–31. Stuttgart, 1926.

Rupprich, Hans. *Die deutsche Literatur vom späten Mittelalter bis zum Barock.* Vols. 1 and 2. Munich, 1970, 1973.

Sabean, David. *Power in the Blood: Popular Culture and Village Discourse in Early Modern Germany.* Cambridge, 1984.

Safley, Thomas Max. *Let No Man Put Asunder.* Kirksville, Mo., 1984.

Salgado, Gamini. *The Elizabethan Underworld.* London, 1977.

Schenda, Rudolf. "Kleinformen der Trivialliteratur aus sechs Jahrhunderten." *Beiträge zur deutschen Volks- und Altertumskunde* 10 (1966): 49–66.

———. *Volk ohne Buch: Studien zur Sozialgeschichte der populären Lesestoffe 1770–1910.* Frankfurt am Main, 1970.

Scherr, Johannes. *Geschichte der Deutschen Frauenwelt.* 4th ed. Leipzig, 1879.

Schmidt, Rudolf. *Die Frau in der deutschen Literatur des 16. Jahrhunderts.* Strassburg, 1917.

Schmitz, Götz. *The Fall of Women in Early English Narrative Verse.* Cambridge, 1990.

Schnucker, Robert V. "La position puritaine à l'égard de l'adultère." *Annales: Economies, Sociétés, Civilisations* 27 (1972): 1379–88.

Schofield, R. S. "The Measurement of Literacy in Pre-Industrial England." In *Literacy in Traditional Societies*, ed. Jack Goody, 311–25. Cambridge, 1968.

Schorbach, Karl. "Die Historie von der schönen Melusine." *Zeitschrift für Bücherfreunde* 1 (1897): 132–42.

Schottenloher, Karl. *Flugblatt und Zeitung: Ein Wegweiser durch das gedruckte Tagesschrifttum.* Berlin, 1922.

Schotter, Anne Howland. "Woman's Song in Medieval Latin." In *Vox Feminae*, ed. Plummer, 19–33.

Schücking, Levin. *The Puritan Family: A Social Study from the Literary Sources.* Trans. Brian Battershaw. New York, 1970.

Scott, George Ryley. *A History of Prostitution from Antiquity to the Present Day.* London, 1936. Rept. New York, 1976.

Scott, Joan W. "Gender: A Useful Category of Historical Analysis." *American Historical Review* 91 (1986): 1053–75.

Scribner, R. W. *Popular Culture and Popular Movements in Reformation Germany.* London, 1987.

Seemann, Erich. "Die Gestalt des kriegerischen Mädchens in den europäischen Volksballaden." *Rheinisches Jahrbuch für Volkskunde* 10 (1959): 192–212.

Shaaber, Matthias A. *Some Forerunners of the Newspaper in England, 1476–1622.* Philadelphia, 1929.

Shahar, Shulamith. *The Fourth Estate: A History of Women in the Middle Ages.* Trans. Chaya Galai. London and New York, 1983.

Shapiro, Susan C. "Sex, Gender, and Fashion in Medieval and Early Modern Britain." *Journal of Popular Culture* 20, no. 4 (1987): 113–28.

Sharpe, J. A. *Defamation and Sexual Slander in Early Modern England: The Church Courts at York.* Borthwick Institute of Historical Research, Borthwick Papers no. 58. York, [1980?].

———. "Domestic Homicide in Early Modern England." *Historical Journal* 24 (1981): 29–48.

———. " 'Last Dying Speeches': Religion, Ideology, and Public Execution in Seventeenth-Century England." *Past and Present* 107 (1985): 144–67.

———. "Plebeian Marriage in Stuart England: Some Evidence from Popular Literature." *Transactions of the Royal Historical Society*, 5th ser., 36 (1986): 69–90.

Shepard, Leslie. *The Broadside Ballad: A Study in Origins and Meaning.* London, 1962.

Shepherd, Simon. *Amazons and Warrior Women: Varieties of Feminism in Seventeenth-Century Drama*. New York, 1981.

Shorter, Edward. *The Making of the Modern Family*. New York, 1975.

Simpson, Claude M. *The British Broadside Ballad and Its Music*. New Brunswick, N.J., 1966.

———. "Ebsworth and the Roxburghe Ballads." *Journal of American Folklore* 61 (1948): 337–44.

Smith-Rosenberg, Carroll. *Disorderly Conduct: Visions of Gender in Victorian America*. New York, 1985.

Springer, Marlene, ed. *What Manner of Woman: Essays on English and American Life and Literature*. New York, 1977.

Spufford, Margaret. *Contrasting Communities: English Villagers in the Sixteenth and Seventeenth Centuries*. Cambridge, 1974.

———. *Small Books and Pleasant Histories: Popular Reading and Its Readership in Seventeenth-Century England*. Athens, Ga., 1981.

Stallybrass, Peter, and Allon White. *The Politics and Poetics of Transgression*. Ithaca, N.Y., 1986.

Stenton, Doris Mary. *The English Woman in History*. London, 1957.

Stone, Lawrence. "The Educational Revolution in England, 1560–1640." *Past and Present* 28 (1964): 41–80.

———. *The Family, Sex, and Marriage in England, 1500–1800*. London, 1977.

———. "Interpersonal Violence in English Society, 1300–1980." *Past and Present* 101 (1983): 22–33.

———. "Literacy and Education in England, 1640–1900." *Past and Present* 42 (1969): 69–139.

———. "The Rise of the Nuclear Family in Early Modern England." In *The Family in History*, ed. Charles E. Rosenberg, 13–57. Philadelphia, 1975.

———. *Social Change and Revolution in England, 1540–1640*. London, 1965.

———. "Social Mobility in England, 1500–1700." In *Seventeenth-Century England*, ed. Paul S. Seaver, 26–70. New York, 1976.

———, and Jeanne C. Fawtier Stone. *An Open Elite? England, 1540–1880*. Oxford, 1984.

Strauss, Gerald. *Law, Resistance, and the State: The Opposition to Roman Law in Reformation Germany*. Princeton, N.J., 1986.

———. *Luther's House of Learning*. Baltimore, 1978.

Stricker, Käthe. *Die Frau in der Reformation*. Quellenhefte zum Frauenleben in der Geschichte, 11. Berlin, 1927.

Stuard, Susan Mosher, ed. *Women in Medieval Society*. Philadelphia, 1976.

Tentler, Thomas N. *Sin and Confession on the Eve of the Reformation*. Princeton, N.J., 1977.

Thomas, Keith. "The Double Standard." *Journal of the History of Ideas* 20 (1959): 195–216.

————. "The Place of Laughter in Tudor and Stuart England." *Times Literary Supplement*, 21 Jan. 1977, 77–81.

————. *Religion and the Decline of Magic*. New York, 1971.

————. "Women and the Civil War Sects." *Past and Present* 13 (1958): 42–62.

Thompson, Roger. "Popular Reading and Humour in Restoration England." *Journal of Popular Culture* 9 (1976): 653–61.

Thrupp, Sylvia L. *The Merchant Class of Medieval London*. Chicago, 1948.

Tillyard, E. M. W. *The Elizabethan World Picture*. London, 1960.

Todd, Janet, ed. *Gender and Literary Voice*. New York, 1980.

Ulbrich, Otto. "Infanticide in Eighteenth-Century Germany." In *German Underworld*, ed. Evans, 108–40.

Underdown, D. E. "The Taming of the Scold: The Enforcement of Patriarchy in Early Modern England." In *Order and Disorder in Early Modern England*, ed. Fletcher and Stevenson, 116–36.

Waage, Frederick O. "Social Themes in Urban Broadsides of Renaissance England." *Journal of Popular Culture* 11 (1977): 731–41.

Wächtershäuser, Wilhelm. *Das Verbrechen des Kindesmordes im Zeitalter der Aufklärung*. Berlin, 1973.

Walker, D. P. *Unclean Spirits: Possession and Exorcism in France and England in the Late Sixteenth and Early Seventeenth Centuries*. London, 1981.

Wallinger, Sylvia, and Monika Jonas, eds. *Der Widerspenstigen Zähmung: Studien zur bezwungenen Weiblichkeit in der Literatur vom Mittelalter bis zur Gegenwart*. Innsbrucker Beiträge zur Kulturwissenschaft, Germanistische Reihe, 31. Innsbruck, 1986.

Warner, Marina. *Alone of All Her Sex: The Myth and the Cult of the Virgin Mary*. New York, 1976.

Warnicke, Retha M. *Women of the English Renaissance and Reformation*. Westport, Conn., 1983.

Waterhouse, Gilbert. *The Literary Relations of England and Germany in the Seventeenth Century*. New York, 1966.

Watt, Ian. *The Rise of the Novel: Studies in Defoe, Richardson, and Fielding*. Berkeley and Los Angeles, 1957.

Weatherill, Lorna. "A Possession of One's Own: Women and Consumer Behavior in England, 1660–1740." *Journal of British Studies* 25 (1986): 131–56.

Weber, Bruno, ed. *Wunderzeichen und Winkeldrucker, 1543–1586: Einblattdrucke aus der Sammlung Wikiana in der Zentralbibliothek Zürich*. Zurich, 1972.

Weber, Marianne. *Ehefrau und Mutter in der Rechtsentwicklung*. Tübingen, 1907.

Weber-Kellermann, Ingeborg. *Die deutsche Familie*. Frankfurt am Main, 1974.

Wehse, Rainer. *Schwanklied und Flugblatt in Großbritannien*. Frankfurt am Main, 1979.

Weisser, Michael R. *Crime and Punishment in Early Modern Europe.* Hassocks, Sussex, 1979.

Wiener, Carol Z. "Sex Roles and Crime in Late Elizabethan Hertfordshire." *Journal of Social History* 8, no. 4 (1975): 38–60.

Wiesner, Merry E. "Frail, Weak, and Helpless: Women's Legal Position in Theory and Reality." In *Regnum, Religio, et Ratio: Essays Presented to Robert M. Kingdon,* ed. Jerome Friedman, 161–69. Sixteenth Century Essays and Studies, 8. Kirksville, Mo., 1987.

————. "Paternalism in Practice: The Control of Servants and Prostitutes in Early Modern German Cities." In *The Process of Change in Early Modern Europe,* ed. Phillip N. Bebb and Sherrin Marshall, 179–200. Athens, Ohio, 1988.

————. "Spinning Out Capital: Women's Work in the Early Modern Economy." In *Becoming Visible,* ed. Bridenthal, Koonz, and Stuard, 221–49.

————. "Women's Defense of Their Public Role." In *Women in the Middle Ages and the Renaissance: Literary and Historical Perspectives,* ed. Mary Beth Rose, 1–27. Syracuse, N.Y., 1986.

————. *Working Women in Renaissance Germany.* New Brunswick, N.J., 1986.

Willen, Diane. "Women in the Public Sphere in Early Modern England: The Case of the Urban Working Poor." *Sixteenth Century Journal* 19 (1988): 559–76.

Wiltenburg, Joy Deborah. "Disorderly Women and Female Power in the Popular Literature of Early Modern England and Germany." Ph.D. diss., Univ. of Virginia, 1984.

Woodbridge, Linda. "New Light on *The Wife Lapped in Morel's Skin* and *The Proud Wife's Paternoster.*" *English Literary Renaissance* 13 (1983): 3–35.

————. *Women and the English Renaissance: Literature and the Nature of Womankind, 1540–1620.* Urbana, Ill., 1984.

Wright, Louis B. *Middle-Class Culture in Elizabethan England.* Ithaca, N.Y., 1958.

Wrightson, Keith. *English Society, 1580–1680.* New Brunswick, N.J., 1982.

————. "The Nadir of English Illegitimacy in the Seventeenth Century." In *Bastardy and Its Comparative History,* ed. Peter Laslett, Karla Oosterveen, and Richard M. Smith, 176–91. London, 1980.

Wrigley, E. A. "A Simple Model of London's Importance in Changing English Society and Economy 1650–1750." *Past and Present* 37 (1967): 44–70.

Wunder, Heide. "Hexenprozesse im Herzogtum Preussen während des 16. Jahrhunderts." In *Hexenprozesse: Deutsche und skandinavische Beiträge,* ed. Christian Degn, Hartmut Lehmann, and Dagmar Unverhau, 179–203. Neumünster, 1983.

Würzbach, Natascha. *Anfänge und gattungstypische Ausformung der englischen Straßenballade, 1550–1650.* Munich, 1981. Translated as *The Rise of the English Street Ballad, 1550–1650.* Trans. Gayna Walls. Cambridge, 1990.
Ziegler, Matthes. *Die Frau im Märchen.* Leipzig, 1937.

Index

Adelger, 198
Adlington, Henry, 166
Admirable New Northern Story, An, 64
Adultery: of husband killers, 163, 216–18; of husbands, 90–91, 93, 160–61, 223; of unruly wives, 102, 104–6, 131, 152–60
Alehouse, 106, 154, 170; as resort of husbands, 82, 86, 94, 128, 224; *see also* Drinking
Alexander of Metz, 62–63, 77
Allen, Edmund, 223
All is ours and our Husbands, 106
Amazons, 193–94
Ambree, Mary, 64, 192
Amussen, Susan, 102, 156, 214
Andächtiger Ruff Von dem H. Leben vnd Marterkampff/der glorwürdigen Jungfrawen Sanct Barbara, 197
Anglicanism, 264
Araignment Of Lewde, idle, froward, and vnconstant women, 215
Aristotle, 79
Askew, Anne, 198
Audience, 28–29, 38–41, 47–48; in England, 29–34; in Germany, 35–38
Augsburg, 37
Authors, 27–29, 39–40; in England, 31–32; in Germany, 36–37

Bachelorhood, ballads in praise of, 65–66
Ballads, 29–34, 40, 44; authors of, 31–32; prices of, 30; sale of, 27, 29, 94
Banquet for Soueraigne Husbands, 100–101

Barbara, Saint, 56, 197
Basel, 37
Batchelor's Delight, The, 129
Benefit of Marriage, The, 85
Binder, Ludwig, 202–3
Boccaccio, 157–58
Bös rauch, Der, 131
Bowne, Tobias, 65, 67
Brednich, Rolf Wilhelm, 36
Bride's Good-morrow, The, 81
Bridewell prison, 171, 187
Bridewel Whores Resolution, The, 171
Brietzmann, Franz, 120
Broadsides, in Germany, 34–36, 44; *see also* Ballads
Buler Artzney, Der, 79
Burke, Peter, 17

Caldwell, Elizabeth, 217, 233, 234
Canterbury Tales, by "Chaucer Junior," 33
Capitalism, 10–11, 19, 20; in England, 24
Carefull Wife's Good Counsel, The, 87
Carnival, 17, 60–61
Catherine, Saint, 56
Catholicism: in Protestant propaganda, 233, 237–38; and street literature, 38; and women, 14, 56–58, 61, 180, 264
Caueat or Warning, A, 169
Censorship, 31, 34, 72
Cent Nouvelles Nouvelles, 157, 160
Chambers, John, 223
Chapbooks, 30, 32–34

Chastity, 23; of heroines, 50–51, 52, 58,
  62–73, 77, 143–44; and rape, 203,
  206; women's valuation of, 102, 254
*Chearful Husband: or, The Despairing Wife,
  The*, 86
Childbirth, *see* Pregnancy
Children, 24–25, 215, 259–60; illegiti-
  mate, 79–80, 176, 233–38; as killers
  of parents, 231–32; as murder vic-
  tims, 213, 224–38, 240, 242, 248–49;
  as victims of witchcraft, 240, 242,
  248–49; *see also* Family, Parents, *and*
  Pregnancy
Chivalry, romances of, 62–63, 145
City Caper, The, 199
Cleopatra, 164–65
Cologne, 37
Concubinage, 16
Constance of Cleveland, 93
*Constant Wife, a kinde Wife, a louing Wife,
  and a fine Wife, A*, 84
*Country Lass, Who left her Spinning-Wheel
  for a more pleasant Employment, The*,
  167
Coupe, William, 36
Courtship, 24, 65–68, 79, 258; *see also*
  Love *and* Marriage
Coy Shepherdess, The, 201
Cressy, David, 33–34, 37
Crew of kind Gossips, A, 106
Crime: and early modern governments,
  17; in street literature, 209–50; *see
  also* Murder, Violence, *and* Witch-
  craft
*Cruell Shrow: Or, The Patient Man's Woe,
  The*, 109
Cuckoldry, 152, 155–56, 256; *see also*
  Adultery
*Cuckold's Haven, Or, The marry'd man's
  miserie*, 153
Cunny, Joan, 242

*Dainty new Dialogue between Henry and
  Elizabeth, A*, 87
Darnton, Robert, 185
Dates, of street literature, 42–44, 261
David, Alice, 218
Davis, Natalie, 9, 254, 263–64
Deloney, Thomas, 31–32, 83, 216
Demography, *see* Population
Demonic possession, 60–62
Devil: and crime, 212; and demonic pos-
  session, 60–62, 225–26, 230; and
  monstrous births, 92, 179–80, 257;
  and murder, 178, 216–21, 224–30,

233–34, 238; and saintly women, 54–
  57, 78; and shrews, 126, 131, 195–
  96; and witchcraft, 23, 238–44, 246–
  47, 249–50; *see also* Madness
Distressed Gentlewoman, The, 62
Ditty delightfull of mother Watkins ale, A,
  149
Donaldson, Ian, 205
Dorothea, Saint, 56
Douglas, Mary, 8
Dovey, Joyce, 62
Dowry, 11
*Drey schoner Hißtorij/Von dreyen
  Heidenischen mörderischen Frawen*, 164
Drinking: economic damage from, 86, 88,
  92, 133–34, 223–24; marital violence
  after, 111, 114, 122–23, 133–36, 221,
  223–24; by wives, 106, 130; *see also*
  Alehouse
*Du junger man merck vnd versteh/Vnd wilt
  du greyffen zu der Ehe*, 40
*Dumb Lady: Or, No, no, not I; I'le Answer,
  The*, 200
*Dumb Maid: or the Young Gallant Trap-
  pan'd, The*, 110

Eberlehrin, Anna, 241, 248
Economy: of Europe, 9–11; of German
  towns, 20, 262–63; of England, 20,
  24, 262
Education, 37
Elderton, William, 32
Elias, Norbert, 18
Elizabeth, Queen, 84
Enfield Common, 150
Engelsing, Rolf, 37
Engraving, copper, 36
Erfurt, 37
Evans, Elizabeth, 165
Eve, 17, 75, 98, 233, 243, 244
Excellent Ballad of George Barnwel, An, 165
Executions, 49, 211, 238; *see also* Torture
Exorcism, 61

Fairing for Maids, A, 65
Fair Maid of Dunsmore, The, 175
Family, history of, 12–14, 24–25, 258–60;
  patterns of crime in, 213–14; privacy
  in, 76
Fashion, 68
Feast, George, 222
First-person voice, 48–50, 69, 211, 215
Flandrin, Jean-Louis, 16
Flower, Margaret, 245

*Forc'd Marriage: Or, Unfortunate Celia,
   The,* 150
France, view of women in, 16
Francis, Katherine, 219
Fräulein von Britania, Das, 204
Frauncis, Elizabeth, 239
Frawen von der Weissenburg, Von der, 163
Fürst, Paul, 122

Gallows confessions, 49, 165–66, 210–12
George, Saint, 198
Gesprech von Fünff Unholden, 246
Goodcole, Henry, 245
Good Wife is a Portion every day, A, 87
Gossip, 101–3, 106; *see also* Neighbors
Governments, 17, 261–62; *see also* Law
Grimmelshausen, 194
Griselda, 50, 64, 93, 144
Guilds, 10
Guy, Robert, 166
Gwyn, Nell, 172

Haß, Cuntz, 106
Have among you! good women, 103
Hee-Diuell, A, 93
Heroines, 47, 50–60; English, 50–52,
   54–55, 62–66, 68–69; German, 50–
   51, 52–54, 56–60, 62–63, 257–58;
   religious, 52–60, 257–58; *see also*
   Saints
Hold your hands, honest Men, 109
Household, 71–72, 76; as center of pro-
   duction, 10; and multiple murder,
   223–32; *see also* Family *and* Marriage
Household Talke, 152
Housework, 94, 101, 130
Housholder's New-Yeere's Gift, The, 85
Howell, Martha, 17–18, 257
Hull, Suzanne, 215
Husbands: duties of, 86–89, 133; vices of,
   92–95, 104; virtues of, 82–83; *see also*
   Adultery, Marriage, Violence, *and*
   Wives

Illegitimacy, 174–75; *see also* Children *and*
   Pregnancy
Impotence, 149–52, 154, 256; *see also* Sex-
   uality
Individualism, 15, 18–20; in England, 24,
   182, 207, 258–59, 264–66; in Ger-
   many, 266
Infanticide, 16, 231, 233–38
Ingram, Martin, 156
Inversion, 9, 157, 184, 206–7
Ita, Saint, 57–58, 60, 93

James, Christian, 54
Jerome, Saint, 244
Jesus, 55–56, 58–60, 180
Joseph, 146–47
*Joviall Crew, Or, The Devill turn'd Ranter,
   The,* 104
Judith, 52, 53, 161–62, 193

Kahn, Coppélia, 156
*Kampffgesprech zwischen einer frawen vnd
   ihrer hausmeit,* 194
Keep a good tongue in your head, 109
Kelly, Joan, 18
Kennow, Margaret von, 193
Knight and the Beggar-Wench, The, 90
Korbmacher, 116–17
Krieg, Walter, 36, 37
*Kurtzweylig Lied/von eynem liederlichen
   man vnd seynem weyb, Ein,* 133–34

*Lamentation of Chloris for the Unkindness of
   her Shepherd, The,* 151
Larner, Christina, 15, 24, 214–15, 245
Last goodnights, *see* Gallows confessions
Law: contrasts between English and Ger-
   man, 262; Roman, 23, 262; *see also*
   Women, legal status of
Lied von einem eelichen volck, Ein, 78
Literacy, 15; in England, 33–34; in Ger-
   many, 37
London, 20–21, 41, 264; literacy in, 33–
   34
Long Meg of Westminster, 64, 191–92,
   194
Lose Mann, Der, 92
Love: and English heroines, 63–65, 68–
   69; and marriage, 71–87, 95, 143–45,
   258; and power of women, 143–46,
   256; religious, 59; *see also* Courtship,
   Marriage, *and* Sexuality
Loves Power, 149
Lucretia, 50, 202–3, 205
Luther, Martin, 12, 14, 24
Lutherans, 61, 264

MacDonald, Michael, 258
Macfarlane, Alan, 14, 24–25, 259, 262,
   265, 266
Madness, 225–26; *see also* Devil
Magdalene, Mary, *see* Mary Magdalene
*Maidens sad complaint for want of a Hus-
   band, The,* 40
Maid Marian, 192
Maid's Comfort, The, 84
Malleus maleficarum, 60, 244

Manners, changes in, 18
Marriage: burdens imposed by, 65–66;
    companionate, 13–15, 20, 256, 260,
    263; discord in, 97–139, 152–56,
    217–23; economic aspects of, 11, 72;
    in England, 24–25; European pattern
    of, 12–13, 259; female dominance in,
    98–106; as happy ending, 63, 68; see
    also Husbands, Love, Shrews, and
    Wives
Married-mans Case, 94
Married wives complaint, 95
Married-womans Case, 94
Mary, Virgin, 15, 58, 180
Mary Magdalene, 58–60, 68
Merchant's daughter of Bristow, The, 63
Mercurius Fumigosus, 128
Meusebach collection, 43
Middle Ages, manners in, 18
Middle classes, German, 20
Midelfort, Erik, 24
Midwives, and witchcraft, 240, 248
Miles, Margaret, 198
*Mirth for Citizens; Or, A Comedy for the
    Country,* 154
Monstrous births, 92, 178–80, 236; see also
    Devil *and* Pregnancy
Morality, public, 17–18
*Most rare and excellent History Of the
    Dutchesse of Suffolke's Calamity, The,*
    83
Most Wicked worke of a wretched Witch, A,
    242
Motherhood, 55–56, 180–81, 196–97,
    215, 259, 264–65; see also Children
    and Pregnancy
Münchheym, Barbara, 36, 57–58
Murder: of children, 213, 224–38, 240,
    242, 248–49; economic factors in,
    224–25, 230–32; of husbands by
    lovers, 163, 215–18; of husbands by
    wives, 212, 214–20; of parents, 231–
    32; of wives by husbands, 214, 220–
    23; see also Crime *and* Violence
Murderers: bands of, 93, 178–79, 231–32;
    as male analogue to witchcraft, 250
Murtherer Justly Condemned, The, 222
My Wife will be my Master, 153

Narrenfresser, 98–99
Nashe, Thomas, 32
Nature, control of, 18–19; see also Reason
Neighbors, and marital relations, 102–3,
    111; see also Gossip
Neun getrewen Hayden, Die, 77

Neun Häuten der bösen Weiber, 103
*New Ballad, Containing a communication be-
    tween the carefull Wife and the comfort-
    able Hus[band], A,* 87
New Lied von eynem bösen weib, Ein, 103
"New Yeeres guift for shrews, A," 126
Nine Skins of Bad Women, 111–16, 123–24
No naturall Mother, but a Monster, 234
Nunneries, 12, 15, 237–38
Nuremberg, 34, 37; censorship in, 72

*Offt Probiertes und Bewährtes Recept oder
    Artzney für die bösse Kranckheit der
    unartigen Weiber,* 122–24
Ortner, Sherry, 8
Ozment, Steven, 14, 266

Page, Mrs., 216–17, 221
Pamphlets: English, 30, 44; German, 34–
    37, 44
Parents: duties of, 83, 123, 236, 259–60;
    as killers of children, 224–38; as
    murder victims, 231–32; power of,
    24, 259; see also Children, Family, *and*
    Motherhood
Parker, Martin, 31–32, 93, 152; and
    murder reports, 219–20, 234; and
    shrews, 100–101, 103, 108–9
Parliament of Women, The, 151
Pasquils Jests, 100
Paul, Saint, 80
Performance, of street literature, 28–29,
    39–40
Perry, Widow, 247
Peterson, Joan, 247
Pinnyng of the Basket, 116, 118–20, 122,
    128
Pitilesse Mother, A, 233
*Pleasant new Songe of a iouiall [jovial]
    Tinker, A,* 187
Poor Man's Counsellor, 82
Popular culture, reform of, 17
Population, 11–12, 20–21
Pornography, 198–202
Portsmouth, duchess of, 172
Pregnancy, 142–43, 196; dangers of, 92–
    93, 176–79, 227, 232, 250, 257; of
    unmarried women, 79, 162, 174–76,
    189–90, 233–38; and witchcraft, 248;
    see also Children, Illegitimacy, *and*
    Motherhood
Price, Laurence, 31, 54, 220
Printing, in Germany, 34
Privacy, in family life, 76

Property, women's rights in, 11, 22; *see also* Women, economic status of

Prophecy, female, 53–56

Prostitution, 16–17, 59, 90–91; economic aspects of, 85, 95, 167, 169–70, 172–73; and female power over men, 162–63, 165–73; in German towns, 166–67; in London, 166–67; and social class, 172–73; and violence, 187–88; *see also* Sexuality

Protestantism, *see* Reformation

Puritans, 14, 21

Ranters, 104

Ranting Whores Resolution, The, 168

Rape, 196–97, 199, 200–206; *see also* Sexuality *and* Violence

Reason, 260–61, 264–65

Recept vur der weiber klappersuecht, Ein, 110

Reformation, 5, 21; and child rearing, 259, 263; and individualism, 15, 19, 263; and marriage, 12, 14, 73–76, 263; and prostitution, 167; and street literature, 34, 38; and women, 14–17, 53, 58, 255, 263–64

Reproduction, 8, 19; *see also* Pregnancy, Motherhood, *and* Sexuality

Robin and Kate; or, A bad husband converted by a good wife, 86–88, 90

Robin Hood, 64–65, 192

Rogers, J. E. T., 30

Rolandt, Der, 91

Roper, Lyndal, 14

Rowlands, Samuel, 106

Sabean, David, 266

Sachs, Hans, 36, 98, 162, 164, 173, 194; and heroines, 52, 161–62, 203; and love, 79–80; and marital discord, 95, 103, 105, 110–13, 123–24, 186; and marital ideals, 76–77; and witchcraft, 246

Saints, female, 15, 50, 56–60, 257–58

Satan, *see* Devil

Saunders, Anne, 215–16

Sawyer, Elizabeth, 239

Schön new Lied/wie ein fraw jren Mann strafft/vnd weret jm er sol nit zum wein geen, Ein, 88

Scolding, *see* Shrews

Scole house of women, 103

Servants, 234, 259

Sexuality, 8, 16–18, 102, 141–82, 256–57, 265; double standard regarding, 17; and social class, 142, 144–45; and

witchcraft, 23, 241–42, 244–45, 261; *see also* Adultery, Love, *and* Prostitution

Shame, 205; and female sexuality, 102, 156, 176–77

Shaming rituals, 102, 156, 253

Shee-diuell, The, 93

Sherwood, Thomas, 165

Shrews, 244, 253–54; and crime, 218–20, 222–23; and the Devil, 195–96; and marital discord, 73, 100–101, 105, 107–10, 114–19, 122–39; and sexual dominance, 152–56; *see also* Marriage, Tongue, Violence, *and* Wives

7 clagenden weiber, 95

Social class: of audience, 38–39; and prostitution, 172–73; and sexuality, 142, 144–45; and violence, 120, 128–29, 183–84

Social mobility, 20, 68, 264–65

Socrates, 244

Solomon's Sentences, 166

Song in Praise of a Single Life, 81

Sorrowful Mother, The, 55

Spanish Virgin, The, 198

Spenser, John, 166

Spiegel einer Christlichen vnd friedsamen Haußhaltung, 76

Stationers' Company, London, 31, 35, 42–43

Steinerin, Veronica, 61

Stile, Elizabeth, 242

Stone, Lawrence, 13, 24, 264

Strange Witch at Greenwich, The, 247

Strangwidge, George, 216–17

Strauss, Gerald, 37

Streitt/zwischen einem bösen Weib/vnd einem versoffnen Mann, Ein, 135

Stretton, Elizabeth, 54, 60

Suffolk, duchess of, 68

Suicide, 227, 228–29, 230–31

Susannah, 51, 77–78

Swetnam, Joseph, 215

Tagweyß/wie man die bösen weyber schlahen sol, 120

Tailors, ridicule of, 90–91, 151–52, 159, 188

Tannhäuser, 164

Thirty Years' War, 21, 35, 184

Thomas, Keith, 24

Tongue, as female weapon, 97, 106–7, 109–10, 155–56; *see also* Shrews

Torture, 23, 178, 209–10, 238

Touch and Go; or, the French Taylor finely Trappann'd, 159
Towns, German, 20–21, 37, 41, 72, 256, 262; prostitution in, 166–67
True Mayde of the South, The, 64
True Relation of the Araignment Of eighteene Witches, A, 242
Truth brought to Light, 247
Tunes, of street literature songs, 29, 42
Two-Penny Whore, The, 170

Underdown, David, 214, 257
Unnaturall Wife, The, 218–19

Valiant Commander with his resolute Lady, The, 84, 192
Violence, 183–207; comic aspects of, 107–8, 119–20, 130–31, 183–85, 188–91; in crime reports, 209–50; decreasing acceptance of, 17–18, 73; and demonic possession, 62; domestic, 73; of husbands, 22, 95, 106–30, 133–37, 153, 222–23; of men, 119; of wives, 107, 126, 129–39, 152, 155, 218–20; of women, 64, 119, 188–96, 207; and sex, 120, 183, 189–91, 197–207; and social class, 120, 128–29, 183–84; *see also* Murder
Virgins A.B.C., The, 40

Wages: of English workers, 30; of German workers, 36; of women, 10–11
Waldis, Burckhard, 227–29
War, 20–21, 184
Warning for all good fellowes to take heede of Punckes inticements, A, 166
Weiber Amastanas, Die, 193–94
Weltlich Joseph, Der, 146–47
Whipping Cheare, 171
Whitney's Dying Letter To his Mistris that betray'd him: With her Answer, 166
Whores, *see* Prostitution
Wick collection, 43

Widows, 78, 231; legal status of, 22
Wiesner, Merry, 262
Wife beating, *see* Violence
Wife lapped in Morels skin, 126–28
Wiles, feminine, 88, 97–98, 141–42, 157–59; in service of virtue, 160–62
Witchcraft, 16, 238–50; economic aspects of, 239, 240–41, 245; and fertility, 247–50; and lust, 241, 244; and misogyny, 23–24, 244–45; and poisoning, 248–49; skepticism about, 246–47; *see also* Devil
Witches of Northamptonshire, The, 239
Wives: economic status of, 10–11, 22, 105–6, 129, 135–36, 256; virtues of, 77–78, 82, 85–90; *see also* Adultery, Husbands, Marriage, Shrews, *and* Violence
Wofull lamentacon of mrs. Anne Saunders, The, 215
Woodcuts, 29, 35–36
Woman's Work is never done, A, 40, 50
Woman to the Plow, And the Man to the Hen-Roost, The, 89
Women: definition of disorderly, 3–4, 7–9, 44; economic status of, 9–12, 17–18, 22, 67, 172, 256–57; legal status of, 15–17, 22; *see also* Motherhood, Shrews, Widows, *and* Wives
Wonderful Praise of a Good Husband, 82
Wonderful Prophecy, A, 54
Wrigley, E. A., 21
Würzbach, Natascha, 39

Young-Mans A.B.C., The, 40
Youth, in street literature audience, 40–41

Zwey Schöne Lieder/wie man ein Braut Geystlich ansingen soll, 74
Zwölff durchleuchtige Weyber des alten Testaments, Die, 52
Zwölff Eygenschafft eines boßhafftigen weybs, Die, 105, 186